The New American Poetry

The New American Poetry

Fifty Years Later

John R. Woznicki

LEHIGH UNIVERSITY PRESS
Bethlehem

Published by Lehigh University Press
Copublished with Rowman & Littlefield
4501 Forbes Boulevard, Suite 200, Lanham, Maryland 20706
www.rowman.com

10 Thornbury Road, Plymouth PL6 7PP, United Kingdom

British Library Cataloguing in Publication Information Available

Library of Congress Cataloging-in-Publication Data
The New American Poetry : Fifty Years Later / edited by John R. Woznicki.
    pages cm
Includes bibliographic references and index.
ISBN 978-1-61146-124-4 (cloth) — ISBN 978-1-61146-125-1 (electronic) 1.
ISBN 978-1-61146-214-2 (pbk
American poetry—20th century—History and criticism. I. Woznicki, John R., editor of compilation.
PS323.5.N49 2013
811'.509—dc23
                                                                    2013035295

~

Contents

~

Acknowledgments

There are always innumerable people to thank when bringing a project of this scope to fruition; so many have provided support in my efforts, including students, colleagues, friends, and family members. My hope is that I will not be negligent in thanking them personally, and when they do finally see this book in print they will recognize the important part they played in its production. There are those, however, who deserve particular mention here for their integral and most special roles. They include Paul Cappucci, with whom I had many vital discussions regarding the idea behind this project and without whose initial support the project would have failed to launch, Marjorie Perloff, who guided me toward potential contributors and provided professional advice, the editors at Lehigh University Press, particularly Scott Gordon and Monica Najar, whose direction proved very valuable, Stephen Nacco, who graciously lent his time to give of his editorial talents, and Regina Betz, for her help with the book's index. The contributors to *The New American Poetry: Fifty Years Later* must also be acknowledged, especially, as they provided the excellent work that makes up this volume and have exacted great patience in waiting for its arrival in print. Finally, I must recognize those closest to me—my wife, Tamara Kendig, and my children, Koren and Joshua, whose daily support, through the provision of spiritual and emotional sustenance, allowed for me to see this book to completion. I am forever grateful for their loving companionship.

I would also like to acknowledge the graciousness of many of the rights' holders, estate executors, and publishing house representatives who understood the importance of this project and provided permissions for use of the work of the artists whom we have studied, especially Joan Blackman, Jill Turnbull, and Raymond Foye, Declan Spring from New Directions, and Victoria Fox from Farrar, Straus, and Giroux. And my acknowledgments would not be complete if I did not recognize the very talented writers and editors who provided the opportunity for response, critics such as Ms. Perloff, Alan Golding, and Jed Rasula, each of the artists included in the original volume and those influenced by it, and Don Allen, who brought to us this treasured anthology some fifty years ago, a volume that will continue to invite response evermore.

Grateful acknowledgement is given to:

"Homage to a Government" from *The Complete Poems of Philip Larkin* by Philip Larkin, edited by Archie Burnett. Copyright © 2012 by The Estate of Philip Larkin. Introduction copyright © 2012 by Archie Burnett. Reprinted by permission of Farrar, Straus and Giroux, LLC.

"Freely Espousing" and "The Morning of the Poem" from *Collected Poems* by James Schuyler. Copyright © 1993 by the Estate of James Schuyler. Reprinted by permission of Farrar, Straus and Giroux, LLC.

Lines from the *Selected Poetry of Amiri Baraka/LeRoi Jones*. Copyright by Amiri Baraka. Reprinted by permission of SLL/Sterling Lord Literistic, Inc.

Lines from *The Collected Poems of Robert Creeley, 1945–1975*, by Robert Creeley. Copyright © 2006 by University of California Press Books. Reprinted by permission by University of California Press Books.

"The Continuity" and "The Problem" by Paul Blackburn. Copyright © 1985 by Joan Blackburn. Used by permission of Joan Blackburn.

"Selected Lines" in *Gunslinger* by Edward Dorn. Copyright ©1989 by Duke University Press. All rights reserved. Republished by permission of the copyright holder: www.dukeupress.edu

"The Song of the Borderguard" by Robert Duncan, from *Selected Poems*. Copyright © 1950 by Robert Duncan. Reprinted by permission of New Directions Publishing Corporation.

"Poem Beginning with a Line by Pindar" and "This Place Rumord to have been Sodom" by Robert Duncan, from *The Opening of the Field*. Copyright © 1960 by Robert Duncan. Reprinted by permission of New Directions Publishing Corporation.

"Apprehensions" by Robert Duncan, from *Roots and Branches*. Copyright © 1964 by Robert Duncan. Reprinted by permission of New Directions Publishing Corporation.

"Passages 25" by Robert Duncan, from *Bending the Bow*. Copyright © 1968 by Robert Duncan. Reprinted by permission of New Directions Publishing Corporation.

"Excerpts" by Ezra Pound, from *The Cantos of Ezra Found*. Copyright © 1934 by Ezra Pound. Reprinted by permission of New Directions Publishing Corporation, Pollinger, Ltd., and Farrar, Straus and Giroux, LLC.

"To a Poor Old Woman" by William Carlos Williams, from *Collected Poems: Volume I, 1909–1939*. Copyright © 1934 by New Directions Publishing Corporation. Reprinted by permission of New Directions Publishing Corporation.

Selected lines from various texts of William Carlos Williams in "'Trying to Build on Their Elders' Work': The Correspondence of Donald Allen and William Carlos Williams" by Paul Cappucci. Copyright © 1959 by William Carlos Williams. Copyright © 1976 by The Estate of William Carlos Williams. Copyright © 2013 by the Estates of Paul H. Williams and William Eric Williams. Used by permission of New Directions Publishing Corporation.

"Now That April's Here" by Gael Turnbull, from *Collected Poems*. Copyright © 2006 by Gael Turnbull. Reprinted by permission of Jill Turnbull.

Lines from "Howl" and "Sather Gate Illumination" by Allen Ginsberg. Copyright © 2001, 2007 by Allen Ginsberg, used by permission of The Wylie Agency LLC and HarperCollins.

Lines from *The Collected Poems of Charles Olson: Excluding The Maximus Poems* by Charles Olson. Copyright © 1997 by University of California Press Books. Reprinted by permission by University of California Press Books.

Lines from *The Maximus Poems* by Charles Olson. Copyright © 1985 by the Estate of Charles Olson. Reprinted by permission by University of California Press Books and the University of Connecticut Libraries. Works by Charles Olson published during his lifetime are held in copyright by the Estate of Charles Olson. Previously unpublished works by Charles Olson are copyright of the University of Connecticut Libraries. Used with permission.

Lines from "The Air of June Sings" by Ed Dorn. Copyright © 1975 by University of California Press Books. Reprinted by permission by University of California Press Books.

"Medusa's hair with snakes. Was thought, split inward" and "In white, she who bathed" by Kathleen Fraser, from *il cuore: the heart—New & Selected Poems (1970–1995)*. Copyright © 1997 by Kathleen Fraser. Reprinted by permission of Wesleyan University Press.

"7 Praises," "Space," "OK Everybody, Let's Do the Mondrian Stomp," "Looking at Some Petroglyphs in a Dry Arroyo Near a Friend's House," "City: Matrix: Bird: Collage," and "Ready for Sunset" by Michael Heller, from This Constellation is a Name, Collected Poems 1965–2010, Callicoon, New York: Nightboat Books, 2012. Copyright © 2012 by Michael Heller. Reprinted by permission of Nightboat Books.

"Writing" by Rachel Blau DuPlessis, from *Tabula Rosa*. Copyright © 1987 by Rachel Blau DuPlessis. Reprinted by permission of Rachel Blau DuPlessis.

"Draft 58: In Situ" by Rachel Blau DuPlessis, from *Torques: Drafts 58–76a*. Copyright © 2007 by Rachel Blau DuPlessis. Reprinted by permission of Rachel Blau DuPlessis.

"Draft 39: Split" and "Draft 43: Gap" by Rachel Blau DuPlessis, from *Drafts 39–57, Pledge*. Copyright © 2004 by Rachel Blau DuPlessis. Reprinted by permission of Salt Publishing.

Non, *Garfield*, and *Force*, by Ron Silliman, from *The Alphabet*. Copyright © 1991 by Ron Silliman. Reprinted by permission of The University of Alabama Press.

Lines from *Dodeka* by John Taggart. Copyright © 1979 by John Taggart. Reprinted by permission of John Taggart.

"In the Sense Of" by John Taggart, from *Standing Wave*. Copyright © 1993 by John Taggart. Reprinted by permission of John Taggart.

"Meditation" by John Taggart, from *Is Music: Selected Poems*. Copyright © 2010 by John Taggart. Reprinted by permission of Copper Canyon Press.

"Of Being Numerous" by George Oppen, from *New Collected Poems*. Copyright © 2002 by George Oppen. Reprinted by permission of New Directions Publishing Corporation.

Lines from *The Dream Songs* by John Berryman. Copyright © 1996 by Noonday Books. Reprinted by permission of Farrar, Straus and Giroux, LLC.

Lines from *Mountain and Rivers Without End* by Gary Snyder. Copyright © 1996 by Gary Snyder. Reprinted by permission of Counterpoint, LLC.

CHAPTER ONE

~

The New American Poetry:
Fifty Years Later

John R. Woznicki

I am happy to introduce you to this collection of critical essays on Donald Allen's 1960 seminal anthology, *The New American Poetry*, an anthology that Marjorie Perloff called in her 1995 essay, "the fountainhead of radical American poetics."[1]

As you may have recognized, Allen's anthology has reached its fiftieth anniversary, providing a unique time for reflection and reevaluation of this preeminent anthology. *The New American Poetry* is referred to in every literary history of post-World War II American poetry. As we know, Allen's anthology was radical in the sense of bringing about change—it was the first to widely distribute the poetry and theoretical positions of poets such as Charles Olson and Allen Ginsberg and the Beats, and it was the first to categorize these poets by the schools (Black Mountain, New York School, San Francisco Renaissance, and the Beats) by which we know them today. Over the course of fifty years, one might agree that this categorization of poets into schools has become one of the major, if not only way, that *The New American Poetry* is remembered or valued; one certain goal of our collection is to, in some way, "pry The New American Poetry out from the hoary platitudes that have encrusted it."[2]

Since the publication of both Allen's original anthology and his updated edition, *The Postmoderns*, there have been a few major critical treatments of *The New American Poetry*, considered as a whole, most notably by Alan Golding (*From Outlaw to Classic* and "*The New American Poetry* Revisited, Again"), Marjorie Perloff (briefly, in a number of her works, but more markedly in her essay, "Whose New American Poetry? Anthologizing in the

Nineties"), and Jed Rasula (*The American Poetry Wax Museum*). To this point critics mostly have examined *The New American Poetry* as an anthology; former treatments of *The New American Poetry* look at it intently as a whole. Though the almost singularly focused study of its construction and, less often, reception has lent a great deal of documented, highly visible and debated material in which to consider, we have been left with certain notions about its relevance that have become imbued ultimately in the collective critical consciousness of postmodernity.

With all due respect to these critics and their touchstone pieces, which have proven to be invaluable in our certain understanding of *The New American Poetry*, our volume, however, goes beyond the analysis of construction and reception and attempts something distinctive, extending those former treatments by treading on the paths they create. This book aims to discover another sense of "radical" that Perloff articulated—rather than a radical that departs markedly from the usual, we invite consideration of *The New American Poetry* that is radical in the sense of root, of harbouring something fundamental, something inherent, as we uncover and trace further elements correlated with its widespread influence over the last fifty years.

We might begin with Perloff, who in her book *21st-Century Modernism* sees the poets and poetry of Allen's anthology as continuing the line of avant-garde work that had begun in modernity.[3] Allen's "modest" anthology is a beginning point for a conceptual examination of anthologies. Allen offers a comparative study of mostly warring anthologies who attempt, like *The New American Poetry*, to be the definitive anthology of its day.[4] Even so, these contemporary anthologies suffer from the "malaise of the midcentury" where, implied by Perloff, an ineffectual struggle ensues as to what and who to include, ending with Perloff's proposition of a model anthology, as one "admit[ing] to a degree of provisionality" that inevitably may resemble Peter Gizzi's *Exact Change Yearbook No. 1: 1995*.[5] As a result, such anthologies can no longer claim to evolve from a simpler environment in 1960 where the raw can separate itself from the cooked, the anti-academic from the academic.[6]

The New American Poetry does indeed attempt to set itself apart from what was perceived to be the stronghold of taste held by academe, thereby positioning itself as an "aesthetically revisionist anthology."[7] Alan Golding reminds us that in the construction of *The New American Poetry*,[8] the milieu was not as simply defined by a desire for something new and a clear path toward reaching whatever new was. The process is complicated by the very notion of newness and, for example, what was considered to be anti-academic (versus perhaps what some thought of as scholarly).[9] Golding's valuable archival work into Allen's letters reveals great vacillation on "evolving ambitions, contents and organization" of the volume,[10] such as whether to include modernist precursors and "continuers,"[11] and the competing influences of poets such as Charles Olson and Robert Duncan, for starters, which shaped the final version.[12] Golding goes on to reveal the conflicts between the expressed groups of the edition, most notably between the Black Mountain and San Francisco poets.[13] Golding also adduces the exclusion of African American poets writing at the time[14] as well as the conflict between Allen and the female poets such as Joanne Kyger who thought themselves worthy to be included and the prevailing male poetic.[15] All of these insights are valuable and interesting and all shed a light on the politics of anthology making in general and for this specific one, in particular.

When Golding does focus on the anthology's reception, admittedly briefly near the end of his essay, he brings up a valuable point: that contemporary readers continue to define *The New American Poetry*'s identity as early critics did, by what he calls the negative mirror critique.[16] From this perspective, *The New American Poetry* is unable to shed the simplistic view that it is merely an oppositional anthology, one whose value only rests in its "Anti" (largely anti-academic stance) and therefore does not or cannot formulate a positive identity separate from its oppositional claim. Here Golding suggests that "all resistance becomes merely reactive, shaped by its opposite, and indeed the critique itself can function as a way of denying cultural resistance any seriousness."[17]

Yet many of us sense that this idea, though a valid one, cannot be solely true. That is, recent commentary that continues to focus on the anthology's development (as if it is stuck in some neurotic, unrealized Lacanian stage) to the exclusion of everything else misses a unique opportunity. Certainly the groundwork that Rasula, Perloff, and Golding lay for us as they focus on the construction of the anthology, its reactive beginnings, its place in the historical and political process of anthologizing, and its indirect, almost reflective role in canon-formation, permit us to see *The New American Poetry* as a fully realized mature entity that can, and should, be seen as possessing generative powers. *The New American Poetry* has a positive identity, a primary progenitor of not just canon-fodder but also many new movements, styles, poets, etc. This book investigates not only how it was entirely shaped but also how it has shaped us, as critics, readers and students of poetry—shaped our identity. When we do look back at its construction, we are readers who have already been influenced by its contents. I would like for readers to see our volume as one that extends in greater fashion the study of *The New American Poetry*'s reception rather than construction, its positive rather than negative value, its proactive rather than reactive activity, a generative rather than a reflective work, and ultimately accepting its own self-exclaimed premise of its being. *The New American Poetry* is a visionary anthology of our time with a vision that extends beyond the boundaries of opposition, one that has not only shaped the canon and continues to do so, but shaped a culture—of critics, students, readers and writers of poetry.[18]

To do so we consider not only the anthology but also the last fifty years of its existence, from matters exchanged in the anthology's conceptual stage to today. We look anew at archival evidence, reread significant poems in new ways, delve deeper into key relationships with key contributors, revise our view of the interactions among these poets to re-contextualize *The New American Poetry* with reference to precursors, contemporaries, successors, and the development of the poets included within it.

To start, Paul Cappucci's essay "'Trying to Build on Their Elders' Work': The Correspondence of Donald Allen and William Carlos Williams" characterizes this correspondence in the two years prior to *The New American Poetry*'s publication. Cappucci's essay focuses on Williams's essay "Measure," which Allen sought to publish in *Evergreen Review* and considered for *The New American Poetry*. Cappucci's archival work is itself reflective in nature, offering further insight into Allen's decision-making process regarding the inclusion of an important precursor such as Williams. Moreover, Cappucci demonstrates, through a careful reading of "Measure," the level of influence Williams had on the New American poets, especially poets such as Gary Snyder who is not usually critically connected to Williams. Though Allen does identify Williams as the most important precursor poet in his introduction, Cappucci's essay implies through its argument how difficult a decision it must have been for Allen to exclude him, while explicitly leaving us with Williams's generative power he had on Allen and *The New American Poetry* poets, and with new legacies to consider.

With legacy in mind, Joshua Hoeynck's "Without a Mammalia Maxima" is an investigation of the interplay between two of the leading poets of *The New American Poetry*, Charles Olson and Robert Duncan, as Golding reminds us of their large parts played in shaping the volume. Hoeynck sees the correspondence between Olson and Duncan as producing a crucial, transformative outcome that, in time, most likely influenced the conceptual development of *The New American Poetry*. As a result, *The New American Poetry* might be seen as an epistemological pivot point for Olson and for the New American poets between an older, Poundian notion of history as the actions of great men and a newer, Whiteheadian notion of cosmos as an interpenetration of physical events and imagination unfolding in time. The essay presents Duncan as midwife to Olson's moving away from the Poundian concept and toward the Whiteheadean one, with Duncan's poem "Apprehensions" and the correspondence between them that surrounds it as a key event. A major outcome of this shift in Olson's thinking was his resolve to drop the character of Maximus from the third volume of *The Maximus Poems* and, by implication, an impetus for Olson's desire to leave the past behind regarding the direction of *The New American Poetry*, as outlined by Golding.

Terence Diggory's essay, "Why *The New American Poetry* Stays News," plots that future direction Olson may have indeed had in mind. Diggory reminds us of *The New American Poetry*'s generative, and thus lasting, quality as a dynamic collection that spoke to many constituents as it tackled, in broad form, the "how to write?" question. There is a subtle discussion of the issue of "intention" in *The New American Poetry*, moving from Olson's dogmatic objective to the more materialist intentions found in many of the poets, thereby providing the background for the emergence of Language poetry. Diggory then goes on to consider how women poets have harvested linguistic "intentionality." Despite the dearth of women poets in the anthology, *The New American Poetry* has proven extremely influential to subsequent generations of women poets like Kathleen Fraser, Alice Notley, and Anne Waldman. They have found value in an anthology that included only four women among forty-four contributors. Rather than finding reflections of themselves in the anthology, these female poets were drawn to new possibilities for writerly practice. Diggory ends his essay with a section on pedagogy, again to emphasize how *The New American Poetry* gave birth to writerly approaches to poetry in the classroom, and prompting us to acknowledge the overwhelming reception of *The New American Poetry* as, one might call, an "instructional" volume, especially on its native ground.

The theme of reception emerges again, albeit more globally, in Ben Hickman's "A Big Kiss for Mother England." Hickman's essay summarizes the reception and influence of *The New American Poetry* in Great Britain, marking the first time since Whitman that U.S. poetry penetrated deeply into British literary circles. Hickman discusses the considerable impact the anthology had on the British avant-garde, which was in many ways libratory and salutary. Hickman also raises some issues of polarization and "poetry wars" in Great Britain that were impossible to resolve. Ultimately, *The New American Poetry* helped legitimize a large body of poetry that countered the influence of the Movement poets of the 1950s and the poetry that followed in its conservative wake.

Just as Hickman's essay orients the reader to the contributions of *The New American Poetry* to British poetry, Joe Moffet's essay, "*The New American Poetry* and the Development of the Long Poem," points out the contribution of *The New American Poetry* to the long poem as a genre. Moffett argues that if the long poem is the measure of poetic ambition (in place of the epic) in American poetry after Whitman, then it is important to look at long poems by the New American poets to see how to value their contribution to American poetry. This essay explores a variety of long poems and a variety of types of long poems by major figures in *The New American Poetry*. Most of the poems discussed did not actually appear in the anthology. Even so, they represent extensions of the principles of the anthology into the most ambitious poems written by the poets. The essay argues for the success and variety of these poems, and thus implicitly for the generative success of *The New American Poetry*.

Megan Swihart Jewell's "Becoming Articulate: Kathleen Fraser and *The New American Poetry*" perhaps announces this volume's first suggestion of *The New American Poetry*'s potential *degenerative* impact. The apparent masculinity of the volume, in many ways, defined the paths of the avant-garde while virtually excluding the feminine principle. The poetic dictums of *The New American Poetry*'s emergent literary schools (as Diggory's essay discusses) instructed contemporary poets in ways of "how to write" while largely excluding radical women poets like Fraser who sought to write outside the gendered poetic narratives engendered by anthologies such as *The New American Poetry*. Innovative women poets have responded to their exclusion by struggling to "unravel their buried history" and to "become articulate," in part by resisting the gender bias and the group construction of poetics and language for which *The New American Poetry* was known.

David Herd's essay "'In the Dawn that is Nowhere': *The New American Poetry* and the State of Exception" anticipates, in theme, a condition of "exception" that also addresses the gender and racial make-up of the contributors to *The New American Poetry*. Herd adduces Hannah Arendt's *The Origins of Totalitarianism* as an analog, in that the work permeated global culture at the time, leading states and nations to homogenize culture and standardize reality through totalitarian practices of exclusion and "conglomeration." Despite Allen's claim to the contrary, his practice as editor did not match the deliberate action toward inclusiveness that Arendt demanded, geo-politically, and in what *The New American Poetry* poets actually practiced poetically. Although the poets in *The New American Poetry* were culturally aware and politically active, led by Olson, they sought a "new stance toward reality" in their deliberate attempt to address the mid-century crisis of nation-hood and, in Herd's view, "articulat[ed] a significant challenge to the assumption of a relation between the practices of art and the apparatuses of the nation-state."

Other critics, as well, have noted the influence of universal cultural phenomenon of the mid-century on the formation of the anthology and the activity of its poets. Peter Middleton fashions an argument that focuses on the later companion anthology to *The New American Poetry, New Writing in the USA*, which Donald Allen and Robert Creeley produced as a lens for looking more closely at *The New American Poetry*. In the later anthology's slight revision—which includes prose as well as poetry—there was a chance for the editors to reassess the principles of *The New American Poetry*. Middleton points out that the two introductory essays to *New Writing in the USA* are more explicit about the criteria for anthologization, and so they address more directly some of the tacit assumptions at work in *The New American Poetry*. In particular, Creeley focuses on the issue of how poetry responds to the increasingly scientific culture of America, and draws attention to the degree of interest in the sciences in *The New American Poetry* group. Middleton employs this altered perspective on *The New American Poetry* to notice just how much the poets are interested in such issues. He concludes that, although the alignment with the radical politics of liberation poetics is the main cause of *The New American Poetry*'s success, the repeated engagement with the issues raised by the increasing scientization of American culture is another reason for its continuing relevance.

In this light, Seth Forrest considers a scientific experimental investigation of phenomena as a topic and as a critical methodology in his essay "Aurality and Literacy" which reflects on the "aural" aspects of *The New American Poetry*, as aided by technology such as the tape recorder. Using techniques such as acousmatic listening, Forrest interprets tape recordings of a number of poems from *The New American Poetry*, and demonstrates how the listening of poets to their own recordings became an element in the composition of the poems. In this sense, recording is transformed from a means for preserving a performance for posterity into an active element in the composition of a poem. The essay makes the point that the New American poets offer an incredibly rich and barely attended to archive of sound performances, now easily available for critical consideration through online streaming. What we learn in part is "how audio recordings have added to the literal textual condition with which editors and scholars need to engage." The principles of recording and the habits of listening are instrumental in understanding the New American poetry.

Like Forrest's essay, Burt Kimmelman's "*The New American Poetry*'s Objectivist Legacy: Linguistic Skepticism, the Signifier, and Material Language" brings us into and keeps us in the twenty-first century. The essay offers us a poet-critic's perspective of the success of and variety contained within what he calls the neo-Objectivist movement that was launched by *The New American Poetry*. Kimmelman moves from Ron Silliman's well-known essay,

"Third Phase Objectivism," to recognize not only one trajectory of neo-objectivism, Language poetry, but also to acknowledge a second trajectory. This includes poets Armand Schwerner, Michael Heller, Harvey Shapiro, and younger poets like Norman Finkelstein and Kimmelman himself, who hearken back to the Objectivists but have not felt the need to repudiate their immediate forbears as do the language poets. Kimmelman acknowledges a third group, to include Rachel Blau DuPlessis and John Taggart, who don't fit easily into the two "schools." However, like the others, they trace themselves from the older Objectivist poets through the mid-century *New American Poetry* poets and share the love of written language as a material phenomenon and a healthy skepticism toward the possible efficacy of language. In some important ways these neo-Objectivists have superseded their *New American Poetry* forbears. Kimmelman finally examines the most recent avant-garde movements in poetry, Flarf and Conceptual Poetry, both of which claim origins in Language poetry. As they are at once contextualized in *The New American Poetry*, these young poets apparently do not fully know why this lineage exists as it does.

Lastly, Carla Billitteri's afterword shows *The New American Poetry* in both a retrospective and a prospective context. That is, Billitteri discusses *The New American Poetry* as both a historical chronicle and as a touchstone to influence future generations of poets—a "beginning" that might be read as an "implex" that carries with it, in Edward Said's idea of the term, both the transitive and intransitive that interoperate at once. As our essayists focus on the anthology's transitive aspects, Billitteri in her commentary looks at the intransitive, seeing the anthology closely resembling a Whiteheadean "prehension" that "respond[s] to the conditions of its own occasion" and produces, ultimately, an interconnected, self-reflexive and sustaining "society."

Though Perloff and Golding's reflections are important and influential parts of the "nexus of occasions" that function within Billitteri's idea of the society that forms around *The New American Poetry*, it is Jed Rasula's work, *The American Poetry Wax Museum*, with which this volume is more closely aligned and dialogues with most directly. Like Rasula, I would consider Allen's original project more intransitive than transitive and have come to see our own project, this anthology of essays, more from this perspective as well. As stated on the book's jacket, Rasula's book is a long and appropriately meandering documentary, a study of "the canonizing assumptions and obsessions" that inform American poetry from 1940–1990. Rasula then separates from the prevailing assumptions on canon-making and goes further than Perloff and Golding in opening up a pathway for less-chartered exploration of *The New American Poetry*. Self-admittedly running between a literary history and a polemic,[19] Rasula expounds on the dangers and detriments of anthologizing in general while citing *The New American Poetry* as a specific example of such hazardous terrain. He sees American poetry as "a matrix of lives lived, not a Jurassic Park of spectacular behemoths"[20] that the literary establishment attempts to make of our poetry, through activities such as anthology-making and canonization. Rasula alerts us of the trouble that ensues in such activities; he speaks of the "anthology war" between the academy-endorsed, "cooked" and "institutionalized" Hall-Pack-Simpson-edited *New Poets of England and America* and the rebelliously "raw" *The New American Poetry*. Rasula's intention, however, as is ours, is neither to re-create "spectacular behemoths" nor to "rerun" the battle as it has been since the battle has begun, but to instead "readjust [. . .] stereotypes."[21]

One such stereotype that Rasula readjusts as he carefully entertains the ideas of *The New American Poetry* poetry's contributors is the idea that, in the rebellion, there is a certain and strategized abandonment of tradition. Rasula shows us in his reading of Creeley's, Duncan's and Gary Snyder's ideas of poetics that their dedication to open form that "stresses form as a biological event," commits them to a "decisively extraliterary sense of 'tradition'."[22] This custom of considering poetry as an extension of the human mind and of human experience has been practiced by the Romantics who have decidedly influenced those who followed—the demarcation, for some, of an American poetic tradition.[23] For Rasula, tradition is acknowledgment,[24] acknowledgment of something wider than what the academy proscribed in the days leading up to *The New American Poetry* and after, "a much vaster assembly now billowed into sight—borne aloft by renegade autodidacts."[25] This breadth of scope, provoked by the idea of poetry as an extension of human experience, looks back into the past and takes into account the entirety of the world, anticipating Rasula's final point in his section on the Anthology Wars that *The New American Poetry* demonstrated the "impetus" to "engage" an "enticing" world poetry whose "circumambient pressure [. . .] overflowed the boundaries of partisan squabbles."[26]

Tradition in this sense is the acknowledgment of everything, everything human, as progenitors of our reality and its effects. This encompasses everything of this world, including that which does not yet exist but only in possibility. This acknowledgment includes the tension and conflict that Perloff, Golding, and Rasula reveal in their historical studies of American poetry of the mid-to-late twentieth century—a "dynamic volatility"[27] that, in essence, does not exclude but, instead, spins like a vortex, productively rather than destructively, to capture all within its path. Perhaps it is this tradition, this breadth of scope, which we might find that is radical in *The New American*

Poetry—a certain expanse that we are hesitant to acknowledge in something so circumscribed as an anthology.

As we have seen, anthologizing is a dangerous business. The capturing and collecting of work, whether artistic or critical, risks creating a Rasula-ian waxen shrine and further politicizing the poetic scene. It is in the light of dynamic volatility, however, with a further nod to Perloff's call for provisionality, that these essays are presented and held together in this anthology. *The New American Poetry* is part of our tradition, as a progressive, generative anthology with the dynamics to produce as an entity that spans and spawns human experience. We look back into the past, distant and recent, and are acknowledging in Rasula's sense only a fraction of some of *The New American Poetry*'s effects.

In this sense then, I eschew formal categories for this book that may be construed as an attempt to politicize our findings. To speak to an inherent logic of organization would be futile, save the natural logic of time that we are guided by as humans. This book's essays therefore are presented in a loosely chronological fashion that initially address the pre-forming of the anthology and then progress toward more contemporary ideas. In this way too I wish to reflect that over the course of fifty or so years since *The New American Poetry*'s initial publication, we should have neither the desire nor the ability to present here a comprehensive summary of critical thoughts on *The New American Poetry*. The very idea of being comprehensive ironically suggests adherence to a standard that *The New American Poetry* poets themselves would have rejected for being absurdly vain or narcissistic.

It is therefore my hope that such an edition will be seen as valuable in adding greatly to poetry scholarship today due to the monumental influence the original collection has had. This volume is a tribute to the endurance and resilience of Allen's anthology. Scholars to this day continue to find *The New American Poetry* and its poets still viable—the work still influential, the echoes still reverberating. I do believe that, in another fifty years, another collection of essays will mark the yet-to-be-conveyed and developed influences that this anthology will have on us as a centennial volume that will celebrate this anthology's contribution to poetry everywhere.

Notes

1. Marjorie Perloff, "Whose New American Poetry? Anthologizing in the 90s," *Diacritics* 26, no. 3–4 (Fall-Winter 1996), 104.

2. Though the idea conveyed here, to reassess *The New American Poetry* for the sometimes misconstrued theoretical and practical legacy it has bequeathed, was a central provocateur in our mounting this project some seven years ago, I was com-

pelled to restate the words of an anonymous editorial reader who said it much more compellingly than I ever could.

3. Majorie Perloff, *21st-Century Modernism: The "New" Poetics*, (Malden, MA: Blackwell, 2002).

4. It is worth noting that on the cover of the reprinted 1999 edition of *The New American Poetry* [see Donald Allen, ed. *The New American Poetry, 1945–60*, (Berkeley: University of California Press, 1999)], it claims it is THE visionary anthology that influenced two generations of readers, a claim that in part led to the creation of our book, as we seek in part the ways in which that claim may be substantiated. Perloff is right, I think, when she suggests *The New American Poetry* is the last anthology able to make a claim such as this, as we are able to in some extended qualitative way, track the influences.

5. Perloff, "Whose New American Poetry," 119.

6. What comes to mind when reading Perloff's essay is an analogy: the contemporary poetry anthology as a contemporary "big-box" supermarket or home improvement center that increases its shelf space to fit every brand of every product in order to appeal to the entirety of the marketplace. Often times in these stores the consumer feels overwhelmed by the amount of choice available; there is no inherent logic to the aisle structure or ordering of the "product" nor are there convenient maps available; and consequently there is no available help to guide the consumer in the right direction or, if guidance is available, the guide's knowledge is suspect. Stores such as these sacrifice quality for the sake of quantity, inherent value for the sake of low cost and thus a new value based on sheer size and volume (a bigger is better phenomena not foreign to contemporary consumer culture.) In this analogy, as I read Perloff, Allen's anthology is the supermarket of past times, where consumers feel more at ease with the shopkeeper's more modest selection and the explicit logic that guided his choices and more careful attention he pays to his customers. Perhaps, when we think of these stores of yesteryear (or, when encountered today, a specialty shop) we are more inclined to think of quality and more apt to place value in the actual wares, rather than in the cheapened junk purchased at the big-box store. The great irony that exists, of course, is that the big-box store passes in our society as being THE place to shop, whether conforming to the bigger-is-better philosophy or, if for no other reason, than there are few specialty shops in existence with which to compete.

7. Alan Golding, *From Outlaw to Classic: Canons in American Poetry*, (Madison: University of Wisconsin Press, 1995), 30.

8. Golding admittedly focuses his attention in his essay *"The New American Poetry* Revisited, Again" on construction rather than reception. See Alan Golding, *"The New American Poetry* Revisited, Again," *Contemporary Literature* 39, no. 2 (1998): 182.

9. Allen himself tells us in his introduction to *The New American Poetry* that, one of the only organizing principles for the poetry contained in his anthology was that it was anti-academic: "one common characteristic: a total rejection of all those qualities typical of academic verse" (see Allen, *The New American Poetry*, xi). And yet Golding reminds us that the term academic as used by Allen here "tends to become

muddied"; there was debate as to what was meant by academic by the contributors themselves. Golding, at length, carefully unpacks the various views on the issue, noting the competition for Allen from Hall, Pack, and Simpson's *New Poets of England and America*, the conflation of the terms academic and scholarly (and educated) by critics, the different views of what constitutes "academic" by poets like Olson, Duncan and Spicer, etc. See Golding, "New American Poetry Revisited," 200.

10. Golding's main focus of his essay is to demonstrate the "instability" of the categories such as "anti-academic" that we have come to accept regarding *The New American Poetry* and to emphasize the "contingences and impurities" that make up the construction of this anthology. See Golding, "New American Poetry Revisited," 205.

11. See Golding, "New American Poetry Revisited," 187. Golding reveals the major influence Charles Olson had on how the volume came into its final shape, especially with regard to the exclusion of certain poetic forerunners and then-current "objectivist" practitioners: in his archival work, Golding reveals Olson's now-famous statement made in a letter to Allen that "I wldn't myself add either of those two units: either the 'aunties' or the grandpas." Also, Paul Cappucci's essay in this volume reveals William Carlos Williams's correspondence with Allen and the factor it played in Allen's thinking as well as the living influence Williams had on the anthology's contributors.

12. Golding documents Olson's explicit influence and, very astutely, portrays Duncan's influence as transmitted through his initial resistance to Allen's anthology, a resistance that Golding shows to be multi-faceted. Joshua Hoeynck's essay in this volume explores the relationship between Duncan and Olson, revealing Duncan's deep-seated philosophy on poetry through the lens of his relationship with Olson that may inform us even further Duncan's initial resistant stances against *The New American Poetry*.

13. Again it is Duncan who, in his resistance, outlines the problems in Allen's regional categories, posturing that he, himself, was a "coterie" and not a "regional" poet and, if needed to be categorized by region, was disassociating himself with the San Francisco "scene" and aligning himself with those poets from Black Mountain, based on aesthetic and not geographical associations. See Golding, "New American Poetry Revisited," 193.

14. Amiri Baraka, as sole African American contributor in the original *The New American Poetry*, points out the exclusivity of the "club" anthologies like *The New American Poetry* represent (see Golding, "New American Poetry Revisited," 196), an idea Golding queries, if not substantiates, in his deliberations of other Afro-American poets with whom Allen was familiar and in contact at the time of his compilation.

15. See Golding, "New American Poetry Revisited," 199. Like African American poets, Golding admits to other reasons, other than the predominately white male circles in which haunted, for the lack of women poets in his volume, poets such as Diane di Prima and Joanne Kyger, who directly confronted Allen in a 1959 letter. Michael Davidson has called the phenomenon a "compulsory homosociality" that dominated the milieu—Rachel Blau DuPlessis suggests that the exclusion of the fe-

male voice was needed to preserve a projective poetics extolled by Olson to "reclaim poetry for masculine discourse" to make poetry a "serious discourse of assertive, exploratory and aggressive manhood." With this in mind, Megan Swihart Jewell's essay in this volume suggests that *The New American Poetry*'s exclusion of women writers challenged contemporary women's writers such as Kathleen Fraser to "become articulate," perhaps in direct response to the lack of women writers in Allen's first edition.

16. See Golding, "New American Poetry Revisited," 206. Golding refers to both former critics such as John Robert Colombo and Karl Shapiro, and more contemporary critics such as Daniel Hoffman, Vernon Shetley and Walter Kalaidjian who see no value presented other than rebellion itself, suggesting that in their rebellion, the poets and its editor become much like that which they rebel against (in terms of its academic formalism in its presentation, the negative criterion for inclusion in the anthology, its negative version of culture poetry, its dependence on traditions its seeks to repudiate, etc.)

17. Ibid.

18. See Golding, *From Outlaw to Classic*, 32–33. Golding himself, in his historical reportage of *The New American Poetry* and its outlaw, avant-garde status that inevitably loses power as it moves toward canonization, is moved to consider "the more positive implications of this process, involving the potential to address, from within, the institutions with which an extracanonical poetics is nominally at odds." Golding addresses some "positive implications" in his last chapter on Language Writing and the Institutions of Poetry, an essay, and one of the few, which examines *The New American Poetry* in this more novel, positive fashion by tracing a lineage from *The New American Poetry*, one that would fit well in our volume.

19. Jed Rasula, *American Poetry Wax Museum: Reality Effects 1940–1990* (Urbana, IL: NCTE, 1996), 58.

20. Ibid.

21. Rasula, 227. Rasula employs an interesting analogy making the battle between Allen's and Hall-Pack-Simpson anthology a "syndicated television program" where, "in the hijinks of the rerun" what he deems earlier in his essay, the "Squares" and the representative "Beats," "face off in 1960 to duke it out for poetry's golden glove award."

22. Rasula, 243.

23. Many critics have traced this influence, most notably Roy Harvey Pearce in his 1962 study *The Continuity of American Poetry* (Middletown, CT: Wesleyan University Press, 1987).

24. Rasula, 246.

25. Ibid.

26. Rasula, 247.

27. This term emerges at the end of Rasula's section on Literary History as Demonology, a section that aims to demonstrate how literary criticism can, has and continues to partake in the simplification and marginalization of certain poetries. With use of this term, Rasula suggests conflict not to be used to demonize and thus polarize, but to be considered a continuous and productive activity.

Bibliography

Allen, Donald, ed. *The New American Poetry: 1945–1960*. Berkeley: University of California Press, 1999.

Golding, Alan. *From Outlaw to Classic: Canons in American Poetry*. Madison: University of Wisconsin Press, 1995.

———. "The New American Poetry Revisited, Again." *Contemporary Literature* 39, no. 2 (1998): 180–211.

Pearce, Roy Harvey. *The Continuity of American Poetry*. Middletown, CT: Wesleyan University Press, 1987.

Perloff, Marjorie. *21st-Century Modernism: The "New" Poetics*. Malden, MA: Blackwell, 2002.

———. "Whose New American Poetry:: Anthologizing in the 90s." *Diacritics* 26, no. 3–4. (Fall-Winter 1996): 104–23.

Rasula, Jed. *American Poetry Wax Museum: Reality Effects 1940–1990*. Urbana, IL: NCTE, 1996.

CHAPTER TWO

~

"Trying to Build on Their Elders' Work": The Correspondence of Donald Allen and William Carlos Williams

Paul R. Cappucci

As is evident in his introduction to *The New American Poetry*, Donald Allen understood Ezra Pound's and William Carlos Williams's far-reaching influence on the younger set of American poets appearing in his anthology. Many of these younger poets—Frank O'Hara, Charles Olson, and Allen Ginsberg—already had credited Williams with influencing their poetic development. Allen's anthology, though, offers one of the strongest and most enduring testimonials about Williams's direct influence on this generation of poets. Whether the extent of this influence was widely appreciated in the academy before its publication, Allen's anthology ensured that more attention would be paid to the Rutherford doctor's poetry. In his preface, Allen lauds the accomplishments of this "older generation" of poets and specifically mentions Williams's later achievements: *Paterson*, *The Desert Music and Other Poems*, and *Journey to Love*. In a letter dated December 23, 1959, Allen wrote to Williams that he wanted his preface to "point out the magnificent achievements of the older generation during the period and that the newer poets have been trying to build on their elders' work."[1] In this same letter, he informed Williams that Grove Press wanted to send him galley proofs of the anthology for review. Such a letter, with its praise and review request, indicates that Williams's influence extended beyond the poets in the anthology to Allen himself. The two men, in fact, corresponded for several years prior to the release of *The New American Poetry*. As editor for the *Evergreen*

Review, Allen actively sought out Williams's poems, book reviews, and the essay "Measure" for publication. This essay examines that correspondence to reveal the depth of Allen's interest in Williams's work and Williams's thoughts about Allen's landmark anthology.

Allen's collaborative approach to the development of *The New American Poetry* has been well documented. In *"The New American Poetry* Revisited, Again," Alan Golding chronicles how this approach shaped the anthology. He documents the role of various poets, most notably Charles Olson and Robert Duncan, whose input and criticism ultimately influenced the anthology's organization and selection of poets and poems. Golding argues, "The collection is as much the product of multiple, interacting poetic communities and affiliations, of correspondence among contributors and editor, as it is the work of an individual editor himself. In this sense, *The New American Poetry* is very much a communal construction or shared enterprise."[2] Very clearly the younger generation of poets contributed to the "communal" effort and "shared" spirit that Golding posits. However, considering that Allen's correspondence with Williams predates the release of his anthology, their interactions offer another vantage point for understanding the anthology's formation. At one point, as Golding notes, Allen even considered including poetry by Williams and several of the older modernists.[3] In the end, though, despite the fact that Allen left Williams's work out, the Rutherford doctor's presence still permeates the anthology.

The correspondence between Allen and Williams began in the late summer of 1957. Allen initiated it in search of possible poems for publication in *Evergreen Review*. At the time, Allen served as an editor for Barney Rosset's newly founded magazine. This avant-garde periodical already had published work by such recognizable figures as Jean-Paul Sartre, Samuel Beckett, and Henri Michaux. Yet it also had published work by younger writers like Allen Ginsberg, Lawrence Ferlinghetti, and Gary Snyder. Allen initially sought to publish Williams's "View of a Woman at Her Bath" for the third issue. However, he subsequently requested permission to publish two more poems: "The High Bridge above the Tagus River at Toledo," which originally appeared in *Spectrum*, and "Sappho," which appeared in *Poems in Folio*. "That would make a superb group of three for us," he wrote Williams, "if it is all right with you?"[4] Williams agreed, "A fine idea. Use the three poems, they will make an attractive assembly—you'll have no trouble from anyone in getting permission to use them."[5] The poems did appear in the remarkable third issue, alongside poems by Frank O'Hara and Hans Namuth's photos of Jackson Pollock.

In this early correspondence, Allen also expressed interest in Williams writing the essay "Measure" for *Evergreen Review*, as well as an article on

Charles Olson to accompany a Grove Press publication of his selected poems.[6] Williams initially put Allen off: "At present and for some time in the future I shall have to pull in my horns . . ."[7] It should be noted that at this time Williams had been quite hobbled by a series of strokes, yet he still managed to work on *Paterson V* and various poetic projects. In the letter cited above agreeing to Allen's request for three poems, Williams softened his stance towards further work with Allen: "Sorry I have felt it necessary to go into temporary retreat, more a subterfuge than a reality."[3] This apology/explanation, along with an invitation to visit him after the "hell" of renovating their "main rooms," opened the door to further interaction between the two men.

Correspondence continued in May of 1958 shortly after Allen's visit to Rutherford. Apparently, as is evident in Williams's letter to Allen, "measure" was their main topic of discussion.

> The basic ideas of my work on "measure" have been seething in my head ever since you were here last week and as usual I have been occupid [sic] in jotting them dawn [sic] as fast as I am able while they are still vivid to me. . . .
> I'll have them copied just as I wrote them. They are still inchoate but, if you use them, I would want to have printed just as they have occurred as an earnes [sic] of the book to come—which I intend to write filling in the as yet unfinished pages, as yet largely unwritten. This will at least put me on record as the man who was a prime mover of the ideas involved. I owe myself that much credit—in view of my recent verses and the Paterson 5 due out in August.[9]

Williams's conversation with Allen clearly inspired the aging poet to sketch out his ideas on the subject. His enthusiasm for the project seems matched only by his desire to get it "on record." In the correspondence, he reiterated his promise to dedicate the published version to Donald Allen. Williams's letter reflects the fact that the two men had moved beyond a staid, formal editor-poet relationship. Allen's interest and persistence concerning "Measure" functioned as a catalyst for Williams's continuing thought on the subject. Williams's personal dedication offered recognition for that contribution. In a subsequent card sent later that month, Williams updated Allen on his effort "to complete this phase of the thing fast" and admitted that he might even have to forego the stenographer and copy it out himself: "that is slow work, one finger method but in this important (to me) work I can't afford not to take infinite pains."[10] The note not only reflects the project's importance to Williams, but the physical obstacles he overcame to convey his ideas and imaginative expression. Allen acknowledged receipt of the news regarding "Measure" and proffered the possibility of printing it in the January issue of *Evergreen Review*.[11]

In this same letter, Allen requested some help from Williams for a different project. With the assistance of José Amaral, Allen selected two poems by Alí Chumacero that he wanted Williams to translate for *Evergreen Review*'s 1959 Mexican issue entitled *The Eye of Mexico*: "Widower's Monologue" and "The Wanderings of the Tribe." Williams agreed to the translations and by June 10, 1958, (two weeks after Allen's request) he submitted both poems to Allen. He described the "surprisingly difficult" nature of the translating process and described his first go around with it as "practicing on a meat chopper." He admits that he had "to take a minimum of liberties with it." Williams's quick turnaround with the translations suggests yet another remarkable instance of his impressive work ethic even at this stage of his life. Allen did not acknowledge receipt of the poems until mid September of 1958. In doing so, he congratulated Williams on the recent publication of *Paterson 5*: "That is the only superbly beautiful poem I've read since 'Asphodel, That Greeny Flower.'" In his letter, he also asked Williams for a translation of Octavio Paz's "Hymn Among the Ruins" that would be included in the Mexican issue of *Evergreen Review*.[12] Williams asked for "a little time,"[13] but he eventually submitted it to Allen the next month.[14] He claimed to "like the poem and the reticenses [sic] that lie behind the intellectual acceptances of the poet. He is a charming man."

Meanwhile, Allen requested Williams's participation in a variety of ventures. He asked for a review of E.E. Cummings's new book of poems entitled 95,[15] which Williams submitted to him less than two weeks later. Allen later asked Williams to write a related review on Charles Norman's biography of Cummings entitled *The Magic-Maker*. Williams wrote the review; however, he was not thrilled with Norman's work. "What is this book?" he writes to Allen, "Kindergarten stuff. There in't [sic] a word about C.s significance as a poet. Not a word about his punctuation etc only the most elemental reference to him as a lyricist of the first order." At the close of his brief letter, he asks Allen for his "candid opinion of the book": Let's hear it."[16] In later correspondence, Allen responded that "it didn't look great to me, but I felt it would be the good to include a brief mention of it."[17] Besides the reviews related to Cummings, Allen also expressed interest in publishing further autobiographical materials from Williams. In a postscript he writes, "I was deeply moved and fascinated by what you told me one afternoon (when I brought Paz over to meet you) about the difficulties you had after the strokes, how you had gone to hospital and how the therapy there had enabled you to get back on your feet again. I keep wishing I'd had a chance to ask you more about that."[18] Williams wrote to Allen the next day and directed him to an article printed in an issue of *The American Scholar* that offered some of this autobiographical material and considered something further for Allen after his present work was completed. It doesn't appear that anything further materialized for Allen, however.

"Measure," though, continued to be the common thread in correspondence between the two men. On September 29, 1958, Allen wrote to Williams about a recent conversation that he had with Allen Ginsberg concerning the essay. According to Ginsberg, Williams thought that *Evergreen Review* had no genuine interest in it. Allen responded strongly, "I hope this is only a mangled version of what you said—for you know I am keenly interested in this important work and want very much to publish part of the book, at least one essay, in *Evergreen Review*. I've even listed it as one of the major pieces we will be printing in future issues." Williams's response was short and direct: "As far as A.G.'s report of my interest in measure is concerned, tell him to shove it up his ass for all it means to me. It is my chief interest in the writing of verse at the moment."[19] By early January of 1959 Williams completed his draft of "Measure" and informed Allen that he intended to send it to Hugh Kenner as well. He informed Allen that he had precedence if he wanted to publish it.[20] Williams then wrote to Allen asking him about possible payment: "I operate on a very restricted income which I must count on."[21] Allen's immediate response expressed his appreciation for previewing the essay. He provided Williams with the conditions of payment, but he also admitted that he would not be able to print the essay in its entirety in the *Evergreen Review.*[22]

The essay eventually appeared in a Fall 1959 issue of *Spectrum* as "Measure—A Loosely Assembled Essay on Poetic Measure." A note from Hugh Kenner preceded the essay and explained the timeline of Williams's drafting: "Dr. Williams planned this essay in the summer of 1958 and drafted it in the following fall and winter. The state of his health in the spring of 1959 brought his work on the project to a halt."[23] This timeline corresponds to the references in the letters between Allen and Williams. There is no dedication to Allen, most likely due to the essay's publication in a different magazine. Kenner does reference the fact that the original had been shortened by one-third due to editorial changes requested by Williams.[24] Williams organizes the essay into six parts: 1) Campion; 2) Chapman; 3) Shakespeare; 4) Sidney Lanier; 5) The American Idiom; and 6) The Variable Foot. The last two sections appear to be the most applicable to the poets and poetry represented in Allen's anthology.

In the section on the American idiom, Williams describes the artist as "a restless man" who continually works to move beyond the perceived genius of others. In the modern era, with the emergence of "Dada and the nihilists,"[25] one has no choice but "to begin again." As Williams contends, "There is always something new to be experienced if we have the wit for it." From Williams's perspective, this desire for "newness" does battle each generation with "traditionalists" who always fear what that newness represents. He invokes as examples Marcel Duchamp's famed painting *Nude Descending a Staircase*, Pound's cantos, and Cummings's poetry. The traditionalists tend to be "school men" and poets are their "mortal enemies"—"even when they are backward at their 'lessons' as today. But in a new country, as this must still be thought of, our compulsions must go to the new."[26] He also concludes the section with combat imagery that pits devotees to the past against pioneers of the future. Despite the hatred inherent in the conflict, Williams argues that "the language itself can have only one conceivable loyalty. . . . it can be nothing if not partisan of the new."[27]

It is in this language—more precisely, the idiom—that the contemporary poet must work. "Our native idiom," Williams writes, "the way we speak in this democracy, is the image our poetry must dig in as a fertile soil."[28] In correcting H. L. Mencken, Williams argues that he would have been more accurate discussing an American idiom rather than an American language. This idiom, as defined by Williams, functions as "a living language, linked to the current thought of the time which it has its part in moulding."[29] That link between time and language seem an essential feature of the poems included in Allen's anthology—from Ginsberg's *Howl* to LeRoi Jones's "In Memory of Radio." Allen's choice of poets reflects the idiomatic experiments of the era.

Several of the poets acknowledge Williams's work in this area. In his biographical note, Robert Duncan claims that "*The Pisan Cantos*, and the first three volumes of *Paterson*, gave us measure."[30] Poets like Jones also seem receptive to Williams's call. In "How You Sound??," included in Allen's *Statements on Poetics*, he acknowledges in conclusion that

> all this means that we want to go into quantitative verse . . . the 'irregular foot' of Williams . . . the 'Projective Verse' of Olson. Accentual verse, the regular metric of rumbling iambics, is dry as slivers of sand. . . . We can get nothing from England. And the diluted formalism of the academy (the formal culture of the U.S.) is anaemic and fraught with incompetence and unreality.[31]

Jones's statement echoes Williams's promotion of cultural newness and the move away from the confines of academia. Allen Ginsberg, a fellow New Jersey poet, also directly acknowledges Williams's role in the area of measure. In "Notes for *Howl* and Other Poems," which also appeared in Allen's *Statements on Poetics*, Ginsberg writes, "I wrote poetry adapted from prose seeds, journals, scratchings, arranged by phrasing or breath groups into little short-line patterns according to the ideas of measure of American speech I'd picked up from W. C. Williams' [sic] imagist preoccupations."[32] Ginsberg's notion of measure and American speech changed throughout his growth as a poet: "Ideally each line of *Howl* is a single breath unit. . . . My breath is long— that's the Measure, one physical-mental inspiration of thought contained in the elastic of a breath. It probably bugs Williams now, but it's a natural consequence, my own heightened conversation, not cooler average-dailytalk short breath. I got to mouth more madly this way."[33] Gilbert Sorrentino mentions Williams's importance to him in his biographical note: "Three great literary markers are Pound, who taught me that verse is the highest of arts and gave me the sense of tradition, Williams, who showed me that our language can produce it, and Creeley, who demonstrated that the attack need not be head on."[34] Lew Welch and Denise Levertov also mention Williams's influence in their biographical notes. Levertov admits, "I feel the stylistic influence of William Carlos Williams, while perhaps too evident in my work a few years ago, was a very necessary and healthful one, without which I could not have developed from a British Romantic with almost Victorian background to an American poet of any vitality."[35]

Williams's essay "Measure" concludes with a discussion of the variable foot. Once again Williams blasts blind allegiance to old notions of measure and conformity. Using a familiar line of attack, he lambastes contemporary practitioners of the sonnet—"It makes my guts turn over. . . . They want to copy them [Dante and Shakespeare], to prove what? That they are also great poets?"[36] As he exhorts in earlier works like *Spring and All*, Williams calls for an end to copying and seeks inventiveness through a new conception of "measure" commensurate with the discovery of a "new continent."[37] This break from past metrical conventions, however, does not result in unbridled freedom. "No verse can be free," Williams writes. "That is solely a confusion in terms: all verse must be measured."[38] Yet Williams struggles to articulate here exactly how that measure may look. He analogizes it to guessing where one's wife goes when she heads out the back door. Upon her return, her look alone gives the answer. "That's what makes life interesting. That is why we are alive—love conquers all. That is the measure that dictates the structure of the lines of our poems."[39]

Later on, he seems to write his way into an explanation of the variable foot. There is an effort, he suggests, "[t]o use cadences dictated by the American idiom."[40] He attempts to use "the fewest possible words" without a dependence on tautology to convey sense. The selected speech terms are then concentrated in a way "so that an alert mind is encouraged to take the leaps necessary to bridge the gaps in the sense left to save time." In Williams's explanation, a poet must recognize the reader's essential role. This recognition functions as a "test" that exposes "mere eccentricity" in the lines from the ability "to reconstruct the sense from the scheme." In such a test, "the reader must be empowered by the interest of the subject, its way, its topography, (not repelled by it) to follow." Through such participation, a reader ultimately "must be rewarded by achieving a satisfaction which awakens him to a maximum followed by a complete rest in which to enjoy his sensations. The passage must come instantly in an epigram to a climax."[41]

For Williams, the creation of such a measure is dependent upon the poet's ability to move beyond an idiom reliant "on a habitual turn of phrase or of thought."[42] He again turns to Pound who had told him "that we are all born with a pattern of speech to which we are native." It is this pattern that a poet utilizes in the design uniquely inherent to a poem. He cites Pound's *Cantos* as an example of such verse, but he also mentions Cummings and Marianne Moore: "The ideas all these poets employ making them make the words dance, come back to a constant repetitiousness that delights or repels their respective audiences." Once these line divisions and units are perceived, readers will discover the inaccuracy of a term like free verse. Williams concludes his essay with a rousing promotion of the invariable foot:

> It is not easy to teach. It is not even easy to apprehend. But the incentive it gives to a choice of words not out of a book leads to surprising assemblies and turns of phrases which are sometimes rewarding in succinctness and vivid interplays when he poet does not feel constrained by the habitual.[43]

It is this break from the habitual that will result in the something new that Williams calls all poets to construct.

It appears that Donald Allen and Williams suspended any further correspondence with each other until the end of the year. In a letter dated December 23, 1959, Allen informed Williams that he had resigned as co-editor of the *Evergreen Review*. He also mentioned the fact that he saw "Measure" in *Spectrum* and "urged Rosset to consider it for possible reprinting in ER. I very much hope he will decide to buy it." The bulk of his letter, however, describes his anthology project, *The New American Poetry, 1945–1960*. He sketches for Williams his organizational approach for the poets:

> I've followed the rather unusual arrangement of dividing the poets into five groups: the first is more or less the poets associated with Origin and Black Mountain Review; the second, the San Francisco Renaissance; the third, the Beat Generation; the fourth, the New York school; and the fifth, what I think of as the new wave: the younger poets who have emerged here and there and who appear to be developing their own individual styles. Then there are statements on poetics by many of the poets, including Olson's Projective Verse essay; biographical notes; and the first attempt at a bibliography of the subject.

My brief preface will try to define the limits of the period but I will point out the magnificent achievements of the older generation during the period and that the newer poets have been trying to build on their elders' work.

Allen's letter offers Williams a sound synopsis of the anthology he published. He then asks Williams if he would like to see a set of the proofs from Grove Press and if he would be willing to write a comment: "They would probably plan to use it on the dust jacket, if that were agreeable with you." Allen's letter and request clearly demonstrate Williams's importance to Allen and Grove Press in regard to how his support could aid the promotion of this avant-garde collection.

Williams promptly responded to Allen on the very next day and welcomed the article. Ever conscious of completing his work assignments, Williams asked Allen to send it soon because, as he writes, "after Floss reads it to me it will take me a little time to get my reply ready for you." He then divulges to Allen that after his summer operation, "I didn't think I would ever write again but I've learned finally never to sell myself short." He closes with a non-sequitur regarding the turn of painters against abstraction.

The conscientious Williams wrote to Allen less than two weeks after receiving the galleys. His letter offers Allen great praise for the anthology. He acknowledges the challenge associated with assembling so many poems from various magazines, as well as the overarching determination of selecting American poems from the specific period, 1945–1960. More important, though, he describes this assembly of poets and poems in the anthology as a "shock of awakening."

"Trends and categories had been uncovered," he writes. "It has been an awakening and a freeing from old form that I have gotten to without shuffling them off." Williams returns to this notion of "freeing" later in the letter, despite the fact that there is some inconsistency in the quality of poems. For Williams, Allen's anthology offers an inclusive presentation of contemporary American verse: "Sectarian views are ignored—Jew, Catholic, or Buddhist does not enter in to the catigories [sic]; all are admitted on equal catigories of thought, that to me is a sine qua non of modern poetic thought. The beatnic [sic] generation without stating it is responsible for that." Williams attributes this equality as an "American phenomenon," a "modern" phenomenon, perhaps even a "Soviet phenomenon." Yet he seems to pull back from that final suggestion and return to an American origin—"but in point of fact it is the American a classless reaction. It has much to do with our sexless modern imagery." This imagery he suggests is rooted in Whitman. He concludes, "There has been a revolution in American taste absolutely circumscribed in

American preferences [*sic*]. Maybe this is linked to our present concepts of astrophysics—I'm willing to accept that it is related to it, but I also think it may be related to our desperation."

Allen eventually responded to Williams on February 16, 1960. He politely thanked Williams for the letter and claimed "to read it from time to time with more understanding." He also referenced Williams's essay "Measure"— both in terms of it publication in Rosset's *Evergreen Review* and Allen's own future project on poetics. Eventually in 1973, Allen did co-edit with Warren Tallman *Poetics of the New American Poetry* (Grove Press), an anthology inclusive of notes, essays, and letters from various American poets regarding poetics. Allen did not include "Measure" here; however, he did include Williams's essays on "Edgar Allan Poe" from *In the American Grain*, "The Work of Gertrude Stein," "Introduction to *The Wedge*," and a 1950 letter from Williams to Robert Creeley.[44] It's unclear how Allen received the Creeley letter, which is filed with the Williams correspondence among his personal papers. Creeley, however, was a significant contributor to the poetry and poetics anthology. In the book on poetics, he quotes Williams extensively, including excerpts from the introduction to *The Wedge*, a book he describes as "a revelation to me."[45] Several other poets reference Williams in some fashion through their various commentary on poetics—Charles Olson, Philip Whalen, Frank O'Hara, Allen Ginsberg, and Denise Levertov. At the conclusion of the essay collection, the editors included a chronology of "significant books, periodicals, and presses of the period."[46] Several of Williams's works are directly referenced: *Poems* (1909), *Kora in Hell* (1920), *Spring and All* (1923), *In the American Grain* (1925), *Paterson* (1946–1951), *The Desert Music* (1954).

It appears that the 1960 letter from Allen is the last written communication between the two men. Allen chose not to use Williams's comments in promotion of his anthology. In his preface, though, he credits Williams among others with setting the foundation for the contemporary poets featured in the anthology. He situates these poets in a postwar period that he describes as "singularly rich" in American poetry. He describes it as a vital, not static time in American poetry and records the accomplishments of the "older generation" (like Williams) and the "second generation" (the poetry of Elizabeth Bishop). He specifically mentions Williams's later achievements: *Paterson*, *The Desert Music and Other Poems*, and *Journey to Love*. He then directly links the younger generation of poets he has assembled to the Williams-Pound line: "Following the practice and precepts of Ezra Pound and William Carlos Williams, it has built on their achievements and gone on to evolve new conceptions of the poem."[47] Besides the poets mentioned earlier who reference Williams, Robert Creeley and Charles Olson also make mention of Williams's influence.[48] Olson seems to offer the most direct acknowledgement of the influence that informs Allen's preface: "But what I want to emphasize here . . . is the already projective nature of verse as the sons of Pound and Williams are practicing it."[49] Such references reflect Williams's import to Allen, as well as his importance to these younger poets. "I stayed up last night reading your anthology," wrote Frank O'Hara in a letter to Allen dated April 28, 1960, "and it is really a beautiful book. The preface is terrific, just right, and the book as a whole is marvelous."[50]

For Williams's part, in a 1960 interview with Walter Sutton, he acknowledged a link to the younger poets in Allen's anthology that were "following the same path."[51] Williams, though, drew a distinction between these poets and his own verse. A particular sticking point for him was their disregard for his variable foot concept: "they don't know exactly, metrically, what they're doing, most of them. They have a tendency to call it free verse, but I object." He expressed particular dissatisfaction with Ginsberg's use of the long line. In contrast, he found Olson's line "much more in the American idiom."[52] Yet he also suggests that Olson's *Maximus* poem "might have been a better poem" if it more closely identified with Gloucester. Of all the poets included in Allen's anthology, Williams aligned himself most closely with Denise Levertov. "I feel closer to her than to any of the modern poets," he told Sutton. "She is more alert—very much more alert to my feelings about words."[53]

The Allen-Williams correspondence serves as a notable entryway into the formation and development of Allen's landmark anthology. As evident in his preface, Allen traced the emergence of these younger poets to the poetic practices of Pound and Williams. Reviewers of the anthology were quick to pick up on the formulization of this poetic line of descent. Harvey Shapiro, in his review for *The New York Times*, wrote that "the new verse is a continuation of the crusade against the English tradition begun years ago by Pound and Williams."[54] Since Allen never appeared to correspond with Pound, his correspondence with Williams reflects his personal desire to connect to that revered, influential older generation of poets. Yet Allen moved beyond simple adoration of Williams and actively sought to integrate him into the happenings of this younger generation, whether it was through publishing poems in the *Evergreen Review* or reviewing galleys for *The New American Poetry*. Through his efforts, Allen linked together several poetic generations and ultimately crystallized through his anthology the scope of a mid-century poetic renaissance rooted in poets like Williams who continued to remain relevant in the American avant-garde.

Notes

1. Letter dated December 23, 1959. All correspondence can be found in the Donald Allen Collection in Mandeville Special Collections Library at the University of California at San Diego. Permission to print Allen's correspondence granted by Michael Williams, literary executor of Donald Allen.

2. Alan Golding, "*The New American Poetry* Revisited, Again," *Contemporary Literature* 39, no. 2 (1998): 81.

3. Ibid., 184.

4. The request appears in a letter dated September 25, 1957.

5. Undated correspondence. All unpublished letters from Williams to Allen are copyright © 2013 by the Estates of Paul H. Williams and William Eric Williams. Used by permission of New Directions Publishing Corporation.

6. Letter dated August 22, 1957.

7. Letter dated September 12, 1957.

8. Ibid.

9. Letter dated May 4, 1958.

10. Card dated May 26, 1958.

11. Letter dated May 27, 1958.

12. Letter dated September 14, 1958. This letter offers compelling evidence for redating the composition of this poem. Based on Paz's recollection of seeing the poem in a 1974 issue of *London Magazine*, this poem previously has been dated as translated in 1955.

13. Undated correspondence.

14. Letter dated October 7, 1958 from Williams to Allen acknowledges the completion of the translation.

15. Letter dated September 29, 1958 from Allen to Williams.

16. Letter dated November 12, 1958 from Williams to Allen.

17. Letter dated November 16, 1958 from Allen to Williams.

18. Letter dated 6 October 1958 from Allen to Williams.

19. Letter dated October 4, 1958 from Williams to Allen.

20. Letter dated January 15, 1958 from Williams to Allen. Based upon the narrative of the correspondence, I believe this date to be mistaken and place it as January 15, 1959.

21. Letter dated January 23, 1959 from Williams to Allen.

22. Letter dated January 25, 1959 from Allen to Williams. Allen notes that the scale of pay is $4.00 for each page of the finished printed material, which approximates to 1 cent per word. He goes on to offer further payment details if the work appears elsewhere and it gets reprinted.

23. Hugh Kenner, "Notes on Measure," *Spectrum* 3, no. 3 (1959): 130.

24. Ibid.

25. William Carlos Williams, "Measure—A Loosely Assembled Essay on Poetic Measure," *Spectrum* 3, no. 3 (1959): 147. All quotes from this essay are copyright © 1959 by William Carlos Williams. Used by permission of New Directions Publishing Corporation.

26. Ibid., 148.
27. Ibid., 150.
28. Ibid., 148.
29. Ibid., 145.
30. Donald Allen, ed. *The New American Poetry: 1945–1960* (New York: Grove Press, 1960), 434.
31. LeRoi Jones, "How You Sound??," in *The New American Poetry: 1945–60*, ed. Donald Allen (New York: Grove Press, 1960), 425.
32. Allen Ginsberg, "Notes for *Howl* and Other Poems," in *The New American Poetry: 1945–60*, ed. Donald Allen (New York: Grove Press, 1960), 414–15.
33. Ibid., 416.
34. Allen, *The New American Poetry: 1945–1960*, 444.
35. Ibid., 441.
36. Williams, "Measure—A Loosely Assembled Essay on Poetic Measure," 152.
37. Ibid., 153.
38. Ibid.
39. Ibid., 154.
40. Ibid., 155.
41. Ibid., 156.
42. Ibid.
43. Ibid., 157.
44. The selection of Williams's "Edgar Allan Poe" essay from *In the American Grain* stands out here in terms of its selection, especially given the numerous essays from which to choose. It strikes me particularly that this same essay was touted by famed art critic Harold Rosenberg early in his career when he aspired to be a poet. He wrote the following to Williams on January 25, 1941: "Reread recently your piece on Poe in The American Grain. That article, which goes counter to every accepted notion about American Literary Tradition, seems to me one of the chief critical embryos of modern U.S. It is too bad that it just lies there, and has never really gotten up and entered the battle" (See Beinecke Library, Williams Collection). One must conclude that Allen and Tallman shared a similar sentiment and sought a way to highlight the essay's relevance in the continuing definition of an American poetic.
45. Donald and Warren Tallman Allen, ed. *The Poetics of the New American Poetry* (New York: Grove Press, 1973), 266.
46. Ibid., 461.
47. Donald Allen, "Preface," in *The New American Poetry: 1945–60*, ed. Donald Allen (New York: Grove Press, 1960), xi.
48. The poets directly referencing Williams in some part of the anthology include the following: LeRoi Jones (425), Robert Duncan (434), Denise Levertov (441), Allen Ginsberg (415; 416), Lew Welch (445), Gilbert Sorrentino (444), Charles Olson (394), and Robert Creeley (409–10).
49. Charles Olson, "Projective Verse," *The New American Poetry: 1945–60*, ed. Donald Allen (New York: Grove Press, 1960), 394.
50. "Letter, Frank O'Hara to Donald Allen, Projective Verse," in *Donald Allen Collection*, Mandeville Special Collections Library (University of California, San Diego).

51. William Carlos Williams, "A Visit with William Carlos Williams: Interview by Walter Sutton," in *Interviews with William Carlos Williams: "Speaking Straight Ahead.*, ed. Linda Welshimer Wagner (New York: New Directions, 1976), 39. Excerpts of this interview are copyright © 1976 by the Estate of William Carlos Williams. Used by permission of New Directions Publishing Corporation.

52. Ibid., 41.

53. Ibid., 40.

54. Harvey Shapiro, "Rebellious Mythmakers," review of *The New American Poetry*, *New York Times*, August 28, 1960, 6.

Bibliography

Allen, Donald, ed. *The New American Poetry: 1945–1960*. New York: Grove Press, 1960.

———. "Preface." *The New American Poetry: 1945–60*, edited by Donald Allen, xi–xiv. New York: Grove Press, 1960.

Allen, Donald, and Warren Tallman, ed. *The Poetics of the New American Poetry*. New York: Grove Press, 1973.

Beinecke Rare Book and Manuscript Library. Yale Collection of American Literature. William Carlos Williams Collection. Yale University.

Ginsberg, Allen. "Notes for *Howl* and Other Poems." *The New American Poetry: 1945–60*, edited by Donald Allen; New York: Grove Press, 1960: 414–18.

Golding, Alan. "*The New American Poetry* Revisited, Again." *Contemporary Literature* 39, no. 2 (1998): 180–211.

Jones, LeRoi. "How You Sound??" *The New American Poetry: 1945–60*, edited by Donald Allen; New York: Grove Press, 1960: 424–25.

Kenner, Hugh. "Notes on Measure." *Spectrum* 3, no. 3 (1959): 130.

"Letter, Frank O'Hara to Donald Allen." *Donald Allen Collection*: University of California, San Diego.

Mandeville Special Collections Library. Donald Allen Collection. University of California, San Diego.

Olson, Charles. "Projective Verse." *The New American Poetry: 1945–60*, edited by Donald Allen; New York: Grove Press, 1960: 386–97.

Shapiro, Harvey. "Rebellious Mythmakers." Review of *The New American Poetry*. *New York Times*, August 28, 1960.

Williams, William Carlos. "Measure—a Loosely Assembled Essay on Poetic Measure." *Spectrum* 3, no. 3 (1959): 131–57.

———. "A Visit with William Carlos Williams: Interview by Walter Sutton." *Interviews with William Carlos Williams: "Speaking Straight Ahead,"* edited by Linda Welshimer Wagner. New York: New Directions, 1976.

———. "Author's Introduction to *The Wedge*." *The Collected Poems of William Carlos Williams*. Volume III. New York: New Directions, 1988: 53–55.

CHAPTER THREE

~

Without a Mammalia Maxima, Charles Olson and Robert Duncan Apprehend a Cosmological American Poetics

Joshua S. Hoeynck

While outlining *The New American Poetry* on September 9, 1959, Donald Allen penned a letter to Charles Olson that articulated his difficulty reconnoitering the landscape of American poetry. Asking Olson's advice about the anthology's organization, Allen writes, "One problem I've always had is finding where (deciding where) the muscle begins."[1] "I've written Bob [Creeley]," he continues, "and asked him what his reaction to this is: to begin with 10 to 15 pages of the older generation, chosen from their work published since 1945: WCW[illiams], [Ezra] Pound (1 canto), M[arianne] Moore, H[ilda] D[oolittle], EEC[ummings], Wallace Stevens."[2] Allen's language belies his fraught position as both editor and reader: the phrases "finding where" and "deciding where" evince tension between his roles as the anthology's coordinator and as an interpreter of poetic, stylistic affinity. For Allen, moreover, the "muscle" includes poets of the Pound era, but as a reader of Olson's poetry, he senses Olson's response might be unfavorable. He proposes to include only "(1 canto)."

"I wldn't [sic] myself add either of those two units: either the 'aunties' or the grandpas," Olson responds on September 12.[3] Offering a different outline, he shapes the contours of the anthology by dividing mid-century American poetry into the Black Mountain School and the Beat Generation: "I. Origin—Black Mountain: Creeley [Robert] Duncan [Michael] Rumaker [John] Weiners [Ed] Dorn [Edward] Marshall and myself / II Beat: Jack [Kerouac]

Allen [Ginsberg] [Philip] Whalen [Gary] Snyder [Gregory] Corso—[Michael] McClure."[4] When Alan Golding considers how Olson's letter compartmentalizes American poetry's content and style, he remarks, "for Olson, the anthology's point was not to trace genealogical connections but to suggest associations among contemporary writers."[5] Golding's emphasis on "associations" between poets further emerges in the letter when Olson skeptically questions dispersing poets from a central axis: he names "the danger" "these 'placements' of Origin-Black Mt, San Francisco / Beat, New York, and the new wave," which "divide up the force and so scatter the center."[6] Against this fear over scattering "the center," however, Allen's final product employs Olson's epistolary advice for organizational purposes, partitioning the poets in the anthology into their respective schools. The letter to Allen then closes by stressing a national poetics, geographically ensconcing *The New American Poetry* and its local "connections among contemporary writers": "yr anthology ought to be the decisive defining factor, that American writing went into a new gear [. . .] none of those older ghosts like—even the papas were international, this thing is most national."[7] Allen follows this request as well, removing modernist poetry from the anthology and only referencing Olson's "older ghosts" in the preface.[8] A significant document for understanding the editorial history of *The New American Poetry*, Olson's letter displays his oftentimes vitriolic relationship to his "aunties" and "grandpas," along with his sense of himself as an American poet with no ties to the European cosmopolitanism functioning in the poetics of Pound and T.S. Eliot.

By directing Allen's attention away from Pound's generation, Olson also engages in a bit of self-promotion, causing his poem, "The Kingfishers," to claim prominence in the anthology. As Burton Hatlen demonstrates, "it has long since won a place among the key texts of modern poetry, and at this point the curious reader can consult at least eight interpretations of the poem."[9] For Hatlen, Olson's "Kingfishers" is "[a] verbal action, a kinetic event" that voices a variety of positions rather than any one settled, final conclusion.[10] Hatlen usefully proceeds through a close reading of this "kinetic event" by analyzing two critical strains available for reading the poem: conservative and radical, a longing for the stasis of a lost order versus an affirmation of constant change.[11] As Hatlen divulges, the poem's critical history highlights its tense opposition of nature to culture, modernity to archaic civilizations, stasis to flux, themes that reverberated throughout the careers of many poets in Allen's anthology. Alongside Hatlen's article, Ralph Maud's investigative study, *The Significance of Charles Olson's Kingfishers*, details the poem's concern with the primordial past and with Olson's sense of a "postmodern archaic." Following some extensive detective work into the poem's references, Maud situates these two concerns in relation to one of Olson's primary intellectual influences:

> Alfred North Whitehead's *Process and Reality*, which Olson used in Spring 1955 before buying his own copy in 1957, is a major intervention between the writing of "The Kingfishers" in 1949 and his being unable to finish a reading of it in 1963. Through Whitehead's *Process and Reality*, there is the possibility of a new stance, where the postmodern "archaic" receives addition from the religious sense of "primordial."[12]

Maud references two points in the poem's life history. First, Olson began to read it at the Vancouver Poetry Festival in 1963 only to find himself unable to finish; second, Olson's reading of Whitehead's *Process and Reality* caused him to re-think how "The Kingfishers" deals with history and with the question of origins. After Whitehead, the conservative strain in "The Kingfishers" became anathema to Olson, which is to say that he rejected the static stance identified by Hatlen while affirming change and paradox.

To summarize: Whitehead's *Process and Reality* considers the philosophies of Descartes, Locke, Hume, and Kant, revising their metaphysical categories and imagining instead a bewildering cosmos of co-dependent things. At its conclusion, the philosophy of organism, as Whitehead names it, defines the primordial stuff of the universe by speculating on "God and the World." The following passage from Olson's copy shows the poet's excitement at Whitehead's expansive definition of the primordial as God's free, eternal yet deficient qualities:

> [God] has a primordial nature and a consequent nature. <u>The consequent nature of God is conscious</u>; and it is the realization of the actual world in the unity of his nature, and through the transformation of his wisdom. <u>The primordial nature is conceptual, the consequent nature is the weaving of God's physical feelings upon his primordial</u> concepts.[13]

Whitehead posits God as a "dipolar" being, consequent and primordial, accounting for first cause and eliminating the idea of a transcendent God from a perplexing cosmos of process and flux. Interestingly, Olson's underlining reveals that Maud rightly notes Olson's notion of a "postmodern archaic"— his interest in researching non-modern human civilizations to discover a means of pushing beyond modernity—receives a cosmic supplement from Whitehead's primordial God. So Whitehead's cosmic thinking about the vastness of external reality induced Olson to stop reading "The Kingfishers" in Berkeley; he recognized the poem did not do enough justice to the nonhuman universe and to the scales of the cosmos' primordial reality.

Given the extensive commentary on "The Kingfishers," proposing an original reading of the poem is difficult, but ignored moments like Olson's failed reading in 1963 point the way forward. The close, cultural and historical analyses do not unpack the life history of the poem's ideas, that is, how the specific images in "The Kingfishers" incite epistolary discussions and new poems that extend Olson's emphasis on the dynamics of the cosmos. Olson influenced Allen to leave Poundian Modernism out of the anthology in late 1959 due to his engagement with the poet Robert Duncan and with Whitehead; both shifted his attention to how the philosophy of organism locates humans amid the cosmos' evolving imaginative, linguistic and actual events. In correspondence from the fall of 1959 to the spring of 1960, as Allen organized the anthology, Olson debated Whitehead's process philosophy with Duncan. While Olson initially read Whitehead's cosmology as a means to establish definite knowledge about the world, Duncan argued *Process and Reality* proposes a universe in which there is "no mammalia maxima," no human center. Their epistolary discussions produced the first part of Duncan's poem "Apprehensions," which he sent to Olson and which turned Olson from the primordial historical events of his early career to Whitehead's notion that humans are mere events in an uncertain world. "The Kingfishers" contains inklings of a poetics that ponders the cosmos' baffling primordial reality, but Olson could not fully imagine a poetics of process and of reality until "Apprehensions" caused him to become a "devotee of the ensemble" of creating and created, cosmic events. By reading Duncan and Whitehead, he arrived at a cosmological poetics in which the poet apprehends an indefinite pluriverse without a "Mammalia maxima." Not just an act of self-promotion then, Olson's comments to Allen about the shape of *The New American Poetry* result from the collision of two contrasting strains of influence: his agonistic Poundian phase (1945–1955), which "The Kingfishers'" use of history exemplifies and which Olson would discard as the 1950s transitioned into the 1960s; and his Whiteheadian phase (1955–1970), which his correspondence with Duncan and *Maximus III* reveal.

Primordial History and "The Kingfishers"

In a foundational article of 1973, Guy Davenport situates "The Kingfishers" squarely within the Poundian tradition, indicating "the poem, like a canto of Pound, is a single ideogram, its components working in synergy," that is, a vortex of energy with constituent parts circulating around a stable, static center.[14] Against Davenport, however, Don Byrd argues that Olson "identifies not with Pound and Eliot but Rimbaud, who goes off in search of a larger space in which to conduct the essential business of living."[15] Either the poem's modernist themes vibrate around a static center and establish an unbroken poetics extending from Pound to Olson, or the poem's language circulates outward and disperses meaning into a "larger space." In "The Kingfishers," after the opening line from Heraclitus's fragments—"what does not change / is the will to change"—Olson's themes oscillate between this duality. The poem's first part describes a party in Washington D.C., Olson's home at the time of composition (1949), where Angkor Vat commands the conversation. Casting primordial reality in human terms, the poet depicts "Fernand," who Maud identifies as the painter John Cernand, and represents him speaking of the extinct civilization:

Yes, Fernand, who had talked lispingly of Albers & Angkor Vat.
He had left the party without a word. How he got up, got into his coat,
I do not know. When I saw him, he was at the door, but it did not matter,
he was already sliding along the wall of the night, losing himself
in some crack of the ruins. That it should have been he who said, "The kingfishers!
who cares
for their feathers
now?"[16]

If, as Davenport argues, "Pound [. . .] set out in *The Cantos* to say how cultures rise and fall," then Olson's concern with "Angkor Vat" places him in the Poundian tradition.[17] And though Davenport differentiates Olson's lack of an economic stance from Pound's overt emphasis on building and trade, the opening of "The Kingfishers" actually concerns economies.[18] Maud discusses Fernand's next comment in the poem—"the pool is slime"—and reveals that Olson references how the sale of kingfisher feathers maintained the upkeep of the ruins: "Angkor Vat's many artificial pools provided the habitat for the birds who financed the national architectural treasure."[19] The poem's opening therefore intimates an economic history in order to connect humans and animals, culture and nature. Maud goes on to note that Olson's "use of the word 'ruins'" may recall Eliot's line from "The Wasteland"— "these fragments I have shored against my ruins"—but he asks, "would it not be possible to stick with the literal here? Gernand was going down the stairs of 'an old building in St. Matthews Court' [. . .] right behind St. Matthews Cathedral" in Washington D.C.[20] "The church," he continues, "[provides] a crack in the ruins for Fernand to lose himself in."[21] Hence, Olson deploys the Christian cultural monument (St. Matthews), the poem's setting (Washington D.C.), and Fernand's conversation about Angkor Vat to foreshadow the landmarks of the United States falling into decay. This is the inevitable fate for nations "that conquer with armies / and whose only right is their power," as Pound puts it in *The Pisan Cantos*.[22] By implicitly comparing the ruins at Angkor Vat to the various ruins surrounding the urban landscape of Washington D.C., Olson also forecasts the first volume of *The Maximus Poems*, where Maximus preaches and warns the dilapidated fishing town of Gloucester against the incursions of the capitalist United States, shadow images replaying Maximus's position against Alexander the Great's invasion of Tyre in 332 B.C. Nonetheless, Olson's phrases imply a deeper uncertainty that counters this cultural reading, for Fernand is "already sliding along the wall of the *night*," not the wall of the church or the wall of a ruin. The language does connect the ruins of Angkor Vat to the detritus produced by the neo-capitalist United States, thus adhering to Pound's *Cantos*, but the "night," "the pool of slime," and Gernand's drunkenness, which Maud identifies, give the poem a bewildering feel. At the outset of "The Kingfishers" and *The New American Poetry*, humans are neither sure nor stable, but thrust against the imposing and indefinite "wall of night," lost at mid-century with the terms of Pound's Modernism (the rise and fall of civilizations) and a cosmic uncertainty authorized by language's slippery metaphors (the "wall of night").

The poem's second part continues to navigate themes of uncertainty and civilization, portraying the "E on the stone" at Delphi along with quotes from Mao Zedong and from encyclopedia passages on kingfishers.[23] The section plays at images of regeneration, and it has occasioned political debate, adding weight to the critical discourse surrounding both "The Kingfishers" and *The New American Poetry*. Olson cites the kingfishers nesting and a letter sent to him by Jean Riboud, which quotes Mao saying, "we must arise and act":

It is true, it does nest with the opening year, but not on waters.
It nests at the end of a tunnel bored by itself in a bank. There,
six or eight white and translucent eggs are laid, on fishbones
not on bare clay, on bones thown up in pellets by the birds.
                                        On these rejectamenta
(as they accumulate they form a cup-shaped structure) the young are born.
And, as they are fed and grow, this nest of excrement and decayed fish becomes
                                        a dripping, fetid mass
Mao concluded:
                    nous devons
                            nous lever
                                    et agir![24]

Scrutinizing Olson's use of Mao's language, Robert van Hallberg indicates Olson's phrases function "on such a high level of abstraction that Mao's particular ideology is irrelevant."[25] By contrast, Sherman Paul suggests that "Mao is an example of the very thing that Olson advises" because he "renews [civilization] by going outside of its traditions, in this instance by bringing western thought (Marxism) to the East."[26] For van Hallberg, the lines exemplify Olson's gradual, career-long rejection of a productive, ideological politics rooted in dialectical materialism, while for Paul, Mao stands as an enabling figure who advances processes of radical change. Nevertheless, the lines juxtapose Mao with a kingfisher building its nest in a cave, paralleling Mao's time in the caves at Yanan to the caves in which kingfishers reproduce. The concurrent political ideals and organic matter produced in both instances do not necessarily have a positive valence. Like the bird, Mao crafts a "dripping, fetid mass" of "rejectamenta" and "excrement," the rot of the body, salient images for a poem only four years removed from World War II and the holocaust. Note Olson's linguistic turns: he opens with a seemingly definite assertion, "it is true," and then follows with indefinite qualifiers, "not on waters" and "not on bare clay." Then the birds lay either "six or eight" eggs: the conjunction leaving us unsure which. The poem deceptively calls for an organic wholeness latent in the regenerative power of the kingfishers and Mao's words, but ironically transports lines from a text of scientific fact, the encyclopedia, into a linguistic construct evincing uncertainty.

After connecting Mao, the birds and the stench of decaying matter, Olson's third part traffics in origins by highlighting the primordial history of America. Maud explicates how Olson borrows the following lines from William Prescott's *History of the Conquest of Mexico*, which describes Aztec priests entreating "the people" to save their gods from Spanish conquistadors:

> In this instance, the priests
> (in dark cotton robes, and dirty,
> their disheveled hair matted with blood and flowing wildly
> over their shoulders)
> rush in among the people, calling on them
> to protect their gods
>
> And all now is war
> where so lately there was peace,
> and the sweet brotherhood, the use
> of tilled fields.[27]

In a poem that opens with "what does not change / is the will to change," these lines represent a primordial American event of epic change, the moment Cortez tore down Aztec gods and claimed the continent for a homogeneous cosmology—monotheism. Davenport contrasts these lines to the kingfisher's nests in the previous section: "the process by which the kingfisher becomes the architect of a nest which it always builds superbly well was developed over millions of years of evolution. Against this continuous line of natural onward-ness the rise and fall of human empires are swift and of indifferent interest to the living universe."[28] Fitting the poem into the Poundian tradition and reproducing the model of twentieth century poetics outlined in Hugh Ken-ner's imperial text, *The Pound Era*, Davenport elides the possibility that Olson vaguely senses nature is a flawed entity; like the wars initiated by Mao and Cortez, Olson's version of nature sometimes takes the shape of a predatory battle. The third part of the poem, for instance, opens with "When the atten-tions change / the jungle / leaps in," framing the section with a personified and primal "jungle" or natural world that preys on the processes of thought by rushing into the brain. "Cat feeds on Mouse / God feeds on God," as Olson's contemporary Jack Spicer put it in *The New American Poetry*.[29] The theme of Pre-Columbian, human sacrifice recurs in the poem's close when Olson declares his interest in "what is slain in the sun," a line that complicates how these lines valorize "tilled fields" and "sweet brotherhood." Indeed, Olson's foray into the historical origins of America uncovers disturbing violence at the heart of cultural and natural orders.

Following the poem's turn to the clash between Aztec priests and con-quistadors, Olson's fourth section deploys Norbert Weiner's text *Cybernetics or Control and Communication in the Animal and the Machine*. With Weiner's book as source, however, the poem briefly and interestingly moves away from its stress on civilization:

> We can be precise. The factors are
> in the animal and/or the machine the factors are
> communication and/or control, both involve
> the message. And what is the message? The message is
> a discrete and continuous sequence of measurable events distributed in
> time.[30]

The final sentence derives from Weiner's introduction and outlines ideas that Olson would rewrite throughout his life—"The message is / a discrete and continuous sequence of measurable events," terms which emerge in his correspondence with Robert Duncan while he advises Allen to cut the older generation from *The New American Poetry*. Nevertheless, these lines highlight tense oppositions, "communication" versus "control," unrelated and "discrete" events versus connected and "continuous" events in a sequence. Maintaining a kind of dialectic of contrasts, Olson posits "factors" that are "in the animal

and/or the machine," which involve "communication and/or control"; the repeated conjunctions upset the copulas, making it unclear whether Olson favors
a static state of being ("is" and "are") or a state of radical change ("and/or").

Dialectically then, "The Kingfishers" opens the anthology emphasizing
a universe of discontinuity versus measure, a cosmos of paradox against a
mathematical universe in which things are known with clarity, and the violent "postmodern archaic" against modernity's empirical stance. The poem
retains this dichotomy at its close, comparing "discrepancy" and "truth":

> Despite the discrepancy (an ocean   courage   age)
>   this is also true: if I have any taste
>   it is only because I have interested myself
>   in what was slain in the sun
>   I pose you your question
>   shall you uncover honey / where maggots are?
>   I hunt among stones.[31]

Opening *The New American Poetry* in 1960 with bodies "slain in the sun," Olson
ties his poem and the anthology to an unsettling vision of humankind and human civilization. A vatic seeker longing for stasis and agency amid these primordial historical events, Olson conceives himself as an archeologist who attempts
to "uncover honey / where maggots are," foreshadowing that other seeker in his
poetry: Maximus of Tyre. Furthermore, he references Pound's "maggots" from
the opening of the *Pisan Cantos*, rounding out the poem's stress on shattered
human civilizations by including fascism's wreck: "that maggots shld / eat the
dead bullock," the slashes recall the slash in "what does not change / is the will
to change."[32] Olson fittingly ends on the line, "I hunt among stones," refusing to
define that after which he hunts and instead positioning humans, and the poet,
as prey animals or cannibals on the "hunt" for food.

"Who Slew the Old Sun": Toward "Apprehensions"

"The Kingfishers" therefore proposes an appropriate reality for a world that
suffered through two of the most violent conflagrations in recorded history,
highlighting deep flaws within nature and human culture while writing tension between stasis and sweeping change, measure and discord. However,
the poem's genetic history reveals more. On December 31, 1956, Olson sent
Robert Duncan a poem entitled "Who Slays the Spanish Sun," explicitly revising the end of "The Kingfishers." In this co-text, Olson appears to indicate
Duncan "slays the Spanish sun," so he changes the original lines, "I have interested myself / in what was slain in the sun." He shifts "what" to "who" and

reverses the sentence's structure, switching from slain objects to subjective agency and from the passive voice to the active, present tense. Something has altered: as Sherman Paul notes, Olson's reading of *Process and Reality* in 1955 revealed that "the only absolute [. . .] is the actual particular occasion, the *event* in which man himself creatively participates."[33] So in this poem, Olson praises Duncan's agency as an active creator within an event, the daily life of the city of San Francisco: "the thing the town is, as it never was able to be without you. Lovely as it is," he writes in the letter before the poem:

> The infestation the sun
>   doesn't breed, what you can't put down,
> San Franciscans, washing your hands
> and your minds. What he won't let you
> wash. Laodicea
>
> Not enlarge
>
> Or sell. Who teaches you what
>
> to enjoy. To enjoy
>   what he got there
> out of your clean clothes. Cruel
> was your loveliness until your loveliness
> fell into his cruel hands, his aimed
> aimlessness. His love
>
> who slew the old sun,
> new North Beach, was shrewder
> than the Sacramento Irish (none got as far
> as Duncan[34]

By comparing San Francisco, a port town like Tyre, to the ancient city of "Laodicea" located in Turkey, Olson connects the profitable commercial trade that sustained Laodicea to the trade that sustains San Francisco. That is, this poem's emphasis on sea-based economies recalls how the opening of "The Kingfishers" includes the birds' feathers as items of trade. Interestingly though, Olson pits the word "what" against the word "who," creating a kind of oppositional rhetorical crescendo: "what you can't put down," "what he won't let you / wash," "what to enjoy," and "what he got there" are set against "who teaches" and "who slew." The stanzas vibrate between sentences constricted by "who" (humans) and by "what" (objects), implicitly referencing the revision within the poem's title: "what was slain" has become "who slays," no longer a history intimating slaughter, but rather a present intimating love. Personifying Duncan's love in the line "His love / who slew the old sun," Olson specifies the poem's dominant pattern, leading the reader away from the bodies slain in the sun to how Duncan's love "slew" the "old sun" from "The Kingfishers." The sonic pun—"old sun" and "Olson"—is also present, paying homage to Duncan's play "The Origins of Old Sun," which Duncan directed at Black Mountain College in 1955 and which made much fun of the college's gargantuan rector. "Slew" maintains the poem's internal rhyme scheme by echoing "new" and "shrew," but it seems to shift back to the past tense. Nonetheless, the verb can be read as a present tense verb—"slew," as in to turn or swing around on a pivot. Like a planet spinning around another heavenly body, "Duncan slew Olson," thus spinning the elder poet's attentions round by circulating epistles to him. These two poets write quasi-collaborative poems through correspondence, such that both fit Charles Altieri's model of productive readers who "take pleasure in and feel enlarged by resisting the demands of our specific material positions."[35] "Who Slays the Spanish Sun" indicates Olson's joy in Duncan's epistles and in his play while confirming Altieri's view: Olson avoids his personal, historical interests and defers to his status as a reader of Duncan's poetry.

But why associate "old sun" with a "Spanish sun"? Olson does rewrite the themes from "The Kingfishers" pertaining to Cortez, a Spaniard, toppling Aztec gods, but a more literal reason exists in the Duncan/Olson correspondence. In 1955, sixteen months before Olson wrote "Who Slays the Spanish Sun," Olson and Duncan exchanged letters that did not circulate from Black Mountain College to San Francisco, but that circulated from Spain to Black Mountain. Vacationing with Jess Collins, Duncan researched the medieval and Renaissance paintings in many of Spain's Catholic Churches. On June 6th of 1955, he wrote a letter to Olson that reveals why Olson includes references to "The Kingfishers" in "Who Slays the Spanish Sun." Duncan describes a painting of Abraham and Isaac: "the starkest terror I have ever seen, in a sacrifice of Isaac and then as one changes, walking around the capital, a terrible jubilation."[36] Upon reading Duncan's comments, Olson may have recalled the scenes of human sacrifice in "The Kingfishers." The letter further induces "Who slays the Spanish Sun" though, because after the discussion of Abraham and Isaac, Duncan protests his love for "kind and kin": "Your poem LOVE relates to POEM—the sense of the appropriate, create and/or avoid, is of measure. The joy for me of Charles Olson, or Robert Creeley, or Denise Levertov is the joy of the work and its visibility."[37] Here, Duncan pits his "terror" against his reading of Olson's 1954 poem entitled

"Love." In that poem, Olson again references "The Kingfishers": "Stories / only / the possibility / of discrete / men," recalling the line "the message / is a discrete and continuous sequence of measurable events" and omitting the theme of continuity.[38] Duncan's personified love in "Who Slays the Spanish Sun" therefore represents the "stories" he tells Olson in letters. Lastly, Duncan's letter highlights his Shelleyian understanding of the one "Poem" to which all poets contribute, a "Poem" that maintains a kind of supra-agency to which the writer submits during the compositional process. For Duncan, the poet experiences the poem or Olson's "stories" as living occasions of love and "visibility," "appropriate" occasions of "measure" related to perceived yet discrete events in reality, terms from "The Kingfishers" and "Love."

In a second letter from Spain, Duncan further defines "visibility" as the function through which a poet attempts to access the limited shape of "measurable events." On August 14, 1955, he distinguishes between medieval art and Renaissance humanism: for the medieval period, "images are signs—and with the 'renaissance' everything is lost of the order; the icons are humanized and become idols."[39] Rejecting anthropocentric art that idolizes humans and favoring art that emerges from "things seen," which become "created things" and then "signs," Duncan highlights creative processes of accretion during which things incite text:

> The created thing then, as now, emerges from the thing seen (the painter's necessary book), the thing embodied as sign in the thing seen/heard (the book, the word, and the letters—the world emerges from vowels and consonants), and the thing as heard (the musician's necessary book—and hence here the trumpet, the harpes and lutes).[40]

During his trip to Spain, Duncan discerns two contrasting visual traditions: one medieval, iconographic, and with signs emerging from "things seen"; the other Renaissance, humanist, and mediated by the imperatives of Catholic dogma. His rich passage to Olson details multiple elements from reality directing the "created thing": first, actual things "seen" and "heard"; second, signs "seen" and "heard." The actual and the imaginative therefore inflect the "created thing" for Duncan, and "the world" "emerges from the vowels and consonants," such that the poem, painting, or concerto creates its own world. Olson would eventually accept this version of the creative process, writing in "Projective Verse II" (1958) that the poem "has one law: it has to occur. And to occur it has to retain and create its own environment."[41] Both found their version of the creative process and the created object corroborated by how the iconographic art of the medieval period crafted a cosmos or environment from the painter's visual, auditory, and imaginative interactions with the actual cosmos. This stress on the collision between the perceiving subject and the cosmos' events is one reason Olson directed Allen to omit the poems of the older generation from the anthology: throughout the 1950s, he and Duncan invested in a perspective that was critical of re‑ naissance humanism, arguably a theme of Pound's first thirty cantos.[42]

Duncan's Spanish letters on human sacrifice, love, medieval icons and renaissance idols thus contributed to Olson's poem "Who Slays the Spanish Sun," but his comments on art history also incited Olson to consider how "icons" emerge from things the poet sees and hears. In his reply of August 24, 1955, Olson connects the word "eikon" to the word "eidos": "have you noticed, by the way, the crazy etymology of yr word icon and this one, idol? That they are both the thing seen, the sign ('you will see a sign')."[43] "If one honestly (wow!) tries to make the picture," Olson continues, "the picture will be iconographic—will be whatever is the polarity of the reductive: (productive? reproductive? You will now see (as I do! why I make as much of eidos as you do of eikon."[44] Speculating about Duncan's exploration of medi‑ eval painting, Olson suggests that the effort involved in "trying to make" or produce a "reproductive" poetry centered on the experience of revelation— "you will see a sign"—emerges from reality. In other words, Olson emphasizes how "things seen" might lead to poems rooted in the perplexing efficacy of the real. Recalling "The Kingfishers," he implies his concern with prolifera‑ tion and tangentially includes the idea of poetry born of "rejectamenta," of a "dripping, fetid mass," but he also adds a third term to that poem's "factors," feedback loops, and images of decay: eidos. The term's "crazy etymology" yields words such as "image," "figure," "see," and "eidolon," which yields the word "apparition."[45]

Interestingly, Duncan employs the word "eidos" at the outset of "Ap‑ prehensions," but he did not write the poem until January and February of 1960 after an intense epistolary discussion with Olson regarding Whitehead's philosophy and *The Special View of History*, Olson's lectures of 1955 and 1956. These lectures are usually taken as the key to Olson's relationship with Whitehead, but his epistolary conversation with Duncan shows him gaining a more robust understanding of Whitehead's philosophy, negotiating the tension between knowledge and uncertainty outlined in "The Kingfishers." Duncan read *Process and Reality* in 1957 after Olson repeated the lectures in San Francisco. There, Olson cast Whitehead as a philosopher whose meta‑ physics allows human knowledge to transition from modernity's mechanistic characterization of nature to a style of thought that enables humans to know everything. Expressing this comfortable epistemology, Olson argues that

"Whitehead has written the metaphysic of the reality we have acquired" and that "the Primordial—the absolute—is prospective, that events are absolute only because they have a future, not from any past."[46] He then suggests that like the absolute events of the cosmos, humans "willfully set in motion egotistical, sublime events" and the subject of the lectures is therefore "actual willful man."[47] Here, the term "event" emerges, so that seven years after writing "The Kingfishers," Olson still trips over the line "The message is / a discrete and continuous sequence of measurable events." Nonetheless, *The Special View of History* is a flawed reading of Whitehead: Olson does not emphasize the implicit uncertainty Whitehead attaches to human knowledge, but rather the agency of "actual willful man" who appears to incite the cosmos' events. The primordial may not be historical, as in "The Kingfishers," but it is decidedly anthropocentric, a style of thought that Whitehead's definition of "an event" resists.

Whitehead first employed the term "event" in *The Concept of Nature*, his 1920 Tarner Lectures on the philosophy of science. Contrasting his notion of an event to empirical science's, he writes, "what we discern is the specific character of a place through a period of time. This is what I mean by an 'event.' We discern some specific character of an event. But in discerning an event we are also aware of its significance as a relatum in the structure of events."[48] For Whitehead, an event is a spatial and temporal instance related to the entire "structure of events" occurring throughout the unified fabric of time and space. In his Lowell lectures of 1925, *Science and the Modern World*, he further indicates an event is "the grasping into unity of a pattern of aspects."[49] Though neither Duncan nor Olson read *The Concept of Nature* or *Science and the Modern World*, their understanding of Whitehead's event derives from *Process and Reality*: "an event is a nexus of actual occasions inter-related in some determinate fashion [. . .]. For example, a molecule is a historic route of actual occasions; and such a route is an 'event'."[50] In Whitehead's scheme, an "actual occasion" is a "drop of experience, complex and interdependent," and an event is the total spatio-temporal "route" of many related actual occasions, that is, a thing's life history amid every other occasion within the cosmic continuum that stretches backward into the thing's past and forward into its future.[51] The molecule is not the event nor is it the occasion; rather, the event is the life-long, sum total of the molecule's temporal relations.

Upon discovering the term "event" in Whitehead's writings, Olson and Duncan incorporated it into their cosmological poetics.[52] While Whitehead's definition pertains to how things become unified into patterns, Duncan characterizes humans and the imagination as events in his letters to Olson of 1960. In his essay of 1963, "Towards an Open Universe," Duncan argues poetry should be faithful to the bewildering dynamism of the universe's immediate events: "the inner structure of the universe itself has only this immediate event in which to be realized. Atomic physics has brought us to the threshold of such a—I know not whether to call it certainty or doubt."[53] He then linguistically defines an event in his 1968 preface to *Bending the Bow* as "a field of ratios in which events appear in language."[54] Duncan's various usages reveal his adherence to Whitehead's definition—"a grasping into unity of a pattern of aspects"—and how he applies Whitehead's notion of the event to poetics. He intimates events pertain to the recognition of the universe's occurring processes; to how the language that emerges during composition influences the poem's pattern; and to how humans extend through time in relation to the events of the imagination. By event, he means the processes of three worlds: the physical world, the imaginative world, and the linguistic world. Moreover, his usages reference "The Kingfishers" and define limits for human knowledge—in the flux, experience is definite, but upon reflection experience becomes perplexing and bewildering.[55] Olson accepted these positions during his correspondence with Duncan, such that after 1960 both poets took an event as the perplexing processes of the cosmos, the poem, and the mind—not a poetics of human history and civilization, but rather a poetics of reality, experience and process. In the context of *The New American Poetry*, Olson's apparent self-promotion—placing "The Kingfishers" first—actually exemplifies his acceptance of new poetic content. By 1960, he and Duncan committed to Whitehead's sense of the ever evolving, perplexing processes of the nonhuman universe.

Nevertheless, it took Duncan's "Apprehensions" to turn Olson from human orders, and the poem emerged when Olson re-articulated *The Special View of History*'s connection between the primordial and human culture. In his Christmas letter of 1959, Olson attests to a lost historical order or center of human civilization, the anthropocentric singularity that critics have read as an element in "The Kingfishers." The letter opens, "My beloved Dunk"— Olson's nickname for Duncan—and then references *The Special View of History*: "I was offering the right stuff—in San Francisco, three years ago come February; and Black Mountain, the spring before—but I know nothing, *nothing* about it."[56] Even after delivering *The Special View of History*, Olson still admits his confusion about *Process and Reality*.[57] A rare moment of humility, his bewilderment about the text precipitates a reversion to an historical vision quite in line with the Poundian Olson on display in parts of "The Kingfishers." "The Ancients," he writes, "(including Alchemie, both European and Tibetan (? or China?) / knew the Necessities of the Soul in / and of the / and for the / Kosmos."[58] Olson's historical center contrasts with his emphasis on the cosmos: on the one hand, he imagines an art in which he functions as a fluid agent of the universe; on the other hand, he asserts an anthropocentric viewpoint. Olson's fictional anthropology in the letter then gives way to generalization: "circum 1200 A.D., among Arabs, as wells as English (Scandinavian?) Gothic, Dante, Giotto," he claims, there were "Ancients" who lived in a time before the alienation of modernity and who maintained a perspective in, of, and for the cosmos.[59] These cultures, Olson argues, knew a way of life that he desires: "my own soul has been bereft all these years of such simple rites as [. . .] the *admission* [emphasis added] that one is living in the presence of a larger life," he confesses to Duncan.[60] Olson's suggestion that his writing ought to acknowledge the human subject's situation within the "presence of a larger life" is not quite commensurable with his vision of history, since he grants a special ability, or *view*, for human beings to be "in, of, and for the cosmos." Pondering Olson's diverging cosmological, historical, and anthropocentric thoughts along with his apparent depression, "my own soul has been bereft," Duncan replies with a lengthy letter that includes the first section of "Apprehensions."

Duncan's response on February 6, 1960, references "Apprehensions" thus: "I'm in the midst of a poem again, projecting a construct of five sections that allows me to come alive, with the nodes—nodes of illumination for the course of the making. 'I was offering the right stuff' and in the enclosed poem 'flames of beauty in old stuff rage.'"[61] While repeating Olson's own commentary on *The Special View of History*, "offering the right stuff," Duncan transforms Olson's fear over his own "soul" into strong confidence concerning how "Apprehensions" includes "illumination," "rage," and "flames of beauty," some rather unsettling aspects of experience that challenge the idea of "actual willful man" setting into motion sublime, egotistical, or primordial events. Instead of human will, Duncan actively stresses the agency of poetic language, indicating the poem itself "allows me to come alive" and therefore intimating that "Apprehensions" controls his life by linguistically controlling his writing.[62] As the letter continues, Duncan asks how Olson's Christmas letter focuses merely on human civilization: "doesn't the adventure of the Kosmos—the atomic reality make man not the center [. . .] Where your Whitehead—that now translates into my Whitehead—where we are events, and that 'we' may be extended as a sum of a progression of imagined events."[63] Contesting Olson's placement of human civilizations at the center of his historical/primordial vision, Duncan testifies to the same anti-humanistic viewpoint he discovered while examining medieval and renaissance art, thereby highlighting a cosmos in which humans do not control the "adventure of the Kosmos." Humans are subsidiary events, he argues, which co-exist with imagined events and actual or atomic events. "I find it difficult," he proposes to Olson, "to think of man as a mammalia maxima, for he is clearly a contemporary instance or possibility (actual) of what a mammal can be along with elefunts [sic] and rats."[64] He critiques Olson's choice of Maximus as the human hero of his long poem; it makes little sense, Duncan suggests, because poems intended to be in, of, and for the cosmos should not be written from the perspective of a human subject, but rather from a perspective that defines humans as events amid many other events in the space-time continuum.

Duncan then differentiates "his Whitehead" from Olson's Whitehead not only by questioning *Maximus*, but also by correcting Olson's *Special View of History*. Exposing Olson's maximal thinking and his desire to discuss human history as primordial reality, Duncan complicates the idea of an ordered, systematic universe:

> There is anyway in Whitehead's scheme an unknowable unknown. And when I work in a poem, the order of the poem arises from two relations.
>   a. a universe—your everything can be known—that a whole poem is a whole poem, as we are at any moment a whole event.
>   b. a kosmos or order or harmony, that includes a void, and cannot possibly be a wholeness, but is a mathematical incomplete [our own versions of harmony, our own scales, are always incomplete and what had been dis-cord is being added.[65]

Duncan might argue that when Olson posits a time in history previous to 1220 A.D. during which humans lived of, for, and in the "Kosmos" or when he suggests in "The Kingfishers" that events are "measurable" without an implicit uncertainty in the measuring process, he underscores a simplistic "universe" where "everything can be known." And yet, Duncan does not leave poetry completely awash in uncertainty; rather, it is the gradual striving toward unity or the addition of discord to "incomplete" "scales" that creates a cosmological "poetics of order in disorder," as Devin Johnston argues.[66] In the letter, Duncan furthers his position on the discord of the universe by supplementing Olson's reading of Heraclitus in *The Special View of History*. He quotes Heraclitus's "Couples are wholes and not wholes; what agrees disagrees, the concordant is discordant" and then sarcastically comments on the epigraph to *The Special View of History*: "And his observation you put here as man is estranged from what is most familiar. It seems to me that the 'peril' and yr. admission [. . .] are one with those apprehensions of love—in peril."[67] Against Olson's epigraph—"man is estranged from what is most familiar"—Duncan characterizes Olson's psychological depression in the Christmas letter of 1959 as a result of his desire to center humans and to give "actual willful man" control of sublime, primordial events. He argues that Olson's "apprehensions of love—in peril" show the Kosmos and their poetics in, of, and for the Kosmos as incomplete processes during which surprising events, actual, linguistic, or imaginative, emerge and inflect the compositional process.

Devotees of the Ensemble: "Apprehensions" and *Maximus III*

Along with his epistolary remarks about *The Maximus Poems*, Duncan sent the first part of "Apprehensions."[68] Given Duncan's comments to Olson on Whitehead's cosmic "unknowable unknown" and given that the poem's title, "Apprehensions," puns on Whitehead's term "prehension" (to seize a thing with the mind), Duncan was reading Whitehead's *Process and Reality* while writing the poem.[69] Prehending apprehensions about a reality of "eidos," images, and apparitions, the first three stanzas invoke Duncan's imaginative vision of something buried in a cave, an internal apprehension that upset him one evening while reading. This ghostly, imaginative event recurs throughout the poem, and at the outset, it is a matter of discord: the event is chiasmatically "hiding in showing" or "showing in hiding":

To open Night's eye that sleeps in what we know by Day
      "If the Earth were animate
it should not experience pleasure when grottoes and cave are dug
      out of its back"
From which argument my mind fell away
or disclosed a falling-away,
and I saw an excavation—but a cave-in of the ground,
hiding in showing or showing in hiding,
a glass or stone, most valuable.
According to the text   ["Renaissance Cosmologies"
                                by Paul-Henri Michel,
Ficino had the idea   *Diogenes 18*]
      life circulates from the earth
      to the stars
"in order to constitute the uninterrupted
      tissue of the whole of nature"
You've to dig and come to see what I mean.
      Eidos, Idea.

"is something to which we gain access through sight."
This defines the borderlines of the meaning.

> For what I saw was only a gleam.
> I did not bring the matter to light.[70]

In *Gnostic Contagion*, Peter O'Leary outlines an extensive, psychoanalytic interpretation of "Apprehensions," and he suggests the line "I did not bring the matter to light" sounds "a note of hesitation" that reveals "an aspect of dread, perhaps even a creative dread."[71] While O'Leary adheres to this characterization of creativity throughout his reading and identifies "Apprehensions" as an expression of Duncan's personal trauma, the letters between Olson and Duncan that induced the poem also link its content to their three categories of event: actual, linguistic, and imaginative.

Though Duncan's opening does reveal dread, it also portrays a cosmos in which the poet attempts to register "things seen" and "signs" in order "to open night's eye," a view of distant stars obscured by day. The stakes between a confessional interpretation of the poem and a cosmological interpretation cluster around one crucial question: what is this vision? At the outset, Duncan casts the hallucination in linguistic discord. After the opening invocation of "night's eye" and the Earth's grottos, the following stanza deploys four coordinating conjunctions to resist disclosing the vision's precise contours. Duncan views an "excavation—*but* a cave-in"; that place is either "hiding in showing *or* showing in hiding"; within that place there is either a "glass *or* stone"; and Duncan's mind during reading either "fell away / *or* disclosed a falling away," such that the vision either shifts his attention *or* makes his mind go blank. Next, he reveals his source text: *Renaissance Cosmologies* in which Ficino imagines "life circulates from the earth / to the stars / 'in order to constitute the uninterrupted / tissue of the whole of nature.'" The citation from Ficino then leads Duncan to recall Olson's "Eidos, Idea" as "something we gain access to by sight." "The vision is macrocosmic," O'Leary remarks, "an idea derived from Ficino that life circulates to the stars in order to ensure the continuity [. . .] of natural life. The body is made of star matter."[72] Despite this cosmic continuity, however, the half-rhymes, like the conjunctions, enhance the indefinite nature of this discrete, imaginative event: "mean," "meaning," and "gleam" urge one to ponder the import of the vision even as Duncan suggests that the "glass or stone" is a mere "gleam," a passing flicker of light. Then there are the rhymes between "sight" and "light," which elicit attention back to "Eidos, Idea" as "something that we gain access to by sight" only after, as Duncan reveals, digging "to come to see what I mean," a direct address to a reader and a pun that connects the act of reading and interpretation to the obscure dug-out Duncan views in his imagination. At the poem's outset, the language creates a perplexing "Kosmos" in the imagination, and if words are the medium by which Olson's "factors" are to be made known, then "Apprehensions" counters the anthropocentric, historical elements in "The Kingfishers" by clearing space for mid-century American poetry to investigate primordial reality as star-matter, the cosmos' fundamental yet immeasurable molecules and visions.

Furthermore, two texts caused Duncan's imaginative event: Marsilio Ficino's cosmology with its argument on the continuity of nature and Olson's Christmas Letter, which claims, "The Ancients (including *Alchemie*, [. . .] knew the Necessities of the Soul in / and of the / and for the / Kosmos."[73] In the opening stanzas, Duncan actively transforms Olson's epistolary comments on human alchemists by envisioning how the Earth creates "a glass" or "a stone" or "a gleam" in its internal depths. His vision does not merely intimate his personal dread, but rather the alchemical powers of an Earth that can feel: "*If the Earth were animate / it should not experience pleasure when grottoes and caves are dug / out of its back.*" The initial, discordant apparition of the "excavation" or "the cave-in" that Duncan sees in the second stanza results from the idea that the Earth has the ability to feel pleasure, and when he considers the lines from Ficino's text alongside Olson's epistolary reference to alchemy, the apparition of the Earth's caves emerges in his mind. The Earth, for Duncan, has the power of alchemy over both mind and matter—hence it is in, of, and for the cosmos—while Olson's human "Ancients" do not have the ability to transform stones. As Duncan's conjunctions intimate, human language cannot even accurately describe the stone when it is an imaginative event in the mind. The fact that Duncan "did not bring the matter" of the Earth's alchemical power and of the gleam, glass, or stone "to light" means exactly that, for the Earth itself creates shining "matter," diamonds for instance, as it spins through the gravitational pressures put upon it by the solar system's planets. Interestingly, however, "The Kingfishers" also deals with matter buried underground, which is not to say that Duncan scrutinized that poem while drafting "Apprehensions," but that both poets shared with Whitehead a concern for that which is hidden and imperceptible: the preface to *Process and Reality* closes, "There remains the final reflection, how shallow, puny, and imperfect are efforts to sound the depths in the nature of things."[74] For *The New American Poetry*, Duncan's emphasis on how words inaccurately represent the unknowable depths of reality tempers Olson's faith in "actual willful man." His statement on poetics at the anthology's close is relevant to both "Apprehensions" and to Whitehead's claim, for it discusses "open composition in which the accidents and imperfections of speech might awake intimations of human beings."[75] The statement relates the sort of accidental visions that inspire "Apprehensions" and an imperfect idea of open composition often overlooked in the critical hubbub surrounding the breath poetics of "Projective Verse."[76]

Continuing to write of the relation between alchemy, the inner Earth, and digging, "Apprehensions" references the Dead Sea Scrolls from the caves at "Qumran," jewels of secret knowledge dug up by archeologists.[77] The poem then shifts back to the dream fragment, which is also an argument between Duncan's poem and Olson's Christmas letter.

> (My mind had slipt again, could not
> keep its place in the sentence)
> "Whenever the subject is not the earth
> but the universe viewd as a whole"
>   "divergences appear"
> And the soul was revealed where it was,
> fearful, rapt, prepared to withdraw
>   from knowing,
> looking down into the six-foot pit where . . .
> Or it was a stone that is most rare
>   moving to see,
> what we call a jewel, hidden there, formd
>   in pressure and the inner fire.[78]

The close of the poem's first section emphasizes Duncan's difficulty representing this vision of the "jewel," "stone," "glass," or "gleam"—"what we call a jewel"—for the thought of the fiery and creative potential of the actual Earth bewilders him. Moreover, this third quotation from Ficino indicates that being in, of, and for the cosmos often leads to visible divergences; the citation highlights the discord that emerges in the human mind when "the subject" of knowledge or of sight, "viewd," is the entire cosmos and not just the Earth. It is "kosmos" versus "universe," as Duncan put it to Olson in his letter; he recognizes poems can deceptively outline portraits of a singular or static universe while the wonders of "Kosmos" escape categorical knowledge. The divergences stressed by Duncan's quotations result in his lack of language for describing his vision, but they are also part of his attempt to register cosmic experiences like fear and wonder. As his letter of February 6 to Olson indicates, he confidently accepts Heraclitus's assertion that "couples are wholes and not wholes; what agrees disagrees, the concordant is discordant." Hence the past tense verbs that structure the stanzas obscure the vision's precise contours; the stuttering alliterative chain in "whenever," "where," "was," "withdraw," and "where"; the passive voice that reveals no absolute position for the "soul" or the contents of the cave; and the "or" that begins the last stanza, harkening back to the conjunctions in the poem's opening and further obfuscating the contents of the excavation/cave-in. The "soul" in the poem deceptively references how Olson's soul was "preparing to withdraw / from knowing" in 1960, not Duncan's: "my own soul has been bereft," Olson confessed in his Christmas letter. The initial discord Duncan hopes to bring into the measures of "Apprehensions" may be the "divergence" between Olson's attempt in *The Special View of History* to valorize "actual willful man" and the "peril of his soul" in the Christmas letter. Furthermore, a thread unites "The Kingfishers" and "Apprehensions," signaling Olson's and Duncan's mutual poetics. This is in the presentation of an imperfect "kosmos" made of Heraclitean paradox—"what does not change / is the will to change" and "the concordant is discordant"—notions in line with the cosmic-poetics they inherited from *Process and Reality*: "That all things flow is the first vague generalization which the unsystematized, barely analyzed, intuition of men has produced"; Whitehead writes, "It is the theme of the best Hebrew poetry in the Psalms; it appears as one of the first generalizations of Greek philosophy in the form of the saying of Heraclitus; [. . .] and in all stages of civilization its recollection lends its pathos to poetry."[79] Duncan's "Apprehensions" and Olson's Christmas letter register that pathos in the knowledge of knowledge's sheer limitation.

Olson deeply admired the first part of the poem and the letter that arrived at his door in early February of 1960, and both documents clinched his decision to erase the character of Maximus from the *Maximus Poems*. Only five months after he posited divisions for *The New American Poetry* and told Allen to omit Pound's generation, Duncan's poem radically changed his poetry. After receiving Duncan's Whitehead letter and "Apprehensions," he enthusiastically responded to Duncan in a language that forecast his removal of the "mammalia maxima":

> Your letter and poem are a joy. I walked right out of the house into the sun and onto the beach which fronts the city to the harbor and the sand is brown and fresh from the winter's storms, and wrinkled like desert sand from the north wind of the past day and until the bitterness of the wind at the sluice near the Tavern turned me up Beach Court and to the gas station (to cash a check to get some breakfast, it was all one thought: the beauty of your own thought, come to me across from a beach on that other ocean—and I am still happy of the thought of your life speaking to me as for some months now Ibn 'Arabi has since 1220— same same marvel of being, that, we are here and can seek to find it truly[80]

Though the letter still references Olson's interests in Arabian mysticism and the idea that "the Ancients" previous to 1220 A.D. knew the necessities of the soul in, of, and for the cosmos, Olson is suddenly walking outside and observing the environment. In this letter, he only "seeks to find it truly," implying that his emphasis on "actual willful man" has become subject to visible signs, images and things. While *Maximus III* does include historical references drawn from Olson's "postmodern archaic," he often subjects them to the seen, perplexing Kosmos and to epochal time: "Out here on the end of the land, it going westward at a known / rate, the ocean approaching from the east daily and equally going / back, the Great Circle of the earth making a straight line over Cap Ann to / Tyre, and further round the world."[81] Shockingly absent, Maximus disappears, and his town, Tyre, is no longer a shadow image for Gloucester's subjugation to neo-American capitalism; rather, Olson links the two towns in the "Great Circle" of "earth" as the continents drift apart below the surface of our direct perception.

Furthermore, when Olson began the third volume in 1963, he opened by stressing processes of observation, to descry, and apprehension, "gloom," in a short, three line poem: "having descried the nation / to write a Republic / in gloom on Watch-House point."[82] "Descry" interestingly indicates Olson's intention not to polemicize about a "Republic," but rather to observe the human and nonhuman "Republic" of reality. As a result of the third volume's hope to descry "Res Publica," a public community of things, Maximus's voice only emerges twice, significantly when Olson states, "It is not I, / even if the life appeared / biographical," a repression of Maximus and his egotistical "I" that opened the long poem in 1950.[83] Olson entertained the idea of eliminating Maximus from the poem as early as 1956, writing to Robert Creeley that "the persons in the poem and the *events* should now take over, strongly— with Mr. Max become a much more fluid agent, no longer the preacher, nor even so much the singer."[84] Nonetheless, it was not until Duncan chided him over his belief in a "mammalia maxima" that he could erase his human hero.

Without a center except the imaginative, linguistic, and actual events of the cosmos, Olson and Duncan concurrently put *The New American Poetry* forward into an observational and linguistic poetics that descries and transforms a plural ensemble of fluid events. They discovered their concern with perplexing cosmic orders in Whitehead's philosophy. Offering a fitting reflection on Whitehead and Olson, Duncan's 1970 essay, "Changing Perspectives in Reading Whitman," connects "composition by field" to the events of the cosmos:

> Dreaming of the ensemble of created and creating forms, Whitman was the poet of primary intuitions, ancestor of Whitehead's *Process and Reality* and of our own vision of creation where now we see all life as unfoldings, as revelations of a field

of possibilities and latencies toward species and individuals hidden in the DNA, a field of generations larger than our humanity. Back of our own contemporary arts of the collagist, the assembler of forms, is the ancestral, protean concept, wider and deeper, of the poet as devotee of the ensemble. Back of the field as it appears in Olson's proposition of composition by field is the concept of the cosmos as a field of fields.[85]

While Duncan's "Apprehensions" and Whitehead's *Process and Reality* directed Olson away from his anthropocentric version of primordial reality, Duncan's "protean," "hidden," and "ancestral" "generations larger than our humanity" summarize the interest he and Olson took in flux of actual things and in a poetics "in, of, and for the cosmos" without a "mammalia maxima." Discussing "the poet as devotee of the ensemble," Duncan relates mid-century American poetry to changing cosmic events—"what does not change / is the will to change." In "the cosmos as a field of fields" or in composition by field, Duncan's and Olson's related texts, including the documents surrounding Allen's anthology, prove fruitful for investigating the discussions that shaped this cosmological American poetics.

Notes

1. Charles Olson and Donald Allen, *Poet to Publisher: Charles Olson's Correspondence with Donald Allen* (Vancouver: Talonbooks, 2003), 58.
2. Ibid.
3. Ibid., 60.
4. Ibid.
5. Alan Golding, "*The New American Poetry* Revisited, Again," *Contemporary Literature* 39, no. 2 (1998): 187.
6. Ibid., 60.
7. Allen, *Poet to Publisher: Charles Olson's Correspondence with Donald Allen*: 61.
8. Allen's link to the "older generation" in the preface lists some of the same poets he mentions to Olson in the letter. The preface reads, "In the years since the war American poetry has entered upon a singularly rich period. It is a period that has seen published many of the finest achievements of the older generation: William Carlos Williams's *Paterson*, *The Desert Music and Other Poems*, and *Journey to Love*; Ezra Pound's *The Pisan Cantos*, *Section: Rock-Drill* and *Thrones*; H.D.'s later work culminating in her long poem *Helen in Egypt*; and the recent verse of E.E. Cummings, Marianne Moore and the late Wallace Stevens." Donald Allen, ed. *The New American Poetry: 1945–1960*, (Berkeley: University of California Press, 1999), xi.
9. Burton Hatlen, "Kinesis and Meaning: Charles Olson's 'The Kingfishers' and the Critics," *Contemporary Literature* 30, no. 4 (1989): 546.
10. Ibid.

11. Ibid., 549–50.

12. Ralph Maud, *What Does Not Change: The Significance of Charles Olson's "The Kingfishers"* (London: Associated University Presses, 1998), 130.

13. Alfred North Whitehead, "Process and Reality," in *Charles Olson Research Collection*, Archives and Special Collections at the Thomas J. Dodd Research Center (Storrs, CT: University of Connecticut Libraries), 345. Olson's underlining.

14. Guy Davenport, "Scholia and Conjectures for Olson's 'The Kingfishers,'" *boundary 2* 2, no. 1/2 (1974): 252. It would seem that Davenport echoes Hugh Kenner's characterization of Pound's poetry in *The Pound Era*, which appeared two years before Davenport's article. Discussing Pound's idea of a vortex, Kenner writes, "a Vortex is a circulation with a still center: a system of energies drawing in whatever comes near." Hugh Kenner, *The Pound Era* (Berkeley: University of California Press, 1971), 239.

15. Don Byrd, *Charles Olson's Maximus* (Urbana: University of Illinois Press, 1980), 9.

16. Charles Olson, ed. *The Collected Poems of Charles Olson* (Berkeley: University of California Press, 1997), 86.

17. Davenport, "Scholia and Conjectures for Olson's 'The Kingfishers,'" 259.

18. Ibid., 261.

19. Maud, *What Does Not Change: The Significance of Charles Olson's "The Kingfishers"*: 28.

20. T.S. Eliot, *The Complete Poems and Plays: 1909–1950* (New York: Harcourt Brace and Co., 1980), 50; Maud, *What Does Not Change: The Significance of Charles Olson's "The Kingfishers"*: 29.

21. Maud, *What Does Not Change: The Significance of Charles Olson's "The Kingfishers"*: 29.

22. Ezra Pound, *The Cantos* (New York: New Directions, 1996), 483.

23. Olson, *The Collected Poems of Charles Olson*, 87.

24. Maud, *What Does Not Change: The Significance of Charles Olson's "The Kingfishers"*: 39; Olson, *The Collected Poems of Charles Olson*, 87.

25. Robert van Hallberg, *Charles Olson: the Scholar's Art* (Cambridge, MA: Harvard University Press, 1978), 19.

26. Sherman Paul, *Olson's Push: Origin, Black Mountain and Recent American Poetry* (Baton Rouge: Louisiana State University Press, 1978), 18.

27. Olson, *The Collected Poems of Charles Olson*, 89.

28. Davenport, "Scholia and Conjectures for Olson's 'The Kingfishers,'" 254.

29. Allen, *The New American Poetry: 1945–1960*, 145.

30. Olson, *The Collected Poems of Charles Olson*, 90.

31. Ibid., 93.

32. Pound, *The Cantos*, 445.

33. Paul, *Olson's Push: Origin, Black Mountain and Recent American Poetry*: 109. Emphasis added.

34. Olson, *The Collected Poems of Charles Olson*, 408. Letter Contained at the University of Connecticut, Storrs: December 31, 1956.

35. Charles Altieri, "Some Problems about Agency in the Theories of Radical Poetics," *Contemporary Literature* 37, no. 2 (1996): 215.

36. Ibid., June 6, 1955.

37. Ibid., June 6, 1955.

38. Olson, *The Collected Poems of Charles Olson*, 299.

39. Ibid., August 14, 1955.

40. Ibid., August 14, 1955.

41. Essay contained at the University of Connecticut, Storrs, "The Principle of Measure in Composition by Field: Projective Verse II," Box 34, pg. 3.

42. This is, perhaps, an over-simplified reading of Pound's *Cantos*, but I am thinking specifically of the investment Pound makes in proportion, stasis, and the "perfect measure," specifically in the first thirty cantos. When he writes, "All rushed out and built the duomo, / Went as one man without leaders / and the perfect measure took form," he describes the raising of the cathedral at Ferrara and emphasizes the kind of perfection in human endeavor about which Olson and Duncan, after reading Whitehead, would have been wary.

43. Ibid., August 24, 1955.

44. Ibid., August 24, 1955.

45. It is also possible that Olson found the term while reading Pound's *Cantos*, specifically the lines from *Canto LXXXI*, when Pound writes,

> Saw but the eyes and stance between the eyes,
> color, diastasis,
>   careless and unaware it had not the
> whole tent's room
> nor was place for the full Eidos
> interpass, penetrate. Pound, *The Cantos*, 540.

However, as Peter Liebergets remarks of these lines, "Pound's notion of vision as well as his sculptural idea of poetry as its expression and inducement to its attainment, may be said to be underscored by his use of the word Eidos, [. . .] [which] connotes the visionary appearance, the perception of it by the poet, and his understanding or knowing the vision." So Pound's version of the term can be distinguished from Olson's and Duncan's. For Duncan, in "Apprehensions," the vision takes the shape of a disturbing apparition that the poet's words cannot objectify, while for Pound "eidos" seems a definite image that provides the poet with knowledge. See Peter Liebregets, *Ezra Pound and Neo-Platonism* (Madison, NJ: Fairleigh Dickinson University Press, 2004), 281.

46. Charles Olson, *The Special View of History*, ed. Ann Charters (Berkeley: Oyez, 1970), 16.

47. Ibid.

48. Alfred North Whitehead, *The Concept of Nature* (New York: Cosimo Classics, 2007), 52.

49. Whitehead, *Science and the Modern World* (New York: The Free Press, 1967), 119.

50. Whitehead, *Process and Reality*, ed. David Ray Griffin and Donald Sherburne (New York: The Free Press, 1978), 80.

51. Ibid., 18.

52. I regret not having the space to provide a full reading of Olson's important *Maximus* poem on Whitehead, "A Latter Note on Letter #15," which closes by stressing what Olson calls "Whitehead's important corollary": "that no event / is not penetrated, in intersection or collision with, an eternal / event / The poetics of such a situation / are yet to be found out." Interestingly, the poem appears to have mixed up Whitehead's terminology. If Olson is closely following Whitehead's argument in *Process and Reality*, and by the measure of his annotations, he most certainly was, then he means to reference Whitehead's "actual occasions" (a spatial-temporal block) and "eternal objects" (abstract ideas). See Charles Olson, ed. *The Maximus Poems* (Berkeley: University of California Press, 1987), 79. Volume II.

53. Robert Duncan, *A Selected Prose* (New York: New Directions, 1995), 12.

54. Duncan, *Bending the Bow* (New York: New Directions, 1968), v. Letter located at the University of Connecticut, Storrs: February 6, 1960.

55. Duncan had also been an avid reader of William James, a major influence on Whitehead's *Process and Reality*. One of Duncan's notebooks from 1970 contains Whitehead's passages copied out in longhand, followed by passages from James's *Essays in Radical Empiricism*, specifically "Does Consciousness Exist?" In effect, Duncan was quite familiar with James's understanding of pure experience, defined in "The Thing and its Relations": "Experience in the immediate seems perfectly fluent" but "when the reflective intellect gets at work, however, it discovers incomprehensibilities in the flowing process. Distinguishing its elements and parts," James continues, "[the mind] gives them separate names, and what it thus disjoins it cannot easily put back together." See William James, *Writings: 1902–1910* (New York: The Library of America, 1987), 782.

56. Letter located at the University of Connecticut, Storrs: December 25, 1959. Olson's emphasis.

57. Olson's experience of the text is not uncharacteristic. Duncan read *Process and Reality* for the first time in 1957 after Olson's lectures in San Francisco, and he wrote to Olson of the experience: "Hovering over Whitehead's Process and Reality which yields, where it yields at all, excitations of 'gray matter'." The initial experience of reading *Process and Reality*, for Duncan, appears to have been more of an excitement or stimulation of the brain, rather than the conveyance of a clear set of concepts. See letter located at the University of Connecticut, June 4, 1957.

58. Letter located at the University of Connecticut, Storrs: December 25, 1959.

59. Ibid., December 25, 1959.

60. Ibid., December 25, 1959. Olson's emphasis.

61. Ibid., February 6, 1960.

62. Duncan had written to Levertov four days earlier, speaking of "Apprehensions" in much the same manner: "And I'm enclosing a poem that could stand on its own as a whole but which I hope to loop out into a sequence on. I just wrote it two days ago so I am still nervous about what it is, walking around its area with vague feeling of what it calls for—" Unfortunately, the Olson archive does not contain the copy that Duncan sent to Olson, so it is impossible to tell what state the draft or the sequence was in when Olson received it. See Albert Gelpi and Robert Bertholf, ed. *The Poetry of Politics, the Politics of Poetry: Robert Duncan and Denise Levertov* (Palo Alto: Stanford University Press, 2006), 240.

63. Letter Located at the University of Connecticut, Storrs: February 6, 1960.

64. Ibid., February 6, 1960.

65. Ibid., February 6, 1960.

66. Devon Johnston, *Precipitations: Contemporary American Poetry as Occult Practice* (Middletown, CT: Wesleyan University Press, 2002), 50.

67. Ibid., February 6, 1960.

68. In his study of Duncan's poetry, *Gnostic Contagion*, Peter O'Leary closely reads "Apprehensions," and he includes a summary of Duncan's correspondence with Creeley during February and March of 1960. Duncan sent each section of the poem to Creeley, and O'Leary details his findings:

> In three separate letters, Duncan sent drafts of 'Apprehensions' to Creeley, each time different successive sections of the poem. One letter, dated 4 February 1960, includes section 1; a second letter dated 15 February includes section 2; and the third, dated 28 March, includes sections 4 and 5. Presumably, since Duncan was sending the whole poem to Creeley as it arrived, a letter between 15 February and 28 March must have contained a draft of the substantial third section. The 'close' of the poem is also missing from this exchange. See Peter O'Leary, *Gnostic Contagion: Robert Duncan and the Poetry of Illness* (Middleton, CT: Wesleyan University Press, 2002), 99.

Among Olson's papers at the University of Connecticut, there is an entire typescript of the poem's five sections, but the correspondence does not indicate when Olson received these documents. It is highly likely, though, that their arrival would have paralleled O'Leary's careful timeline.

69. O'Leary includes an endnote on Duncan's awareness of the term "prehension" from Whitehead's cosmology, writing, "Duncan, who read *Process and Reality* in the mid-1950s, would have been aware that 'Apprehensions,' particularly in its terminological adaptation, 'prehension' (roughly the most concrete element in any actuality), is an important word in Whitehead's philosophy of the organism." Ibid., 239.

Whitehead defines "prehension" in his second chapter, "The Categorical Scheme," stating, "each actual entity is analyzable in an indefinite number of ways. In some modes of analysis the component elements are more abstract than in other modes of analysis. The analysis of an actual entity into 'prehensions' is that mode of analysis that exhibits the most concrete element in the nature of actual entities [. . .]. A prehension reproduces in itself the general characteristics of an actual entity: it is referent to an external world, and in this sense will be said to have a 'vector character'; it involves emotion, and purpose, and valuation, and causation." See Whitehead, *Process and Reality*, 19.

70. Robert Duncan, *Roots and Branches* (New York: New Directions, 1964), 30–31.

71. O'Leary, *Gnostic Contagion: Robert Duncan and the Poetry of Illness*, 100.

72. Ibid.

73. Letter located at the University of Connecticut, Storrs: December 25, 1959. Emphasis added.

74. Whitehead, *Process and Reality*, xiv.

75. Allen, *The New American Poetry: 1945–1960*, 401.

76. Ibid.

77. Duncan, *Roots and Branches*, 31.

78. Ibid., 32.

79. Whitehead, *Process and Reality*, 208.

80. Letter Located at the University of Connecticut, Storrs, 2/8/1960.

81. Olson, *The Maximus Poems*, 105. Volume III.

82. Ibid., 9. Volume III.

83. Ibid., 101. Volume III.

84. Letter located at the Creeley Archive: Stanford University, Box 117, Folder 8. Emphasis added.

85. Duncan, *A Selected Prose*, 66.

Bibliography

Allen, Donald, ed. *The New American Poetry: 1945–1960*. Berkeley: University of California Press, 1999.

Allen, Donald, and Charles Olson. *Poet to Publisher: Charles Olson's Correspondence with Donald Allen*. Vancouver: Talonbooks, 2003.

Altieri, Charles. "Some Problems About Agency in the Theories of Radical Poetics." *Contemporary Literature* 37, no. 2 (1996): 207–36.

Bertholf, Robert, and Albert Gelpi, eds. *The Poetry of Politics, the Politics of Poetry: Robert Duncan and Denise Levertov*. Palo Alto: Stanford University Press, 2006.

Byrd, Don. *Charles Olson's Maximus*. Urbana: University of Illinois Press, 1980.

Davenport, Guy. "Scholia and Conjectures for Olson's 'The Kingfishers'." *boundary 2* 2, no. 1/2 (1974): 250–62.

Duncan, Robert. *Bending the Bow*. New York: New Directions, 1968.

———. *Roots and Branches*. New York: New Directions, 1964.

———. *A Selected Prose*. New York: New Directions, 1995.

Eliot, T.S. *The Complete Poems and Plays: 1909–1950*. New York: Harcourt Brace and Co., 1980.

Golding, Alan. "*The New American Poetry* Revisited, Again." *Contemporary Literature* 39, no. 2 (1998): 180–211.

Hatlen, Burton. "Kinesis and Meaning: Charles Olson's 'The Kingfishers' and the Critics." *Contemporary Literature* 30, no. 4 (1989): 546–72.

James, William. *Writings: 1902–1910*. New York: The Library of America, 1987.

Johnston, Devon. *Precipitations: Contemporary American Poetry as Occult Practice*. Middletown, CT: Wesleyan University Press, 2002.

Kenner, Hugh. *The Pound Era*. Berkeley: University of California Press, 1971.

Liebregts, Peter. *Ezra Pound and Neo-Platonism*. Madison, NJ: Fairleigh Dickinson University Press, 2004.

Maud, Ralph. *What Does Not Change: The Significance of Charles Olson's "The Kingfishers."* London: Associated University Presses, 1998.

O'Leary, Peter. *Gnostic Contagion: Robert Duncan and the Poetry of Illness*. Middleton, CT: Wesleyan University Press, 2002.

Olson, Charles. *The Collected Poems of Charles Olson*. Edited by George F. Butterick. Berkeley: University of California Press, 1997.

———. *The Maximus Poems*. Edited by George F. Butterick. Berkeley: University of California Press, 1987.

———. *The Special View of History*. Edited by Ann Charters. Berkeley: Oyez, 1970.

Paul, Sherman. *Olson's Push: Origin, Black Mountain and Recent American Poetry*. Baton Rouge: Louisiana State University Press, 1978.

Pound, Ezra. *The Cantos*. New York: New Directions, 1996.

van Hallberg, Robert. *Charles Olson: The Scholar's Art*. Cambridge, MA: Harvard University Press, 1978.

Whitehead, Alfred North. *The Concept of Nature*. New York: Cosimo Classics, 2007.

———. "Process and Reality." *Charles Olson Research Collection*. Storrs, CT: University of Connecticut Libraries.

———. *Process and Reality*. Edited by David Ray Griffin and Donald Sherburne. New York: The Free Press, 1978.

———. *Science and the Modern World*. New York: The Free Press, 1967.

CHAPTER FOUR

Why *The New American Poetry* Stays News

Terence Diggory

"Literature is news that STAYS news," Ezra Pound declared in *ABC of Reading*.[1] In one sense, then, to claim that *The New American Poetry* (1960) stays news fifty years after its publication is to claim that the work it introduced (New American poetry without the italics) has met the test of time, achieved the permanent status of "literature." However, the New American poetry also stays news today in another sense that was not true of the work of Pound or Eliot at the time when *The New American Poetry* anthology was published, less than fifty years after "Hugh Selwyn Mauberley" (1920) or *The Waste Land* (1922). By 1960, there was a widespread consensus about how to read Pound and Eliot, in part because the poets themselves had devoted considerable energy to building that consensus. "How to Read"[2] was the title of an essay of 1929 that Pound later expanded into *ABC of Reading* (1934). During the 1940s, the method of reading that modernist poets demanded became institutionalized as both a critical and a pedagogical method through the influence of the New Critics. Such institutionalization in turn produced the "academic" verse of the 1950s, against which the New American poets rebelled. If the rebellion continues today, if *The New American Poetry* stays news, it is not only because the poets wrote differently but also because they offered to be read differently. In the words of Roland Barthes, who developed a theory of such reading at the same time that the poets were working out the practice, "the goal of literary work (of literature as work) is to make the reader no longer a consumer, but a producer of the text."[3] *The New American Poetry* stays news because it continues to produce new work. Rather than

Pound's question, "How to Read," the poets of *The New American Poetry*, like their closer predecessors Gertrude Stein (1932) and William Carlos Williams (1936), address the question, "How to Write."[5]

The writer's block erected by the monuments of High Modernism is evident in Williams's response to Eliot's *The Waste Land*: "Our work staggered to a halt for a moment under the blast of Eliot's genius which gave the poem back to the academics."[4] Williams's rhetoric is close to that of Donald Allen in his preface to *The New American Poetry*; indeed, the work in which Williams's statement appears, his *Autobiography* (1951), is closer in date to Allen's anthology than to the date of *The Waste Land*. However, Williams's original experience of reading Eliot has remained fresh enough in his memory to register a significant difference between his charge against the "academics" and Allen's. When Allen claims that the poets of his anthology share "a total rejection of all those qualities typical of academic verse,"[6] the term "academic" refers to a mode of writing. Williams, by contrast, seems to be describing a shift between a mode of writing—"our work"—to a mode of reading, that of "the academics," who would have the knowledge to translate Eliot's many foreign phrases and explicate his mythical allusions. In other words, *The Waste Land* assigns priority to the work of reading over the work of writing. The institutionalization of this priority, in the years intervening between the 1920s and the 1950s, produced the type of "academic verse" that Donald Allen opposes. As David Perkins puts it in his history of twentieth-century poetry, "Young poets began to write for the kind of 'close reading' or 'explication' they had been taught in the classroom."[7] They began to write "with their eyes on the myth / And the missus and the midterms," as Kenneth Koch puts it, less academically, in one of the more memorable works in *The New American Poetry*, "Fresh Air."[8]

A reader with "eyes on the myth" would have felt well-prepared to enter *The New American Poetry* through the opening poem, Charles Olson's "The Kingfishers," aptly described by James Breslin as "a poetic text that comes to the reader laden with quotations and learned allusions."[9] The news conveyed in *The New American Poetry* was not Olson's modernism, at least insofar as Olson perpetuated the hieratic stance of his predecessors. Another New American poet, Frank O'Hara, complained of Olson, "he's extremely conscious of the Pound heritage and of saying the important utterance, which one cannot always summon up and indeed is not particularly desirable most of the time."[10] O'Hara's focus on "most of the time" in his own poems has proved to be more influential than Olson's mythologizing. However, another remark by O'Hara, from the same interview just quoted, points to the type of reading that both Olson and O'Hara helped to stimulate, and that constitutes the primary influence of *The New American Poetry* as a whole. Speaking five years after the anthology's publication, O'Hara remarks, "It's only recently that young poets . . . have made people see what there was there [in Olson], or is there I should say, by their own work and by the intensity of their interest."[11] Olson's work is the sort that produces new work, and O'Hara learns to read Olson through the eyes of the new producers.

The generative power of poetry is persuasively asserted in Olson's essay on "Projective Verse," the text that opens the section of "Statements on Poetics" at the conclusion of *The New American Poetry*. Endorsed early on by Williams, who quoted an extensive excerpt in his *Autobiography*, Olson's essay continues today to circulate more widely in discussion of contemporary poetry than his poems do. It is a key statement of a poetics of process, conveyed in the image of speed that excited younger poets from the Beats to the New York School: "get on with it, keep moving, keep in, speed, the nerves, their speed, the perceptions, theirs, the acts, the split second acts, the whole business, keep it moving as fast as you can, citizen."[12] "'Put down anything so long as you keep writing' would be a fair enough paraphrase,"[13] scoffed Tom Gunn, who had aligned himself with what he would regard as a more demanding aesthetic through his inclusion in *The New Poets of England and America* (1957).[14] As a counterstatement to that anthology, *The New American Poetry* implies that to "keep writing" is a worthy goal in itself. Olson's essay, in this respect, belongs to the "How to Write" genre mentioned above. It presents the act of reading explicitly as an extension—or in the terms of the essay, a "projection"—of the act of writing. This is "the already projective nature of verse as the sons of Pound and Williams are practicing it," Olson explains. "Already they are composing as though verse was to have the reading its writing involved."[15]

In the recollections of the sons (and daughters) of *The New American Poetry*, there is abundant evidence that they were reading in the manner Olson envisioned. As if to confirm Olson's description of the poem as "a high-energy construct,"[16] David Shapiro observes, "I am always impressed by how many people were lit up by the Donald Allen anthology."[17] He names O'Hara's "Ode to Michael Goldberg," Olson's "The Kingfishers," and Ginsberg's "Howl" as poems that stood out for him in particular. This is a diverse selection, and Shapiro highlights diversity as a source of energy in the anthology as a whole: "that was a very good anthology because it contains differences; people like Frank did not like Charles Olson very much."[18] There was room for difference not only among the writers represented in the anthology, but between the writers and their readers—room for the readers to become writers in their own way. "Here were more than 400 pages of what living American poets were doing, and thus indications of the many places I myself could go," recalls Tony Towle.[19] For Lewis Warsh, the map provided by *The New American Poetry* suggested the possibility of further exploration: "It was just a matter of time before we realized that our real work wasn't simply to mine the tradition of the poets of that world, but to create our own."[20] Warsh's collaborator in editing *Angel Hair* magazine, Anne Waldman, sketches in some details of the world she hoped to create: "I felt—coming after—the need to define the ongoing hybrids of the New American Poetry lineage further, to include more women, and a more polysemous relation to language and its 'intentionality,' and to define the pedagogy of such a lineage so that it might flourish and continue, building on an ever-expansive poetics."[21]

While the concept of "intentionality" highlights the implicit invitation to readers of *The New American Poetry* that they read as writers, attention to "pedagogy" calls into question who is included in that invitation, as well as what type of texts they are encouraged to read. Interconnections among these issues have become evident as the desire "to include more women," as Waldman expresses it, has been realized in the tradition growing out of *The New American Poetry*.

Intentionality

At the simplest level—simpler than the level at which Waldman applies these terms—pedagogy is a mode of intentionality traditionally found in literature. The author intends to teach. Olson is a classic pedagogue in this respect, and this is another way in which Olson's presence in *The New American Poetry* makes that volume Janus-faced, backward- as well as forward-looking. The influence of Olson's "Projective Verse" essay owes much to its pedagogic rhetoric: "I am dogmatic, that the head shows in the syllable."[22] But Olson also adopts a very similar stance in his poetry. In "Maximus, To Himself," he claims to have "offered / what pleasures / doceat allows,"[23] alluding to Pound's prescription,[24] derived from classical rhetoric, that a poem should both instruct and please (*ut doceat . . . ut delectet*), but assigning priority to instruction. In the manner of Pound, Olson practices what might be termed a bold pedantry, a defiant statement of dogma for dramatic effect, as opposed to a timid pedantry, the resigned recital of life's lessons in the "academic" verse opposed by Donald Allen. Nevertheless, a major force in the forward-looking thrust of Allen's anthology was a rejection of academic stance even in the Pound-Olson sense. New American poems do not intend to teach. "The reader can do with them what he likes," according to John Wieners,[25] a former student of Olson's at Black Mountain College. The now-classic statement of this attitude is O'Hara's "Personism: A Manifesto," rejected by Allen for *The New American Poetry* but later included in *The Poetics of the New American Poetry* (1973). "But how can you really care if anybody gets it, or gets what it means, or if it improves them," O'Hara asks,

> Improves them for what? for death? Why hurry them along? Too many poets act like a middle-aged mother trying to get her kids to eat too much cooked meat, and potatoes with drippings (tears). I don't give a damn whether they eat or not.[26]

While rejecting pedagogy as his intention, O'Hara can appear to offer simply the inverse of Olson, celebrating the pleasures of the body over Olson's "dance of the intellect."[27] In "Ode to Joy," one of his poems included in *The New American Poetry*, O'Hara imagines a condition where "there'll be no more music but the ears in lips and no more wit but tongues in ears and no more drums but ears to thighs."[28] However, orgiastic energy assumed an intentionality more clearly parallel to Olson's in the work of the Beat writers, particularly Allen Ginsberg. Like Olson, Ginsberg addressed himself to an entire culture; more than Olson, Ginsberg seemed eager to abandon the lectern for complete immersion in the culture he addressed: "Down to the river! Into the street!" as he proclaims at the end of "Howl," Part II, the concluding excerpt printed in *The New American Poetry*.[29] By the time *The New American Poetry* was published, Ginsberg's direct challenge to contemporary society had already made him the most widely recognized poet included in the anthology. For most of the 1960s, the extreme expressionism of the Beats, harnessed to an explicitly oppositional politics, kept the *New American Poetry* news. But the close connection to the news of the day made the reception of poetry subject to some extent to the political climate, which darkened dramatically in 1968 with the intensification of the war in Vietnam, the assassinations of Martin Luther King Jr. and Robert Kennedy, and the suppression of protestors at the Democratic convention in Chicago. The consequent disillusionment spread to a critique of reigning paradigms of intentionality in poetry, whether pedagogic, as in Olson, or revolutionary, as in Ginsberg. Without abandoning either intention, the critique that developed over the next decade reconceived the work of writing as an activity of language itself, rather than an author in the guise of either teacher or prophet. It is no mere coincidence that Roland Barthes's essay "The Death of the Author" is dated 1968.

The concept of "the death of the author" is an essential corollary to the concept of reading as productive rather than merely receptive, the starting point for my argument. "The birth of the reader must be requited by the death of the Author," Barthes declares.[30] However, this exchange does not involve the simple transfer of subjectivity from author to reader. The readings produced or "written" in a text express neither the author's nor the reader's feelings but rather certain possibilities inherent in language as code, a system for generating meanings. Intentionality resides in language. In Barthes's terms, "it is language which speaks, not the author."[31] Its mode of speaking does not refer to some world of meaning (internal feelings, external nature) that lies outside language, a misconception that Barthes criticizes in the Surrealists: "Surrealism . . . could doubtless not attribute a sovereign place to language, since language is system, and what this movement sought was, romantically, a direct subversion of the codes—an illusory subversion, moreover, for a code cannot be destroyed, only 'flouted.'"[32] Transferred to the American context, this became the critique of the New American poetry that emerged from the disillusionment of the 1960s. Sixties radicalism imagined "an illusory subversion" in seeking to destroy the codes; the more sober radicalism of the ensuing decades worked with the codes, hoping at most only to "flout" them. This is the historical progression implied, for instance, in a recent formulation by Barrett Watten: "the notion of poetic vocabulary moves beyond the expressivist uses of much open work (as, for example, in the process poetics of New American poets such as Charles Olson and Robert Duncan, whose work depends on open horizons of meaning) in granting a predetermined, objectified language an autonomous existence whose ultimate meaning will be engaged but not determined by the poet."[33]

The schema of moving "beyond" expressivist to constructivist uses, as Watten presents it, would seem to leave *The New American Poetry* buried in the past, as old news, rather than news that stays news. As a strategy of literary politics, this schema has proved effective, enabling the Language writers, of whom Watten is an important representative, to brand their movement as "new" in contrast to the "old" New Americans.[34] As a version of literary history, however, Watten's schema risks serious distortion. While Language writing may have been new in combining theoretical concepts such as the "death of the author" with poetic practice, the practice itself was not new. "Granting a predetermined, objectified language an autonomous existence," as Watten describes it, is a practice that corresponds to the theoretical concept of linguistic "materiality." In practice, the writer does not refer to some extrinsic meaning through language, employed as a transparent medium, but rather engages with the materials of language itself to set in operation the meaning-generating power of its codes. Increasingly, and thanks in part to the theoretical tools developed in Language writing, readers have come to recognize this practice of writing in *The New American Poetry*. For instance,

Ron Silliman, a close associate of Watten, has recently offered the following generalization:

> What all New American Poetry tendencies mostly have in common is a general emphasis on the materiality of language. Whether it's in the compositional strategies of the Black Mountain poets, ever seeking a more accurate method of scoring the page for sound, in the oracular excesses of a Beat poet going "overboard" verbally, via spontaneous bop prosody, as Kerouac put it, or in the densely crafted imagery of Ginsberg's *hydrogen jukebox* or Michael McClure's ecstatic lion roars, or in the softer and more ironic variant offered up by O'Hara et al, every one of these poetries comes alive precisely because it resists the conception of a transparent referential language.[35]

Silliman goes on to suggest that this "emphasis on the materiality of language" was new in contrast to the transparency presumed by the "School of Quietude," Silliman's disparaging term for the establishment aesthetic represented in *The New Poets of England and America.*

Within *The New American Poetry*, the range of attitudes toward linguistic materiality may be represented by comparing Gary Snyder's "Riprap" and LeRoi Jones's "In Memory of Radio." Snyder offers a simile based on physical material: "Lay down these words / Before your mind like rocks."[36] This is a conception grounded in the modernist tradition, as seen, for instance, in William Carlos Williams's description of the work of Marianne Moore: "With Miss Moore a word is a word most when it is separated out by science, treated with acid to remove the smudges, washed, dried and placed right side up on a clean surface."[37] Despite the emphasis on materiality, language in this conception is not accorded the full autonomy proposed by Barthes or the Language writers. Whether on a mountainside, as in Snyder's case, or in a laboratory, as in Williams's, the ruling order is natural rather than linguistic. In contrast, LeRoi Jones (later Amiri Baraka) exposes language as a matter of code, revealed through the decoding technique that was a common feature of the radio drama Jones recalls:

> & Love is an evil word.
> Turn it backwards / see, see what I mean?
> An evol word. & besides
> who understands it?[38]

We are not far here from the practice of anagrams that fascinated Ferdinand de Saussure, the linguist who is most responsible for the theory of language as autonomous system.[39] We are far from the "speech-based poetics" often assigned to the New American poetry in contrast to the poetics of Language writing.⁴⁰ Jones's use of the ampersand and the slash mark in the passage just quoted derives from the practice of "scoring the page for sound" that Silliman describes as a mode of materiality among the Black Mountain poets (Olson et al.), and that Jones fully acknowledges in his statement on poetics in *The New American Poetry*, entitled "How You Sound??" In his poem, however, Jones slyly satirizes the nostalgia for speech by writing "In Memory of Radio," and by performing an act of decoding that relies on the visual dimension of writing: "see, see what I mean?" The paranoid "I" who desperately claims to own this meaning is equally a target for decoding. Rather than occupying a stable position of authorial intention, this "speaker" is subject to reversals as arbitrary as the reversal of letters in a word. The movement from "see what I mean?" to "who understands it?" enacts the death of the author.

Returning to Barthes's suggestion that the death of the author coincides with the birth of the reader, we can now ask specifically how the materiality of language, as treated in *The New American Poetry*, encouraged readers to behave as producers of text. The evidence in the case of Ted Berrigan is especially clear. Although Berrigan is usually described as a "second generation" poet of the New York School, he saw himself as an inheritor of the full range of New American poetry: "Beats, with O'Hara on the left & Creeley on the right."⁴¹ Within the small circle of writers he belonged to in Tulsa, Oklahoma, Berrigan recalled, "we held our breaths and eagerly awaited the Don Allen anthology."⁴² When it arrived, Berrigan "was suddenly given an extremely close reading by O'Hara's poem WHY I AM NOT A PAINTER." Flouting the conventions of "close reading," associated with the New Criticism, Berrigan assigns greater autonomy to the act of reading by fusing it with the activity of the text. No reading could be "closer" than that. No author is required. Nor, in the "sudden" experience of being read by a text, is there a need for a theory of the death of the author. Carter Ratcliff has noted the parallels between that theory and the collaborative experiments of Berrigan and the poets and artists who eventually gathered around him in New York. Yet Ratcliff insists: "feeling no need to score theoretical points, they simply left such obstacles behind as they moved out into the open spaces where the new is possible."⁴³

"Why I Am Not a Painter" helped to show Berrigan the way into those open spaces by dramatizing the role of materiality in the creative process, both of painting and of writing. On the one hand, the distinction between the two media appears merely arbitrary. O'Hara says he would rather be a painter, but he just happens to write poems rather than make paintings. On the other hand, as presented in the poem, Mike Goldberg's creation of a painting called "Sardines" contrasts with O'Hara's creation of a sequence of prose poems called "Oranges" in a way that recalls the contrast between the two types of materiality evident in Snyder's and Jones's poems, discussed above. Painting is a physical medium. When words enter into it—as in the case of the word "sardines" that Goldberg had placed at an early stage of his composition because "it needed something there"[44]—they become absorbed into the physical material and lose their identity as words. "All that's left is just / letters," O'Hara observes of a later stage of the composition.[45] On the other hand, poetry is a coded medium. Painterly material—like the color orange—cannot enter the code as such, but only set it in motion. Once that happens, the code will proceed to generate its own material:

> One day I am thinking of
> a color: orange. I write a line
> about orange. Pretty soon it is a
> whole page of words, not lines.
> Then another page.[46]

This generative property of linguistic code makes the reading experience "writerly," ultimately creative, though not in the romantic sense that identifies creativity with originality.

Viewing lines as material rather than expression, as O'Hara does in "Why I Am Not a Painter," encouraged Berrigan to experiment with a process of composition that would seem to repudiate the ethos of originality associated with the concept of the Author. He constructed new poems out of lines from other poems. For instance, the title of John Ashbery's "'How Much Longer Will I Be Able to Inhabit the Divine Sepulcher . . . ,'" another poem that appears in *The New American Poetry*, shows up as a line in Berrigan's "Personal Poem #7" and "Sonnet II." The sonnet is one of several that Berrigan produced by mining his "Personal Poems" for material, following a set procedure: "taking one line from each [poem in the group], at random, going from first to last poem then back again until 12 lines, then making the final couplet from any 2 poems, in the group."[47] No doubt, as Reva Wolf has noted, Ashbery's title entered into this process because his entire poem reads like a collage of quotations.[48]

Berrigan's practice of "found" poetry is an extreme case, useful because it highlights the materiality of language in *The New American Poetry* as a stimulus to "writerly" reading, though it is surely not the only form such reading took. A response of more wide-ranging implications is the re-conceiving of poetic subjectivity or "intentionality" as a consequence of conceding greater autonomy to language. In another account of his response to reading O'Hara, Berrigan stated: "I had seen there, in his poem 'Why I'm [sic] Not a Painter' for example, how I could write too. As soon as I found it out I almost forgot it, right away, because I wasn't ready to write yet in my own voice."[49] Although the notion of poetic "voice" is traditionally associated with "expressivist" rather than "constructivist" poetics, to recall Barrett Watten's distinction, the constructivist reading of O'Hara's poem that I have just given above does not contradict a reading of the poem as a performance of what O'Hara called "Personism," that is, a "voicing" of the poem—a plausible translation of the word "persona"—that is constructed in the process of writing it. As I have noted, Berrigan constructed some of his sonnets out of a group of poems that he called "Personal Poems," after the "Personal Poem" by O'Hara that serves as a pendant to his "Personism" manifesto.[50] Berrigan's method for writing his "Personal Poems" was simple: "I would notate what was going on at that particular time," he explained.[51] "The painting / is going on, and I go, and the days / go by," O'Hara writes in "Why I Am Not a Painter."[52] At the opening of an essay on "Voice," Berrigan's widow, the poet Alice Notley, offers the following definition, recalling also the "page" that forms from the accumulation of words in O'Hara's poem: "time implies a voice, and though there might exist a sort of 'page' meant to be taken in all at once and not linearly, the page would most probably have been constructed linearly, letter by letter, and that linear construction is the author's voice. An author's voice is existence and presentation in time."[53]

Women

Later in the same essay, Notley argues that the issue of voice has a special urgency for women poets, because they do not inherit the collective voice of the tradition dominated by men.[54] Each woman will have to construct her own voice, an experimental project that might be expected to find encouragement in the generally experimental orientation of *The New American Poetry*. Kathleen Fraser reports her response to one of the poems that represented Barbara Guest in that anthology, "Parachutes, My Love, Could Carry Us Higher." What captured her when she heard Guest read that poem in 1964, Fraser recalls, was "the precariousness of emotional suspension and the suggestion of imminent shattering . . . [sic] the condition of the tenuous, spoken out of a peculiarly interior experience, yet as far afield as one could imagine from the battering 'confessional' model much favored in certain East Coast poetry circles at that time."[55]

A voice "spoken out of a peculiarly interior experience" defines the genre of lyric poetry, made suspect, along with the concept of voice itself, by the Language writers' emphasis on linguistic materiality. However, Fraser argues for Guest, as I have argued for Berrigan, that "personal" or lyric utterance becomes in the work of these writers a construction out of linguistic material rather than an expression of some pre-existing "self." Fraser concludes: "The speaker's hold on language is at stake: Guest's location of self is disclosed as structural."[56] In "post-language" writing, as the work of experimental poets emerging in the 1990s is sometimes called, a greater openness to "lyric as experimental possibility" has become one of the principal markers of the new.[57] The leading role played by women poets in this investigation was recognized in a major conference held at Barnard College in 1999: "Where Lyric Tradition Meets Language Poetry: Innovation in Contemporary American Poetry by Women." The poet Marjorie Welish delivered a paper at the conference, entitled "The Lyric Lately,"[58] that explores the work of Barbara Guest in much the same spirit as Fraser's memoir.

Of course, anyone familiar with the table of contents of *The New American Poetry* might question to what extent recent experiment by women writers can be seen as a continuation of the work of that anthology as a whole. Barbara Guest is one of only four women whom Donald Allen included in a roster totaling forty-four poets. In the revised version of the anthology that Allen and George Butterick issued in 1982, entitled *The Postmoderns*,[59] Guest and Denise Levertov are carried over, while the other two women from the first edition, Helen Adam and Madeline Gleason, are dropped. Three new women, Diane di Prima, Joanne Kyger, and Anne Waldman, are added to a slightly reduced roster of thirty-eight poets overall. In the conventional calculus of identity politics, these are alarming statistics. However, an essential premise of my argument here is that the news of *The New American Poetry* depends not simply on who wrote it but also on who read it and how. Women like Di Prima, Kyger and Waldman, Fraser, Notley and Welish read *The New American Poetry* not to find a reflection of their identity as women but to find a structure of intentionality from which they could produce new writing. "We are *writerly* readers," declare the editors of an anthology of critical essays on contemporary experimental writing by women.[60]

In a talk entitled *Dr Williams' Heiresses*,[61] Notley constructed an amusing fable to describe her sense of women's place in the lineage of the New American poetry. "Gertrude Stein & William Carlos Williams got married," the story goes. They produced two legitimate children, Frank O'Hara and Philip Whalen, both "male-female." Charles Olson, Williams's illegitimate child by "the goddess Brooding," "was too big to be as male-female as he would have liked." Notley acknowledges that "it was striking how there were no females in this generation," nor in the first generation of children produced by O'Hara, Whalen and Olson, "but the male-females also produced a second wave of children of which there were many females," a development subsequently documented by Libbie Rifkin and Kimberly Lyons.[62] Notley admits that, in the absence of mothers (all "evaporative non-parental" goddesses), it was difficult to recognize one's father as one's father. Nevertheless, her identification of O'Hara, Whalen and Olson as "male-females" suggests that she has finally arrived at that recognition. Implicitly, she has also recognized three of the major poets included in *The New American Poetry*.

Anne Waldman has similarly re-envisioned her relationship to Charles Olson, to the point of dating her "birth" as a poet to her attendance at Olson's marathon performance at the Berkeley Poetry Conference in 1965.[63] Echoing Notley's suggestion that Olson may have wanted to be more "male-female" than he usually seemed, Waldman's description of his performance also recalls "the suggestion of imminent shattering" that Fraser observed in Barbara Guest's poem. Waldman calls this process "dissipative,"[64] with none of the negative ethical connotations that term used to connote.[65] In Waldman's account, Olson was breaking up on stage, "up there in front of you: very scary, but also moving, profound, and vulnerable."[66] As his energy was dispersed, it became available to the audience. "The energy is dissipated like an agape feast, in which one shares the body, symbolized by food," Waldman explained in reference to a poem she wrote in part to commemorate the event.[67] Rather than a teacher, offering instruction, Olson becomes in Waldman's eyes "the poet as tribal shaman, speaking and moving and being embarrassing not just for himself or herself, but for you, the audience."[68]

To view Olson as shaman may appear merely to shift his role from that of teacher to that of prophet, like Allen Ginsberg, another father-figure whom Waldman has described as a shaman.[69] Unlike either of these roles, however, that of the shaman, as Waldman understands it, does not "set the poet up"[70] but rather takes the author down, in a kind of ritual performance of his death (the male pronoun seems appropriate in light of the previous discussion of gender). Barthes refers to the shaman to illustrate the absence of the role of author in what he quaintly calls "ethnographic societies," where "narrative is never assumed by a person but by a mediator, shaman, or reciter, whose performance (i.e., his mastery of the narrative code) can be admired, but never his 'genius.'"[71] Following Barthes's lead, Waldman relies not only on ethnography but also linguistics to define the sort of intentionality involved in such performance:

The strength of our own 'linguistic revolution' of the twentieth century (according to Saussure and Wittgenstein) is the recognition that meaning is not merely something 'expressed' or reflected in language but is actually produced by it. Art is not to be seen as the expression of an individual subject. Rather, the subject is just the place or medium where the truth of the world speaks or enacts itself, and it is this truth we hear.[72]

Of course, there is a difference between Barthes's assumption that "the narrative code" speaks in the shaman's performance and Waldman's assumption that "the truth of the world speaks," but the difference is no greater than that between the purely linguistic materiality in LeRoi Jones's "In Memory of Radio" and the naturalized materiality in Gary Snyder's "Riprap." As David Shapiro remarked, Donald Allen wisely made room to accommodate such diversity in *The New American Poetry*. Of fundamental importance for the continuing influence of that anthology, what makes it stay news, is the common orientation to language as productive, an orientation shared by writers and by readers, who thus also perform as writers. Waldman's poem commemorating Olson's performance at Berkeley takes its title from the conclusion of "Letter 6" of *The Maximus Poems*: "Eyes in all heads, / to be looked out of."[73] The image aptly describes the outlook of, and the outlook for, *The New American Poetry*.

Pedagogy

The "sublime democracy" implied in such a vision, as Waldman understands it,[74] depends upon the development of a pedagogy that can extend beyond a "lineage," the term Waldman adopts from the transmission of Buddhist teaching.[75] The writers I have discussed belong in various ways to the lineage of *The New American Poetry*, which usually entails transmission not only through text, as in Berrigan's first encounter with O'Hara. It is also through personal contact, as in Waldman's encounter with Olson or Fraser's with Guest. In her effort "to define the pedagogy of such a lineage," Waldman has helped to develop scenes for personal contact, for instance, at the Poetry Project in New York City or the Jack Kerouac School of Disembodied Poetics at Naropa Institute (now University) in Boulder, Colorado. However, their function as scenes necessarily limits the possibility of transferring the pedagogy elsewhere.

In theory, the critique among Language writers of the "personism" underlying the notion of lineage removes this limitation.[76] In fact, dropping also the New American objection to all things "academic," Language writers have achieved more widespread recognition within the mainstream academy for the principles they share with the New Americans: the materiality of language and the "writerly" process of reading. Nevertheless, these principles have not transformed pedagogical practice to anywhere near the extent that the principles of the New Criticism did. In the introduction to an anthology attempting to address this situation, Joan Retallack and Juliana Spahr observe that what they broadly refer to as "innovative" poetries "appear to be a kind of permanent revolution since they haven't been absorbed by the academy's more stubbornly reductive pedagogies."[77] The observation prompts an ironic response to the question posed in my title: lack of "absorption" into the classroom has kept the New American poetry new, whereas the pedagogical success of the New Criticism produced the staleness in poetry that the New Americans reacted against.

Poetry and Pedagogy, the anthology edited by Retallack and Spahr, abundantly demonstrates that specific, transferable pedagogic strategies have evolved from the principles of the New American Poetry, although that lineage is somewhat effaced in the "post-Language" viewpoint of Retallack and Spahr. In their preface, they acknowledge that "Kenneth Koch's *Wishes, Lies and Dreams* [1970] was widely used by teachers in elementary and high schools to wrest poetry exercises out of the 'imitation of great models' mode."[78] Koch's name does not appear again in *Poetry and Pedagogy*, but one of his former students at Columbia University, Bob Holman, closes the book with a list of exercises for "poetry performance." One example is "Teach Olson's 'Projective Verse' and O'Hara's 'Personism: A Manifesto' back to back. Toss in some Surrealist and Futurist Manifestos. Then have the class invent schools of poetry, characters who write in that style, and write 'their' poems."[79] Koch produced such a performance with an invented South American movement he called *Hasosismo*.[80]

Perhaps the most famous set of exercises growing out of the New American poetry is the list of "Experiments" devised in Bernadette Mayer's workshops at the Poetry Project during the 1970s, referred to in *Poetry and Pedagogy* in Jim Keller's account of a class he taught at Bard College.[81] Mayer, who assigned readings by Barthes in her workshop, was interested in weaning students from a sense of owning words as authors.[82] Several of the workshop exercises are in the spirit of Berrigan's "found" poetry: "Experiment with theft & plagiarism in any form that occurs to you."[83] Anne Waldman developed a similar list for her workshops at Naropa,[84] as did Charles Bernstein for his "creative reading" classes in the Poetics Program at the University of Buffalo.[85] On the web page where his list is posted, he acknowledges his debt to Mayer, whose workshop he attended in New York.

Many reasons could be cited for the failure of these techniques to make a greater impact on mainstream academic institutions. *The New American Poetry* and readers' responses to it, as I have sketched them here, highlight two reasons in particular. First, *The New American Poetry* encourages "writerly" response, where reading and writing blend in a single process. In contrast, academic institutions separate these activities, emphasizing reading in "literature" classes and even further separating two types of writing, "creative" and "expository." The institutional critique undertaken by Language writers has identified this separation as a problem,[86] and in practice they have sought to overcome it. This is why Bernstein refers to his workshops as "creative reading,"[87] even though his assignments would strike most teachers as "creative writing" exercises. The point is to engage students in the materiality of language, so the same exercises can apply whether the "source text" is one's own writing or the work of another.[88] Again, the pedagogical experiments of Kenneth Koch stand in the background. Using similar exercises, he followed up *Wishes, Lies, and Dreams*, subtitled *Teaching Children to Write Poetry*, with *Rose, Where Did You Get That Red?* (1973), subtitled *Teaching Great Poetry to Children*.[89] The title of *Rose* refers to a poem that one child wrote in response to Koch's invitation to get inside the "poem idea' that produced Blake's "The Tyger."

The reference to "Great Poetry" in Koch's subtitle, with its implications of canon, points to a second source of resistance to experimental pedagogy. Perhaps it should be called interference rather than resistance, because in this case the problem stems as much from the contradictory goals of experimental poets themselves as from the structure of academic institutions. The goal of directing attention to new texts interferes with the goal of promoting new kinds of attention to any texts. For instance, the question posed by Retallack and Spahr in the title of their introduction to *Poetry and Pedagogy* is not "how to teach poetry?"—a question of pedagogy—but "why teach contemporary poetries?"—essentially a question of canon. The issue of canon comes into focus more clearly when Retallack and Spahr add the term "innovative" to "contemporary poetry." Their assumption, which I share, is that the kinds of texts that I have identified with *The New American Poetry* promote "writerly" reading. It does not follow, however, that this type of reading can be applied only to a certain type of text. Writing *The Sonnets* helped Ted Berrigan gain new insight into Shakespeare.[90] More teachers of literature are likely to be won over to a new approach to teaching if it promises news about Shakespeare rather than (or at least in addition to) news about Berrigan.

There may be a lesson to be learned here from that first generation of women poets who tuned in to the news of *The New American Poetry* despite the small number of women included in the anthology. Discovering the location of self to be structural, as Fraser discovered in the case of Guest, some women read *The New American Poetry* in order to write it rather than to see their "identity" reflected in it. The so-called "canon wars" have proved to be a battle in the larger war of "identity politics," waged on the field of aesthetics. *The New American Poetry* promises a more open field, a truly "sublime democracy" in which all kinds of texts are acknowledged to share in the materiality of language, and all readers engaged in that materiality are acknowledged also to be writers. Stripped of the aesthetic category "poetry," and the identity category "American," *The New American Poetry* will still be news.

Notes

1. Ezra Pound, ABC of Reading (New York: New Directions, 1960), 29.

2. Pound, *Literary Essays*, ed. T.S. Eliot (New York: New Directions, 1968), 15–40.

3. Roland Barthes, *S/Z*, trans. Richard Miller (New York: Hill and Wang, 1974), 4.

4. William Carlos Williams, *The Autobiography* (New York: New Directions, 1951), 146.

5. Gertrude Stein, *How To Write* (Barton, VT: Something Else Press, 1973); William Carlos Williams, "How To Write," in *Interviews with William Carlos Williams*: "Speaking Straight Ahead, ed. Linda Welshimer Wagner (New York: New Directions, 1976).

6. Donald Allen, ed. *The New American Poetry: 1945–1960* (Berkeley: University of California Press, 1999), xi.

7. David Perkins, *A History of Modern Poetry 2: Modernism and After* (Cambridge: Harvard University Press, 1987), 8.

8. Allen, *The New American Poetry: 1945–1960*, 233.

9. James E. B. Breslin, *From Modern to Contemporary: American Poetry, 1945–1965* (Chicago: University of Chicago Press, 1985), 74.

10. Frank O'Hara, "Interview with Edward Lucie-Smith," in *Standing Still and Walking in New York*, ed. by Donald Allen (San Franscisco: Grey Fox, 1983), 13.

11. Ibid., 21.

12. Allen, *The New American Poetry: 1945–1960*, 388.

13. Thom Gunn, "Outside Factions," Review of Charles Olson, *The Distances*, and Other Titles, *Yale Review* 50:4, (Summer 1961): 596.

14. Donald Hall, Robert Pock, and Louis Simpson, eds. *The New Poets of England and America* (New York: Meridian, 1957).

15. Ibid., 394.

16. Ibid., 387.

17. David Shapiro, "Pluralist Music," *Rain Taxi* (2002), http://www.raintaxi.com/online/2002fall/shapiro.shtml.

18. Ibid.

19. Tony Towle, *Memoir 1960–1963* (Cambridge, MA: Faux Press, 2001), 31.

20. Lewis Warsh, "Introduction," in *The Angel Hair Anthology*, ed. Lewis Warsh and Anne Waldman (New York: Granary Books, 2001), xx.

21. Anne Waldman, "Premises of Consciousness," in *The Poem That Changed America:"Howl" Fifty Years Later*, ed. Jason Shinder (New York: Farrar, Straus and Giroux, 2006), 269.

22. Allen, *The New American Poetry: 1945–1960*, 390.

23. Ibid., 15.

24. Pound, *Literary Essays*: 78.

25. Allen, *The New American Poetry: 1945–1960*, 425.

26. Donald and Warren Tallman Allen, ed. *The Poetics of the New American Poetry* (New York: Grove Press, 1973), 353–54.

27. Allen, *The New American Poetry: 1945–1960*, 390.

28. Ibid., 250.

29. Ibid., 190.

30. Roland Barthes, "The Death of the Author," in *The Rustle of Language* (Berkeley: University of California Press, 1989), 55.

31. Ibid., 50.

32. Ibid., 51.

33. Barrett Watten, *The Constructivist Moment: From Material Text to Cultural Poetics* (Middletown, CT: Wesleyan University Press, 2003), 12.

34. Eleana Kim, "Language Poetry: Dissident Practices and the Making of a Movement," http://home.jps.net/~nada/language6.htm; Shapiro "Pluralist Music"; Mark Wallace, "Emerging Avant-Garde Poetries and the 'Post-Language Crisis'," http://wings.buffalo.edu/epc/authors/wallace/emerging.html.

35. Ron Silliman, "Four Contexts for Three Poems," *Conjunctions* 49 (2007): 298.

36. Allen, *The New American Poetry: 1945–1960*, 308.

37. William Carlos Williams, *Selected Essays* (New York: New Directions, 1969), 128.

38. Allen, *The New American Poetry: 1945–1960*, 357.

39. Jean Starobinski, *Words Upon Words: The Anagrams of Ferdinand de Saussure*, trans. Olivia Emmet (New Haven: Yale University Press, 1979).

40. Wallace, "Emerging Avant-Garde Poetries and the 'Post-Language Crisis.'"

41. Daniel Kane, *All Poets Welcome, The Lower East Side Poetry Scene in the 1960s* (Berkeley: University of California Press, 2003), 42.

42. Ted Berrigan, "Review of Frank O'Hara, *Lunch Poems*," *Kulchur* 17 (1965): 91.

43. Carter Ratcliff, "Schneeman and Company: How to Do Things with Words and Pictures," in *Painter Among Poets: The Collaborative Art of George Schneeman*, ed. Ron Padgett (New York: Granary Books, 2004), 25.

44. Allen, *The New American Poetry: 1945–1960*, 243.

45. Ibid., 244.

46. Ibid.

47. Ted Berrigan, *The Collected Poems*, ed. Alice Notley with Anselm Berrigan and Edmund Berrigan (Berkeley: University of California Press, 2005), 668.

48. Reva Wolf, *Andy Warhol, Poetry, and Gossip in the 1960s* (Chicago: University of Chicago Press, 1997), 94.

49. Ted Berrigan, *Talking in Tranquility: Interviews with Ted Berrigan*, ed. Stephen Ratcliffe and Leslie Scalapino (Bolinas, CA: O Books, 1991), 47.

50. Frank O'Hara, *The Collected Poems*, ed. Donald Allen (Berkeley: University of California Press, 1995), 335–36.

51. Ted Berrigan, *On the Level Everyday: Selected Talks on Poetry and the Art of Living*, ed. Joel Lewis (Jersey City, NJ: Talisman House, 1997), 91.

52. Allen, *The New American Poetry: 1945–1960*, 243–44.

53. Alice Notley, "Voice," in *Coming After: Essays on Poetry*, ed. Alice Notley (Ann Arbor: University of Michigan Press, 2005), 147.

54. Ibid., 151–52.

55. Kathleen Fraser, "Barbara Guest: The Location of Her (A Memoir)," in *Translating the Unspeakable: Poetry and the Innovative Necessity*, ed. Kathleen Fraser (Tuscaloosa: University of Alabama Press, 2000), 127.

56. Ibid., 128.

57. Steve Evans, "The American Avant-Garde after 1989: Notes Toward a History," in *The World in Time and Space: Towards a History of Innovative American Poetry in Our Time*, ed. Edward Foster and Joseph Donahue (Jersey City, NJ: Talisman House, 2002), 655; Wallace, "Emerging Avant-Garde Poetries and the 'Post-Language Crisis'"; Wallace, "On the Lyric as Experimental Possibility," http://wings.buffalo.edu/epc/authors/wallace/lyric.html

58. Marjorie Welish, "The Lyric Lately," *Jacket* 10 (1999).

59. Donald Allen and George F. Butterick eds., *The Post-moderns: The New American Poetry Revisited* (New York: Grove Press, 1982).

60. Laura Hinton and Cynthia Hogue, ed. *We Who Love to Be Astonished: Experimental Women's Writing and Performance Poetics* (Tuscaloosa: University of Alabama Press, 2002), 5.

61. Alice Notley, *Dr Williams' Heiresses* (Berkeley: Tuumba, 1980).

62. Kimberly Lyons, "The Itineraries of Anticipation (Women and The Poetry Project)," http://home.jps.net/~nada/lyons.htm; Libbie Rifkin, "'My Little World Goes On St. Mark's Place': Anne Waldman, Bernadette Mayer and the Gender of an Avant-Garde Institution," *Jacket* 7 (1999).

63. Anne Waldman, *Vow to Poetry: Essays, Interviews, and Manifestos* (Minneapolis: Coffee House Press, 2001), 204.

64. Ibid.

65. Heather Thomas, "'Eyes in All Heads'": Anne Waldman's Performance of Bigendered Imagination in Iovis I," in *We Who Love to Be Astonished: Experimental Women's Writing and Performance Poetics*, ed. Laura Hinton and Cynthia Hogue (Tuscaloosa: University of Alabama Press, 2002), 204–05.

66. Waldman, *Vow to Poetry: Essays, Interviews, and Manifestos*, 27.

67. Ibid., 210.

68. Ibid., 27.

69. Waldman, "Premises of Consciousness," 268.

70. Juliana Spahr, *Everybody's Autonomy: Collective Reading and Connective Identity* (Tuscaloosa: University of Alabama Press, 2001), 57.

71. Barthes, "The Death of the Author," 49.

72. Waldman, *Vow to Poetry: Essays, Interviews, and Manifestos*, 212.

73. Ibid., 205–08; Charles Olson, "Letter 6," *The Maximus Poems*, ed. George F. Butterick (Berkeley: University of California Press, 1983): 31–34.

74. Ibid., 209.

75. Waldman, "Premises of Consciousness," 269.

76. Bob Perelman, "'fucking / me across the decades like we / poets like': Embodied Poetic Transmission," in *Don't Ever Get Famous: Essays on New York Writing after the New York School*, ed. Daniel Kane (Champaign, IL: Dalkey Archive Press, 2006).

77. Joan Retallack and Juliana Spahr, ed. *Poetry and Pedagogy: The Challenge of the Contemporary* (New York: Palgrave Macmillan, 2006), 4.

78. Ibid., xi.

79. Ibid., 295.

80. Kenneth Koch, "Some South American Poets," in *The Art of Poetry: Poems, Parodies, Interviews, Essays and Other Work*, ed. Kenneth Koch (Ann Arbor: University of Michigan Press, 1996), 66.

81. Retallack, *Poetry and Pedagogy: The Challenge of the Contemporary*, 226–27.

82. Kane, *All Poets Welcome, The Lower East Side Poetry Scene in the 1960s*, 196.

83. Bernadette Mayer and the Members of the St. Mark's Church Poetry Project Writing Workshop, "Experiments," *In the American Tree*, ed. Ron Silliman (Orono, ME: National Poetry Foundation, 1986), 558.

84. Waldman, *Vow to Poetry: Essays, Interviews, and Manifestos*: 297–305.

85. Charles Bernstein, http://www.writing.upenn.edu/bernstein/experiments.html

86. Bernstein, "'A Blow is Like an Instrument': The Poetic Imaginary and Curricular Practices," in *Beyond English Inc.: Curricular Reform in a Global Economy*, ed. Claude Mark Hurlbert, David B. Downing, and Paula Mathieu (Portsmouth, NH: Boynton-Cook, 2002), 48; Alan Golding, *From Outlaw to Classic: Canons in American Poetry* (Madison: University of Wisconsin Press, 1995), 86; Ron Silliman, "Canons and Institutions: New Hope for the Disappeared," in *The Politics of Poetic Form: Poetry and Public Policy*, ed. Charles Bernstein (New York: Roof Books, 1990), 158, 67.

87. Bernstein, "'A Blow is Like an Instrument': The Poetic Imaginary and Curricular Practices," 49.

88. Bernstein, http://www.writing.upenniedu/bernstein/experiments.html.

89. Kenneth Koch, *Rose, Where Did You Get That Red? Teaching Great Poetry to Children* (New York: Random House, 1971); Koch, *Wishes, Lies, and Dreams: Teaching Children to Write Poetry* (New York: Chelsea House, 1970).

90. Berrigan, *On the Level Everyday: Selected Talks on Poetry and the Art of Living*, 90–91.

Bibliography

Allen, Donald, ed. *The New American Poetry: 1945–1960*. Berkeley: University of California Press, 1999.

Allen, Donald and George F. Butterick, eds. *The Postmoderns: The New American Poetry Revisited*. New York: Grove Press, 1982.

Allen, Donald, and Warren Tallman, ed. *The Poetics of the New American Poetry*. New York: Grove Press, 1973.

Barthes, Roland. "The Death of the Author." *The Rustle of Language*. Berkeley: University of California Press, 1989.

———. *S/Z*. Translated by Richard Miller. New York: Hill and Wang, 1974.

Bernstein, Charles. http://www.writing.upenn.edu/bernstein/experiments.html

———. "'A Blow Is Like an Instrument': The Poetic Imaginary and Curricular Practices." *Beyond English Inc.: Curricular Reform in a Global Economy*. Edited by Claude Mark Hurlbert, David B. Downing, and Paula Mathieu. Portsmouth, NH: Boynton-Cook, 2002: 39–51.

Berrigan, Ted. *The Collected Poems*. Edited by Alice Notley with Anselm Berrigan and Edmund Berrigan. Berkeley: University of California Press, 2005.

———. *On the Level Everyday: Selected Talks on Poetry and the Art of Living*. Edited by Joel Lewis. Jersey City, NJ: Talisman House, 1997.

———. "Review of Frank O'Hara, *Lunch Poems*." *Kulchur* 17 (1965): 91–94.

———. *Talking in Tranquility: Interviews with Ted Berrigan*. Edited by Stephen Ratcliffe and Leslie Scalapino. Bolinas, CA: O Books, 1991.

Breslin, James E. B. *From Modern to Contemporary: American Poetry, 1945–1965* Chicago: University of Chicago Press, 1985.

Evans, Steve. "The American Avant-Garde after 1989: Notes toward a History." *The World in Time and Space: Towards a History of Innovative American Poetry in Our Time*. Edited by Edward Foster and Joseph Donahue. Jersey City, NJ: Talisman House, 2002: 646–73.

Fraser, Kathleen. "Barbara Guest: The Location of Her (a Memoir)." *Translating the Unspeakable: Poetry and the Innovative Necessity*. Edited by Kathleen Fraser. Tuscaloosa: University of Alabama Press, 2000: 124–30.

Golding, Alan. *From Outlaw to Classic: Canons in American Poetry*. Madison: University of Wisconsin Press, 1995.

Gunn, Thom. "Outside Faction." Review of Charles Olson, *The Distances*, and Other Titles. *Yale Review* 50:4 (Summer 1961): 585–96.

Hall, Donald, Robert Pack, and Louis Simpson, eds. *The New Poets of England and America*. New York: Meridian, 1957.

Hinton, Laura, and Cynthia Hogue, ed. *We Who Love to Be Astonished: Experimental Women's Writing and Performance Poetics*. Tuscaloosa: University of Alabama Press, 2002.

Kane, Daniel. *All Poets Welcome, the Lower East Side Poetry Scene in the 1960s*. Berkeley: University of California Press, 2003.

Kim, Eleana. "Language Poetry: Dissident Practices and the Making of a Movement." http://home.jps.net/~nada/language6.htm.

Koch, Kenneth. *Rose, Where Did You Get That Red? Teaching Great Poetry to Children*. New York: Random House, 1971.

———. "Some South American Poets." *The Art of Poetry: Poems, Parodies, Interviews, Essays and Other Work.* Edited by Kenneth Koch. Ann Arbor: University of Michigan Press, 1996: 61–71.

———. *Wishes, Lies, and Dreams: Teaching Children to Write Poetry.* New York: Chelsea House, 1970.

Lyons, Kimberly. "The Itineraries of Anticipation (Women and the Poetry Project)." http://home.jps.net/~nada/lyons.htm.

Mayer, Bernadette, and the Members of the St. Mark's Church Poetry Project Writing Workshop. "Experiments." *In the American Tree.* Edited by Ron Silliman. Orono, ME: National Poetry Foundation 1986: 557–60.

Notley, Alice. *Dr Williams' Heiresses.* Berkeley: Tuumba, 1980.

———. "Voice." *Coming After: Essays on Poetry.* Edited by Alice Notley. Ann Arbor: University of Michigan Press, 2005: 147–57.

O'Hara, Frank. *The Collected Poems.* Edited by Donald Allen. Berkeley: University of California Press, 1995.

———. "Interview with Edward Lucie-Smith." *Standing Still and Walking in New York.* Edited by Donald Allen. San Franscisco: Grey Fox, 1983: 3–26.

Olson, Charles. "Letter 6." Charles Olson. *The Maximus Poems.* Edited by George F. Butterick. Berkeley: University of California Press, 1983: 31–34.

Perelman, Bob. "'fucking / me across the decades like we / poets like': Embodied Poetic Transmission." *Don't Ever Get Famous: Essays on New York Writing after the New York School.* Edited by Daniel Kane. Champaign, IL: Dalkey Archive Press, 2006: 195–214.

Perkins, David. *A History of Modern Poetry 2: Modernism and After.* Cambridge: Harvard UP, 1987.

Pound, Ezra. *ABC of Reading.* New York: New Directions, 1960.

———. *Literary Essays.* Edited by T.S. Eliot. New York: New Directions, 1968.

Ratcliff, Carter. "Schneeman and Company: How to Do Things with Words and Pictures." *Painter among Poets: The Collaborative Art of George Schneeman.* Edited by Ron Padgett. New York: Granary Books, 2004: 11–28.

Retallack, Joan, and Juliana Spahr, ed. *Poetry and Pedagogy: The Challenge of the Contemporary.* New York: Palgrave Macmillan, 2006.

Rifkin, Libbie. "'My Little World Goes on St. Mark's Place': Anne Waldman, Bernadette Mayer and the Gender of an Avant-Garde Institution." *Jacket* 7 (1999).

Shapiro, David. "Pluralist Music." *Rain Taxi* (2002), http://www.raintaxi.com/online/2002fall/shapiro.shtml.

Silliman, Ron. "Canons and Institutions: New Hope for the Disappeared." *The Politics of Poetic Form: Poetry and Public Policy.* Edited by Charles Bernstein. New York: Roof Books, 1990: 149–74.

———. "Four Contexts for Three Poems." *Conjunctions* 49 (2007): 283–99.

Spahr, Juliana. *Everybody's Autonomy: Collective Reading and Connective Identity.* Tuscaloosa: University of Alabama Press, 2001.

Starobinski, Jean. *Words Upon Words: The Anagrams of Ferdinand De Saussure*. Translated by Olivia Emmet. New Haven: Yale University Press, 1979.

Stein, Gertrude. *How To Write*. Barton, VT: Something Else Press, 1973.

Thomas, Heather. "'Eyes in All Heads': Anne Waldman's Performance of Bigendered Imagination in Iovis I." *We Who Love to Be Astonished: Experimental Women's Writing and Performance Poetics*. Edited by Laura Hinton and Cynthia Hogue. Tuscaloosa: University of Alabama Press, 2002: 203–12.

Towle, Tony. *Memoir 1960–1963*. Cambridge, MA: Faux Press, 2001.

Waldman, Anne. "Premises of Consciousness." *The Poem That Changed America: "Howl" Fifty Years Later*. Edited by Jason Shinder. New York: Farrar, Straus and Giroux, 2006: 260–71.

———. *Vow to Poetry: Essays, Interviews, and Manifestos*. Minneapolis: Coffee House Press, 2001.

Wallace, Mark. "Emerging Avant-Garde Poetries and the Post-Language Crisis." http://wings.buffalo.edu/epc/authors/wallace/emerging.html.

———. "On the Lyric as Experimental Possibility." http://wings.buffalo.edu/epc/authors/wallace/lyric.html

Warsh, Lewis. "Introduction." *The Angel Hair Anthology*. Edited by Lewis Warsh and Anne Waldman. New York: Granary Books, 2001: xix–xxvii.

Watten, Barrett. *The Constructivist Moment: From Material Text to Cultural Poetics*. Middletown, CT: Wesleyan University Press, 2003.

Welish, Marjorie. "The Lyric Lately." *Jacket* 10 (1999).

Williams, William Carlos. *The Autobiography*. New York: New Directions, 1951.

———. "How to Write." *Interviews with William Carlos Williams: "Speaking Straight Ahead."* Edited by Linda Welshimer Wagner. New York: New Direction, 1976: 97–100.

———. *Selected Essays*. New York: New Directions, 1969.

Wolf, Reva. *Andy Warhol, Poetry, and Gossip in the 1960s*. Chicago: University of Chicago Press, 1997.

CHAPTER FIVE

"A Big Kiss for Mother England": *The New American Poetry* in Britain

Ben Hickman

"I can't remember anyone writing anything I considered interesting in those days who didn't have a well-worn copy on their bookshelf. It was a breath of air in a stifling room."[1]

So recalls the British poet Tom Raworth of *The New American Poetry*, in an email to me. The stifling room was the scene of the 1950s, dominated by the Movement, a group of anti-Modernist poets who were essentially one half of the "academic" alliance of Anglo-American poetry, while what Raworth considered interesting was the beginnings of what Eric Mottram has called the "British Poetry Revival," a loose avant-garde grouping of writers that eventually included Raworth, inspired by American and European experimental examples. For the sake of clarity, in outlining the nature of *The New American Poetry*'s reception in the Great Britain I will follow this opposition, as well as Mottram's shorthand phrase for the British avant-garde and the prevalent but highly contested and occasionally meaningless term "academic." The aim here, that is, is to show how Allen's anthology gave impetus to poets searching for a poetry and poetics challenging a set of assumptions about class, history and aesthetic form that had crystallized in the British, in a way that could and did provide a model, a rallying point and a source of authority for a radical and vibrant British avant-garde. The absurdity of Andrew Motion and Blake Morrison's contention that, after the demise of the Movement, in the 1960s and 1970s "very little . . . seemed to be happening . . . in British poetry"[2] can be best illustrated through British poets' reading of *The New American Poetry*.

Reviewed virtually nowhere in Great Britain, and certainly not in the mainstream literary press, and expensive at 14 shillings and sixpence (Al Alvarez's 1962 *The New Poetry* was about a third of the price), *The New American Poetry* nonetheless remains the single most influential book on British avant-garde poetry. Though not instantly entering the poetry-reading public's consciousness, or even its purview, the attentiveness of the margins of British poetry guaranteed *The New American Poetry*'s short- and long-term impact. In the most immediate terms, the book's effect is easily sketched. Within five years of *The New American Poetry*'s appearance, almost all of the poets included, most of whom in 1960 were simply unheard of in Great Britain, had seen their work published in one form or another in the country. Many, including Charles Olson, Robert Duncan, Denise Levertov, Robert Creeley, Ed Dorn, Larry Eigner, Gary Snyder, Michael McClure, and John Ashbery had found British publishers for collections by the end of the decade, in some cases with mainstream presses, with the likes of Olson, Creeley, and Snyder even becoming "exceedingly available in British bookshops."[3] Even the British academy, though admittedly a marginal part of it, was inviting New American poets such as Ed Dorn into ranks.[4] Many of the little magazines that sprang up in the 1960s were operated on the basis of making avant-garde poetry from the United States available along with the British poetry that was consciously following the its example.[5] The viability of Better Books in the 1960s as "an astonishing resource for [The New] American poetry," according to Eric Mottram,[6] would have been impossible without the readership created by Allen's anthology. Indeed, founder Tony Godwin had sought the assistance of a contributor, Lawrence Ferlinghetti, to help "bohemianize" the operation—the City Lights store manager was sent from San Francisco. Fulcrum Press, meanwhile, publishing the likes of Snyder, Dorn, Eigner, Lee Harwood, Tom Raworth, and Roy Fisher, routinely had first print-runs of 3,000 copies. Conferences and readings featuring American poets sprang up everywhere, the most notable being the International Poetry Incarnation at the Royal Albert Hall in 1965, which 7,000 attended to hear radical British poets read alongside the likes of Ginsberg and Gregory Corso. Even *The Times Literary Supplement*, the establishment literary review *par excellence*, was forced to admit that "the whole scene has been transformed" by British followers of *The New American Poetry* like Ian Hamilton Finlay, Gael Turnbull, Michael Horovitz, and Anselm Hollo, all of whom were included in the weekly's "The Changing Guard" issue (August 6, 1964) and were "worth studying even if the standard is not always high" according to the editorial. "British Poetry" had been changed, or at least now had a competitor.

The New American Poetry was a reference point that previously disparate avant-garde British poets could gather around. Andrew Crozier, who presented an American poetry supplement to the wide readership of the Cambridge-based literary quarterly *Granta* just four years after *The New American Poetry* and clearly modeled on its example, echoed Allen's preface in identifying the rallying-point of his own avant-garde anthology, *A Various Art*: "one of the means by which many [British Revival poets] identified each other was an interest in a particular aspect of post-war poetry, and the tradition that lay behind it—not that of Pound and Eliot but that of Pound and Williams."[7] Though it is clear that other vehicles prepared ground for the reception of such alternative poetries (the San Francisco issue of *Evergreen Review*, for example) none were so broad and comprehensive, or encouraged so much *further* reading than *The New American Poetry*. The volume's selection of forty-four poets, especially along with a well-finished poetics, was a window, and an enticing one, onto poetic scenes that were evidently much larger. Though Peter Riley remembers that "very few of the poets in the book were set aside or ignored—almost every name was investigated,"[8] eventually British poets tended to focus their energies on individuals, spurred by the strength of *The New American Poetry*'s varying styles, poetic philosophies and politics. A selective list of influences and relationships can be illustrative: Lee Harwood (New York School, especially Ashbery), John James (New York School, especially O'Hara), Peter Riley (Jack Spicer), J. H. Prynne (Olson and Dorn), Gael Turnbull (Black Mountain and Ginsberg), Andrew Crozier (Olson, back to the Objectivists), Barry MacSweeney (McClure), Tom Pickard (Creeley and Dorn), Chris Torrance (Spicer), Allen Fisher (Olson, Spicer, Barbara Guest), and Jeremy Hilton (Robert Duncan). When one considers that most of the American poets here, with some very notable exceptions, were completely unknown and unavailable in the United Kingdom, and indeed sometimes obscure and unpublished in the United States, the impact of *The New American Poetry* on the complexion of British poetry, even considered as a mere bibliography of the American avant-garde, becomes quantifiable.

Quantity is one thing, but looking into the precise qualities of *The New American Poetry*'s impact in Britain opens up questions not so easily answered by lists or publication histories. How was it that these poets, who had "already created their own tradition, their own press, and their public," according to Allen,[9] could talk to another tradition, to another, quite different, public? Why did so many British poets look to America in the first place? What specific forms did *The New American Poetry* and its poets take as a model? What has it meant for British poetry beyond the 1960s?

Allen's contention that his poets were "already exerting strong influence abroad"[10] was pre-emptive; even so, it is not quite true to say that *The New American Poetry* simply wrote its iconoclastic proclamations on the dead white skull of conventional British poetry. Just as *The New American Poetry* prepared the ground for a fundamental rethinking of the legacy and possibilities of modernism in post-war Britain, it did not itself come out of nowhere, and had the ground prepared for it by a number of enthusiasts and vanguardists. The two stories—British poets and presses laying the foundations for *The New American Poetry* and vice versa—are not always easy to separate, but the lay of the land can be broadly mapped out. Some British poets, indeed, were *in* the anthology, as publishers. Gael Turnbull was one, whose Migrant Press had published or distributed work by Creeley, Olson's *Maximus Poems* and Ed Dorn's *What I See in the Maximus Poems* before *The New American Poetry*. Turnbull himself, who lived in California from 1958 to 1964, was passing on the advice on the American avant-garde received from Cid Corman and others to important British poets. Roy Fisher remembers meeting Turnbull while he still lived in England: "I met Gael Turnbull and I was exposed in one day to Olson, Creeley, Bunting, Zukofsky, Duncan, Ginsberg, Corso, Ferlinghetti, Ray Souster, and, most of all, William Carlos Williams."[11] *Migrant Magazine*, meanwhile, was a hugely important vehicle despite only running for eight issues from July 1959 to September 1960. Emerging from Turnbull's home in Ventura and shipped around the United States, Canada, and the United Kingdom, *Migrant* was responsible for introducing Levertov, Eigner, Dorn, Creeley, and Olson to audiences both sides of the Atlantic (though they had appeared less regularly in other British little magazines of the 1950s such as *Window*, *The Poet*, *Artisan* and *Nine*). Olson himself had certainly "arrived" in Britain before Allen's anthology, and would have made his mark without *Migrant*. Elaine Feinstein, as Olson's "Letter" to her in *The New American Poetry* indicates, as well as other British poets including Turnbull and critics such as Ronald Mason were all well-enough acquainted with the poet's work to be in correspondence with him about some serious matters of poetics. J. H. Prynne, who began a correspondence with Olson around the time of *The New American Poetry*'s publication, was also initiating what would be a long-term fascination with Olson at Cambridge University, itself soon to become a center of avant-garde poetry and poetics under Prynne's leadership. Robert Duncan was another who was visible in the United Kingdom, if not widely understood—his work was being reviewed in establishment journals like *Poetry Review* early on in his career, but was being criticized for its "sprawl" and for "lacking in tension and rhythmic control."[12] Charles Tomlinson and even the habitually conservative Donald

Davie, who called Olson's "Projective Verse" "the most ambitious and intelligent attempt by a poet of today to take his bearings, and to take a future course,"[13] were making efforts to introduce the range of American poetry to British readers at a time when even William Carlos Williams couldn't find a publisher in the country. The Beats, of course, were well known for many other reasons. It is not clear what is meant by *Agenda*'s ambiguous remark in an editorial to its September 1960 issue that "without American poetry English poetry would be almost non-existent."[14] However, given that it was said in the context of introducing Williams's "The American Idiom" essay, which was printed in the issue, we can guess that it saw Allen's "Pound and Williams" tradition already emerging in Great Britain.

When it did arrive, *The New American Poetry* had intended and unintended consequences in Britain. One of the intentions of the anthology, which had an almost identical resonance on both sides of the Atlantic, was its militant anti-academicism. Indeed, anyone seeking a single "movement" among the anthology's various groupings was told where to look: the poets have "one common characteristic," according to Allen: "a total rejection of all those qualities typical of academic verse."[15] Allen's anti-academic offensive spoke to certain British poets because they had experienced the same decade of formalist, academic, conservative verse—in America it was the so-called Middle Generation, in the United Kingdom it was the Movement. The similarity between the two poetic scenes is not surprising—after all, American academic verse defined itself by looking to England, a point I will pick up shortly. *The New American Poetry*'s rival, the formalist *New Poets of England and America*, summed the scene up:

> The problem of an audience—of a community of informed and open discussion and dissent, concerned and yet free from commercial or vested interest—is inseparable from the question of the vitality of art. In our time, the university, rather than literary cliques, the poetry societies, the incestuous pages of little magazines, is capable of nurturing and supporting such an audience.[16]

The Movement's poetry of "academic principles [with] an intellectual backbone"[17] represented a similar conception of audience. There were reactions to this institutionalization of poetry even in the academy's ranks. Al Alvarez's *The New Poetry* (1962) attempted to rid British poetry of the old, scholarly, Middle-England guard while keeping things firmly in the mainstream. It was clearly a dry well: Alvarez's famous "Gentility Principle" introduction, with its posturing iconoclasm, was hypocritical. Lambasting the Movement for writing "academic administrative verse"[18] was one thing, but the accusation lost its teeth when the anthology included generous selections from most of the Movement poets that were in Robert Conquest's *New Lines* anthology of Movement poetry (1956). Alvarez's strategy was to try to use four Americans at the start of the book as catalysts for English innovation. The problem was that it was hard to see how these Americans (Robert Lowell, John Berryman, Anne Sexton, and Sylvia Plath) were not "gentile" themselves, especially if you had just been reading Charles Olson or Allen Ginsberg. For many, the book did little to redeem British poetry because its poems were so rooted in academic *standards*. What Eric Mottram called "the 1950s Axis orthodoxy" was not so much challenged by attempts like Alvarez's to rearrange the priorities of mainstream academic poetry, but repackaged with an emphasis on greater "emotion" and less scholarly subject matter.

The problem for the avant-garde, though, was the academic itself. In some cases this led to anti-intellectualism (as in the case of Jeff Nuttall), but it could also lead to a different *kind* of academicism (or so it was claimed) as with the Cambridge School. The 1960s counterculture objected particularly to the New Criticism's removal of the author and, it seemed, individualism, as in Michael Horovitz's "Afterwords" to his groundbreaking, Beat-inspired *Children of Albion* anthology (1968).[19] Others responded to the elitism of a poetry scene so dependent on a critical apparatus, with Lee Harwood noting that the Beats proved to him that "you don't have to have gone to a public school and Oxford and Cambridge before you can write,"[20] while others still, such as British concrete poet Bob Cobbing, saw the very power structures of the British university *per se* as the problem, helping to run as he did in 1968 along with other British intellectuals like R. D. Laing, the London Anti-University. Whatever the nuances, the consensus among British avant-garde writers was that the academy was stifling creativity, excluding forms of experience and perpetuating reactionary politics—and that academic verse it was bad for poetry, bad for the imagination and bad for society.

The influence of *The New American Poetry*'s "total rejection of . . . academic verse," was to show the possibility of a serious poetry that was not academic, and an intellectually powerful art that did not need to be built on T.S. Eliot's "historical sense" or New Critical tenets. While Lowell was busy working out the poet's role in society in metrical patterns and vocabulary borrowed from metaphysical poetry, readers could find O'Hara describing poetry in the medium of sardines in the delightfully irreverent "Why I Am Not a Painter";[21] while New Criticism was insisting on the ontological autonomy of the poem, LeRoi Jones and Allen Ginsberg were placing it firmly in the political world; Olson even showed in "Projective Verse" how a poet could make use of Elizabethan prosody without limiting the engagement to academic discussions of anapaests, dactyls and "defective feet."[22] The lessons were well-learned in Britain: from Tom Raworth's parodies of academic language to the irreverent, demotic or simply unofficial vocabulary of poets like Barry MacSweeney, a new "poetic diction" was being born; popular culture was also seen entering British verse with much greater frequency; there was a mixing of art forms that forced poetry far from university grounds. Overall, though, what was to replace "the academic" was not always consistent. British avant-gardists increasingly juxtaposed it to *genuine experience* in a way that challenged the New Critical separation of world and artwork: "Recently I read, "pain is a great incentive / to art." / Which proves two things; / I've been reading again, / and you can not trust the printed word / until you have experienced that which it proposes."[23]

The link between English departments and England itself was never far away from this anti-academy rhetoric, in a way that had unique potential for British poets. Like the Anglophobic *The New American Poetry*, which was a reaction to a formalist Anglophilia seen as both academic and conservative, for British poets the liberation from "Eng Lit" was a weapon to be used against the little Englandism of the Movement. Gael Turnbull's critique of the Movement, "Now That April's Here," makes the link between the group's parochial chauvinism and academic poetic practice clear:

> It's raining on the Brussels sprouts.
> The fire is smoking in the grate.
> Macmillan says he has no doubts.
> Will Oxford beat the Cambridge eight?
>
> Some bright intervals tomorrow.
> Sixpence on a football pool.
> Seven percent if you want to borrow.
> Charles is settling down at school.
>
> Put the Great back in Great Britain.
> Write a letter to *The Times*.
> Lots of fun with Billy Butlin.
> It's a poem if it rhymes.[24]

The poem seems to sum up the opposite of *The New American Poetry* for British poets as well as their own anathema: art that is uncritically formal, imperialistic yet parochial, unambitious yet chauvinistic, academic yet narrow-minded.

If *The New American Poetry* influenced British poetry, it was precisely because it did not address it. Even James Schuyler, who was no Anglophobe, displayed uncharacteristic vitriol in the book for "the campus dry-heads who wishfully descend tum-ti-tumming from Yeats out of Graves with a big kiss for Mother England."[25] The principal aim of *The New American Poetry* was to establish a distinctly American poetry that had not been seen in the United States since Whitman. In part turning to France, but mainly emphasizing the sufficiency of American traditions, *The New American Poetry* was unabashed, like avant-gardists in the other arts such as John Cage and Jackson Pollock, about "American exceptionalism." The possibilities of the imagination were offered by the political traditions and geographic make-up of the country, whether as myth or felt reality. The strident nationalism of Olson's "To Gerhardt, There, Among Europe's Things" was eventually dropped as the volume's opening poem in favor of "The Kingfishers," but the volume nonetheless made its case for the vitality of a specifically *American* tradition. The wide open spaces of Olson and Duncan's work re-introduced for the first time since Whitman the possibility of an American sublime, all kinds of Americana were made suitable subjects for poetry by the likes of O'Hara, Schuyler, and Ginsberg, while the "Statements on Poetics" section made the volume feel in some way self-sufficient. Even the book's organization, with contents divided geographically, was clearly modeled on the localism of William Carlos Williams—with the major exception to the spread being Boston, because for Allen, Boston is not a local place but an Anglophile colonial outpost. The trend was noticed by *The New American Poetry*'s establishment detractors: by 1962, in the second edition of *New Poets of England and America*, Donald Hall would complain of the "uncritical Anglophobia" of a certain class of American poet. The English tradition that had seemed so inescapable in the 1950s was suddenly being thrown on the proverbial scrapheap by a group of uneducated *parvenus*.

Whatever has been the result of this cultural nationalism for American culture now, in 1960s Britain the implications were clear. Some observers would argue that, partly as a result of *The New American Poetry*'s efforts, "British poetry and American poetry [wouldn't be] on speaking terms"[26] for some years. A British anthologist wrote in 1962 of the results of American poetry's "Chinese box of semantic ingenuities":

> American and English poetry is no longer homogeneous, though written in approximately the same language. Contemporary American poetry—which, thanks to the excessive interest taken in it by American universities, is now an industry rather than an art—seems to be wandering off in the direction of the decorative, where style and technique is all.[27]

Others, however, saw things quite differently. Nathaniel Tarn even suggests the book's influence was greater in the United Kingdom than its place of origin. He reflected on how there was "an America in England and an England in America"[28]—the America in England being the avant-garde, and the England still existing in America embodied in poets like Wilbur, Nemerov, and Lowell. Dom Silvester Houédard (or *dsh*), a British concrete poet of the period, similarly observes:

> EITHER you see the modern movement as happening to american poetry (whether written in GB or USA) OR you see it as happening to english poetry (whether written in USA or GB); in 1st case you restrict English poetry to victorian-georgian-neoelizabethan: in 2nd case you see wild zigzag life well f i (Whitman) Pound Stein Sitwell Cummings Eliot Auden Williams Spender Olson Ginsberg Corso Horovitz Heliczer Hollo & the jazzpoetry of now . . . [29]

Roy Fisher, a major if not the major British avant-garde poet of the 1960s, would talk of his "exercises in de-Anglicizing England"[30]—exercises made possible from his models of Williams and Olson. In essence, *The New American Poetry* had initiated a choice for British poets that was national as much as aesthetic between a nationalistic Little Englandism on the one hand and a perceived American internationalism on the other. Eric Mottram refers to poets "who distinctly reject the Movement and all it stands for, and whose experience of American poetry has activated their work,"[31] with implications that went far beyond the practice of poetry.

The appeal in Britain of a de-Anglicized American poetry over an "American poetry [that] seems to have all the traditional British virtues,"[32] as John Bayley put it at the time, is best understood as motivated by four factors: two of which, namely issues of class and empire, are political-historical and two—approaches to the past and poetic philosophy—aesthetic. Clearly, however, that British poets looked to America in the 1960s in no way marks them out from political, commercial and other cultural areas of British society that had been increasingly viewing the United States as a model (and in many cases as a patron) ever since the beginning of the Marshall Plan. Successive British governments had eagerly taken up a junior-partner role to the new American superpower after the Second World War, switching from an independent nuclear power to one dependent on the United States for supply, and trying to act as the United States' spokesperson in Europe (culminating in its humiliating rejection for membership of the European Common Market in 1963). Meanwhile Fordism, advertising, Hollywood, jazz, Abstract Expressionism, and many other forms of Americana were all having a huge impact on British culture long before *The New American Poetry*. Even in the academy, Britain went from a place where, as Charles Tomlinson writes, "A boy from the provinces, going up to read English at Cambridge in 1945, as I did, would have learned little of American poetry from his university teachers,"[33] to one where the new subject of "American Studies" (which was promoted at arm's length by the United States government) was available at many institutions, some of which had British Revival Poets like Eric Mottram and Roy Fisher teaching them.[34]

It would clearly be naive to separate British poets from broader cultural, political and economic areas of the country increasingly looking to the United States. British avant-garde poetry had special interests within this, however, given its own specific politics and constituency, not to mention what it felt were the specific implications of this cultural shift for poetry as an art form. Foremost among the issues raised was class. When Conservative Prime Minister Harold Macmillan declared in 1959 that "The class war is over and we have won it,"[35] it was clear who the "we" was. The Movement was the poetic spokesperson of this misleading consensus politics, with Donald Davie in all his critical works and manifestoes for the Movement insisting on the necessity of "consensual" centrism against the radicalism of some trade unions and the counter-culture. "Political alternatives to social democracy," according to Davie, "are too costly in terms of human suffering."[36] It was clear to those seeking alternatives to Davie's "rational conservativism," however, that all the Movement's talk of democracy and consensus was a veil for a reactionary politics intent on perpetuating the class and wealth divides in British society. The relative prosperity of the 1950s had caused problems for the Movement, which had built its stoical poetic of common-sense following the post-war "age of austerity" (1945 to about 1951); the plea to "keep calm and carry on" in a continuation of World War II politics of class collaboration was wearing thin. Rightly or wrongly, British poets looking to America saw a classless society in the United States, or at least a poetry scene that was untainted by the conservative elitism of certain attitudes toward class. Tom Raworth wrote in a letter to Ed Dorn:

> one day I found *Evergreen 2* . . . the San Francisco scene one—with Howl and all which started me off reading more and more of the Americans . . . there are English poets still, over here, but "English" and "poets" . . . you know the sort of thing. It's odd . . . poetry over here is, I think, still a "class" thing . . . There's no flow, no use of natural language. The whole thing is so artificial and contrived . . . Nothing has the power to move.[37]

The "Movement" of course, had no ambitions to "move"—in aesthetic as in political terms, its aims were for quietism based on cozy resignation. "A neutral tone is nowadays preferred," wrote Davie in his famous poem, "Remembering the Thirties."

The snobbery of the poetry itself contrasts clearly with its American-inflected Revival counterparts, particularly in the limitations it imposed on subject matter. While its conservative sensibility allowed the Movement to conclude, absurdly, that "nobody wants any more poems on the grander themes for a few years,"[38] its antidemocratic bent was anxious about "meagreness and triviality of subject matter":[39] the result was a middling poetry anxious to uphold thematic decorum without overstepping the mark into the ambitious. There are no poems about red wheelbarrows in Movement verse, but neither are there speculations on the meaning of the *polis*. If a book ever veered between these two extremes, and not always with consistency, it was *The New American Poetry*: for every Robert Duncan there is a Frank O'Hara among the anthology's contributors. Olson, meanwhile, was a poet who could be seen swinging wildly from the quotidian concrete to the grand mythical abstract within a single poem—Ginsberg was another. J. H. Prynne, interrupting occasionally tortuous speculation on economic reality with all manner of assembled objects, and Allen Fisher, whose fragmented particulars were part of a revaluation of the concept of place, were just two poets who saw in the new American avant-garde as a liberation from poetic principles that were inseparable from conservative class politics. Stephen Spender, certainly not a poet Prynne or Fisher owed anything to, was to say in 1973 that, unlike British poets, American artists "express an American total-sum of present-day consciousness, not of a civilization confined to one class or to an elite. The American writer seems open to everything that happens in his country. His attitude is summed up in the idea of 'projectiveness.'"[40]

This is not to say that class was not an issue in Britain, as it clearly was despite all the rhetoric of a society that had "never had it so good." It is true to say, though, that poets looked to America in an attempt to transcend rather than abolish class distinctions that had a cultural element in Britain far more at odds with economic reality than in other countries. This is certainly in correspondence with the Emersonian democratic self of most of *The New American Poetry*'s poets, but was more evident in the volume's poems that simply had no anxieties about such matters (and, in some cases, no anxieties about politics at all). What the New American poets were, above all, was classless: academic affiliation was a sign of respectability in British poetry at the time, but here were these Americans "living by clerking, surveying, gardening etc.,"[41] "working on a tanker,"[42] or enjoying the itinerant lives of freedom that had been mythologized in Jack Kerouac's *On the Road*. British poets suddenly felt comfortable *addressing* poems to an audience beyond petit-bourgeois academia, as in the Welsh poet John James's Olson-inflected

"An Open Letter to Jim Workman, Landlord, at the Rose and Crown, Withy Mills, North Somerset":

> your lame foot & stick
> suggest pain
> carry your
> trunk, head, arms
> hands, the drink in
> your hand, a glass
> mug, pint, bringing
> it to us
>
> & if I brought you a poem
> what would you do with it?
> what would your hawk's nose,
> your dry sniff, pulled down
> corners of the month . . .[43]

This is not the attempt at "rescuing from silence the class into which he was born"[44] that Tony Harrison and other left-wing British poets less associated with the American avant-garde were attempting, but rather a gesture toward the inclusion of broader forms of experience as a result of a liberation from the narrow class concerns of the Movement.

Attempts to reverse the imperial decline of Britain were accepted as part of the plan to perpetuate the class system. As one journalist, Peregrine Worsthorne, observed in 1959: "The Right is acutely aware that the kind of Britain it wishes to preserve depends on Britain remaining a great power . . . Everything about the British class system begins to look foolish and tacky when related to a second-class power on the decline."[45] The Conservative government of the time was intent on retaining British prestige: at times in the 1950s, military spending accounted for around ten percent of GNP, more than double that of its main competitors, while hospitals and schools went unbuilt. Britain was not, however, conducting itself in a manner altogether commensurate with a major world power. The decolonization of its empire had been farcically conducted at times; and there was the 1956 disaster of Suez, in which British forces invaded Egypt following the nationalization of the canal, only to withdraw in humiliation seven days later after the United States and United Nations exerted public pressure. The country's international position was summed up in 1962 when the then-U.S. Secretary of State Dean Acheson said: "Great Britain has lost an Empire and has not yet found a role."[46] In 1969, however, with the dismantling of empire and the pacifist counter-culture in full swing, Philip Larkin wrote this:

HOMAGE TO A GOVERNMENT
Next year we are to bring the soldiers home
For lack of money, and it is all right.
Places they guarded, or kept orderly,
Must guard themselves, and keep themselves orderly.
We want the money for ourselves at home
Instead of working. And this is all right.

It's hard to say who wanted it to happen,
But now it's been decided nobody minds.
The places are a long way off, not here,
Which is all right, and from what we hear
The soldiers there only made trouble happen.

Next year we shall be easier in our minds.
Next year we shall be living in a country
That brought its soldiers home for lack of money.
The statues will be standing in the same
Tree-muffled squares, and look nearly the same.
Our children will not know it's a different country.
All we can hope to leave them now is money.[47]

Tragic armchair general or swaggering chauvinist, Larkin was as out of touch with public opinion as he was with economic reality. If Larkin was "a citizen of some commonwealth" as Davie admiringly opined,[48] then it was a commonwealth many young British poets did not want to be part of. Ironically, it was the American counterculture, which had recognized the imperial ambitions of its own country, which provided an example addressing the issue. Davie lamented that "impressionable sections of British society were swept by recurrent tides of sympathy for the mostly young Americans who were protesting at the nation's warfare in Vietnam" leading to an "avid and responsive audience" for an American poetry that had not been "screened first by the New York and subsequently by the London literary establishments."[49]

Lee Harwood is a case in point, in his early career mixing the self-consciousness of the New York School with the politics of Black Mountain and the Beats. *The White Room* (1964–67) is a major collection of poetry by any standards, but it also stands as a document of an American mode applied to the archetypal British issues of empire. The eponymous section of the book[50] seems to be a complex parable of the end of empire, and opens with an apparently repainted room that "meant that the toy soldiers had to all be rearranged," despite "the same flags still hanging" and "the "last words" / of an important general's speech / talking of history, religion and tradition."[51] "The Doomed Fleet" explores the tension between an empire that has lost all meaningful purpose and power, but still has the ability to cause meaningless damage and pain. The poem begins:

> The entire palace was deserted, just as was
> the city, and all the villages along the 50 mile
> route from the seaport to the capital.
> It was not caused by famine or war—
> "It was all my fault,"
>
> The troops of desperate cavalry were ridiculous.
> The naval guns could pick off
> whatsoever their whim dictated,
> but there was only one commander-in-chief.[52]

The reflexivity of the imperial regime, echoed ironically in the self-consciousness of the poem, seems to ensure its survival, whatever the circumstances, as empire seems to determine the vocabulary through which it is to be thought: "The men's minds were set—/ they didn't understand "pity." The very word / had been deliberately deleted from all the books / scattered among the fleet."[53] The paradox of "soldiers in the castle who select the dance records" and a castle itself whose "walls were beyond all hope of restoration"[54] causes subsequent poems to balance, as many of Ashbery's ominous landscape poems of the same period do, precariously between observation and self-implication. Language itself, whether as "whim dictated" or "books / scattered among the fleet," is dangerous in this context as a tool for setting "men's minds." Though "all the previous locations are now impossible," there is still "the agreed colour in the atlas key"[55] to be overcome. The application of New York School self-reflexivity to the menace of empire is an unexpected episode in the story of *The New American Poetry*, but one that would have implications for the survival of Black Mountain and especially Ashberyan modes in Britain.

However, *The New American Poetry* was probably an example for post-imperial Britain for its flexible approach to the past generally as much as anything else. The change from Eliot's "Return to the Sources"[56] to Olson's Heraclitean "will to change"[57] would have been obvious to any reader opening *The New American Poetry*:

> I am no Greek, hath not th' advantage,
> And of course, no Roman:
> he can take no risk that matters,
> the risk of beauty least of all.

But I have my kin, if for no other reason than
(as he said, next of kin) I commit myself, and,
given my freedom, I'd be a cad
if I didn't. Which is most true.

It works out this way, despite the disadvantage.
I offer, in explanation, a quote:
si j'ai du gout, ce n'est guères
que pour la terre et les pierres

Despite the discrepancy (an ocean courage age)
this is also true: if I have any taste
it is only because I have interested myself
in what was slain in the sun

    I pose you your question:
shall you uncover honey / where maggcts are?

    I hunt among stones[58]

Robert van Hallberg has said, "Olson is posthistorical man: the change he urges is the transition out of history."[59] An overstatement no doubt, but the claims to hunt among stones rather than classical texts is clearly a different approach to the starting-point of Eliot and his disciples like Lowell that "the poet should know everything that has been accomplished in poetry."[60] The change is partly a move from the *literary* history Eliot equates with civilization generally, and partly toward a more inclusive conception of the past—in Olson's case, encompassing geological, economic, archival and many other elements.

The democratization of the past from a literary vault into an "open field" is part of the generally less oppressive force of the past in *The New American Poetry* compared to *New Lines, New Poets of England and America*, or *The New Poetry*. While Davie was lamenting that "Our poetry suffers from the loss, or the drastic impoverishment, of the traditional images of celebration,"[61] U.S.-inspired poets like Michael Horovitz were praising the "NOW" of the new poetry.[62] There were clearly many variations on this in *The New American Poetry*: Ashbery engaged deeply with the past, but inattentively, to shine a light on the present; Ginsberg's ideas about orality and breath insisted on a kind of primordial, creative presence; O'Hara wrote a radical poetry of the present tense; even a religious poet like Brother Antoninus could be found praising God for "making" "most instantly, / On the very now";[63] many others simply rejected the possibility of an atemporal meditative space for poetry so typical of much "traditional" verse from Coleridge to Lowell. Clearly, there could be problems with this; as Marjorie Perloff observed in the 1970s: "the modesty . . . of [mainstream] contemporary British poetry has much to do with the poets' persistent and perhaps burdensome sense of tradition, a tradition their American counterparts dismiss with what is all too often a frightening insouciance."[64] The consequences were equally varied within the British avant-garde. Perhaps the most significant development was the import of the "happening." Horovitz wrote in his *Children of Albion* anthology: "We went on the road in spontaneous accord, to revive the oral traditions by which the word had resounded through the ages."[65] Horovitz's Poetry in Motion outfit, which organized poetry readings throughout the country, was inspired by the possibilities of presence shown by the Beat and Black Mountain experiments in the communication of poetry. Some of the significant aural concrete poetry of the British Poetry Revival, such as that of Bob Cobbing, also came out of this. O'Hara's chatty "I do this, I do that" poems were brought to a British milieu by John James and many others, while the twentieth-century tradition of fragmentation, carried mainly by David Jones in Britain hitherto, and largely cut off in its tracks by a reading of Eliot that emphasized *Four Quartets* over *The Waste Land*, also re-emerged, but gutted of its underlying mythical architecture. Inspired by the collage of James Schuyler, John Ashbery, Michael McClure and other poets, young British poets like Tom Raworth, Lee Harwood, and Allen Fisher went on to become bricoleurs making their own poetry of the contemporary. Elsewhere, a kind of automatic writing reigned, but largely unconcerned with any subconscious and inspired by the kind of experiential mimesis demanded by Olson's precept that "one perception must must must MOVE, INSTANTER, ON ANOTHER."[66]

The question of form in its narrowest sense is the most visible measure of *The New American Poetry*'s impact. Hard as it is to imagine, free verse, let alone experimental forms, had virtually disappeared from British poetry in the 1950s—those who could command a significant readership being largely limited to survivors of modernism like David Gasgoyne and David Jones. In terms of this, 1960 is a watershed moment. In 1961, the most successful postwar work of formal experimentation, Roy Fisher's *City* was published, with other collections of the 1960s variously following the oracular versification of Ginsberg (Michael Horovitz's 1963 *Declaration: a poem in twelve parts, spelled out for the human voice*), Olsonian lineation (J. H. Prynne's *The White Stones* of 1968), or the prosaic non-style of Frank O'Hara (John James's *Mmm . . . Ah, Yes*, 1967). The use of disjunctive or unconventional syntax, seen in the majority of poets in *The New American Poetry*, was also taken up by many poets, particularly in Cambridge. Davie's insistence in 1952 that "to dislocate syntax in poetry is to threaten the rule of law in civilized community,"[67] is easily ridiculed, but had mainly only received a different emphasis under *The New American Poetry*'s influence—that this was a *good* thing. Certainly the link would be realized more fully later in the United States with Language Poetry, but some poets associated with Cambridge such as Veronica Forrest-Thomson and especially Prynne had began to explore its implications.[68]

The way in which this formal experimentation was contextualized by a theoretical engagement with poetry was perhaps the biggest influence. The anti-philosophical sensibility of British poetry in the 1950s was thoroughgoing and far more pronounced in the United Kingdom than in the United States at the time—indeed, mainstream British poetry's resistance to philosophy, relative to Europe and America, remains one of its major characteristics. The outlook of the British poets that dominated the 1950s was what it called "empiricism." The Movement would describe itself as "empirical in its attitude to all that comes,"[69] but in truth this attitude was far less an engagement with the thought of John Locke than it was an abdication of abstract thought and an appeal to so-called British common sense. The approach was clearly intellectually as well as politically conservative: though its principal aim was not to sully the waters of poetry with philosophy, its main effect was to create a stagnant, uncritical basis for poetry that was, in its own terms, unchangeable. Empiricism as a term did mean something, though, insofar as it signified an intention to accept the world as it appeared. Such acceptance was not part *The New American Poetry*'s project, politically or phenomenologically. Charles Olson specifically says in "The Human Universe" that "external reality is more than merely the substance which man takes in."[70] As the "Statements on Poetics" section of *The New American Poetry* shows, unlike British poets of the 1950s (who barely had a "poetics" between them), Olson and others, variously through readings of Martin Heidegger, A. N. Whitehead, and all manner of Eastern philosophies, were questioning reality. The philosophical preoccupation of *The New American Poetry* is epistemological, but the questions raised in "Statements" section are diverse: concerning, for example, the sources of creativity (Duncan),[71] the nature of description (Creeley),[72] the distinction between "disclosure" and representation (Spicer),[73] and questions of sound and identity (Jones).[74] Nor are these speculations limited to the statements appended to the book. Many of the poems themselves had the capacity to carry detailed considerations of large philosophical ideas: three of the anthology's most impressive works, Olson's "The Kingfishers," Duncan's "A Poem Beginning with a Line by Pindar," and Spicer's "Imaginary Elegies" define themselves by their capacity to question the intellectual assumptions that had made Middle Generation and Movement poetry alike seem so complacent and comfortable. Admittedly, these questionings were sometimes more mystical than rigorous elsewhere in *The New American Poetry*, but the figures behind the book—Stevens, Williams, Pound, and Olson himself—ensured that the questions themselves were never simply taken as read.

The British avant-garde's antipathy to what Michael Horovitz called the "backwash of nineteenth-century materialism"[75] had, therefore, an example of its transcendence. In this there is evidently a *geist* that goes beyond the individual poets picked up from *The New American Poetry* by British poets, which raises a key question about the anthology's reception in the United Kingdom: did the British get an Olsonian poetics from the book? There are many reasons for thinking that they did. Firstly, the anthology invites such a reading anyway: Olson is the first poet and has about twice as much space as anybody else, he heads up the Black Mountain section of poems, which is the first and largest in the book, and the "Statements on Poetics" section. Various references to Olson, implicit and explicit, in other poems and prose pieces, give the idea of an Olsonian tradition. Olson's own role in helping to edit the volume[76] perhaps also played a part in furthering his specific ends. Many British poets, however, were predisposed to an Olsonian tradition and facilitated the reading of it into *The New American Poetry*. Firstly, more than any other contributor, Olson gave voice directly to the fundamental problems of mainstream British verse of the 1950s, the lazy empiricism that was providing "a p[iss] poor crawling actuarial "real"—good enough to keep banks and insurance companies, plus mediocre governments, etc. But not Poetry's Truth."[77] Secondly, the ideas of "composition by field" had a democratizing element, as much as it liberated poetry from kind of fetishism of the past that Eliot and Pound had insisted upon. Thirdly, Olson was an internationalist, at least compared to the parochialism of the British poetry of the period, however much this internationalism had an imperialism of its own. There are other aspects: in "Projective Verse" one of the fullest theorizations of free verse hitherto seen, the unashamed relegation of English traditions from a privileged position of authority, the emphasis on the "high energy construct" over the low energy of common sense, and so on. Olson, indeed, seems to represent at both aesthetic and theoretical levels, most of what I have been talking about as motive forces behind *The New American Poetry*'s success in Britain, unified into a comprehensive and original poetics.

In the actual event, it is clear that Olson was the most influential figure for the heyday of the British Poetry Revival. R. F. Langley, another poet associated with Cambridge, equated American poetry and Olson in a way that was typical: "I didn't start writing until I found out about American poetry . . . It was really Olson who convinced me that I might write something myself."[78] Immediately after *The New American Poetry*'s appearance, probably more British poets were in touch with Olson, discussing poetics and civilization generally, than any other American poet: J. H. Prynne, Tom Raworth, Peter Riley, Elaine Feinstein, Gavin Selerie, Nathaniel Tarn, Gael

Turnbull, Andrew Crozier and Anselm Hollo could all be named among his correspondents. Certainly the most influential of these poets—Prynne and Crozier—were, though in different ways, committed Olsonians. As late as 1987, Crozier, who had produced an Olsonian American-poetry supplement in Britain twenty-three years earlier ("the spirit of Olson informs this whole collection," it said), could be found introducing an anthology of British avant-garde poetry with an assertion that its overriding spirit was "the tradition . . . of Pound and Williams,"[79] a coded reference to Olson. Even among detractors, Olson would often be the fall guy for the entire project of *The New American Poetry*. Furthermore, it should be noted that Olson not only influenced younger poets; the success of his example it can be argued, prepared the ground for the wider acceptance of some older poets' work on both sides of the Atlantic as well: Roy Fisher and Basil Bunting (whose *Briggflatts* was not published until 1965) being just two examples.

The story after the decade of *The New American Poetry*'s immediate reception is one of mixed fortunes for both the British avant-garde and the New American poetry it was using and promoting. The New American poets had inspired a vital and original movement in British poetry that had taken root and allowed some of the poets of *The New American Poetry* to take root in the country also. In *The New British Poetry* (1988), Ken Edwards speaks of the influence of Revival poets as disseminators of the American avant-garde and major figures in their own right: "[younger poets] have *started* by discovering the work of Prynne, Mottram, Raworth, Harwood, Cobbing or Roy Fisher, only then proceeding backwards through these to Pound, Williams, Olson, Ashbery or O'Hara, and then perhaps on to the current work being done in America and Europe."[80] If the former were still not taught at universities, meanwhile, the latter certainly were beginning to be, representing a challenge to New Critical orthodoxy and the "Great Tradition" on another front. By 1970 Great Britain had a poetic avant-garde that was evidently here to stay, that had common ground and a shared tradition, and that still exists, with many of its principles intact.

On the other hand, this avant-garde has been far less visible in Britain than the tradition sparked by *The New American Poetry* in the United States. The so-called "Poetry Wars" seem symptomatic of the problems that *The New American Poetry* could cause when transplanted to a British context. From 1971 to 1977, after the general council of the Poetry Society had been overrun with a group of avant-gardists (including Allen Fisher, Lee Harwood, and Barry MacSweeney) elected in 1970, Eric Mottram, elected as editor of *Poetry Review*, would unapologetically introduce radical British and American poetry to the most mainstream, middlebrow magazine of them all, culminating in a backlash that eventually involved the state itself. The publication of poetry by Americans was one of the major sticking points, with the eventually successful reactionary elements in the society standing on a platform of excluding American poets.[81] Mottram's "treacherous assault on British poetry" was similar to Allen's attack on the then-mainstream American verse, but the lack of common ground between the two camps in the United Kingdom made audiences much harder to find for the radicals and absorption much harder to accept for the mainstream. This was largely *caused* by the different traditions they had come from: at least the poets of the Allen and Pack/Hall anthologies had Pound, and perhaps Stevens and Auden, in common—the British "Poetry Wars" pitched Olsonian or New York School-influenced poets against a mainstream that had mainly never heard of Olson or Ashbery, or at least did not recognize their legitimacy. Even where anti-experimental poets and critics were increasingly forced to take note of the New American poetry tradition, it did not necessarily lead to a healthy intercourse between self-appointed mainstream and avant-garde groupings: the way in which some British poets were emboldened by American examples was sometimes read as a unfounded arrogance by detractors then forced into defensive or rebarbative positions of their own, leading to little hope of reconciliation.[82] By 1981 Stephen Pereira, the editor of the British poetry magazine *Angel Exhaust*, would lament: "The radicals have nothing to do with the Establishment and vice versa."[83] Eric Homberger had earlier noted that "The gap between academic verse and its opposite . . . became a permanent feature of the landscape, to the consequent impoverishment of both."[84] A series of further skirmishes were staged between the two in the 1980s and 1990s, though to smaller audiences. Though Thom Gunn's appraisal of Allen's attack on the formalist verse of the 1950s as "the academy against bohemia, metre against free verse, the considered against the spontaneous, or at its most desperate Howard Nemerov against Gregory Corso, a zombie against a buffoon,"[85] was unnecessarily reductive, it seemed less so when applied to some of the battles raging thirty years later, when the various categories of avant-garde/mainstream, experimental/tradition and even, within the avant-garde, Cambridge/London, was fast becoming an alternative to reading. In the long run, *The New American Poetry* polarized British poetry in a way that was damaging to it, and to both sides' attempts to find an audience. A question is posed by this story: was the United Kingdom ready for *The New American Poetry*? This cannot be answered in these brief concluding remarks, but needless to say that, as well as inspiration, *The New American Poetry* came with problems that were not always adequately addressed by British poets.

There are many aspects of *The New American Poetry*'s impact that should have been discussed here, but have not been because of space. *The New American Poetry*, probably because of its own lack of diversity, had little effect on minority poetries or ethnopoetics, and probably because of the pre-eminence of the phallocentric Olson, little interest for women. LeRoi Jones's appearance in *The New American Poetry* as "*The* Negro"[86] was at best mirrored in the British poetry the followed, as was Allen's underrepresentation of women, both of which would not be righted until *The New British Poetry*, which dedicated half its contents to black and feminist poetry. Likewise, the geographical diversity of reaction to *The New American Poetry*, from Northumbria to Cambridge, and from Scotland to London, is also an important consideration that, with greater space, could have been detailed. The influence of the New American poetry on publishing practices has also been only briefly discussed here, though, as Jeff Nuttall noted at the time, the likes of Grove Press and New Directions were beginning "to demonstrate that the only thing preventing poetry becoming a mass commodity . . . was orthodox publishing."[87] The small presses and homemade editions, and Pack's "incestuous pages of little magazines," were doubtless inspired by *The New American Poetry* poets who had "already created their own tradition, their own press, and their public"[88] in similar ways. The impact of *The New American Poetry as an anthology* was also to be significant: subsequent anthologists on the margins of British poetry, such Horovitz in *Children of Albion* or Crozier in *A Various Art* were given permission to include un- or under-published poets, to group together poets under common objectives but not within a single "school" or "movement," by Allen's pioneering example. The feedback, the echo of *The New American Poetry* through British poetry heard in America is also worthy of discussion: the 1965 issue of *Sum*, edited by Andrew Crozier as "Thirteen British Poets," the 1971 anthology edited by John Matthias, *Twenty-three Modern British Poets*, and the 1982 Festival of British Poetry held in New York are just three examples of the cross-fertilization that *The New American Poetry* gave rise to.

It is finally hard to say what British poetry would have been like without *The New American Poetry*, but hopefully what is detailed here of its prevalence, its vibrancy and its rigor as a model for a new kind of British poetry in the 1960s and beyond has shown what is was like with it. Liberated from pre-war notions of class, able to encompass traditions beyond "English Poetry" and emboldened by a conscious project of poetics, the British avant-garde represented perhaps an even more radical divergence from its national poetry's status quo than its American counterpart. The results were not always as successful, but they were enough to change the British poetry from a parochial backwater of formalism into a scene that increasingly and irreversibly had to take note of radical, questioning and diverse experiments in poetry, and a new conception of the poetic itself.

Notes

1. Tom Raworth, Email to author, July 1, 2010.
2. Andrew Motion and Blake Morrison eds. *The Penguin Book of Contemporary British Poetry* (Harmondsworth: Penguin, 1982), 11.
3. Donald Davie, *Under Briggflatts* (Manchester: Carcanet, 1989), 49.
4. One can also see the book's importance for individual figures in another way by surveying the reputation in Britain of poets who could have been included but, for one reason or another, were not. Robert Bly, W. S. Merwin, Cid Corman, Jerome Rothenberg, and especially Louis Zukofsky were all candidates in hindsight, but their non-appearance has perhaps been the primary reason for their relative obscurity in Britain to this day.
5. See Roger Ellis, "Mapping the UK Little Magazine Field," in *New British Poetries: the Scope of the Possible*, eds. Peter Barry and Robert Hampson (Manchester: Manchester University Press, 1993).
6. Eric Mottram, "Poetic Interface: American Poetry and the British Poetry Revival, 1960–1975," in *Forked Tongues? Comparing Twentieth-Century British and American Literature*, eds. Ann Massa and Alistair Stead (Harlow: Longman, 1994), 196.
7. Andrew Crozier and Tim Longville, eds. *A Various Art* (Glasgow: Paladin, 1990), 12.
8. Peter Riley, Email to author, July 8, 2010.
9. Donald Allen, ed. *The New American Poetry: 1945–1960* (New York: Grove Press, 1960), xi.
10. Ibid., xii.
11. Quoted in Simon Jarvis, "A Burning Monochrome: Fisher's Block," *The Thing About Roy Fisher: Critical Studies*, eds. Kerrigan and Robinson (Liverpool: Liverpool University Press, 2000), 189.
12. "Review of *The Opening of the Field*," *Poetry Review* 53, no. 1 (1962): 42.
13. Donald Davie, *Ezra Pound: Poet as Sculptor* (Oxford: Oxford University Press, 1964), 246.
14. "Editorial," *Agenda* 3, no. 1. See inside flap for quote.
15. Allen, *The New American Poetry: 1945–1960*, xi.
16. Donald Hall, Robert Pack, and Louis Simpson, eds. *The New Poets of England and America* (New York: Meridian, 1962), 182.
17. Robert Conquest, ed. *New Lines* (London: Macmillan, 1956), xvi.
18. Al Alvarez, ed. *The New Poetry* (Harmondsworth: Penguin, 1966), 23.
19. Michael Horovitz, *Children of Albion* (Harmondsworth: Penguin, 1968).
20. Quoted in Robert Sheppard, *The Poetry of Saying: British Poetry and its Discontents* (Liverpool: Liverpool University Press, 2005), 41.

21. Allen, *The New American Poetry: 1945–1960*, 243–44.

22. See Cleanth Brooks and Robert Penn Warren, *Understanding Poetry* (New York: Thomson, 1988), 493–523.

23. David Chaloner, "Inspiration is Just a Guy Called Art," in *A Various Art*, eds. Andrew and Tim Longville Crozier (Glasgow: Paladin, 1990), 55.

24. Gael Turnbull, *Collected Poems* (Exeter: Shearsman, 2006), 88.

25. Allen, *The New American Poetry: 1945–1960*, 418.

26. Donald Davie, *Thomas Hardy and British Poetry* (New York: Oxford University Press, 1972), 184.

27. David Wright, ed. *The Mid Century: English Poetry 1940–1960* (Harmondsworth: Penguin, 1965), 17.

28. Nathaniel Tarn, *Views From The Weaving Mountain: Selected Essays In Poetics and Anthropology* (Albuquerque: University of New Mexico Press, 1991), 58.

29. Horovitz, *Children of Albion*: 368.

30. Roy Fisher, "Interview," *Gargoyle* 24 (1976): 95.

31. Mottram, "Poetic Interface: American Poetry and the British Poetry Revival, 1960–1975," 165.

32. John Bayley, "New Poets of England and America (2nd ed.)," *Agenda* 3, no. 1 (1963): 9.

33. Charles Tomlinson, "Some American Poets: A Personal Record," *Contemporary Literature* 18, no. 3 (1977): 279.

34. See Marcus Cunliffe, "The Growth of American Studies in British Universities," *The Guardian* (1963).

35. Quoted in Steven Fielding, *The Labour Governments 1964–1970: Labour and Cultural Change* (Manchester: Manchester University Press, 2003), 63.

36. Davie, *Thomas Hardy and British Poetry*: 172.

37. Quoted in Eric Mottram, "The British Poetry Revival 1960–75," *New British Poetries: the Scope of the Possible*, ed. Peter Barry and Robert Hampson (Manchester: Manchester University Press, 1993), 34.

38. Kingsley Amis, "Kingsley Amis," in *Poetry of the 1950's*, ed. D. J. Enright (Tokyo: Kenkyusha, 1958), 17.

39. Ibid.

40. Stephen Spender, "England and America," *Partisan Review* 40, no. 3 (1973): 349.

41. Allen, *The New American Poetry: 1945–1960*, 432.

42. Ibid., 444.

43. John James, *Mmm . . . Ah, Yes* (London: The Ferry Press, 1967), 14.

44. Tony Harrison, "Interview with Peter Lennon," *The Times* (1984): 14.

45. Quoted in John Seed, "Hegemony Postpones: the unravelling of the culture of consensus in Britain in the 1960s," *Cultural Revolution? The Challenge of the Arts in the 1960s*, ed. Bart Moore-Gilbert and John Seed (London: Routledge, 1992), 17, 18.

46. Quoted in Lawrence J. Butler, *Britain and Empire adjusting to a post-imperial world* (London: I.B. Tauris, 2002), 167.

47. Philip Larkin, *High Windows* (London: Faber, 1974), 29.

48. Davie, *Thomas Hardy and British Poetry*, 73.

49. Davie, *Under Briggflatts*, 49.

50. Lee Harwood, *The White Room* (London: Macmillan, 1968), 89–104.

51. Ibid., 89.

52. Ibid., 92.

53. Ibid., 93.

54. Ibid., 95.

55. Ibid., 101.

56. T.S. Eliot, "War-Paint and Feathers," *Athenaeum* (1919), 1036.

57. Allen, *The New American Poetry: 1945–1960*, 2.

58. Ibid., 7.

59. Robert van Hallberg, *Charles Olson: the Scholar's Art* (Cambridge, MA: Harvard University Press, 1978), 18–19.

60. Eliot, "War-Paint and Feathers," 1036.

61. Davie, *Thomas Hardy and British Poetry*: 72.

62. Horovitz, *Children of Albion*: 327.

63. Allen, *The New American Poetry: 1945–1960*, 122.

64. Marjorie Perloff, "The Two Poetries: An Introduction," *Contemporary Literature* 18, no. 3 (1977): 264.

65. Horovitz, *Children of Albion*, 323.

66. Allen, *The New American Poetry: 1945–1960*, 388.

67. Donald Davie, *The Purity of Diction in English Verse* (London: Chatto and Windus, 1952), 99.

68. Indeed, Edward Larrissy and Lawrence Kramer have both suggested that what originally marked British poetry's development of the achievements of the American avant-garde was the expression of a radical distrust of language. See Edward Larrissy, "Poets of A Various Art: J. H. Prynne, Veronica Forrest-Thomson, Andrew Crozier," in *Contemporary British Poetry: Essays in Theory and Criticism*, ed. James Acheson and Romana Huk (New York: SUNY Press, 1996), 63–66; Lawrence Kramer, "The Wodwo Watches the Water Clock: Language is Postmodern British and American Poetry," *Contemporary Literature* 18, no. 3 (1977).

69. Conquest, *New Lines*, xv.

70. Charles Olson, *Collected Prose*, ed. Donald Allen and Benjamin Friedlander (Berkeley: University of California Press, 1997), 161.

71. Allen, *The New American Poetry: 1945–1960*, 400–07.

72. Ibid., 408.

73. Ibid., 413.

74. Ibid., 424–25.

75. Horovitz, *Children of Albion*: 325.

76. See Alan Golding, "*The New American Poetry Revisited*, Again," *Contemporary Literature* 39, no. 2 (1998): 185–87.

77. In "Letter to Elaine Feinstein," Allen, *The New American Poetry: 1945–1960*, 399.

78. Quoted in Ian Brinton, *Contemporary Poetry: Poets and Poetry Since 1990*. (Cambridge: Cambridge University Press, 2009), 28.

79. Longville, *A Various Art*, 12.

80. Ken Edwards, "Introduction to Some Younger Poets," in *The New British Poetry*, eds. Fred D'Aguair, Gillian Allnutt, Ken Edwards, and Eric Mottram (London: Paladin, 1988), 267.

81. See Peter Barry, *Poetry Wars: the Battle for Earl's Court* (London: Salt Publishing, 2006), 50–51.

82. See especially Alan Brownjohn, "A View of English Poetry in the Early Seventies'," in *British Poetry Since 1960*, eds. Michael Schmidt and Grevel Lindop (Manchester: Carcanet, 1972).

83. Quoted in Ellis, "Mapping the UK Little Magazine Field," 83.

84. Eric Homberger, *The Art of the Real: Poetry in England and America Since 1939* (London: Dent, 1977), 179.

85. Thom Gunn, "The Postmodernism You Deserve," *Threepenny Review* 57 (1994): 6.

86. LeRoi Jones, *Raise Race Rays Raze* (New York: Random House, 1971), 25.

87. Jeff Nuttall, *Bomb Culture* (London: Paladin, 1970), 162.

88. Allen, *The New American Poetry: 1945–1960*, xi.

Bibliography

Allen, Donald, ed. *The New American Poetry: 1945–1960*. New York: Grove Press, 1960.

Alvarez, Al, ed. *The New Poetry*. Harmondsworth: Penguin, 1966.

Amis, Kingsley. "Kingsley Amis." *Poetry of the 1950s*. Edited by D. J. Enright. Tokyo: Kenkyusha, 1958.

Bayley, John. Review of *New Poets of England and America*. 2nd ed. *Agenda* 3:1 (Aug-Sep 1963): 9–13.

Brooks, Cleanth, and Penn Warren, Robert. *Understanding Poetry*. New York: Thomson, 1988.

Brownjohn, Alan. "A View of English Poetry in the Early Seventies." *British Poetry Since 1960*. Edited by Michael Schmidt and Grevel Lindop. Manchester: Carcanet, 1972.

Butler, Lawrence J. *Britain and Empire: Adjusting to a Post-imperial World*. London: I. B. Tauris, 2002.

Crozier, Andrew, and Tim Longville, eds. *A Various Art*. Glasgow: Paladin, 1990.

Cunliffe, Marcus. "The Growth of American Studies in British Universities." *The Guardian*, 2 February 1963.

Davie, Donald. *Ezra Pound: Poet as Sculptor*. Oxford: Oxford University Press, 1964.
———. *Thomas Hardy and British Poetry*. New York: Oxford University Press, 1972.
———. *Under Briggflatts*. Manchester: Carcanet, 1989.
Edwards, Ken. "Introduction to Some Younger Poets." *The New British Poetry*. Edited by Gillian Allnutt, Fred D'Aguair, Ken Edwards, and Eric Mottram. London: Paladin, 1988.
Eliot, T.S. "War-Paint and Feathers." *Athenaeum*, October 17, 1919.
Ellis, Roger. "Mapping the UK Little Magazine Field." *New British Poetries: The Scope of the Possible*. Edited by Peter Barry and Robert Hampson. Manchester: Manchester University Press, 1993.
Fielding, Steven. "'But Westward, Look, the Land is Bright!' Labour's Revisionists and the Imagining of America, c. 1945–64." *Twentieth Century Anglo-American Relations*. Edited by J. Hollowell. London: Palgrave, 2001.
———. *The Labour Governments 1964–1970: Labour and Cultural Change*. Manchester: Manchester University Press, 2003.
Fisher, Roy. "Interview." *Gargoyle* 24, 1976.
Golding, Alan, "*The New American Poetry* Revisited, Again." *Contemporary Literature* 39.2 (Summer 1998): 180–211.
Gunn, Thom. "The Postmodernism You Deserve." *Threepenny Review* 57 (1994): 6–8.
Hall, Donald, Louis Simpson, and Robert Pack, eds. *New Poets of England and America*. New York: Meridian, 1962.
Harrison, Tony. "Interview with Peter Lennon." *The Times*, 21 December 1984.
Horovitz, Michael. *Children of Albion*. Harmondsworth: Penguin, 1968.
Hyde, Lewis, ed. *On the Poetry of Allen Ginsberg*. Michigan: University of Michigan Press, 1984.
Homberger, Eric. *The Art of the Real: Poetry in England and America Since 1939*. London: Dent, 1977.
James, John. *Mmm . . . Ah, Yes*. London: The Ferry Press, 1967.
Jarvis, Simon. "A Burning Monochrome: Fisher's Block." *The Thing About Roy Fisher: Critical Studies*. Edited by Kerrigan and Robinson. Liverpool: Liverpool University Press, 2000: 173–192.
Larkin, Philip. *High Windows*. London: Faber, 1974.
Motion, Andrew, and Blake Morrison, eds. *The Penguin Book of Contemporary British Poetry*. Harmondsworth: Penguin, 1982.
Mottram, Eric. "The British Poetry Revival 1960–75." *New British Poetries: The Scope of the Possible*. Edited by Peter Barry and Robert Hampson. Manchester: Manchester University Press, 1993: 15–50.
———. "Poetic Interface: American Poetry and the British Poetry Revival, 1960–1975." *Forked Tongues? Comparing Twentieth-Century British and American Literature*. Edited by Ann Massa and Alistair Stead. Harlow: Longman, 1994: 152–68.
Nuttall, Jeff. *Bomb Culture*. London: Paladin, 1970.
Olson, Charles. *Collected Prose*. Edited by Donald Allen and Benjamin Friedlander. Berkeley: University of California Press, 1997.

Perloff, Marjorie. "The Two Poetries: An Introduction." *Contemporary Literature* 18.3 (Summer 1977): 263–278.

Review of *The Opening of the Field*. *Poetry Review* 53:1 (Jan-Mar 1962): 42–43.

Sheppard, Robert. *The Poetry of Saying: British Poetry and its Discontents*. Liverpool: Liverpool University Press, 2005.

Seed, John. "Hegemony Postpones: The Unravelling of the Culture of Consensus in Britain in the 1960s." *Cultural Revolution? The Challenge of the Arts in the 1960s*. Edited by Bart Moore-Gilbert and John Seed. London: Routledge, 1992.

Spender, Stephen. "England and America." *Partisan Review* 40:3 (1973): 349–69.

Spicer, Jack. *The Collected Books*. Santa Rosa: Black Sparrow, 1980.

Tarn, Nathaniel. *Views from the Weaving Mountain: Selected Essays in Poetics and Anthropology*. Albuquerque: University of New Mexico Press, 1991.

Tomlinson, Charles. "Some American Poets: A Personal Record," *Contemporary Literature* 18.3 (Summer 1977), 279–304.

Turnbull, Gael. *Collected Poems*. Exeter: Shearsman, 2006.

van Hallberg, Robert. *Charles Olson: The Scholar's Art*. Cambridge, MA: Harvard University Press, 1978.

Wright, David, ed. *The Mid Century: English Poetry 1940–1960*. Harmondsworth: Penguin, 1965.

CHAPTER SIX

~

The New American Poetry and the Development of the Long Poem

Joe Moffett

The American Tradition of the Long Poem

When Donald Allen published his 1960 anthology *The New American Poetry*, there was little to indicate that he was presenting what would become one of the most influential literary anthologies of the postwar period. Figures who are now literary giants—Olson, Ginsberg, Ashbery—had yet to receive the critical attention they would later garner. Instead, the book presented a number of poets whose fame and influence would come later and thus the presentation to the public is as much an introduction to the poets as it is a celebration of their achievements.[1]

It is no coincidence that the writers collected in this anthology who eventually became major literary figures all published significant long poems.[2] As the twentieth-century equivalent of the epic poem, the long poem becomes the measure of a poet's ambition and attempt to ascend the literary ladder to canonicity. Critics typically trace the modern American long poem back to Whitman's "Song of Myself."[3] In 1961 Roy Harvey Pearce argued Whitman's poem was "an American equivalent of an epic."[4] If such were the case, gone was the didactic function of the historical epic. So too was the heroic figure absent, replaced instead by a modern "I" who attempts to encapsulate a society in his person rather than represent a figure driven by pursuit of his own glory, such as Achilles.[5] The conventional narrative structure was also altered. If one looks at the first, 1855 edition of "Song of Myself," the poem lacks the divisions and poeticisms of the later 1892 "deathbed" edition. Instead, the poem moves freely from stanza to stanza, anticipating some of the

more untamable poems of modernism. Even Ezra Pound, who was as forceful
a literary figure in modernism as anyone, felt he had to acknowledge Whitman's precedence, however begrudgingly, in "A Pact."

In one of the best studies of the genre, Margaret Dickie associates the
long poem with modernism.[6] In her view, the long poem captures the large
ambition of leading modernist poets such as Pound and William Carlos Williams. The outstanding literary achievements of modernism—especially T.S.
Eliot's *The Waste Land*, which many postmodernist writers viewed as one of
the, if not *the*, definitive works of modernism—established the long poem
as an essential endeavor for the serious poet. Eliot, writing about "minor"
poets, memorably remarks, "The difference between major and minor poets
has nothing to do with whether they wrote long poems, or only short poems—though the very greatest poets, who are few in number, have all had
something to say which could only be said in a long poem."[7] Of course, the
long poem becomes such an enigma for some poets that it often proves interminable; such is the case, of course, with Pound's *Cantos* and, later, Olson's
Maximus Poems. John Berryman jokes in *The Dream Songs*,

> The only happy people in the world
> are those who do not have to write long poems:
> muck, administration, toil [. . .]
>
> . . .
>
> A Kennedy-sponsored bill for the protection
> of poets from long poems will benefit the culture.[8]

Berryman captures the sense that the long poem had become an inevitable
endeavor, and he indicates the drain the project places on the poet. Ironically, the fun he pokes at the long poem here takes place within the context
of his own long poem and accordingly the struggle of writing the long poetic
work is captured.

Using the basic divisions that Allen's anthology created, I want to look
at various long poems written by leading figures among the New American
poets in the present essay. We will see that while the long poem becomes
an essential undertaking for these writers, how each poet interprets the
challenge of writing the long work and indeed what constitutes a long
poem varies. As Susan Stanford Friedman points out, the very length of a
piece long enough to be considered a "long poem" is subject to argument
and the poems under study here vary from the five hundred page *Maximus*
to the fifteen page "Howl."[9] I stand with Margaret Dickie in believing that
it is the ambition of the poet that the long poem is defined by, rather than
by a simple page count.

I want to focus on the three groups represented in Allen's book which I feel made the largest contributions to the development of the long poem, and so I will begin with the Black Mountain poets, continue on through the New York poets, and finish by looking at the Beats. Throughout, my primary interest is in demonstrating continuities and discontinuities within the groups and across the groups. Of course, using these labels perpetuates something of fiction since the writers within any given group are not monolithic in their beliefs or approaches to poetry, and there remains a good deal of cross-pollination between categories. Nevertheless for the sake of clarity and organization, I will proceed with the divisions. We will see that each of the poets works within the long poem tradition to expand, revise, or reinterpret what came before him. This exercise offers us one unit of measure of the New American poet's considerable contribution to the development of American verse in the twentieth century.

The Black Mountain Poets

Because of the year of his birth—1910—Olson represents a figure who bridges the modernists and postmodernists. Most of the postmodernist poets were born in the 1920s and came of age in the immediate postwar years, playing a pivotal role in shaping the verse that would be published in the Atomic Age. Olson is the first poet presented in *The New American Poetry* anthology and in this way heralds the new poetry to follow. This is not to mention that the essay on poetics included in the book by Olson, his "Projective Verse," is probably the most influential of the manifestos included in the collection and was famous enough to be parodied by New York poet Frank O'Hara in his "Personism" essay. Among his insights, Olson advocates the importance of the typewriter to score the poem with a spatial displacement of lines that he would utilize to a great degree in his work. He speaks of "field composition," where the poet is free to capitalize on the page's space. He echoes fellow Black Mountain poet Robert Creeley's dictum that "form is never more than an extension of content." That is, he establishes an approach to poetry where the poet does not seek to fit his content into a predetermined form but rather allows form and content to work symbiotically in expressing his vision.

Among the poets I look at here, only Olson and Ginsberg published at least parts of their long poems in Allen's anthology. When the book was edited, most other poets had yet to write the work that might be seen to help define their careers. Olson labored on his *Maximus Poems* from 1950 to his death in 1970. Initially he saw the poems as a short series, but the project continued to grow until it constituted a long work that followed on the heels of great modernist poems such as Williams's *Paterson* and Pound's *Cantos*. In fact, *Maximus* resembles *Paterson* in that Olson focuses on one locale as Williams had done with his town in New Jersey. For Olson, the location instead is the fishing village of Gloucester, Massachusetts, a place he visited on vacations as a boy, and where he eventually settled once the experimental school for which he served as rector, Black Mountain College near Ashville, North Carolina, closed its doors in 1957. In Olson's mind, Gloucester becomes an essential "polis," which must resist the pull of commercialism and postwar global economics that mark the rest of the nation. Olson asserts in its place "an actual earth of value" and part of what happens in the poem, as I have demonstrated elsewhere, is that Olson's persona of Maximus gives way as the poet's hope for the town turns to hopelessness. He laments, "once more drawn into the / plague of my own unsatisfying possible identity as / denominable Charles Olson."[10] The poem thus charts the dissolution of the poetic conceit and becomes more focused on cosmic themes in its second and third installments as it moves away from a focus on Gloucester's fate.

Among the poems by Olson that appear in Allen's *The New American Poetry* are "I Maximus of Gloucester to You," "The Songs of Maximus," and "Maximus to Himself." The latter poem is the one most often anthologized and stands as one of Olson's best individual lyrics. The poem encapsulates the author's theme of personal estrangement in an increasingly complex civilization marked by bewildering technology and the inundation of the effects of capitalism. In *Maximus* this intrusion of capitalism into the local is figured as the newly constructed Route 128, which Olson argues now bridges Gloucester with the rest of the nation. In "Maximus to Himself," the speaker calls himself a "wind and water man"—a figure intimately connected with the elements. Yet he also notes that he had to "learn the simplest things last, which made for difficulties." He ends the poem by speaking of an "undone business," which the reader can interpret as his ongoing battles with what he sees as the deterioration of the nation and he offers an image of "the sea / stretching out / from my feet."[11] Olson consequently establishes a theme of spatial concerns, which had long been one of his preoccupations.

In his critical work on Herman Melville, *Call Me Ishmael*, Olson had forcefully argued, "I take SPACE to be the central fact to man born in America."[12] He goes on to point out how the history of the West has followed a westerly line and the United States is the product of salient impulses within the Western spirit. Olson's concern with space can be seen to carry over into his Black Mountain College student Edward Dorn's own long poem *Gunslinger*. In a document later published as "A Bibliography on America for Ed Dorn," Olson admonishes his pupil to "dig one thing or place or man until you yourself know more abt that than is possible to any other man," complete a "saturation job."[13] Dorn can be seen to follow this advice with his exploration of conceptions of the American West in his long poem, a topic he understood well having lived in Idaho in the time leading up to his writing of *Gunslinger*.

Dorn's experience of space in his long poem is quite distinct from Olson's, however. Whereas space seems to be a positive force in *Maximus*, both representing the promise of Western expansion in European and American history, as well as the increasing spatial displacement of poems on the page as *Maximus* goes on,[14] in *Gunslinger* there is almost an agoraphobia that marks its characters. His poem is constellated around a quest motif of which I will discuss later, but for now I would like to look at a short passage near the end of the poem. Dorn's group of travelers is faced with what they take to be the terrifying expanse of the West:

> We survey the Colorado plateau,
> There are no degrees of reality
> in this handsome and singular mass,
> or in the extravagant geometry
> of its cliffs and pinnacles.[15]

Although the group might admire the "handsome . . . mass" that lies in front of them, there is also a lack of "reality," a disconnection with the landscape itself. The reality of the West as a geographical area is contrasted to its mythical status projected in books, TV, and movies as a landscape to be tamed and controlled. This incongruity establishes a sense of fear in the characters as they are faced with the reality of their own superficial images. If the reality of the West does not correspond to the image upon which it is built, how can such characters as the title figure, Slinger, whose very being is tied to images of the West, understand himself?

These ontological questions reverberate throughout the poem. The group is composed of a motley tribe, including Slinger, who spouts clichés recycled from the genre of his derivation: the TV and movie Western. Also, the group includes a talking horse humorously named Claude Levi Strauss, as well as a character who dies midway through the narrative and is preserved in a vat of LSD—a clear jab at the mind-altering preoccupations of the poem's time period. This character's name causes narrative confusion as he is simply called "I." With this approach, Dorn begins the poem in seemingly first person manner, only for the reader to realize the poet implies something like the death of subjectivity with the passing of the character. Michael Davison argues that "I" can be seen as "the last vestige of the self-conscious, rationalizing ego."[16] The death of I can also be read as an inversion of the Whitmanian "I" in the American long poem who sings of himself at the beginning of "Song of Myself." In his use of the signifier I, Dorn reveals a high spirited and playful approach to the long poem, which as we shall see with some other poets of his fully postmodernist generation (Dorn was born in 1929), becomes a default mode of the postmodernist long poem. By contrast, Olson's sometimes angry condemnations of current society strike a very different note and do not bear the same self-reflexive, ironic mode represented by Dorn and others.[17]

Playfulness in the long poem might be seen to stem from the mock epic tradition. Whether one speaks of Ariosto's *Orlando Furioso* or Byron's *Don Juan*, the mock epic tradition carries within it the seeds of postmodernist playfulness. Like those earlier works that subvert literary conventions by poking fun at the epic, a genre that Bakhtin memorably argues "has not only long since completed its development, but one that is already antiquated,"[18] postmodernist long poems such as Dorn's seek to expand the genre beyond the restrictions of seriousness of intention that mark modernist long works. As we shall see, Kenneth Koch's long poem also works along such lines, and other poems such Ginsberg's, while not being as humorously motivated, question social mores and what is proper decorum in contemporary poetry.

Marjorie Perloff calls *Gunslinger* a "dazzling anti-epic of the Wild West"[19] and part of the narrative structure of the poem focuses on its characters' search for the elusive, eccentric billionaire Howard Hughes. This motif can be seen to engage the economic issue Olson presents from a different angle: instead of saying the financial underpinnings of America are negative, one can point out that desire for economic success is an essentially American pursuit, as Hughes represents. In fact Olson's beloved New England has been shown to be a commercial venture from the start.[20] We can see then how Dorn builds on and reworks themes we find first in Olson and in this process witness how one generation responds to the one that came before it. The long poem becomes a particularly vital genre to observe these kinds of relationships.[21]

Whereas Olson works in a disjunctive mode inspired by Pound, Dorn produces a story, albeit a somewhat jumpy one. This return of narrative in postmodernist verse was first recognized by Marjorie Perloff in *Dance of the Intellect*[22] and later analyzed at great length by Brian McHale, who in his book on the long poem offers two structural models that he argues many postmodernist writers utilize: an architectural mode and a narrative one.[23]

Of course, Dorn's poem falls into the latter category. One finds narrativity utilized elsewhere in postmodernist long poems, including Koch's *Seasons on Earth*, as we shall see in a moment, as well as in later works such as Rita Dove's *Thomas and Beulah* and James Merrill's *The Changing Light at Sandover*.

Another important Black Mountain poet (and one often associated with the San Francisco Renaissance as well), Robert Duncan, also attempts to capture the spirit of the 1960s in his long poem, *Passages*. Among its concerns, the poem communicates the history of the Vietnam conflict. Pound memorably described the epic as "a poem containing history" and that is precisely what Duncan's long poem becomes, among other things. In "Passages 25," for example, subtitled, "Up Rising," we find the speaker railing against the policies of then-President Johnson in Vietnam. The speaker observes,

> this specter that in the beginning Adams and Jefferson feard and knew
> would corrupt the very body of the nation
>> and all our sense of our common humanity
> this black bile of old evils arisen anew,
> takes over the vanity of Johnson;
> and the very glint of Satan's eyes . . .
>> . . .
> now shines from the eyes of the President
>> in the swollen head of the nation[24]

And so Duncan's long poem becomes a mouthpiece for political dissent and might be viewed in company of another work from the era, Galway Kinnell's *Book of Nightmares*, a kind of demonic Whitmanian long poem, which offers a dark, apocalyptic vision to rival Duncan's. *Passages* becomes a time capsule of the distinctive poetry of protest that the era produced, which as James Mersman points out is different from that of the World War II period by the transparency with which poets would register their discontent. Rather than adopting the elaborate personae produced by poets during previous wars, Vietnam poets would often speak in their "own" voice.[25] We will see momentarily how Ginsberg also brings a particularly political approach to the long poem.

Duncan's poem was published as separate pieces in a series of individual volumes. Nathaniel Mackey would adopt this approach as well with his *Song of Andoumboulou*. This practice adds another dimension to the format of the long poem. It establishes the question of whether a sequence is the same thing as a long poem. Finally settling this question is beyond the scope of the present essay, but it is worth mentioning that one solution presented to this problem was M. L. Rosenthal and Sally Gall's decision to speak of the "modern poetic sequence" rather than the long poem.[26] This method allows the critics to cast a wider net and include poets such as Emily Dickinson and W. B. Yeats who did not write long poems but nevertheless engaged in producing sequences alongside writers associated with the long poem tradition, such as Olson. In Dickinson's case, such an argument is based on reconstructing the fascicles that held her poems originally. One might argue, based on poems such as Duncan's, that the sequence carries many attributes of the long poem, including its tentative and sometimes improvisatory structure and its disregard for past generic conventions. The success of the long poem (or sequence) in twentieth-century poetry was indeed dependent on the adaptability of the form to the various desires of the poets.

The New York Poets

While Dorn's and Duncan's poems both capture the spirit of the 1960s in different ways, *Gunslinger* better reflects New York poet Kenneth Koch's *Seasons on Earth* than Duncan's sometimes rather bald political commentary in *Passages*. Both *Gunslinger* and *Seasons* become invested in images proliferated by popular culture and both adopt the freeform sense of play that informs postmodernist literature generally.[27] I have argued elsewhere that the proliferation of images associated with mid-century capitalist America marks Koch's poem.[28] In terms of its structure, *Seasons* bears a sense of "weak narrativity," as McHale terms it. McHale argues that this weak narrativity entails "telling stories 'poorly,' distractedly, with much irrelevance and indeterminacy, in such a way as to *evoke* [emphasis added] narrative coherence while at the same time withholding commitment to it and undermining confidence in it."[29] In this way postmodernist poets revisit the narrative mode of the traditional epic with an eye toward undermining narrative conventions through the use of parodic strategies.

Seasons on Earth begins by telling the story of Ko, a Japanese baseball player, but then modulates into a tale of high adventure including a character named Joseph Dah, who works as a parody of the action painters of Koch's period in New York. The poem eventually evolves into a narrative that includes Disney characters who compete in a car race on the roads of Greece. These Disney characters act in ways one does not associate with children's cartoons. Minnie Mouse warns Clara Cow at one point:

> "Clara, beware!" cried Minnie. "I'll not let you
> So carry on with Mick while I'm alive!
> even if you make him now, he'll soon forget you

> When we go speeding off upon our drive
> Over the million roads of Greece. Upset you?
> Too bad! He's mine! You, just when we arrive,
> Start making cow eyes at him. Your tough luck!
> Alone with him tonight I'll squeal and fuck!"[30]

Clearly, Koch's poem disrupts our sense of what cartoon characters are capable of. Koch increases the absurdity of his use of the Disney characters by having Mickey and the gang live on Mount Olympus. In this way, they are elevated to the position of our equivalent of Greek gods. Of course, this blending of high and low culture is a hallmark of postmodernism, and Koch's poem, along with Dorn's, is probably the best example of the phenomenon in the long poem.[31]

In fact, the line between the high and low becomes so blurred that when Mickey meets his demise, he is resurrected—like a sort of Christ figure—by "high" artists. The artists create an image, the narrator tells us,

> by the joint efforts
> Of fifty painters in the USA,
> England, and Greece . . . to protest the severance
> Of Mickey from real life. The painters, they
> Felt that a work so huge construed in reference
> To this event might touch him where he lay.
> By some strange chance it does. In comics sleep
> On Sunday papers, he begins to squeak.[32]

The spirit of Koch's poem holds much in common with the mock epic tradition. Koch alludes to *Don Juan* in his introduction to the poem and his epigraph is drawn from Ariosto.[33] Koch clearly aligns himself with major figures of a subversive tradition and presents himself as a further link in a chain that leads back centuries. As is evident in the examples above, he even employs the ottava rima favored by Byron, but also employed by Yeats to more serious ends. Koch was an advocate of the pedagogic value of imitation in learning to write poems, and he himself is the author of a number of humorous imitations. In works such as his playful *Art of Love*, a contemporary revision of Ovid's *Amores*, or his ars poetica *The Art of Poetry* that recalls Horace, he pokes fun at classics rather than reinterpreting them, as Olson attempts.

James Schuyler was not as playful a poet as Koch, but nevertheless his often overlooked long work "The Morning of the Poem" is a *tour de force* in which the poet presents a rambling long poem that further expands the possibilities of the form. The speaker begins, not sure of the date: "July 8 or

July 9, the eighth surely, certainly 1976 that I know."[34] The jagged lineation of the poem recalls the early version of "Song of Myself." The action of the poem is simple: the speaker wakes up, as he says, to "take a piss" and the poem recounts the associations and thoughts that run through his mind in that short time. The poem projects a unity of time, as if it were all uttered at once. But of course this is only an illusion, just as much later Campbell McGrath's long poem, "The Bob Hope Poem," would chronicle the thoughts of an individual inspired by a tabloid story on the famous entertainer. This speaker also considers his personal life and larger themes such as the history of Chicago and the economic basis of Western society, all during the course of a single snowy Chicago afternoon. Despite the illusion of a unity of time in his poem, McGrath spent nine years working on the piece.

The meditative long poem, such as Schuyler's is, can also be witnessed in Welsh poet David Jones's late modernist *The Anathiemata*. This poem considers the intertwining of history and culture, while the basic setting for the piece is the thoughts of the speaker as he attends a Catholic Mass. Rather than focusing on the historic or religious themes that occupy Jones's poem, Schuyler's poem is more personal in nature, meditating for instance on the speaker's relationship to an individual revealed to be a painter. Early in the poem the speaker concedes,

> How easily I could be in love with you,
>   who do not like to be touched,
> And yet I do not want to be in love with you,
>   nor you with me[35]

In this way the poem becomes a consideration of love and art. Art of course is a major theme in the New York poets' work generally, making an appearance in each of the long poems by the poets I focus on here. While one might make the argument that all art is essentially about the problematic nature of its own creation, the long poems by the New York poets I analyze all foreground their metapoetic nature and thereby highlight their own artificialities as art objects.

In Schuyler's poem, the speaker's thoughts shift from childhood memories, to homosexual encounters, to the place of art in society and our lives, and specifically the role of writing. To the unnamed addressee of the poem, the speaker admits,

> this is not.
> your poem, your poem I may
> Never write, too much, though it is there and
>   needs only to be written down

> And one day will and if it isn't it doesn't matter:
>   the truth, the absolute
> Of feeling, of knowing what you know, that is
>   the poem[36]

The speaker makes an implicit argument about the poetic nature of such large concepts as truth and the absolute, which he notes can be found not only in literature, but also in the process of simply living. Life can take the place of the poem, and the poem in this case is very much a meandering recollection of the life. Late in the piece, the speaker tells his addressee, "You've slipped out of my poem."[37] At this point the speaker has admitted to himself that the poem is more about him and his status as an artist than it is about the painter being addressed.

Art has always been an important subject for Schuyler's fellow New York poet John Ashbery, who even worked as an art critic for a time. The poet with the largest reputation today of any of the New American poets, Ashbery has published numerous long poems, including *Flow Chart*, several longer works in *Three Poems*, and more recently *Girls on the Run*. Particularly vital, however, are his early long poems: the watershed moment of *Tennis Court Oath* and its "Europe" and his next book's "The Skaters," both of which use popular culture sources, especially turn of the century children's books.[38] Perhaps most important, however, is Ashbery's "Self-Portrait in a Convex Mirror," a uniquely ekphrastic long poem in conversation with Parmigianino's sixteenth-century masterpiece of the same name. Whereas Schuyler's poem is initially addressed to an anonymous painter, Ashbery's poem constitutes an address to the famous Mannerist artist, describing the painting and the artist's work—and the artist himself in fact—as especially difficult. The poem is, then, an ars poetica at the same time it is ekphrastic, as most such poems are. Ashbery speaks of the problem of

> A whispered phrase passed around the room
> Ends up as something completely different.
> It is the principle that makes works of art so unlike
> What the artist intended. Often he finds
> He has omitted the thing he started out to say
> In the first place.[39]

While clearly more abstract and scholarly in tone than Schuyler's piece, Ashbery's poem nevertheless similarly communicates the difficulty of writing. Ultimately the speaker must ask Parmigiano, "I beseech you, withdraw that hand, / offer it no longer as a shield or greeting."[40] The speaker has

talked himself into believing in the inevitable failure of art not only to express something in general, but specifically he laments the loss of the initial
spark to create that has somehow become lost in the shuffle.

Ashbery's poem is probably the most decorated of postwar long poems. In
the year of its publication, 1976, the book it appeared in (bearing the same
title) was awarded the three main literary prizes in the United States: the
Pulitzer, the National Book Award, and the National Book Critics Circle
Award. Despite this critical attention, "Self-Portrait" criticizes "those ass-
holes / Who would confuse everything with their mirrors games,"[41] which
illustrates the playful undertone of the work. The play on words with the
term "mirror" stands out. Parmigianino was literally engaging in a mirror
game as he created his optically warped self-portrait and this new perspective
allowed him to expand the options of a venerable artistic genre. Of course,
the speaker has in mind not Parmigianino but those who interpret the work
and miss the point of it. Clearly, "asshole" comes from a different level of
speech than "beseech" in the quote above, and we see Ashbery, like Koch before him, pushing boundaries and experimenting with tone. The long poem
undergoes further development in the hands of Koch and Ashbery, adopting
new subjects and different levels of discourse. As Koch put it in his preface
to *Seasons*, he was seeking to overcome the restrictions placed on poetry by
modernism and the New Critics:

> *The Waste Land* gave the time's most accurate data,
> It seemed, and Eliot was the Great Dictator
> Of literature. One hardly dared to wink
> Or fool around in any way in poems,
> And Critics poured out awful jereboams
> To *irony, ambiguity,* and *tension*—
> And other things I do not wish to mention.[42]

Koch identifies, and pokes fun at, those terms held in high esteem by poets
and critics of the 1940s and 1950s—irony, ambiguity, etc.—and thereby
explains why he felt a need to take his work in another direction. Ashbery is
not as direct in his subversion of literary conventions, but he is careful to begin his poem with sweeping statements that the poem eventually undoes in
its playfulness. The high rhetoric found early on in "Self-Portrait," in which
the speaker makes grand statements such as "The soul establishes itself,"[43]
"the soul has to stay where it is, / Even though restless,"[44] and "the soul is
not a soul, / Has no secret,"[45] must be read with the metaphysical conceit
"soul" in quotation marks. It is as if the speaker of the poem finds he must
initially establish his theme with broad rhetorical gestures, but by the end he
realizes he was only interested in art to start with and with his own personal

grappling with those who came before him. Correspondingly, the "soul" gives way to a consideration of art and aesthetics take the place of metaphysics.

The Beats

Ginsberg's "Howl" proves much more visceral than Ashbery's "Self-Portrait," and Ginsberg draws more directly on the work of Whitman, who writes freely about the self and sexuality. The Whitmanesque cadences of otherwise disparate poems such as Duncan's *Passages* and Schuyler's *The Morning of the Poem* are also evident in Ginsburg's "Howl." While these three poems might be seen to entertain very different ways of looking at culture, they are united in the sense that each goes about defining in hitherto unseen ways the role of the individual in society and his or her use of poetry as a tool for public utterance.

Whereas "Song of Myself" might commence with the speaker declaring, "I sing myself and celebrate myself" in a self-conscious rhetorical move aimed at asserting the primacy of the self in post-epic discourse, Ginsberg begins "Howl" with a bare, "I saw the best minds of my generation destroyed by madness."[46] There is little sense that the speaker must contend with a new approach, as Whitman reveals. Instead, Ginsberg builds on Whitman in furthering an essential quality of the American long poem, which entails the replacement of the epic hero with the everyday individual. However, it quickly becomes apparent that Ginsberg celebrates the *counterculture* individual. This strategy at once pays homage to Whitman's elevation of the everyday individual, but also goes beyond by looking specifically at marginalized figures, a version of what contemporary postcolonial theory would call the "subaltern," whose voice has been silenced historically. These figures include not only such groups as African Americans, but also the mentally ill, with whom the speaker identifies by evoking his time in a psychiatric hospital, called Rockland in the poem, with an individual known as Carl Solomon.

Through such moves, "Howl," like the other examples we have seen, offers yet another approach to the long poem. In particular, Ginsberg's poem is extraordinarily frank about sexuality. Whereas one of modernism's paradigmatic works, *The Waste Land*, laments the breakdown of modern sexuality as a perfunctory exercise in its "Fire Sermon" section, Ginsberg's poem celebrates open sexuality, of many types deemed deviant at the time. He speaks of those

> who let themselves be fucked in the ass by saintly motorcyclists, and
>   screamed with joy
> . . . .
> who copulated ecstatic and insatiate with a bottle of beer a sweetheart a

> package of cigarettes a candle and fell off the bed, and continued along
> the floor and down the hall and ended fainting on the wall with a
> vision of ultimate cunt and come eluding the last gyzym of consciousness [47]

Passages such as these allow Ginsberg to become one of the leading poets to speak openly about sexual experiences, particularly same sex relationships. He moves away from the conceit of writing to an unspecified "you" to hide the subject of his poems as a homosexual lover, as used by W. H. Auden and later by Ashbery. Instead, Ginsberg writes freely about homosexual encounters, even more so than Schuyler. He is deeply invested in presenting an image of a large subculture who is oppressed by the majority. Schuyler, on the other hand, presents a more personal vision of a rather insular world of poets and painters.

In fact, Ginsberg's speaker is careful not to elevate his own status as poet above the others. He speaks of those

> who scribbled all night rocking and rolling over lofty incantations
> which in the yellow morning were stanzas of gibberish[48]

The role of the poet is not more important than that of his subjects, but rather he suffers the same psychological pressures that render his work "gibberish" in the end. "Howl" itself, of course, Ginsberg realizes, will be considered gibberish by some in the literary establishment of the time, not least of all because of its form. In the examples above, one can mark the extraordinarily long line utilized by Ginsberg, inherited from Whitman. Whitman's use of lists, drawn from the repetitions of the Bible, finds a home in Ginsberg's work as well. Yet Ginsberg's penchant for oddly modified nouns, such as "saintly motorcyclists" and "ultimate cunt" above, reveal his own spin on the Whitmanian approach. Such descriptions become part of Ginsberg's unique lexicon and a key aspect of his aesthetics.

Another significant long poem by Ginsberg from this period, "Kaddish," proves a poetic case study of the individual under intense psychological pressure. The subject this time is the speaker's mother's mental illness. She tells him at one point, "Don't be afraid of me because I'm just coming back from the mental hospital—I'm your mother."[49] That admission does little to comfort the bewildered child and the form of the poem, with its numerous dashes and prosaic construction, reflects the tentative nature of his recollections, as if the speaker is unable to versify the memories that flood back as he recalls his mother's life.

Again the poem turns to sexual details at key moments. Ginsberg demonstrates the extent to which Freudian views of human behavior had influenced modern poets by this time:

One time I thought she was trying to make me come lay her—[. . .] dress
up round her hips, big slash of hair, scars of operations [. . .] I was cold—later
revolted a little, but not much—seemed perhaps a good idea to try—know the
Monster of the Beginning Womb [. . .].[50]

The speaker here is surprisingly little conflicted in his Oedipal desire for his
mother, although the reality of her physical body, with its scars revealing
her troubled past, marks her as a woman not conventionally desirable. Thus
Ginsberg takes the long poem in a different direction than his fellow New
American poets and instead allows the form to work as a tool for the expression of personal inner turmoil and struggle. One finds this quality also in
work from the period by figures such as Robert Lowell in his *Life Studies*, and
especially Berryman's *Dream Songs*. Yet Ginsberg's openness with homosexuality and in particular his demonstration in "Kaddish" of the psychodrama of
childhood reflect a singular contribution to the form.

Among other important long poems from poets associated with the Beats
is Gary Snyder's *Mountains and Rivers Without End*. Snyder worked on his
poem for forty years and in that way it is another example of the lifelong
long poem, although this one does not prove to be interminable like Olson's
Maximus or Pound's *Cantos*. Snyder's poem is unique among the texts discussed here in that it reflects its author's longstanding engagement with Buddhism. In fact, Snyder's poem might be the largest scale discussion of Eastern
principles to be found in the American long poem. The Beats are often
credited with introducing Buddhism to wider audiences at the midcentury
point, and important works such as Ginsberg's "Sunflower Sutra" (included
in Allen's anthology) and Kerouac's *The Dharma Bums* readily bear Buddhist
influences. But for Snyder, Buddhism became more a way of life than a passing phase as it was for the other writers. In terms of more recent long poems,
one might point to Armand Schwerner's *Tablets* and its author's interest in
Zen Buddhism, as well as Charles Wright's *The Appalachian Book of the Dead*
project, as other examples of long poetic works that deal extensively with
Eastern spirituality.

Certainly, one quality of Ginsberg's poetics that we see reflected also in
Snyder's is a forthrightness with the body and sexuality. At one point, the
speaker of *Mountains and Rivers* declares, "The root of me / hardens and lifts
to you, / thick flowing river, // my skin quivers I quit // making this poem."[51]
We might note a key difference with Ginsberg, however, is that sexuality in
Snyder's poetry tends to be connected with a spirituality rooted in the natural world, as here where the speaker in a sense becomes a part of the river.
The use of present tense is interesting as it implies the speaker is making the
poem while he experiences his erection standing in the river. Such a move

recalls Schuyler's argument about life constituting its own kind of poem, and here again we see a metapoetic moment folded into a statement about the extension of literature into life. This argument, of course, indicates that rather than be cut off from life, literature is very much a part of our everyday existence, and we witness the poet responding to our wider culture that seems to have little use for literary endeavors.

One aspect of the poem that distinguishes it from the others we have looked at is its focus on working class issues. Snyder spent time in the Pacific Northwest as a logger and so the poet tends to describe blue collar jobs when he offers images of the United States: "trucks on the freeways, / Kenworth, Peterbilt, Mack, / rumble diesel depths / like boulders bumping in an outwash glacial river."[52] Of course, as I have said, Whitman was engaged in celebrating the everyday individual, but Snyder puts his own spin on an old theme by tying such professions to older movements of the earth, as he does with his evocation of glaciers here. Such an awareness of deep time is Snyder's gift among the poets reviewed here, rivaled only by Olson.

In sections such as "Jackrabbit," Snyder speaks of the limits of human knowledge, particularly as we are cut off from instinct. In sharply chiseled lines that recall the spare lineation of Williams, the speaker addresses the animal:

> Great ears shining,
> you know me
> a little. A lot more than I
> know you.[53]

Aside from its focus on the epistemological limits we have imposed on ourselves, the poem underscores the fact that humanity is still part of nature and that with greater effort, we may be able to come into communion with nature again. The current distance between humanity and the animal world is reinforced by a later section, "Under the Hills Near the Morava River," which describes a modern excavation of a woman's body where "She lay there midst // Mammoth, reindeer, and wolf bones."[54] Similar to Seamus Heaney's "bog" poems that constitute their own kind of long poem, Snyder's poem illustrates the past and present that coincide in the moment of excavation. The woman is found amongst the bones of various animals, and in this way she is more connected with the earth than the contemporary individual.

Two aspects of Snyder's poem that pick up themes we have witnessed elsewhere are a playfulness with language and the ekphrastic nature of his title. Snyder is particularly fond of found language, such as in the section

"Three Worlds, Three Realms, Six Roads" with its subtitles, "Things to Do Around Seattle," "Things to Do Around Portland," Things to Do Around a Lookout," "Things to Do Around a Ship at Sea," and so on. These subsections contain simple inventories of activities and in this way Snyder evokes the lists one might find in a popular magazine or how-to book. Later in *Mountains and Rivers*, the section "Instructions" riffs off a set of instructions for changing the oil in a vehicle. The poem begins, "Fuel filler cap—haven't I seen this before? The / sunlight under the eaves, mottled / shadow, on the knurled rim of / dull silver metal."[55] Again, we witness Snyder's fusion of the natural and the human-made, woven together in an interplay of introspection and vivid imagery.

The human-made is not entirely faulty, of course, and in art, as we saw with others poets, Snyder finds redemption. The title of the poem is drawn from Asian landscape painting. Snyder notes, "The East Asian landscape paintings invite commentary. In a way the painting is not fully realized until several centuries of poems have been added."[56] Accordingly, Snyder's poem provides commentary on centuries old practices and combines Eastern and Western influences. In fact, Snyder calls his long poem a "sutra," a spiritual discourse in the Buddhist tradition.[57] Indeed, the spirituality of the poem is confirmed in the layers of art, self, and world, especially the natural world, that come to be tied together in a synthetic vision of human wholeness. Art, whether it be painting or writing, serves as the reservoir for these deeper connections of existence.

Conclusion

One could certainly point to tangible examples of the direct influence of the New American poets and their work on the long poem on others who followed them. The so-called Language poetry, for example, is difficult to imagine without taking into account the work of the New American poets. Susan Howe could not have produced her "Thorow" section of *Singularities*, which uses eccentric placement of poetry on the page and muses on such themes as the connections of language and history, were it not for Olson's groundbreaking efforts in *Maximus*. The work of another Language poet, Charles Bernstein, such as his *The Lives of the Toll Takers*, is inconceivable without the playfulness of writers like Ashbery and Koch blazing a trail before him.

And yet one does not have to look for examples of direct influence to appreciate the profound contribution the New American poets have made to the ever-evolving tradition of the long poem. From the satirical fun of Dorn's

Gunslinger to the personal reveries of Schuyler, from the mediation on art by Ashbery to the Eastern influences of Snyder, the New American poets offer an extraordinarily broad palette of possibilities for later poets to draw from. From this perspective, it is easy to see why Donald Allen's anthology has assumed a central place in the recent history of American letters. He offered what might have been the most eclectic mix possible of poets who would help rewrite what is possible in American poetry and in the long poem in particular. For that reason alone it is easy to see why, fifty years later, we can still be engaged, excited, and awed when we open the covers of Allen's collection and begin to explore or revisit the work of the writers introduced there.

Notes

1. Tuma offers a useful contextualization of *The New American Poetry* and its place in American and British poetics of the postwar period, especially in regard to other anthologies. Keith Tuma, *Fishing by Obstinate Isles: Modern and Postmodern British Poetry and American Readers* (Evanston, IL: Northwestern University Press, 1998), 48–50; 80–93.

2. For this chapter, I have sought to employ a broad scope rather than focus on an individual writer or group of writers. While this approach does not allow me to look at any of the writers or their works in great depth, it does offer me the chance to demonstrate the contribution of the New American poets to the development of the long poem. In that way, I see the function of this essay more as a survey of achievements and recognition rather than an in-depth critical analysis of select pieces. My scholarly work has been almost exclusively in the long poem, and I know of no other survey of the unique contributions of the New American poets to the genre.

3. The importance of Whitman to the twentieth-century long poem, as well as Ashbery's poem that I discuss here, is chronicled in Thomas Gardner, *Discovering Ourselves in Whitman: The Contemporary American Long Poem* (Urbana: University of Illinois Press, 1989); Jeffery Walker, *Bardic Ethos and the American Epic Poem* (Baton Rouge: Louisiana State University Press, 1989). Other important works on the postwar long poem include books by Peter Baker, *Obdurate Brilliance: Exteriority and the Modern Long Poem* (Gainesville: University of Florida Press, 1991); and Lynn Keller, *Forms of Expansion: Recent Long Poems by Women* (Chicago: University of Chicago Press, 1997).

4. Roy Harvey Pearce, *The Continuity of American Poetry* (Princeton: Princeton University Press, 1961), 81.

5. Bernstein offers a useful summary of the ways in which the "modern epic," as he terms it, reworks generic expectations. See Michael André Bernstein, *The Tale of the Tribe: Ezra Pound and the Modern Verse Epic* (Princeton: Princeton University Press, 1980), 14.

6. Margaret Dickie, *On the Modernist Long Poem* (Iowa City: University of Iowa Press, 1986).

7. T.S. Eliot, *On Poetry and Poets* (New York: Farrar, Straus, and Cudahy, 1957), 47.

8. John Berryman, *The Dream Songs* (New York: Noonday, 1996), 376.

9. Susan Stanford Friedman, "When a 'Long' Poem is a 'Big' Poem: Self-Authorizing Strategies in Women's Twentieth-Century 'Long' Poems," *LIT* 2 (1990).

10. Charles Olson, *The Maximus Poems*, ed. George F. Butterick (Berkeley: University of California Press, 1983), 450.

11. Ibid., 16.

12. Olson, *Collected Prose*, ed. Donald Allen and Benjamin Friedlander (Berkeley: University of California Press, 1997), 17.

13. Ibid., 306–07.

14. McHale describes the ontological dimension of the spatial displacement of text on the page in Brian McHale, *Postmodernist Fiction* (New York: Routledge, 1987), 170–90.

15. Edward Dorn, *Gunslinger* (Durham: Duke University Press, 1995), 146.

16. Michael Davidson, "'To Eliminate the Draw': Narrative and Language in *Slinger*," in *Internal Resistances: The Poetry of Edward Dorn*, ed. Donald Wesling (Berkeley: University of California Press, 1985), 120.

17. Alan Wilde offers a useful distinction between modernist and postmodernist forms of irony. He associates "Disjunctive irony" with modernism and says it "strives, however reluctantly, toward a condition of paradox"; it "both recognizes the disconnections and seeks to control them." Postmodern irony is "suspensive irony," "with its more radical vision of multiplicity, randomness, contingency, and even absurdity, abandons the question for paradise altogether—the world in all its disorder is simply (or not so simply) accepted." He notes that with postmodern irony "an indecision about the meanings or relations of things is matched by a willingness to live with uncertainty." See Alan Wilde, *Horizons of Assent: Modernism, Postmodernism, and the Ironic Imagination* (Baltimore: Johns Hopkins University Press, 1981), 10, 44.

18. M. M. Bakhtin, *The Dialogic Imagination*, trans. Caryl Emerson and Michael Holquist (Austin: University of Texas Press, 1994), 3.

19. Marjorie Perloff, "Introduction," in *Gunslinger*, ed. Edward Dorn (Durham: Duke University Press, 1995), v–vi.

20. Joseph S. Wood tells us that "[f]or all its religious context, New England was a commercial venture from its inception." Joseph S. Wood, *The New England Village* (Baltimore: Johns Hopkins University Press, 1997), 33.

21. See Chapter 2 in Joe Moffett, *The Search for Origins in the Twentieth-Century Long Poem: Sumerian, Homeric, Anglo-Saxon* (Morgantown: West Virginia University Press, 2007). Included is an illustration of this theme in practice between Olson and Schwerner in his *Tablets*.

22. Marjorie Perloff, *Dance of the Intellect: Studies in the Poetry of the Pound Tradition* (Evanston, IL: Northwestern University Press, 1985).

23. Brian McHale, *The Obligation Toward the Difficult Whole: Postmodernist Long Poems* (Tuscaloosa: University of Alabama Press, 2004).

24. Robert Duncan, *Bending the Bow* (New York: New Directions, 1968), 82–83.

25. James F. Mersman, *Out of the Vietnam Vortex: A Study of Poets and Poetry Against the War* (Lawrence: University of Kansas Press, 1974), 25.

26. Joseph Conte similarly overcomes the limitations of the designation "long poem" by speaking of "serial" and "procedural" forms, although he focuses on a very narrow category of poets, all of whom are associated with experimental American verse. See Joseph Conte, *Unending Design: The Forms of Postmodern Poetry* (Ithaca: Cornell University Press, 1991).

27. A blind reviewer for this chapter pointed out to me, correctly, that tying popular culture to postmodernism is no new concept and indeed might be ripe for re-evaluation. I agree; to me, one of the most useful aspects of the resurgent interest in modernist studies has been works by figures such as Chinitz and Entin who show that modernist writers maintained a much closer relationship with popular culture than previously credited. While that may be the case, I would argue we see little among those writers traditionally labeled modernist writers (Chinitz is focusing on Eliot; Entin on figures such as Williams), that approaches the way popular culture is an essential part of the fabric of their long poems as it is for two of the writers I look at here: Dorn and Koch. In this way, there appears to me to be a difference of degree and not kind between the way modernist and postmodernist writers handle popular culture. See David E. Chinitz, *T. S. Eliot and the Cultural Divide* (Chicago: University of Chicago Press, 2003) and Joseph B. Entin, *Sensational Modernism: Experimental Fiction and Photography in Thirties America* (Chapel Hill: University of North Carolina Press, 2007).

28. See Joe Moffett, "Simulation, Popular Culture, and the Postmodern Long Poem: The Case of Kenneth Koch's *Seasons on Earth*," *The Journal of the Midwest Modern Language Association* 40, no. 2 (2007).

29. Brian McHale, "Weak Narrativity: The Case of Avant-Garde Narrative Poetry," *Narrative* 9, no. 2 (2001): 165.

30. Kenneth Koch, *Seasons on Earth* (New York: Penguin, 1987), 143.

31. Recent work in modernist studies has sought to illustrate the influence of popular culture on works of modernism. For example, David Chinitz argues that T.S. Eliot has been used as a "straw man for modernist 'contamination anxiety'" of high art being compromised by popular culture. Chinitz calls for a more comprehensive view of Eliot that exceeds seeing him simply as the poet who dismisses the "Shakespherian Rag" in *The Waste Land*. David E. Chinitz, *T. S. Eliot and the Cultural Divide* (Chicago: University of Chicago Press, 2003), 5.

Other recent work includes Joseph B. Entin's *Sensational Modernism*, which shows how certain modernist writers, particularly William Carlos Williams, Pietro di Donato, and Richard Wright, do not stand aloof from the popular, but rather engage it directly, at times reflecting the sensational nature of then-contemporary media outlets. Joseph B. Entin, *Sensational Modernism: Experimental Fiction and Photography in Thirties America* (Chapel Hill: University of North Carolina Press, 2007), 13–17.

Despite the efforts of critics like Entin and Chinitz, one must note that even if modernist writers are shown to entertain an interest in popular materials, their appropriation of these materials never begins to approach the attitude of poets like Koch and Dorn where their poems enlarge the subject matter of the long poem to include these "low culture" sources. In fact, the postmodernist long poem, as these poets define it, becomes impossible to imagine without the incorporation of these culture-wide influences.

32. Koch, *Seasons on Earth*, 238.

33. Ibid., 21.

34. James Schuyler, *Collected Poems* (New York: Noonday, 1993), 259.

35. Ibid.

36. Ibid., 262.

37. Ibid., 291.

38. Lehman points out that the sources of these poems are popular children's literature. In the case of "Europe" it is an "Edwardian book for girls" called *Beryl of the Bi-plane* and in "The Skaters" the inspiration comes from a book called *Three Hundred Things a Bright Boy Can Do* published in 1911. See David Lehman, *The Last Avant-Garde: The Making of the New York School of Poets* (New York: Anchor, 1999), 121–22, 60.

39. John Ashbery, *Selected Poems* (New York: Penguin, 1985), 201.

40. Ibid., 203.

41. Ibid., 200.

42. Koch, *Seasons on Earth*, 7.

43. Ashbery, *Selected Poems*, 188.

44. Ibid., 188–89.

45. Ibid., 189.

46. Allen Ginsberg, *Collected Poems: 1947–1980* (New York: Perennial, 1984), 126.

47. Ibid., 128.

48. Ibid., 129.

49. Ibid., 217.

50. Ibid., 219.

51. Gary Snyder, *Mountains and Rivers Without End* (Washington D.C.: Counterpoint, 1996), 72.

52. Ibid., 66.

53. Ibid., 31.

54. Ibid., 96.

55. Ibid., 61.

56. Ibid., 159.

57. Ibid., 158.

Bibliography

Ashbery, John. *Selected Poems*. New York: Penguin, 1985.

Baker, Peter. *Obdurate Brilliance: Exteriority and the Modern Long Poem*. Gainesville: University of Florida Press, 1991.

Bakhtin, M.M. *The Dialogic Imagination*. Translated by Caryl Emerson and Michael Holquist. Austin: University of Texas Press, 1994.

Bernstein, Michael André. *The Tale of the Tribe: Ezra Pound and the Modern Verse Epic*. Princeton: Princeton University Press, 1980.

Berryman, John. *The Dream Songs*. New York: Noonday, 1996.

Chinitz, David E. *T. S. Eliot and the Cultural Divide*. Chicago: University of Chicago Press, 2003.

Conte, Joseph. *Unending Design: The Forms of Postmodern Poetry*. Ithaca: Cornell University Press, 1991.

Davidson, Michael. "'To Eliminate the Draw': Narrative and Language in *Slinger*." *Internal Resistances: The Poetry of Edward Dorn*. Edited by Donald Wesling. Berkeley: University of California Press, 1985: 113–49.

Dickie, Margaret. *On the Modernist Long Poem*. Iowa City: University of Iowa Press, 1986.

Dorn, Edward. *Gunslinger*. Durham: Duke University Press, 1995.

Duncan, Robert. *Bending the Bow*. New York: New Directions, 1968.

Eliot, T.S. *On Poetry and Poets*. New York: Farrar, Straus, and Cudahy, 1957.

Entin, Joseph B. *Sensational Modernism: Experimental Fiction and Photography in Thirties America*. Chapel Hill: University of North Carolina Press, 2007.

Friedman, Susan Stanford. "When a 'Long' Poem Is a 'Big' Poem: Self-Authorizing Strategies in Women's Twentieth-Century 'Long Poems.'" *LIT* 2 (1990): 9–25.

Gardner, Thomas. *Discovering Ourselves in Whitman: The Contemporary American Long Poem*. Urbana: University of Illinois Press, 1989.

Ginsberg, Allen. *Collected Poems: 1947–1980*. New York: Perennial, 1984.

Keller, Lynn. *Forms of Expansion: Recent Long Poems by Women*. Chicago: University of Chicago Press, 1997.

Koch, Kenneth. *Seasons on Earth*. New York: Penguin, 1987.

Lehman, David. *The Last Avant-Garde: The Making of the New York School of Poets*. New York: Anchor, 1999.

McHale, Brian. *The Obligation Toward the Difficult Whole: Postmodernist Long Poems*. Tuscaloosa: University of Alabama Press, 2004.

———. *Postmodernist Fiction*. New York: Routledge, 1987.

———. "Weak Narrativity: The Case of Avant-Garde Narrative Poetry." *Narrative* 9, no. 2 (2001): 162–67.

Mersman, James F. *Out of the Vietnam Vortex: A Study of Poets and Poetry against the War*. Lawrence: University of Kansas Press, 1974.

Moffett, Joe. "Simulation, Popular Culture, and the Postmodern Long Poem: The Case of Kenneth Koch's *Seasons on Earth*." *The Journal of the Midwest Modern Language Association* 40, no. 2 (2007): 4–18.

———. *The Search for Origins in the Twentieth-Century Long Poem: Sumerian, Homeric, Anglo-Saxon*. Morgantown: West Virginia University Press, 2007.

Olson, Charles. *Collected Prose*. Edited by Donald Allen and Benjamin Friedlander. Berkeley: University of California Press, 1997.

———. *The Maximus Poems*. Edited by George F. Butterick. Berkeley: University of California Press, 1983.

Pearce, Roy Harvey. *The Continuity of American Poetry*. Princeton: Princeton University Press, 1961.

Perloff, Marjorie. *Dance of the Intellect: Studies in the Poetry of the Pound Tradition*. Evanston, IL: Northwestern University Press, 1985.

———. "Introduction." *Gunslinger*. Edited by Edward Dorn. Durham: Duke University Press, 1995: v-xviii.

Schuyler, James. *Collected Poems*. New York: Noonday, 1993.

Snyder, Gary. *Mountains and Rivers Without End*. Washington D.C.: Counterpoint, 1996.

Tuma, Keith. *Fishing by Obstinate Isles: Modern and Postmodern British Poetry and American Readers*. Evanston, IL: Northwestern University Press, 1998.

Walker, Jeffery. *Bardic Ethos and the American Epic Poem*. Baton Rouge: Louisiana State University Press, 1989.

Wilde, Alan. *Horizons of Assent: Modernism, Postmodernism, and the Ironic Imagination*. Baltimore: Johns Hopkins University Press, 1981.

Wood, Joseph S. *The New England Village*. Baltimore: Johns Hopkins UP, 1997.

CHAPTER SEVEN

Becoming Articulate:
Kathleen Fraser and
The New American Poetry

Megan Swihart Jewell

Although it only included the works of four women writers, Donald Allen's
The New American Poetry provided innovative feminist poet Kathleen Fraser
with alternative compositional models that would later become integral to her
fullest exploration of language, gender, and poetic form.[1] While her more radical formal experimentation would take place in the 1970s and 1980s, Fraser in
essays and interviews has discussed the initial possibility of becoming articulate as represented to her by Allen's anthology. Born in 1937, Fraser belongs
to what Lynn Keller has termed an "in-between generation" of experimental
poets. She was too young to be included in Allen's anthology, and was only in
peripheral association with poets defined as Language School writers.[2] Fraser
was, however, associated with the New York School and Black Mountain
poets in the 1960s, and, as she recalls, transformed in her practices by the
poets from those schools. Specifically, Fraser cites Charles Olson's manifesto
"PROJECTIVE VERSE" as particularly important for herself and for other
feminist poets who felt limited by conventional "left-margin poetics."[3] Despite
what Fraser has referred to as Olson's "territorial inclusive/exclusive boy-talk,"
she writes that his essay provided an "immense, permission-giving moment"
to move away from traditional formal constraints and to more openly explore
the relationship between gender, language, materiality, and page space.[4] In an
essay from 1996, Fraser describes the influence of Olson's poetics. Fraser writes,

> Expanding onto the FULL PAGE—responding to its spatial invitation to play
> with typographic relations of words and alphabets, as well as with their de-
> notative meanings, has delivered visual-minded poets from the closed, airless

containers of the well-behaved poem into a writing practice that foregrounds the investigation and pursuit of the unnamed.[5]

Some of the "visual-minded" poets she cites include Susan Howe and Hannah Weiner, with the sought-after "unnamed" signifying a distinct form of feminine subjectivity.[6]

Yet, it would be more than ten years after first encountering Olson's work in *The New American Poetry* that Fraser would be able to appreciate his emphasis on the structural, as opposed to lyrical, composition that it represented for her own poetry.[7] At the moment of first encountering Olson and his work, Fraser could not overcome Olson's misogyny, the ways in which, as she witnessed first-hand, "women just didn't count" within his coterie of male poets.[8] In essays, interviews, and editorial statements, Fraser cites Olson's sexism as representative of the early 1960s New American poetry scene, which she characterizes as an environment as fraught in terms of gender discrimination as it was a site for artistic possibility. As she recalls it, this gender bias revealed itself specifically for Fraser in editorial and other poetry networks, excluding or largely ignoring women as well as in the lack of critical attention given to innovative Modernist women poets. Fraser has noted the tremendous influence of Allen's volume; she has used Olson's "Projective Verse" in the classroom to help her women students develop a sense of voice.[9] Yet, she is also quick to point out the gender discrimination in the largely male poetry communities at the time of its publication. Indeed, this period of becoming articulate as a poet marks a critical period for Fraser not only developing her own poetic voice, but of becoming aware of the struggles involved for women in doing so.

When reflecting upon *The New American Poetry*, Fraser links her early experiences negotiating gender in the early 1960s New York poetry scene to her later experiences creating alternative spaces for innovative women's writing, most visibly represented by the feminist poetics journal *HOW(ever)*, which she edited from 1983 to 1991. While the models offered by the New American poets were influential to the development of her poetry, the gendered contexts surrounding the period of publication of *The New American Poetry* were instrumental to Fraser's later work forming alternative communities composed of and for women writing innovative poetics. Fraser's innovative aesthetics—in all phases of her more than forty-year career as a poet—have and continue to be shaped by the formal innovations carried out by many of the poets first published in Allen's collection. Her most recent book of poems, *movable TYYPE* (2011), for instance, manifests the complexly multiplied process of her sense of visuality, typography, and collaborative production that was first inspired by her reading of Allen's volume. It is Fraser's autobiographical accounts, however, her candid prose marking an intervention in criticism, that underscores the equally important gendered conditions under which "New American" poetry was produced. Fraser's prose essays, most of which are collected in *Translating the Unspeakable: Poetry and the Innovative Necessity* (1999), tell the story of the production and reception of late-century feminist avant-garde poetics, and her experiences with the "New American Poets" directly connect to Fraser's work creating alternative communities of exchange among other women poets. Her story, one composed of the tangled narratives of feminist avant-garde poetics and Second Wave politics, is that which is in need of emphasis fifty years later when thinking back upon *The New American Poetry*. A retrieval of Fraser's original concerns, and a re-iteration of her subsequent efforts to create alternative spaces for feminist poets, promotes a crucial reconsideration of the ways in which the gender imbalance of Allen's anthology—and the accompanying assumptions about women's relationship to poetic innovation—might continue to be reproduced by poets, anthologists, and critics alike.

Framing Feminist Innovative Writing

Fraser's necessarily qualified statements about *The New American Poetry* are familiar examples of how narratives of poetic influence do not apply neatly to the innovative women poets of her own or later generations. Poetic innovation has historically been seen as the province of men in terms of the discourses surrounding how it is both imagined and received. Rachel Blau DuPlessis asks whether there exists a "female Olson," in an essay addressing the masculine aggression signified by his manifesto.[10] As Steve Evans puts it, "discussions of avant-garde poetry can carry on for generations without ever seriously confronting discussions of gender."[11] Linda Russo points out that *The New American Poetry* has served to reproduce this imbalance. Russo writes,

> Because it has taught poetry-readers for decades to recognize "the new" and because what it presents has been taken for "the new," as we understand it "the new" wasn't produced by women. What is the mote in the mechanism of representation, beyond the obvious problematic of sexism, that yields up an overwhelming patrilineage? The nomenclature and genealogies that *The New American Poetry* created and preserves and through which we see poetic production and assign significance shows itself to be a problem for locating, and so talking about, women writers of that generation.[12]

Russo calls attention to the fact that each of the poetic schools included in *The New American Poetry* included, at best, only one token woman poet in what is its fundamentally patrilineal organizational scheme. Women writing at this time fall in-between the lines of demarcation in large part established by Allen's collection; their works are either not seen as significant or not believed to exist. If, as Language poet Ron Silliman has proclaimed, *The New American Poetry* is "unquestionably the most influential single anthology of the last century," then, for women, the question remains as to what extent its largely male composition delimited the interpretation of poetic innovation.[13] Ultimately, following DuPlessis, to what extent does newness signify a particularly masculine endeavor whereby the aggressive production of something new comes at women's expense?

In addition, when assessing the influence of *The New American Poetry*, one must be especially cognizant of the ways in which summative forms of influence, especially if couched in terms of retrospection, can overwrite the complexly gendered narratives of innovative women writers. Ann Vickery acknowledges the problems associated with tracing influence, and so she attempts to avoid the narrative elisions and disrupt the biases of traditional literary historiography in her alternative "feminist genealogy" of innovative women poets associated with the Language School.[14] Vickery notes that "[B]ecause literary history traditionally treats gender as a normative category, it becomes an invisible effect. Taken for granted, gender is naturalized into the structures of critical narrative."[15] Vickery draws upon innovative language-oriented poet Johanna Drucker's poem *From A to Z* to argue that a feminist genealogy, in contrast, "draw[s] attention to the vicissitudes of cultural activity by foregrounding the exchanges of this activity rather than the objects that are a part of it," and therefore wholly "politicize[s] the structures that frame a text's production, reproduction, and reception."[16] Vickery also cites Drucker's statement from a published forum on women's writing and theory in order to emphasize the gender politics involved in the discursive formation of poetics as a field:

> Even if NOTHING in the writing practice [has] to do with the writing—publishing it, seeing it received, being identified with it publicly and professionally, querying its historical position, etc. are ALL involved with gender issues.[17]

For Vickery, a feminist genealogy requires "an additional level of critique that engages with historically specific cultural formations and through which an aesthetic circulates and shapes possible roles for women."[18] It is a mode of inquiry entailing a focus on material structures of poetic production. It therefore requires a set of representational strategies that attends to the gender dynamics informing the construction of the poetics; otherwise, as in the past, accounts of the poetics become a form of addition that hides its subtractions.

The ways in which gendered poetic narratives have elided the poetics of Fraser and other women poets writing innovatively in the decades after the publication of Allen's anthology have been examined by several critics in what is now an established body of scholarship on innovative women writers; such omissions, misrepresentations or otherwise problematic interpretations have arguably led to the construction of a field. Beginning in the 1980s and 1990s, critics such as Vickery, Lynn Keller, Christanne Miller, Linda A. Kinnahan, Elizabeth A. Frost, Cynthia Hogue, and DuPlessis (who writes both traditional and non-linear experimental essays) have explored these issues in studies that elucidate the complicated process for these innovative women writers of becoming articulate, of seeking out poetic and theoretical models, forming their own or associating with other poetic and visual arts communities, and anthologizing or otherwise promoting their work within a context where structures of poetic production and reception center on male poets. Fraser herself worked to establish an earlier critical forum in *HOW(ever)*, and has otherwise collaborated with several scholars in interviews and personal correspondence. Importantly, she will frequently underscore the detailed, even anecdotal nature of events and interactions—those more often than not omitted from traditional criticism—in order to help bring about a clearer understanding of the gender dynamics informing her work.

Both Fraser's collaboration with other scholars and emphasis on interpersonal details can be interpreted as a strong gesture of resistance to formal literary historiography, as can Fraser's approach to criticism. She has published several semi-autobiographical essays that similarly foreground her personal exchanges as fundamental to a critical interpretation of the gender politics informing her poetic career. A focus on Fraser's lived experiences as she expresses them in essays and personal interviews allows for an important reiteration of several of these critical issues regarding gendered poetic structures. As she recounts them, her experiences with "New American" poets call full attention to the gendered contexts that continue to mediate the reception of women innovative poets.

Fraser's poetry, editorial work, and her teaching demonstrate a consistent concern with women's creative agency and the possibility of its expression in an experimental poetic mode. The trajectory of her career reflects the complex relationships between feminist politics and innovative aesthetics. Since 1966,

Fraser has published nineteen volumes of poetry, and a collection of her criti-cal essays in addition to founding and editing *HOW(ever)*. She taught creative writing at Iowa Writer's Workshop, Reed College and, for more than fifteen years, at San Francisco State University, where she founded the American Poetry Archives. Her work appeared throughout the past decades in numer-ous mainstream and innovative feminist anthologies ranging from Florence Howe's *No More Masks! An Anthology of Twentieth Century American Women Poets* (1973), Laura Chester's *Rising Tides: Twentieth Century Women Poets* (1973) and *Deep Down: The New Sensual Writing by Women* (1988), Mag-gie O'Sullivan's *Out of Everywhere: Linguistically Innovative Poetry by Women in North America and the UK* (1996), and *Moving Borders: Three Decades of Innovative Writing by Women* (1998). Howe's and Chester's anthologies are often characterized as more mainstream feminist texts, given their emphasis on presenting what might be viewed as highly accessible poems written in a literal mode. Fraser's inclusion in these anthologies has to do with the empha-sis of these collections on presenting women's experiences as written from the overlooked perspective of female poets. Further, Fraser's poetry at this time contained a more recognizably woman-centered emphasis on domesticity, personal relationships, and body-image acceptance that would have appealed to these more or less essentialist, recovery-driven editors.[19]

Yet, while fully supporting Second Wave feminist causes, Fraser became by the 1970s in large part dissatisfied with the "immediately-accessible language of personal expression" characterizing mainstream feminist poetry, noticing a growing divide between mainstream and innovative practice.[20] As Keller writes for feminist poets at this time, the formal elements characterizing both in-novative and more literal poetry were seen as equally useful for exploring gendered concerns:

> Before the seventies, a woman writer could at least partially suspend the di-visions of the anthology wars in order to make headway in issues related to gender: she could find liberating and even courageously innovative models in work that gave direct expression to women's experience *as well as* in mys-teriously oblique, disjunctive, and visually attuned work like Guest's. Fraser's poems of the mid-sixties themselves suggest that she did not then choose between them—and I mean not only the mentoring friendships but also the poetic examples of the feminist who uses language instrumentally and the linguistically innovative one.[21]

Yet, even though she aligned early on with more mainstream feminist mod-els, Fraser had been seeking a more complex aesthetic than personal expres-sion for exploring gender issues. While beginning her career as a poet, Fraser first felt uninspired by female confessional poets of the 1950s and 1960s, such as Sylvia Plath, who relied heavily on lyric conventions.[22] Kinnahan writes that this "aesthetics of female subjectivity validated by the masculine stamp of approval but unexamined for its interest in linguistic complexities dissatisfied Fraser."[23] Fraser later identified the style adopted by Second Wave feminist poets in the 1970s, as it retained the lyric perspective of the Confessional poets, as inadequate for fully examining gendered poetic stances: "while seriously committed to gender consciousness, a number of us carried on an increasing skepticism toward any *fixed* rhetoric of the poem, implied or intoned. We resisted the prescription of authorship as an exclusively unitary proposition—the essential 'I' positioned as central to the depiction of reflectivity."[24] Fraser, who was more inspired by the "linguistic innovations" of Virginia Woolf and Gertrude Stein, has also written about her inability to find a productive working community within these mainstream groups: "I recognized [in Woolf and Stein] a structural order of fragmentation and a linguistic resistance to law-abiding traditional models that confirmed my perspective. . . . Yet, ironically, this fascination with the innovative works of modernist women writers marginalized me even further from the official women's writing community."[25]

This marginalization eventually came at the expense of exclusion from institutional accounts of feminist poetry.

> The feminist poetry that has been institutionalized within women's studies programs and teaching anthologies can be restrictively organized around a normative concept of "experience" that renders all but the most tentative formal innovations by women inadmissible and anathematizes theoretical reflection on poetic practice (by poets themselves, by their readers) as an overly intellectualized interference with the immediate pleasures afforded by cathartic identification.[26]

For Fraser, this canonical exclusion was represented specifically by the appearance in 1985 of *The Norton Anthology of Women's Literature*, which largely excluded innovative poetry. Fraser writes,

> [I]n 711 pages of contemporary writing by women, not a single representation of current innovative practice is in evidence, no reference to the more than 100 women writing and publishing in English, radically opening up the terrain of contemporary literature since the late Sixties.[27]

The omission of women innovators, although done in a volume dedicated to feminist recovery, replicated the same exclusionary structures among male poets that Fraser had witnessed and took note of as an early feminist in the 1960s. She writes that "[t]he male power structure we'd learned to recognize and analyze as the basis of the canon-forming profession of literature suddenly had its able female counterpart. This was not any less stifling."[28]

Additionally, innovative women's writing in the 1980s was elided by the critical shaping of the Language School, most usually viewed as the next generation of poetic innovators after the New American poets. In the introduction to her *Out of Everywhere* anthology of experimental women poets, O'Sullivan writes that although "excluded from 'women's canons,'" innovative feminist poetics does "connect up with linguistically innovative work by men who have themselves also transcended the agenda-based and cliché-ridden rallying positions of mainstream poetry."[29] Yet, while these women poets were engaging in similar forms of experimentalism, given the longstanding gender bias bound up with both the avant-garde and the creation of literary schools, the individual projects of women experimentalists largely disappeared from or were tokenized within that categorization. As Marianne DeKoven puts it in an oft-quoted statement from 1986:

> [a]s long as an experimental writer whose "signature" is female aligns herself with the language poets, for example, as many of them sometimes do, she has a place on the literary map. The price she pays, which is familiar to all of us, is two-fold: the question of gender will be erased, declared a non-issue, and, at the same time, it is less likely than if her signature were male, that she will become one of the stars, even in that tiny firmament.[30]

At this time, Silliman and Douglas Messerli were producing the first two Language Poetry anthologies, *In the American Tree: Language, Realism, Poetry* (1986) and *"Language" Poetries* (1987), respectively. Hank Lazer characterized them as "the two most important anthologies of contemporary American poetry since Donald Allen's *The New American Poetry* in 1960."[31] Like *The New American Poetry*, these anthologies were significant to defining innovation as a largely male practice.[32] Silliman includes the work of twelve women poets among the forty poets in the volume. While Vickery writes that the inclusion of women "reflects the gradual social change wrought by feminism," critic Linda Renfield concluded that (in Silliman's anthology) women's voices remained "irreducibly marginal."[33] Vickery writes that both *In the American Tree* and *"Language" Poetries* served to significantly bolster the reputations of certain women poets such as Susan Howe and Lyn Hejinian while "writers such as Kathleen Fraser, Joan Retallack, Leslie Scalapino,

Rosmarie Waldrop . . . were effectively rendered marginal in terms of their reception to Language projects."[34] Thus, in the production and organization of what were the next important anthologies of avant-garde poetics since *The New American Poetry*, the tokenism and marginalization of women innovators remained largely intact.

Importantly, Fraser has connected the framing of the Language School to the same structures that marginalized women writers in the 1960s, and strongly pushed against such group constructions in her own critique of the Language School in the 1980s.[35] Drawing on Vickery's account of the ways in which critical groupings have elided women innovators, Kinnahan emphasizes the ways in which "framing terms" have interfered with the reception of the works of Fraser and other innovative women poets. She writes,

> [T]he framing term *feminist poetry* has not historically admitted avant-garde/ experimental/innovative approaches, while the framing term *Language* writing has generated a history built up around men from which linguistically innovative writings by women functioning outside of this frame are not brought into the constructed literary history that dominates.[36]

The work of Fraser and other women writing innovatively strays not only from mainstream feminist poetry, but also from these longstanding narrative frameworks of avant-garde production that had earlier informed, as Russo points out, the organization of *The New American Poetry*. Clearly drawing upon her experiences with the poetic avant-garde in the early 1960s New York scene, Fraser responds to the implicit gender-blindness accompanying Language writing,

> [A]mbivalence toward upper-case Language Writing exists in many women whose writing history had been until, the early Seventies, formed largely by male teachers, editors, and critics whose tastes conformed to experiences, aesthetic values, pleasures, and struggles *as* men in a social/political world where access to print was assumed. A growing awareness of this suddenly glaring fact—its clout and assumption of the word—has posed serious questions for women writers who struggle for language access to their own experience.[37]

Fraser writes that developing feminist poets share with the Language poets a desire to "reinvent, deconstruct, find syntactical and experimental detours out of the dominant and often turgid mainstream."[38] Yet, as with the earlier poetic movements: "there is an undeniable wariness in simply following the diagrams and preferences of the new language formalists who are, once again, male-dominated in their *theoretical* documents."[39] In Fraser's view, the formation of a new school signifies that women poets are *once again* being denied opportunity for expression by the gender dynamics of a male-dominated field. She writes that a woman would be better off to "attend first to the unraveling of her own buried history of/in language before it gets classified, theorized, tamed," further observing that for women "the [language-oriented] distaste for *any* self-referentiality introduces (yet again) the concept of prohibition."[40] In her estimation, the formation of the Language movement necessarily entails a gendered poetic mechanism historically conditioned to limit women's expression, with the Language-oriented emphasis on a wholly impersonal poetics only serving to doubly silence them. Again, while not fully discounting Language School projects, Fraser, given her experiences with New American poetry formations, necessarily re-politicizes them in terms of gender: "For a writer whose awareness has been tuned by the growing need to claim her own history and present tense, Language Writing's directives are often encountered—if not intended—as the *newest* covenant."[41]

"A Definitely Male Network": Fraser's Early Years in New York

The preceding statement on Language writing is just one example of how Fraser was influenced by the male bias accompanying avant-garde production maintained within "a definitely male network."[42] If one looks back on Fraser's more than forty years of work as an innovative feminist poet, teacher, and editor, it is clear that the sexism evident in the male-dominated poetry formations in the early 1960s has shaped her wariness for new poetry movements. As Fraser recalls,

> [t]hrough the Sixties, various movements emerged and ran parallel courses, all sharing two observable similarities. They each had male theorists setting forth the new aesthetic dogma, usually asserted in public correspondence or theoretical repudiation of each other's poetics. Each poetics constellation or school had its token woman poet.[43]

A focus on the specific autobiographical instances informing Fraser's observations underscores the connections between the time when she was a young poet associated with the "New American" poets and the work she has done creating spaces for the recognition of women writing innovative poetics.

After graduating from Occidental College in 1959, Fraser moved to New York where she worked as a journalist at *Mademoiselle*, viewing her position writing fashion copy as "a sort of word discipline."[44] In New York, she first studied poetry with Stanley Kunitz and later became involved in the New York poetry and art scene, where she met Frank O'Hara and Barbara Guest and studied in a workshop led by Kenneth Koch.[45] At New York School poetry readings and gallery exhibitions, she began to notice that men were the designated leaders and promoters of these developing movements. As she recalls about her experiences with Koch: "I watched uneasily as he divided us into male poets and female sex objects who wrote poetry."[46]

Fraser in 1960 had just read Simone de Beauvoir's *The Second Sex* and was "waking up," as she now phrases it, to the gender biases located within poetry communities, the ways in which women were not associated at this time with serious artistic production, and were thus confined to marginal roles within these male-dominated groups. The book, as she notes, was her first "politicization."[47] As Fraser writes about this time,

> We literary women had all been taught our manners and, with few exceptions, in the Sixties, women writers sent out their work and waited to be taken up by powerful male editors and mentors who were willing to discover them and authenticate their reality as writers. Women mentors and editors were in very short supply, still captured by their own tentative power base.[48]

At this time, Fraser was also in the process of re-assessing the traditional all-male poetry canon that she studied in college. Fraser recalls as a student admiring W. B. Yeats's poem "Leda and the Swan" only to have it infuriate her upon re-reading after her early experiences with seeing how women were both sexualized and tokenized at this time in New York. That Yeats's swan, the God Zeus, had the unquestionable power in this poem to hold Leda in his grasp, to execute a brutal rape and then move on, angered her in its symbolic representation of women's roles at this time. Men, like the Swan, were wholly able to "take what they need," while women were always grounded, serving as their "support system."[49] This "taking up" of women poets by "powerful male editors" remains a permanent symbol for Fraser of *The New American Poetry* scene.

Fraser's association with Guest at this time influenced the development of both her visual poetic experimentation and her feminism. In New York, in 1964, Fraser recalls that Guest was one of few "identifiable women writers within a "definitely male network" of poets and painters.[50] She writes about hearing in 1964 Guest read her poem "Parachutes, My Love, Could Carry Us

Higher," which was one of the four of her poems included in Allen's anthology. Noting that Guest's poem was, for her, "the beginning of a new plane of ecstatic response to poetic language," Fraser was particularly struck by its more structural, non-lyrical elements that demonstrated what was for her a new sense of artistic restraint.[51] Fraser writes that Guest's poem represented "the condition of the tenuous, spoken out of a peculiarly interior experience, yet as far afield as one could imagine from the battering 'confessional' model much favored in certain East Coast poetry formations."[52] In addition, Fraser has described in numerous essays and interviews how Guest's technique has influenced her own practice with regard to her more visual use of language as a painterly material and view of "painting as a base for how she saw the world."[53] She writes that "Guest's words are clues along a path that is actually the painting of that path. Her page can be dense and opaque with the brushed overlays of a fully covered canvas, but as often trusts the phrasal conviction of minimal gesture—the swift notation invited by sketchbook practice."[54] Yet, while Guest was, as Sara Lundquist describes, "a defining and foundational 'member'" of the New York School, her work was often excluded from representations of it, including the first major collection of its poets, *An Anthology of New York Poets* (1970) edited by David Shapiro and Ron Padgett.[55]

Fraser's autobiographical accounts of this period link this and other forms of representational exclusion to the sexism within these networks. Witnessing the ways in which women were ignored at readings and events, Fraser in particular recalls Koch's "cruel" treatment of Guest, and the ways in which he excluded her when promoting New York school events.[56] Fraser notes that Guest's reaction to this exclusion was foundational to her politics: "Guest was hidden, not about to reveal her pain. That's what turned me into a feminist."[57] In the 1980s and 1990s, Fraser devoted much time to Guest in essays and in her editorial work in *HOW(ever)*, placing Guest within what Fraser would term an alternative "tradition of marginality" to describe innovative women writers.[58] In "Barbara Guest: A Memoir," in addition to giving careful attention to her poetics, Fraser emphasizes Guest's generosity toward other aspiring women poets. Fraser writes that "it was the exception in the Sixties, when the word *mentor* more than often implied token male sponsorship based on dubious power relations. Her friendship was offered in dignity, assumed reciprocity of value and complementarity of interests."[59] Fraser emphasizes the importance of the example Guest provides for women: "[She] continues to provide a model for those of us engaged in finding full parity for women in the reading/writing community, beyond token representation."[60]

Coming into Voice in the Academy

After leaving New York, Fraser taught creative writing at Iowa and at Reed College. In 1967, she eventually moved to San Francisco, where she found echoes of New York School male poetry networks in her work with female students who lacked a sense of voice as well as a lack of supportive women mentors. Patrick Prichett observes that the "signal ambit of Kathleen Fraser's remarkable poetic career has encompassed the feminist concern with exclusion, marginality, and the generation of 'voice,'" and the first years of Fraser's life in the academy was motivated by both discovering her own poetic voice and helping other women to do so.[61] In an extensive interview with poet Suzanne Stein, Fraser states that this concern with voice was "what my teaching was about for five years."[62] When teaching poetry workshops, Fraser noticed how the male students were more at ease. Fraser recalls how her experiences with women students in her classrooms replicated a gendered pattern that she had experienced as a student. Fraser tells Stein about her students:

> They were very smart and wonderful writers, but they could not speak publicly and I really understood that because I was very much that way when I was in school. I would have something to say and then a really articulate graduate student, usually a man, would immediately come in with this incredibly evolved—what seemed to me at the time as brilliant—statement . . . and I was undone.[63]

At this time in her life, Fraser became strongly concerned with the gendered structures denying women full access to these critical interpretative communities. As she tells Stein, this process of speaking within them "was absolutely core to what I was struggling with at that time." Fraser notes,

> I had been noticing things for a very long time, unequal situations time and time again. I kept noticing these patterns in these completely different programs where the women in the classroom would not be entering into the conversation. No one was stopping them, really, but they couldn't seize the moment fast enough. There would be people who were accustomed to speak and seize the moment and they would tend to be men—this was before any of us were noticing it as a conscious problem or project, but I was noticing it a lot and thinking about it a lot. By the time I got to San Francisco State, I had women coming into my office when I was doing the Poetry Center describing situations in class and being turned away . . . being told that they wouldn't be able to be poets . . . (they became very good poets, by the way).[64]

Her students' inability to "seize the moment" in a classroom as well what Fraser interpreted as their desire for affirmation reflects the unequal power relations that she witnessed in New York, where women poets were traditionally passive objects waiting to be taken up within an unquestionably male network. Her experiences with her students led to Fraser's interrogation of the ways in which women were long denied access to the male-dominated communities associated with poetry's interpretation and production, and so she began to explore in both her teaching and poetics a more female-centered model as a form of empowerment.

In the interview with Stein, Fraser also discusses her relationship with Frances Jaffer, with whom she would later form a writing group along with poet Beverly Dahlen, and with whom she would collaborate with in establishing *HOW(ever)*. The centerpiece poem in the collection *Something (even human voices) in the foreground, a lake* (1984), "Medusa's hair with snakes. Was thought, split inward," is dedicated to Jaffer and to other women whom she felt were "needing to speak but being acutely aware of the judgment that is seeing them as inadequate to the task."[65] Fraser notes that the poem is uncharacteristic of her works in its concern with mythology and was written a few years earlier than the other poems in the volume.[66] Yet, the invocation of the threatening figure of Medusa, who turned men to stone with her glances, serves well in subverting the gender dynamics within modes of communication that render women voiceless. Her use of myth on another level alludes to her concern with Yeats's "Leda and the Swan," and the sexist editorial practices of the New York poets in the 1960s.

With its non-linear, associative form suggesting a more female-centered model, the poem actively explores the different ways in which men and women have been conditioned to communicate. The poem begins with a speaker asserting that "I do not wish to report on Medusa directly," its defiant "I" conveying that modes of directness have been oppressive to women in academic and other contexts. As Fraser emphasizes, the poem is concerned with women's ability to seize voice in aggressive contexts from which they have been historically prohibited. As she tells Stein, "Frances had been part of that struggle."[67] The next line describes the difficult process of coming into voice for Medusa, Jaffer, and other female figures. It reads: "After she gave that voice a shape, it was the trajectory itself / in which she found her words floundering and pulling apart." About this line, Fraser describes the visceral process it represents for women struggling to develop a voice. These first lines, she remarks, "follow the trajectory, the journey, the traveling of the voice out into the air literally. The voice begins to split apart to stutter, to not be able to follow in a narrative logical clarity because of the anxiety of the people judging in this space."[68] She cites the fierceness of the imagery as replicating the terror involved with the process of learning to speak "in the company of any kind of authority, which was often men, but sometimes women."[69] The second stanza moves on to explore the barriers to communication, with the first line reading "[s]ometimes we want to talk to someone who can't hear us."[70] The third and fourth stanzas enact this disconnect between sexes, noting the historically-gendered patterns of language access:

> When he said "red cloud," she imagined *red*
> but he thought *cloud* (this dissonance in which she was feeling trapped,
> out-of-step, getting from here to there)
>
> Historical continuity
> accounts for knowing what dead words point to[71]

The poem continues with another description of the physical violence involved into coming into voice, of becoming articulate. Fraser writes,

> Medusa trying to point with her hair
> That thought turned to venom
> That muscle turning to thought turning
> to writhing out.[72]

Becoming articulate is portrayed as a particularly complex set of negotiations between interpretation and representation in the remainder of the poem. Additional stanzas center on Medusa's figurative re-casting in mythology and literal recasting in stone, as in Gian Lorenzo Bernini's sculpture of her, which Fraser had viewed prior to composing the poem. Eternally threatening, Medusa is repeatedly subdued, cast in stone by Bernini, or, as in the poem, buried "in backyard weeds" or mounted "above his sails, her hair splitting tongues."[73]

Composed much later than "Medusa," but included in the same volume, the prose poem "In white, she who bathed" subtly depicts the ways in which a masculinist perception of female ways of knowing has served to silence women. In its entirety, the poem reads,

> Everywhere, rooms are leading to other rooms. The brain, she thinks, is her corridor and her strict casement when she is a window. It is believed that she understands partially, but cannot speak, except haltingly, and about nothing in particular.[74]

In this poem, women's halting speech is construed by a presumably male presence as a lack of intelligence or mental acuity. Halting speech is un-recognizable when the moment must always be seized. The first sentence of this poem seems to marvel at the gendered labyrinth of (mis-)communication while the next line represents a woman struggling with how she might perceive others, herself, or be perceived. In the last sentence, the female interpretative process is speculated about, and then, unable to be understood, dismissed as feminine. Like "Medusa's Hair with Snakes," this poem deals with longstanding gendered patterns that obstruct communication at the expense of women's voice. While Fraser notes that she ultimately felt that men were also victims of the historical patterns of incommunicability, that "they had been impressed and suppressed by the history of public discourse," it was women's coming into voice that was central to her concerns as a teacher and, later, to her founding of *HOW(ever)*.[75]

From the New York School to *HOW(ever)*: Founding "a Sisterhood of Exploration"[76]

At San Francisco State, Fraser's reading group with Jaffer and Dahlen generated the idea of forming *HOW(ever)*.[77] The first issue of appeared in May 1983, with a run of nine years and twenty-four issues.[78] Along with Jaffer and Dahlen, Fraser enlisted feminist scholars Carolyn Burke and DuPlessis and then, two years later, poet-critic Susan Gervitz in order to provide a forum for women poets who were writing experimentally, but without much visibility. *(HOW)ever* was intended to put editorial control in the hands of women and so retained an all female editorial and submission policy in the hopes of creating an alternative tradition.[79] In addition, the journal's aim was to cultivate a dialog between contemporary women poets and scholars studying modernist women experimentalists. The format of *HOW(ever)* contains discrete components intended to cultivate interchange between poets and critics, resisting traditional critical categories from which Fraser had felt alienated. Each issue included creative work, author's working notes, critical commentary, and reader correspondence. As Kinnahan writes,

> The thematic, theoretical, and structural relationships between poem, critical essay, and notes form an integral part of the journal's feminist project. In the process, the textual space of *HOW(ever)* both comments upon and puts into practice strategies of writing and reading geared toward exploring the relationship of language structures to female experience. Such exploration takes place as a process of sharing materials and ideas, of teaching new concepts, of recovering forgotten ground, of producing new knowledge, of producing a reading community.[80]

Again, Fraser's work in the academy brought about this need for community, "an even more powerful urge to help break down and dismantle the concrete wall," as she witnessed the hesitation to speak in more than a few of her women students.[81] In large part, therefore, *HOW(ever)* was established to allow more women to speak to women. Fraser writes that when working in three different university writing programs, "[I]t became clear that this performance anxiety—in the charged field of authority and fluency—was not confined to a few 'problem' individuals," and it was this structure of the male-dominated field that inhibited Fraser and that she consequently felt compelled to change.[82] Emphasizing the aggressive nature of these interpretative communities in direct regard to the founding of *(HOW)ever*, Fraser continues,

> The inability to enter into public conversation was pervasive. One noticed it in the lopsided post-panel exchanges often held among writers after community literary events: women were seldom heard from. The mandate for more equitable participation was clear, but the ability to carry it out was waylaid. I, too, was convinced that I did not have the scholarly training required to speak with sufficient authority in public exchanges where writing practice and theory were being tested and defined. Although I valued analytical skills necessary to thinking and writing, I did not feel comfortable pursuing the combative tone that often accompanied the arguments I imagined as necessary to these public exchanges.[83]

From its inception, *HOW(ever)* would be organized in resistance to structures of a male-dominated field under which women poets were denied the opportunity to develop their voices in traditional academic forums left our or otherwise under-represented within academic canons. Fraser writes,

> There was no longer any question in my mind. I had to give time to making a place where our issues could be aired and some new choices put forward in women's poetry—asserted and selected by women—including a revival of modernist figures and a closer look at contemporary work discounted by critics. I wanted a serious yet *informal* conversation among poets and scholar/teacher/critics (Fraser's emphasis).[84]

Informality is placed in opposition to stifling decorum, and had male writers been involved in the editorial process, "[t]here would have been a more heavily weighted set of histories to stare down, a male style of logic and argument with its confident and enlightened pressures always there to be negotiated."[85] Women have long been alienated from the discourse associated with male interpretative communities, in Fraser's experience, and therefore *HOW(ever)* was a place for women poets to take a "jump" into "unofficially recognized realm involved the development of a new descriptive language."[86]

In her prose essays, Fraser has consistently traced the origins of HOW(ever) to a process of both becoming aware of and overcoming the limitations of her "own era's established models of good behavior."[87] Fraser's story underscores the ways in which the gender expectations for women at the time of *The New American Poetry* have significantly influenced the trajectory of her own and others' poetics. In the introduction to *Translating the Unspeakable*, Fraser identifies her own experience as representative of that of other women poets of her generation and right away underscores the founding of HOW(ever) as designed to rectify the gender imbalances that she first witnessed as a young poet among New York and other "New American" poets. Becoming articulate as a feminist, Fraser then took note of the larger structures of gendered communication bound up with the study of poetry as she moved into the academy and witnessed women's alienation from traditional and other poetic discourses. Fraser's mentorship of women poets and establishment of a reading group thus resulted in the founding of (HOW)ever, a collaborative space showcasing the current works of women writing innovatively as well as the critical works of women studying the forgotten first generation of Modernist female innovators. After HOW(ever), Fraser collected older and continued to compose detailed prose accounts of her lived experiences as an innovative feminist poet negotiating the entrenched gender biases of poetic innovation. This practice, as well as her continued willingness to collaborate with feminist critics on innovative women's writing, represents an intervention into the "internalized voice of a male-dominant academic method."[88] Ultimately, her accounts allow one to connect those formal critical discourses to those self-same alienating features of the male poetry communities to which she was first exposed—and took quick note of—at the time when *The New American Poetry*—with its inclusion of only four women—was the primary model of poetic innovation.

Notes

1. The four women included in Allen's 1960 edition were Helen Adam, Madeline Gleason, Barbara Guest, and Denise Levertov.

2. Most of poets who were primarily active in the 1960s were born in the late 1920s. Poets associated with the Language movement were born in the late 1940s and early 1950s. Lynn Keller, "Just one of the Girls:—/normal in the extreme": Experimentalists-To-Be Starting Out in the 1960s. *differences: A Journal of Feminist Cultural Studies* 12, no 2. (Summer 2001): 47.

3. Kathleen Fraser, *Translating the Unspeakable: Poetry and the Innovative Necessity* (Tuscaloosa: University of Alabama Press, 1999), 175.

4. Ibid., 175–6.

5. Ibid., 175.

6. Ibid. Fraser adds that "The dimensionality of the full page invites multiplicity, synchronicity, elasticity [. . .] perhaps the very female subjectivity proposed by Julia Kristeva as linking both cyclical and monumental time."

7. Kathleen Fraser, "Conversation with Suzanne Stein," Jan. 17, 2007, *PennSound: Kelsey Street Press*, http://writing.upenn.edu/pennsound/x/Kelsey-Street.php.

8. Ibid.

9. Kathleen Fraser, phone conversation with author, November 27, 2012.

10. Rachel Blau DuPlessis, "Manifests," *Diacritics* 26, no. 3 (1996): 44. For DuPlessis, Olson's notion of space is as of a virgin territory to be occupied by masculine projections.

11. Steve Evans, "After Patriarchal Poetry: Feminism and the Contemporary Avant-Garde. Introductory Note," *differences: A Journal of Feminist Cultural Studies.* 12.2 (Summer 2001): i.

12. Linda Russo, "Introduction: a Context for Reading Joanne Kyger," *Jacket*, no. 11 (April 2000), http://jacketmagazine.com/11/kyger-russo.html.

13. Ron Silliman, "Monday June 11, 2007," *Silliman's Blog: A Weblog Focused on Contemporary Poetry and Poetics*, http://ronsilliman.blogspot.com/2007/06/donald-allen-theres-no-such-thing-as.html.

14. Ann Vickery, *Leaving Lines of Gender: A Feminist Genealogy of Language Writing* (Middletown, CT: Wesleyan University Press, 2000).

15. Ibid., 14.

16. Ibid.

17. Ibid.

18. Ibid., 15.

19. Keller, "Just one of the Girls . . . ," 54. Keller does a close reading of Fraser's poetry from the 1960s, concluding that "While Fraser's poetic personas have freed themselves from the traditional position of passive object defined by the male gaze, they are rarely able to deviate from the decade's 'normal' gender roles—any more than Fraser herself is able to push the lyric beyond the free-verse possibilities opened by the generation of Rich and Creeley."

20. Fraser, *Translating*, 31.

21. Keller, "Just One of the Girls . . . ," 51.

22. Linda Kinnahan, *Lyric Interventions: Feminism, Experimental Poetry, and Contemporary Discourse* (Iowa City: University of Iowa Press, 2005), 60.

23. Ibid., 60.

24. Fraser, *Translating*, 176.

25. Ibid., 32.

26. Evans, "After Patriarchal Poetry," i-ii.

27. Fraser, *Translating*, 136–137.

28. Kathleen Fraser, "The Jump: Editing (How)ever," *Chain*, no. 1 (Spring-Summer 1994), 43.

29. Maggie O'Sullivan, *Out of Everywhere: Linguistically Innovative Poetry by Women in North America and in the UK* (Hastings, UK: Reality Street Press, 1996), 9.

30. Marianne Dekoven, "Gertrude's Granddaughters," *Women's Review of Books*, no. 4 (November 1986), 12.

31. Vickery, *Leaving Lines of Gender*, 138.

32. Ibid. Vickery points out how they "quickly became handy pedagogical tools," given the extent to which they were more accessible than the small press journals in which Language poets were previously publishing.

33. Ibid. In a chapter on innovative anthologizing, Vickery provides a detailed study of how gender issues inform the composition of both anthologies in terms of the representative creation of a school, as well as how those two significantly influential Language poetry anthologies later informed the first collections dedicated solely to innovative women, *Out of Everywhere* and *Moving Borders*.

34. Ibid., 141.

35. Fraser began her career just prior to the formation of Language poetry movements. Although she had significant exposure to the West Coast Language poetry scene, she remained largely on its peripheries. Fraser's 1982 essay "Partial Local Coherence: Regions with illustrations (Some notes on 'Language' writing)" prefigures DeKoven's critique of the ways in which the formation of a Language School canon excludes women writers.

36. Kinnahan, *Lyric Interventions*, 9.

37. Fraser, *Translating*, 76.

38. Ibid.

39. Ibid.

40. Ibid.

41. Ibid. My emphasis.

42. Ibid., 126.

43. Ibid., 30–31.

44. Corine Robins, "Four Young Poets," *Mademoiselle*, 1959. Reprinted in *Empty Mirror: Magazine of the Arts*. June 2, 2012, http://www.emptymirrorbooks.com/images/poets/hart/mllereview.html.

45. At this time, Fraser studied with Kenneth Koch and Robert Lowell at the New School for Social Research and with Stanley Kunitz at the Poetry Center at the YMHA.

46. Fraser, *Translating*, 23.

47. Kathleen Fraser, phone conversation with author, November 27, 2012.

48. Fraser, *Translating*, 31.

49. Kathleen Fraser, phone conversation with author, November 27, 2012.

50. Fraser, *Translating*, 126.

51. Ibid.,127.

52. Ibid.

53. Fraser, "Conversation with Suzanne Stein."

54. Fraser, *Translating*, 125.

55. Sara Lundquist, "The Fifth Point of a Star: Barbara Guest and the New York 'School of Poets,'" In *Barbara Guest: This Art*. ed. Catherine Kaspar. Special Issue, *Women's Studies*, no. 30: (2001), 12.

56. Kathleen Fraser, phone conversation with author, November 27, 2012.

57. Ibid.

58. Kinnahan, *Lyric Interventions*, 47. Fraser discusses Guest in the following critical essays, from *Translating the Unspeakable*, "Tradition of Marginality" and "Line. One the Line. Lining up. Lined with. Between the Lines. Bottom Line," and "Barbara Guest: The Location of her (A memoir)."

59. Fraser, *Translating*, 127.

60. Ibid.

61. Patrick Pritchett, "An Excerpt from and Book Review of *il cuore: the heart: Selected Poems 1970–1995*," *Electronic Poetry Center*, November 12, 2011, http://epc .buffalo.edu/authors/fraser/review.html.

62. Fraser, "Conversation with Suzanne Stein."

63. Ibid.

64. Ibid.

65. Ibid.

66. "Medusa" was first included in a Fraser's manuscript *Leda and the Swan*, which was lost in a theft while she was in Italy.

67. Ibid.

68. Ibid.

69. Ibid.

70. Kathleen Fraser, *il cuore: the heart—New and Selected Poems (1970–1995)* (Middletown, CT: Wesleyan University Press, 1997), 67.

71. Ibid.

72. Ibid.

73. Ibid., 67–68.

74. Ibid., 68.

75. Fraser, "Conversation with Suzanne Stein."

76. Rachel Blau DuPlessis, "postcards." *HOW(ever)*, volume 6, no. 4 (January 1992), http://www.asu.edu/pipercwcenter/how2journal/archive/print_archive/0192post .html.

77. Translating, *Tradition*, 35.

78. In 1999, *How2*, an online version of *HOW(ever)*, appeared under various editorships as a continuation of the print journal. The site contains archives of the original *HOW(ever)* and *How2*. *How2's* current URL is http://www.asu.edu/ pipercwcenter/how2journal/.

79. See Kinnahan for an extensive reading of *HOW(ever)* and a more detailed account of the politics of an alternative tradition.

80. Kinnahan, *Lyric Interventions*, 30.

81. Fraser, *Translating*, 2.

82. Ibid.

83. Ibid., 2–3.
84. Ibid., 35.
85. Fraser, "The Jump."
86. Ibid.
87. Fraser, *Translating*, 1.
88. Fraser, "The Jump."

Bibliography

DuPlessis, Rachel Blau. "postcards." *HOW(ever)*, volume 6, no. 4 (January 1992). http://www.asu.edu/pipercwcenter/how2journal/archive/print_archive/0192post.html.

———. "Manifests." *Diacritics* 26, no. 3 (1996): 31–53.

Evans, Steve. "After Patriarchal Poetry: Feminism and the Contemporary Avant-Garde. Introductory Note." *differences: A Journal of Feminist Cultural Studies* 12, no. 2 (Summer 2001): i–v.

Fraser, Kathleen. *il cuore: the heart—New and Selected Poems (1970–1995)*. Middletown, CT: Wesleyan University Press, 1997.

———. *Translating the Unspeakable: Poetry and the Innovative Necessity* Tuscaloosa: University of Alabama Press, 1999.

———. "Conversation with Suzanne Stein." 17 January 2007. *PennSound: Kelsey Street Press*. http://writing.upenn.edu/pennsound/x/Kelsey-Street.php.

Keller, Lynn. "'Just one of the Girls:—/normal in the extreme': Experimentalists-To-Be Starting Out in the 1960s." *differences: A Journal of Feminist Cultural Studies* 12, no 2. (Summer 2001): 47–69.

Kinnahan, Linda. *Lyric Interventions: Feminism, Experimental Poetry, and Contemporary Discourse*. Iowa City: University of Iowa Press, 2005.

Lundquist, Sara. "The Fifth Point of a Star: Barbara Guest and the New York 'School of Poets.'" *Barbara Guest: This Art*. Edited by Catherine Kaspar. Special Issue, *Women's Studies*, no. 30 (2001): 11–41.

O'Sullivan, Maggie. *Out of Everywhere: Linguistically Innovative Poetry by Women in North America and in the UK*. Hastings, UK: Reality Street Press, 1996.

Pritchett, Patrick. "An Excerpt from and Book Review of *il cuore: the heart: Selected Poems 1970–1995*." *Electronic Poetry Center*. November 12, 2011, http://epc.buffalo.edu/authors/fraser/review.html.

Robins, Corine. "Four Young Poets," *Mademoiselle*. 1959. Reprinted in *Empty Mirror: Magazine of the Arts*. 2 June 2012. http://www.emptymirrorbooks.com/images/poets/hart/mllereview.html.

Russo, Linda. "Introduction: a Context for Reading Joanne Kyger." *Jacket*, no. 11 (April 2000). http://jacketmagazine.com/11/kyger-russo.html.

Silliman, Ron. "Monday June 11, 2007." *Silliman's Blog: A Weblog Focused on Contemporary Poetry and Poetics*. June 11, 2007. http://ronsilliman.blogspot.com/2007/06/donald-allen-theres-no-such-thing-as.html.

Vickery, Ann. *Leaving Lines of Gender: A Feminist Genealogy of Language Writing* Middletown, CT: Wesleyan University Press, 2000.

CHAPTER EIGHT

~

"In the Dawn that is Nowhere": *The New American Poetry* and the State of Exception

David Herd

"The Visionary Anthology that Influenced Two Generations of Poets and Readers"

To assert, as The University of California Press does on the cover of the 1999 edition of *The New American Poetry*, that an anthology is (or was) "visionary" is to make a claim about the way the future has turned out. There are various ways to pitch such a claim, especially at it relates to poetry; "visionary" is not quite "prophetic," though it does hint in the direction of poetry's special powers. A less mystical formulation of the relation between a work and its subsequent future is offered by Ed Dorn who, in considering the durability of Charles Olson's achievement—an achievement closely tied to the durability of *The New American Poetry*—suggested that Olson's work "*anticipates* a millennium already underway in 1950."[1] "Anticipatory," though less appropriate as sales pitch, better indicates the qualities of writing at issue, suggesting a watchfulness in the present capable of discerning subsequent events. Alternatively, to take up Olson's language from the beginning, one might say that where an anthology has retained purchase on the future, what's at issue is that the work is still of "use."

The question I want to ask is what, in 1960, or between 1945 and 1960, can *The New American Poetry* be thought to have envisaged? In answering that question it is necessary at the outset to distinguish between the claims Allen made for the anthology in his "Preface," and the insight or foresight demonstrated, though his editorial emphases, by the poets themselves. This is in no sense to diminish Allen's role. It is to suggest, however, that the anthology projected successfully into the future despite certain editorial emphases, and that Allen's real insight—the way he was exemplary as an editor—was to trust to the practice of certain key poets, not least Olson. *The New American Poetry*, this is to say, has proved durable despite certain editorial constructions, but also because, against the background of those constructions, Allen had the nerve to promote poets whose work appeared to him best to be articulating and apprehending new realities.

One area of editorial blindness, as has been well observed, regarded the question of identity. In putting together his list of contributors, Allen singularly failed to envisage the revolutions in race and gender politics that were already, at the time of the anthology's conception, in an advanced stage of preparation. This thinking, or failure to think, about the question of identity generates only an implicit editorial claim; that aesthetically advanced poetry in America in the 1950s was a white male pursuit. A different area, if not of editorial blindness quite, then lack of foresight, connects to one of the two substantive claims Allen makes in his "Preface;" that, as he puts it, the new poetry, "has shown one common characteristic: a total rejection of all those qualities typical of academic verse."[2]

There is a truth in this of course, to do with the influence of the New Criticism, but Allen's claim was slackly formulated. The slackness lay in his failure to specify what the "qualities typical of academic verse" were, a specification that, in turn, might well have exposed the limitations of the adjective. What the claim certainly didn't anticipate was the degree to which the poetry he was presenting, and more so its successors, would come to mesh with the practices of the academy.

The editorial construction I am most interested in, however, not least because, as I argue, it conflicts seriously with the poetry's actual insights, has to do with Allen's second substantive claim, the claim of nation. This is what Allen says on that subject:

> These poets . . . are our avant-garde, the true continuers of the modern movement in American poetry. Through their work many are closely allied to modern jazz and abstract expressionist painting, today recognized throughout the world to be America's greatest achievements in contemporary culture. This anthology makes the same claim for the new American poetry, now becoming the dominant movement in the second phase of our twentieth-century literature and already exerting strong influence abroad.[3]

From one point of view this *was* visionary, in its incipient exceptionalism, in its claim on emerging American dominance, cultural or otherwise. Seeing an opportunity for American poetry to ride shotgun to American painting and music, what Allen anticipated was a world in which, for reasons of dominance, the pure products of America were going global. From the point of view of poetics, however, the identity Allen asserted between nation and artistic practice seems, now, somewhat unreflective. More to the point, I want to argue, his insistence in his preface on "our avant-garde" significantly misrepresented the way the poetry itself construed the issue of nation.

The intention of this essay is to begin to uncouple the material of the anthology from certain aspects of its editorial presentation. Insofar, that is, as Allen mediated *The New American Poetry* to potential audiences, the anthology now looks decidedly time-bound. Where Allen still seems brilliantly anticipatory is in his assessment of the strength and durability of certain poetic positions and developing bodies of work, not least among them that of the anthology's guiding spirit, Olson.

Allen's faith in Olson was evident, if originally invisibly so, in the anthology's basic parameters. His early plan for the anthology included an introductory section of recent work by high Modernist forbears, followed by a section presenting a middle Modernist generation. As Allen notes in the "Afterword," Olson vetoed that idea:

> I wldnt [sic] myself add either of these two units: either the "aunties" or the grandpas. If the thing we are now in is it is in its own character, and there isn't any one of us who isn't bound together in that way, than by any of those older connections. . . . Those connections strike me as smudging the point; 1950 on.[4]

The reasons for Olson's insistence on the date were complex and, no doubt in some respects, self-motivated. What Allen's adherence to the proposed time-frame shows is the value he placed on Olson's view. More visibly, Allen's sense of Olson's importance to the new poetries was clear from the bulk of the poet's presence at the beginning of the book. It is apparent also in the editorial preface, where Allen gives Olsonian poetics explicit priority. "Projective Verse" and the letter to Elaine Feinstein, are thus taken to present: "the dominant new double concept: 'composition by field' and the poet's 'stance toward reality.'"[5]

The argument here is that Olson's "stance toward reality," for all that it could sometimes itself collapse into exceptionalist rhetoric, was fundamentally at odds with Allen's stance toward the nation; that what in fact one finds in Olson's stance is a poetic, or rather a prosody, equal to crises in the idea of nationhood, crises that radical narratives of the state were already registering and anticipating. The particular narrative of state and nation I want to consider as point of comparison is that provided by Hannah Arendt in *The Origins of Totalitarianism*. Which brings us back to a date: the year 1950.

The Year 1950

For Olson, as his letter to Allen showed, the year 1950 had a foundational significance. Certainly it had been an important year, aesthetically, for him. It was the year he published "Projective Verse," in *Poetry New York*, and the year also he published the poem that would become the first of *The Maximus Poems*, "I, Maximus of Gloucester, to You" (both subsequently reprinted in *The New American Poetry*). What Olson wanted further to establish, however, above and beyond his own development, was that 1950 marked a beginning of a new period in poetics. In his insistence on the date one hears echoes of Pound's emphasis on turning points, or reverberations, perhaps, of the composition of *Moby-Dick*. 1950, that is, was to be understood, like 1914 or the summer of 1850, as a moment of aesthetic re-beginning, a re-beginning to be identified in the poet's new "stance toward reality." Wary as one needs to be about the vatic overtones of such a claim, there are reasons also to entertain it. Dorn dated the new millennium, a millennium marked by "terror and pandemia," from that mid-century moment. Allen, likewise, was persuaded that the aesthetic shift achieved in 1950 constituted the commencement of a new period.

The further reason to entertain the claim is given by the work of the moment itself. From 1949 to 1950, spurred by the radicalism of Black Mountain, under the influence of Frances Boldereff, and driven by revelations of the most devastating realities of the Second World War, Olson (alongside poet colleagues, most notably Duncan) was in a state of creativity so intense one can think of it as discovery. The question, then, bearing on the "visionary," or "anticipatory," or just still usable quality of *The New American Poetry* is: what should we take Olson's new "stance toward reality" to have registered? What new realities, in 1950, did "composition by field" begin to make visible?

At which point I want to leap to Arendt. "Summer 1950" was the date Arendt inscribed at the end of her preface to *The Origins of Totalitarianism*.[6] Written, and subsequently revised, in the United States, while Arendt was contributing to such journals as the *Nation* and *Partisan Review*, *The Origins of Totalitarianism* coincides closely with the production of *The New American Poetry*. Begun in 1945 and finished in 1950, Arendt's book was first published in the United States in 1951. It was reissued, following significant revision, in the States in 1958, and then published for the first time in Britain in 1961, the year *The New American Poetry* first appeared there. Arendt's narrative of state and nation was thus contemporary with the evolution of *The New American Poetry*. What she looked to present, as a matter of urgency at the end of the Second World War, was the new human reality toward which Olson was trying to adjust poetry's stance.

She was hardly alone; there are any number of other writers, émigré or otherwise, one might invoke. The particular reason for settling on Arendt's book as counterpoint to *The New American Poetry* is that it has itself proved darkly anticipatory. To be specific, the argument of her chapter "The Decline of the Nation State and the End of the Rights of Man" was revived by Giorgio Agamben as the basis for his presentation of the nation in *State of Exception*. What Arendt presents so grimly, and brilliantly, in other words, in that part of her account, is that reality of national self-definition which results inexorably in exclusion and internment. Allen didn't see this in 1960, and it's not what The University of California Press had in mind in 1999 when they described *The New American Poetry* as "visionary." What we can see from the vantage of the present moment, however, is that a number of the more prominent New American poets were writing out of deep anxiety towards the question of territory; that those Allen called "our avant-garde" were in fact articulating a significant challenge to the assumption of a relation between the practices of art and the apparatuses of the nation-state.

Arendt presented a broad-brushed account of the new reality she was seeking to establish in her Preface of 1950. The book

> was written . . . to discover the hidden mechanics by which all traditional elements of our political and spiritual world were dissolved into a conglomeration where everything seems to have lost specific value, and has become unrecognizable for human comprehension, unusable for human purpose.[7]

There is an interlacing of terms here that speaks directly to the priorities of what Allen, generalizing out of Olson, called the poet's "stance toward reality." One aspect of that new stance—a necessary corrective—was that specific value, the value of specifics, must be regained. Only, Arendt implies, with a recovery of specific value can a world be reestablished that is usable for human purpose. What Arendt is arguing for, it is no great stretch to suggest, is what Olson would term a Human Universe, one marker of which would be a cognitive insistence on specificity and use. What Arendt argues for also, however, is a new kind of map against which such values can be fixed. What recent political realities clearly demonstrate is that

> human dignity needs a new guarantee which can be found only in a political principle, in a new law on earth, whose validity this time must comprehend the whole of humanity while its power must remain strictly limited, rooted in and controlled by newly territorial entities.[8]

This being the preface, Arendt holds back the substance of her argument. The basic parameters, though, are clear enough. What she is looking to sketch is an environment in which specifics are accorded a new measure of dignity, and in which that measure—she calls it a guarantee—leads to a rethinking of international relations, a redefinition, as she puts it, of territorial entities. It is not such a leap, I'd like to propose, to the Olson of Black Mountain, insisting absolutely on singularities while working through the documents of myth and history towards a revised sense of how territories interrelate; to the Olson, for instance, who applied for a Fulbright in 1951 to make a study of Sumerian culture in Baghdad. The new "stance toward reality" that Allen identified in Olson and established as central to *The New American Poetry*, this is to say, involved both an explicit commitment to specificity *and* a commitment to a poetics of internationalism. How really that stance can be thought to be visionary, or anticipatory, or just still useful, is better understood through Arendt's development of her opening position.

The development I'm interested in is that which Arendt offers in "The Decline of the Nation State and the End of the Rights of Man." Written in 1957, for the second edition of the book, that chapter supplements her primary narrative, exploring the legacy rather than the origins of the thinking that produced totalitarianism, especially its legacy for the identity of the nation state. It is not possible, here, to communicate the full force of Arendt's argumentation. To try to summarize, though, as Arendt wrote in 1957, what she observed was a reality in which "the nation-state was no longer capable of facing the major political issues of the time."[9] This, as she set it out, was the consequence of the series of complex historical interactions that had made mainstream race-thinking possible, and which, following totalitarianism's terrible reinforcement, was the real consequence of the Second World War. The name for that consequence was "statelessness":

> The newest mass phenomenon in contemporary history, and the existence of an ever-growing new people comprised of stateless persons, the most symptomatic group in contemporary politics.[10]

For the aetiology of that phenomenon Arendt looked to the shift, closely tracked through late nineteenth and early twentieth-century international relations, from a model of the state underpinned by a commitment to equality before the law, to an idea of nation in which the law became "an instrument of the nation."[11] Sovereignty, Arendt patiently observes, became by this process identical with the definition of citizenship, which in turn became distinct from the claim to humanity as such. What nationhood had come to mean, in other words was the power to exclude, to place people outside its jurisdiction.

Dismayed by the reality she found herself describing in the 1950s—a reality in which "the number of stateless people—twelve years after the end of the war—[was] larger than ever"—Arendt pressed deep into the contradictions of the prevailing idea of the nation-state. Only in the modern environment, as she argued, with its "completely organized humanity" (a humanity organized according to the principle of national identity), "could the loss of home and political status become identical with an expulsion from humanity altogether." "Before this," as she put it,

> what we must call a "human right" today would have been thought of as general characteristic of the human condition. . . . Only the loss of a polity itself expels him from humanity.[12]

What Arendt was detailing, as Agamben appreciated, was the state of exception, that state in which a person is outside the law but subject to the law's force, the territory of exclusion in which human rights should, in theory, operate, but in which, in practice, a person's vulnerability is re-exposed. For Arendt this constituted a crisis in which, to reiterate, "the nation-state was no longer capable of facing the major political issues of the time." What was required, it followed, was a new kind of polity, a polity that registered people in the specificity of their mere existence, a polity in which expulsion would not be the routine and symptomatic practice it had increasingly become. None of which is registered in the rhetoric of Allen's claims for *The New American Poetry*, in the presentation of *"our* avant-garde." It is, though a governing concern of much of the writing itself. Or to put it the Olson way, "Polis is this."

"That presumption in a sacred place"

Anticipatory as it turned out to be of a number of highly significant poetic careers, and therefore instrumental as it was in shaping a poetic future, *The New American Poetry* now seems, even so, curiously restricted in the sense it presents of postmodern writing. What one barely glimpses, because in that context one barely glimpses him, is the range of poetic developments that have emerged out of Ashbery. As Allen states, the poetic predecessors most clearly invoked by the poets he presents are Pound and Williams; not, therefore, as they might have been, Stein and Stevens. What one gets little warning of, then, from the *New American Poetry*, is either the ludic postmodernism of, say, James Tate, or the turn to LANGUAGE out of the poems of *The Tennis Court Oath*. These strains are not altogether absent, and the New York School, in so far as it manifests them, is generously represented; but such strains do not prevail. What one finds instead, on revisiting *The New American Poetry*, is a postwar book, a book whose collective sense of a postmodern departure is shaped by a felt need to engage with the realities of the postwar period. One measure of this, in contradistinction to a turn to language, is a marked (though not of course universal) insistence that language should reconstitute its relation to bodies, one measure of which is the attention *The New American Poetry* pays to the dead.

Ed Dorn's poem, "The Air of June Sings," is an example of this. The poem finds, or sets, the speaker and his daughter in a cemetery. The poem is elegiac, of course; as elegy, though, it has a particular kind of concern. As the speaker states

> a 6 inch square of sandstone, flush with the earth
> is more proper for the gone than blurred and faded flags.
> Than the blurred and faded flags I am walking with in the graveyard.[13]

The poem does not disclose the character of "the blurred and faded flags," though in mentioning them it does establish a distinction between kinds of symbol, between the square of sandstone, which is appropriate, and the flags, which are not. It is this distinction that gives Dorn's elegy its specific character. Thus, as the speaker goes on to say:

> My eyes avoid
> the largest stone, larger than the common large, Goodpole
> Matthews,
> Pioneer, and that pioneer sticks in me like a wormed black cherry
> in my throat, No Date, nothing but that zeal, that trekking
> and Business, that presumption in a sacred place, where children
> are buried, and where peace, as it is in the fields and the country
> should reign. A wagon wheel is buried there. Lead me away
> to the small quiet stones of the unpreposterous dead.[14]

Dorn's poem is fuelled by the resentment that the person the speaker addresses has been treated less notably than the "Pioneer" he here observes. The point of the poem, though, is not the commonplace that death is, or should be, a leveler. The point lies more precisely in the phrase, "that presumption in a sacred place." This poem, like many of the more durable poems in *The New American Poetry*, sets out to establish a place that is sacred, a territory, however limited, which is unaffected by presumption, where the presumption, in this case, takes the form of national markers.

It would be good to dwell on Dorn's poem, and especially on the implications of his term "presumption." But there are other significant examples. Robin Blaser is represented by five poems, three of which make the matter, but more importantly the manner, of dying their subject. In "Poem by the Charles River," Blaser sees how:

> Fish feed on fish
> and drop those beautiful bones [. . .]
> These fish die easily.

This ecology contrasts, in the anthology, with the fourth part of Blaser's poem "A Part Geometry Lesson":

> That's it. All those dead children
> What calm eyes. A machine gun
> tore them out of the grass.[15]

The manner of death is the issue, hence, also, "Poem," in which Blaser anticipates the moment when he will "pay death's duty," and where the point of the poem is only to try to imagine:

> what I think is that there's a sparrow in an old
> man's heart and it flies up—
> Thus
> in the wrinkling flesh the discovery of disgust.[16]

Like Dorn, Blaser is not writing elegy in any straightforward sense. What matters to him is that death, or more precisely dying, should become part of the discourse and what he attends to, therefore, is the way dying occurs. He does not, as Dorn does, or as Duncan does, explicitly invoke either a language of ceremony or an idea of the sacred. What he seeks to ensure, though, is a cultural setting, the setting of the poem, in which the end of the body can be contemplated as such.

It is an issue that comes back, in the context of *The New American Poetry*, to Olson. Read as postwar poetry, as poetry explicitly concerned with the legacies of the politics that generated the war, the poems Olson is represented by in Allen's anthology read, collectively, as works of mourning. It is a complex picture. The two longest poems in the Olson section of the anthology are elegies: "The Death of Europe," subtitled "a funeral poem for Rainer M. Gerhardt," and "As The Dead Prey Upon Us," a poem in memory of the poet's mother. Elegy, in a characteristically large sense, the largest sense perhaps, was arguably Olson's major mode. It was a major mode for him because, as in both of the anthologized examples, but as also, say, in his great poem "The Librarian," elegy granted him access to his most pressing themes: legacy, continuity, influence, rupture. As Olsonian elegy is presented in *The New American Poetry*, however, it comes charged with a specific question: how to bury the dead. Consider the opening of Section II of "The Kingfishers":

> They buried their dead in a sitting posture
> serpent cane razor ray of the sun
>
> And she sprinkled water on the head of the child, crying
> "Ciao-coatl! Ciao-coatl!"
>
> Where the bones are found, in each personal heap
> with what each enjoyed, there is always
> the Mongolian louse.[17]

Written in 1949, and the poem in which Olson first arrived at the poet's new "stance toward reality," "The Kingfishers" is a work of fragile physiologies, which, in its method of composition by field, sets out to grant those physiologies their necessary space. Here, at the beginning of section II, the question of physiology becomes, as in Dorn's poem, a question of ceremony and sacredness, except that where Dorn arrived at the question in a nearby cemetery, Olson, the intellectual comparativist, makes the issue international. It is a question, for him, of setting specifics against a redefined sense of territorial relation. What's necessary for Olson, as for Dorn and Blaser, is a poetic methodology that allows bodies to appear as such.

"To Bend the Ear of the Outer World"

I will return, by way of conclusion, to the implications of what Allen called "the dominant new double concept: 'composition by field' and the poet's 'stance toward reality.'" Briefly, though, I want to stay with the bodies of *The New American Poetry*, the live ones this time, not the dead.

There are instances in the anthology of bodies that are sure of themselves, or at least instances of bodies that are sure of others. In Paul Blackburn's poem "The Once-Over," for instance, the speaker is pretty sure of himself, and more so of the blond woman he is gazing at. "Sure" is a Blackburn word in fact, as in his poem, "The Problem":

> My wife broke a dollar tube of perfume.
>   The arab
> who owns the perfume shop, insisted
>   it was good luck.
> Sure it was.[18]

Blackburn is unusual in being "sure." For the most part the bodies presented by *The New American Poetry* are fragile, acutely aware of their basic vulnerability. Frank O'Hara sets up the terms in "In Memory of my Feelings," where, in the voice of the serpent in the closing section, he offers himself up for scrutiny. "I am not quite you," the speaker suggests, "but almost, the opposite of visionary." It's an important phrase, "not quite . . . but almost," establishing a principle of commensurability between speaker and addressee, and where the likeness consists not in the visionary but in its opposite, here fragility. As O'Hara says, beautifully:

> the prey
> is always fragile and like something, as a seashell can be
> a great Courbet, if it wishes. To bend the ear of the outer world.[19]

Again the phrasing is precise: "the prey is always fragile *and* like something" (my italics), "not quite you," perhaps, "but almost"; the point of commonality, the way people are like one another, lying precisely in that common fragility. Which leaves O'Hara's injunction: "To bend the ear of the outer world."

"Bending the ear of the outer world," and especially bending it to—or on the subject of—the fragile body, could well be taken (as much as any single injunction might be taken) to be the guiding ethical principle of *The New American Poetry*. It is Allen Ginsberg's objective, clearly enough, in *Howl*, that work being, memorably, "the absolute heart of the poem of life butchered out of their/ own bodies good to eat a thousand years."[20] It is John Weiners' subject in "Poem for Painters" where, in our age, bereft of nobility, "we go driven by forces over which we have no control."[21] It is Duncan's subject in "The Song of the Borderguard," where the theme and difficulty of border crossing is variously expressed, and where the poem closes by identifying itself "naked as a line of poetry in a war." It is variously the issue also, in "Poem Beginning with a Line by Pindar," with its framing territorial question, "Who is it that goes there?" and its repeated presentation of "bodies" out of context, bodies, as the poem says, "not in a landscape."[22]

As with other recurring questions in the anthology, however, it is Olson who frames the fragility of the body in its larger context; his poem "The Distances" setting various bodies in various contexts of power. Like "The Kingfishers," "The Distances" is explicitly a "composition by field," the various elements of the poem standing in difficult and unresolved relation to one another, so that the reader is involved in establishing how Zeus, Pygmalion, Galatea, Augustus, and the German Inventor in Key West combine to make the poem's meaning. How they compare is in a shared preoccupation with

the manipulation of physiologies. Crucial though—in the context of arguments about territory and specificity, and against the background of Arendt's
articulation of the need for a new guarantee for human dignity—is the frame
Olson's poem tries to construct; the way it imagines bodies in conjunction
with distance, the way it aims to place specifics:

> O love who places all where each is, as they are, for every moment,
> yield
> > to this man
> > > that the impossible distance
> be healed.[23]

"Composition by Field"

The claim I made, at the outset, was that Olson's "stance toward reality" is
fundamentally at odds with Allen's stance toward the nation; that what one
finds in Olson's stance is a poetic, or rather a prosody, equal to crises in the
idea of nationhood. I pressed that claim through Arendt's account of the
"The Decline of the Nation State and the End of the Rights of Man" because
Arendt, more than any commentator of her time, registered the implications
of nationhood for contemporary politics. Arendt matters here also because in
her argument she prepared the ground for Agamben's discussion of the *State
of Exception*, a book occasioned by, but in no sense limited to, recent realities of American self-definition. The argument turned to *The New American
Poetry*'s presentation of the vulnerable body because in that presentation one
finds a shared (if by no means collective) effort to establish settings in which
the body as such, not as bearer of status, might be properly considered. Still,
though, there's the deferred formal claim with which to deal.

Allen's contention was that the "poet's stance toward reality" and "composition by field" amounted to the "dominant new double concept" of the new
poetry. This still seems right. Olson's influence on poetics is apparent in many
of the statements that conclude the anthology. More to the point, in the context of the anthology, composition by field seems axiomatic to much of the new
practice itself: to O'Hara, say, James Schuyler, Philip Whalen, or LeRoi Jones.
(An exception is Ginsberg, in whom, specifics, though material to the production, aren't guaranteed as such but instead fuel the machinery of the voice.)
What Olson arrived at, or at least gave articulation to, in "Projective Verse" in
1950 thus still seems, as Allen argued, to have been a decisive advance.

Given the order of the advance—a new "stance toward reality"—and
given the historical conditions in which that advance was made, one perhaps

doesn't have to advertise the poet's awareness of his moment. The fact is, though, that Olson was, again in a large sense, as politically attuned as a poet might be. As he announced to the Pacific Northwest Writers' Conference in Washington in August 1947:

> What bores me, and angers me as much in writing as in foreign policy, are those who clutch old answers in a new, terrifying world.[24]

In Olson's mind, the new writing he was struggling to bring in to being was intimately linked to a reality still shaped by the old answers of foreign policy.

Olson's new answer in writing, however, is in no sense governed by an image of policy, or rather, gets far below anything a policy maker might register as thought. What Olson proposes for the page itself is a means of composition in which all elements of writing are registered. Thus:

> every element in an open poem . . . must be taken up as participants in the kinetic of the poem just as solidly as we are accustomed to take what we call the objects of reality.

Equally important, those objects:

> which occur at any given moment of composition (of recognition, we can call it) are, can be, must be treated exactly as they do occur therein and not by any ideas or preconceptions from outside the poem, must be handled as a series of tensions (which they also are) are made to *hold*.[25]

That, as O'Hara might say, is for the "composition by field" part—where what the new method calls for is a recognition and treatment of specifics as such; that they might be "handled as a series of tensions"; that they, the specifics, might be made to "hold." At the level of writing then, of prosody, one finds a pressing analogy. Olson, like Arendt, is determined to resist "conglomeration."

More important in his context, though, is the poet's stance "toward reality," where the issue is, as Olson puts it, "the degree to which the projective involves a stance toward reality outside a poem as well as a new stance toward the reality of the poem itself."[26] This is a question of the poet's conduct, for which, as opposed to "lyricism" and "objectivism," Olson proposes the term "objectism." The point of that term is to signal that the poet must understand his or her relation to other objects, that he or she is an object among objects. Which means that on the question of the outside, there is no outside; not that there is no reality, but that the idea of "outside" does not describe it. What Olson formulated, in other words, in 1950, was a poetic method that refused exclusions, that tried to conceive of itself in such a way that, for the poem at least, all elements hold good.

"In the dawn that is nowhere"

I close with two images—one out of Duncan, one out of Olson—both of which return questions of poetic method to questions of territory. Duncan closes "A Poem Beginning With a Line by Pindar" this way:

> In the dawn that is nowhere
> I have seen the willful children
> clockwise and counter-clockwise turning.[27]

Olson, interpreted by Butterick, opened the third volume of *The Maximus Poems* this way:

> having descried the nation
> to write a republic
> in gloom on Watch-House Point[28]

Deeply concerned with the relation of bodies to power, Duncan's poem ends up "nowhere," permissive as that state is of "clockwise and counter-clockwise turning," of different ways of doing the same thing. Olson, always more the politician, opted for an actual space, but one, as he hoped, in which the practices of the nation might be held at bay; where instead of a "nation" he might "write a republic," the difference predicated on an open stance.

Notes

1. Quoted in Tom Clark, *Charles Olson: The Allegory of a Poet's Life* (Berkeley, North Atlantic Books, 2000), xiv.

2. Donald Allen (ed.), *The New American Poetry 1945–1960* (Berkeley and Los Angeles, University of California Press, 1999), xi.

3. Ibid., xi-xii.

4. Ibid., 448.

5. Ibid., xiv.

6. Hannah Arendt, *The Origins of Totalitarianism* (London: George Allen and Unwin Ltd, 1967), xxxi.

7. Ibid., xxx.

8. Ibid., xxxi.

9. Ibid., 261.

10. Ibid., 277.
11. Ibid., 230.
12. Ibid., 297.
13. Allen, *New American Poetry 1945–1960*, 104.
14. Ibid., 105.
15. Ibid., 138, 139.
16. Ibid., 140.
17. Ibid., 6.
18. Ibid., 72.
19. Ibid., 249.
20. Ibid., 189.
21. Ibid., 365.
22. Ibid., 41, 50.
23. Ibid., 39.
24. Clark, *Charles Olson*, 124.
25. Allen, *New American Poetry 1945–1960*, 391.
26. Ibid., 394.
27. Ibid., 57.
28. Charles Olson, *The Maximus Poems* (Berkeley: University of California Press, 1983), 377.

Bibliography

Agamben, Giorgio. *State of Exception*. Translated by Kevin Attell. Chicago: University of Chicago Press, 2005.

Allen, Donald, ed. *The New American Poetry 1945–1960*. Berkeley: University of California Press, 1999.

Arendt, Hannah. *The Origins of Totalitarianism*. London: George Allen and Unwin Ltd., 1967.

Clark, Tom. *Charles Olson: The Allegory of a Poet's Life*. Berkeley: North Atlantic Books, 2000.

Olson, Charles. *The Maximus Poems*. Berkeley: University of California Press, 1983.

CHAPTER NINE

Science and *The New American Poetry*

Peter Middleton

In 1967 Penguin published *The New Writing in the USA*, edited by Donald Allen and Robert Creeley, one of a series of anthologies including *African Writing Today*, *South African Writing Today*, *Latin American Writing Today*, and *German Writing Today*. As the title hints, this was what we might call the Tauchnitz or export version of *The New American Poetry 1945–1960*, making it a revealing lens for re-examining its predecessor. By echoing the title of Donald Allen's earlier anthology instead of calling the new anthology something like "American Writing Today," the publishers and editors signalled an unusually close relationship between the literary scopes of the two anthologies. The Penguin anthologies in the series were not, however, solely collections of poetry; they included fiction, drama and essays as well as poetry, and they shared a pre-planned format. So the inclusion of Richard Brautigan, William Burroughs, Jack Kerouac, John Rechy, Michael Rumaker, Hubert Selby Jr., and Douglas Woolf, as well as fiction from Robert Creeley and Edward Dorn, marks a significant difference from Allen's collection. A "New American Poet" is now presented as part of a larger movement of fiction writers and dramatists, a shift that put pressure on the editors to explain the shared aesthetic. Both editors duly contributed revealing introductions. The new anthology was an opportunity for some rethinking of just who should be admitted to the movement, notably to remedy one of the main flaws of the earlier anthology, the evident injustice of excluding Louis Zukofsky, an omission which cost him dearly. Now Zukofsky is represented by a section from "A"-13, written around the year of Allen's anthology, which gives his sentiment that poets now write for the bass drum and "oneself" appears to be one of the few still attuned to the "intimacy of one response."[1] The poignancy of this must have registered with Creeley, a poet similarly uninterested in writing loud, political poems, preferring to embed his finely worked vernacular lyrics within intimacies of family and friendship.[2]

Given the necessary reduction in the pages available for poetry, *The New Writing in the USA* also makes some significant adjustments to its list of inclusions. The core figures remain with the exception of Robert Duncan who refused permission to use "Apprehensions" saying he was "disenchanted with anthologies"[3] while James Koller, Joanne Kyger, and George Stanley make an appearance, and a considerable number of poets are dropped, including Paul Blackburn, Larry Eigner, Joel Oppenheimer, and Philip Lamantia. It is unclear whether we should believe Allen's lament that strict publishing constraints meant the editors were unable to find room for other writers, since blaming the parsimony of the publishers is often a get-out clause for editors. But by far the biggest change is the way that this whole literary movement is pitched to readers, and for this we have Creeley to thank. In a substantial introductory essay he diverges from Allen's prefatory characterization of the New American writers as "'hip'" practitioners of a "*new* realism"[4] [my italics], turning away from what he dismisses as "the usual critical vocabulary"[5] to a sometimes strained discourse populated by abstractions such as "things," "particulars," "space," "reality" and "self" that variously "take place," and "act," abstractions which despite their seeming blandness Creeley treats as points of great intensity.[6] These abstractions provide a poetics for the New American poetry based on a network of allusions to the sciences, a new emphasis that is supported by the choice of many poems with scientific leanings. In this chapter I shall explore the implications of dressing the New American poets in lab coats.

Donald Allen's essay comes first in the anthology, under the title "Writer as Native: Preface." Allen characterizes the writers selected for the anthology as "new," repeating the modernist claim to priority that had been evident in his choice of title for the earlier anthology. These writers look back to the high modernists and "turn away from the sterile examples of the writers of the thirties and forties."[7] What does this new fecundity entail? Williams showed how it was possible to write about "the actual conditions of the American experience"[8] while Pound "showed the possibilities of creating a high culture by opening the portals to the Classical and Oriental cultures."[9] In other words, Allen's poetic values have two foundations, an appeal for empirical accuracy as signalled by the insistence on the "actual," and a desire for American culture to engage with other, non-European literary traditions in order to make possible a "high culture" in America. As we shall see, this is one of the dividing lines with Creeley, who similarly shares a commitment to observation, accuracy of representation, and a reinvigorated realism, but has no interest in creating an elevated culture. Allen also characterizes the writers as part of a community, explaining that the "chief architects" of "the larger community thus formed"[10] were Ginsberg, Olson, and his co-editor Creeley (not apparently Duncan), a claim that is about as close as Allen gets to saying what sort of structural connection there is between these poets. We might also wonder about the writers who are deliberately excluded by Allen. Isn't there something historically insensitive in the airbrushing out of the movement supposedly "sterile examples of the poets of the thirties and forties" when these included poets such as the Objectivists (George Oppen would win the Pulitzer Prize for *Of Being Numerous* in 1969), and activists like Muriel Rukeyser who would produce another major work, *The Speed of Darkness* (widely credited as the first great Second Wave feminist work of poetry) just a year after the Allen and Creeley anthology?

In 1960, Allen felt little need to justify using the adjective "new" to describe his chosen poets, as if this quality were self-evident. Now in 1967, perhaps because of the inclusion of prose or just because the passing of time had been an opportunity for skeptics to question the criteria on which the New American poetry was constituted, he clearly felt that it required more argument. Any critic claiming that a poetry is "new" is endorsing a primarily modernist perspective which values art in temporal terms insofar as it sets itself apart from the immediate let alone the more distant past, making novelty a necessary though not sufficient claim to value, so that the claim to be new has to be justified in terms of some formal or thematic break with the past. What then makes *these* writers new? His answer is to argue that this poetry is "civic" (we can hear the voice of Robin Blaser here, whom Allen credits as an advisor for this introduction), "intellectually alert," more "critically ethical and humane" than that of the older generation of writers who had lost touch with modernism and, most strikingly, it is capable of a new "eloquence," a term he probably uses because it derives from the tradition of rhetoric as a foundation of the civic, public sphere.[11] In effect, these poets have "a heightened awareness of all the terms and possibilities of our present, our reality" and "strive to regain that eloquence which is only possible when the voice of the poet is that of the whole man."[12] Such language may have been little more than a tacit acknowledgement of the then widespread celebration of drugs that would "open" consciousness, but it can also be understood as a gesture towards the rigors of observation and analysis that a new realism might entail. This at least turns out to be how Creeley thinks of it, though he avoids any hint that artificiality or eloquence distinguish the anthologized writers.

Creeley's introduction is a surprise after Allen's. This supposedly "New American" writer never uses the word "new" to describe this poetry, downplays questions of high modernist literary influence, talks primarily about poetics despite the wider remit of the collection, and supplants the civic with the scientific. His very first sentence—"Nothing will fit if we assume a place for it"[13]—echoes the Pragmatist idea of scientific method as inviting new empirical evidence to confirm, refute, or revise a theory. Creeley presents a world in which writers are faced by rules, by theories which no longer fit the facts, so that like scientists, during what Thomas Kuhn calls a "paradigm shift," they are "driven back upon the particulars of their own experience, the literal *things* of an immediate environment."[14] We should notice that the tangibility of "things" is opposed to the intangibility of literary "eloquence," perhaps even that new eloquence which Allen claimed to hear in New American poetry. In this opening section of his four part introduction, Creeley presents three touchstones: a passage from Robert Duncan's "Ideas on the Meaning of Form"; a passage from William Carlos Williams's introduction to *The Wedge* in which Williams outlines a poetics that follows the grain of ordinary language, a passage that Creeley cited many times; and Ginsberg's famous account of how he composed *Howl* by deciding to "open secrecy"[15] and to write without fear of exposure or ridicule. What unites all three of these passages is an insistence on a poetics that is as accurate as possible in its treatment of direct experience, a poetics of exact observation of self and world in which, in Duncan's words, "men and things were beginning to mix and cross boundaries of knowledge."[16]

Experience is a concept that John Dewey and earlier American Pragmatists had made foundational for knowledge and inquiry, but as Richard Bernstein explains, had by the 1950s come to seem an unhelpfully vague bit of intellectual debris from the past. How could inquiry as a search for knowledge arise from ordinary experiences which are not in themselves self-conscious? According to Bernstein's reading of Dewey, inquiry is instigated by situations that in themselves contain tensions or conflicts that are "problematic for us."[17] Just how such inquiry can proceed however always remained uncertain for Dewey:

> Therefore, it would seem that those ideas which function as theories and hypotheses in scientific experimentation and organization are not copies of sensations nor suggested by past experience, by past observation, but that they have a free, imaginative quality that no direct sensation or observation can have.[18]

The awkwardness of Creeley's terminology is partly due to his recognition that it is now insufficient to appeal to experience alone as a ground for reliable knowledge of the world; experience needs to be aligned with newer, more organized forms of experientially based attention and curiosity of the kind exemplified by the sciences. Poets must write about *"what is real"*[19] [his italics], and to do so they will need to understand precisely what the real world is actually like. By way of further explanation, Creeley cites a substantial passage from Olson's essay, "Equal, That Is, to the Real Itself." Olson writes that in the nineteenth century "an idea shook loose, and energy and motion became as important a structure of things as that they are plural and have mass" and the human being became an object of inquiry, "a thing among things."[20] Olson does not use the word science to name these nineteenth century developments so Creeley makes this connection explicit, adding immediately after the passage from Olson that "this recognition had come primarily from scientific thinking, as it might be called."[21] "As it might be called"? How else might such language be described? The final clause is there to defend against the idea that Olson is merely calling for poets to treat scientific knowledge uncritically as truth, rather than calling for recognition of the contribution that poets and novelists have made alongside the sciences to our knowledge of the nature of things.

From this point on, Creeley himself adopts a more evidently scientific terminology of his own, arguing that the two great fundamentals of physics, space and time, are also fundamental to the New American poetry, whose nature is therefore "to move in the field of its recognitions."[22] On one level this assertion of an equivalence between physics and poetry amounts to no more than affirming that poetry should not be displaced by science, that poetry is as objective a form of knowledge as that produced by science. On another level this amounts to the more ambitious argument that when poets use their senses keenly, and observe what happens as scrupulously as possible without preconceptions, their poetry can be an enactment of knowledge rather than a reproduction of existing knowledge from outside the poem:

> One cannot describe it [the "actual"], so to speak. Either one acts in an equal sense—becomes the issue of a term "as real as real can be"—or else there is really nothing to be said. Again, the writing here collected seems to me distinct in point of its distance from the usual habit of *description*—by which I mean that practice that wants to "accompany" the *real* but which assumes itself as "objectively" outside that context in some way. Certainly it is possible to minimize or otherwise distort one's concern in a given matter or relation. Yet one is either there or not, and being there, cannot assume some "not being" so as to "talk about it."[23]

The "usual habit" that he mentions would be the then widespread belief in philosophical and literary spheres that a description is no more than a label, a meaning dependent on what is labelled, the object, person or event which guarantees its validity. Creeley's reasoning is in line with the emergence of a renewal of Pragmatism in American thought, associated with amongst others, Wilfrid Sellars, who argued in 1957 that "although describing and explaining (predicting, retrodicting, understanding) are *distinguishable*, they are also, in an important sense, *inseparable*."[24] Arguments about description are indeed deeply entwined with American philosophy, and are currently the live edge of one of the most controversial and influential recent studies of epistemology, John McDowell's *Mind and World*, a study of just where perception and cognition meet. Description is also central to our leading contemporary exponent of Pragmatism today, Robert Brandom.

In his recent outline of his pragmatist theory of language, *Reason in Philosophy*, Brandom glosses Sellars's claim by saying that "in order to understand the content of the description, we must know something about what other descriptive contents its applicability gives us sufficient reason to apply, which other descriptions would give us reason to apply that one, and which further descriptions it rules out."[25] Brandom calls this a revision of pragmatism based on the insight that because "the *inferential* relations sentences stand in to one another are an essential element of the *meanings* that they express"[26] our verbal interactions depend not only on logical but also on normative concepts. This may still sound mere a matter of logic and linguistic abstraction, but not so, because these normative concepts are irreducibly social constructions, and when we invoke them, implicitly or explicitly, "what we are doing is claiming authority and undertaking responsibility, altering our commitments and entitlements in ways that depend on what is a reason for what."[27] Although he does not consciously use this type of philosophical vocabulary, Creeley, like Olson and many of his contemporaries, was deeply influenced by the American pragmatist tradition, and in his preface is effectively arguing that by avoiding bad habits of "description," the New American poets are committed to "claiming authority and undertaking responsibility, altering . . . commitments and entitlements" in poetic form. They are making sense through poetry of material, cultural, and affective worlds.

But we can also locate a scientific source for Creeley's reasoning here. The underlying thought not only derives from Pragmatism, it also echoes the text of Werner Heisenberg's widely read *Physics and Philosophy* (published in 1958). Perhaps because Heisenberg was still a questionable public figure not yet forgiven for his association with the Nazi nuclear program, Creeley does not credit him as the source of his ideas about the embeddedness of the observer in what is observed. In *Physics and Philosophy*, Heisenberg explains that, counter-intuitively, there is a "subjective element in the description of atomic events, since the measuring device has been constructed by the observer, and we have to remember that what we observe is not nature in itself but nature exposed to our questioning."[28] Scientists need to be reminded of this "uncertainty principle" because the old, "classical physics started from the belief—or should one say from the illusion?—that we could describe the world or at least parts of the world without any reference to ourselves."[29] The problem with trying to treat an object of study as wholly separate from the rest of the world (which includes the observer) is that observer and object necessarily interact during the process of measurement. Creeley's echoes of Heisenberg suggest that the new poetry is to be understood not just in some general way as being as much a site of reliable investigation of the human world as physics is of the material world, but also as something closer to science because it too measures the inherence of uncertainty in all acts of perceptually based understanding. The poetics of the New American poetry is for Creeley a literary analogue to the methods of quantum physics, and the poem is a site of inquiry rather than a record of discoveries made elsewhere.

Heisenberg is not the only modern scientist who provides a conceptual language for Creeley's interpretation of the poetics of the New American poetry. Creeley's conclusion contains another. Here is the final resounding endorsement of the new poetry expressed in remarkably airless abstractions: "That undertaking most useful to writing as an art is, for me, the attempt to *sound* in the nature of the language those particulars of time and place of which one is a given instance, equally present. I find it here."[30] "Particulars of time and space of which one is a given instance"? What could this possibly mean? Is the poet meant to celebrate what William Bronk, in his poem "The Thinker Left Looking Out the Window," drily calls "grossness . . . all the atoms he carried with him?"[31] Given the apparently personal authenticity of this affirmation ("that undertaking most useful to writing as an art is, *for me*") it is surprising to realize that Creeley is actually echoing very closely another popular science book, Erwin Schrödinger's lectures on *What is Life?*, published in 1944. *What is Life?* had become a classic of modern popular science literature that was widely credited with having influenced many biologists, not least James Watson and Francis Crick, who discovered the structure of DNA. Schrödinger, one of the leading first generation quantum physicists, answers the question in his title by drawing on theories of entropy from both statistical and quantum mechanics, and applying these insights to recent biological research into the mechanisms of heredity. In a formulation that Creeley borrowed for his introduction, Schrödinger tells his audience at the start of the first lecture that his aim is to ask whether physics can help us understand the workings of living organisms: "How can the events in space and time which take place within the spatial boundary of a living organism be accounted for by physics and chemistry?"[32] Instead of laying claim to complete knowledge over these events, Schrödinger concedes that they cannot yet be fully explained by the methods of physics, and that recent genetics research by Max Delbrück and others strongly suggests that "living matter, while not eluding the 'laws of physics' as established up to date, is likely to involve 'other laws of physics' hitherto unknown, which, however, once they have been revealed, will form just as integral a part of this science as the former."[33] When Creeley echoes Schrödinger's central question he is also alluding to this idea that there might be new physical laws to be discovered and hinting that poetry may be capable of joining the search. This after all is the aspiration that opens Olson's essay "Human Universe," reprinted in *The New Writing in the USA*, an essay which begins with the ringing assertion that "there are laws, that is to say, the human universe is as discoverable as that other."[34]

Rather than treating Allen's prefatory remarks as dissonant with Creeley's, we could argue that what Allen represents as the responsible, critical ethics of the New American poets is largely the same as what Creeley represents as the self-reflexive acts of the observer who is explicitly part of what is observed. Is the enactment of the real that Creeley endorses, the act that is equal to the real, then a new humanist ethics? Or to put it in terms of Creeley's scientific commitments that I have been making explicit, is the scientific stance actually a way of articulating a new ethics (and perhaps a politics too)?

When Creeley ends his essay by saying he finds in the work collected in *The New Writing in the USA* this understanding of the need for a recognition of how the observer is embedded in the observed material world of spacetime, his claim is easily supported from within the choice of poems in the anthology, a consonance which is revealing. An editorial hand has been able to locate material by the New American poets that provides just such an emphasis. The choice of poems readily demonstrates just how much what Creeley understands to be the New American poetics of observation and inquiry aligns itself with scientific ideals. In "Hermit Poems," Lew Welch challenges his readers to "step out onto the Planet. / Draw a circle a hundred feet round" and see how many things they can locate that "nobody understands."[35] In "Love Poems," Jack Spicer ruefully notes that the distances he feels in his lovelorn condition, and the distances of poetry, don't behave like the scientists say—"Distance, Einstein said, goes round in circles"[36]—which would mean that both love and poetry would return. Even the wave particle duality of the California beach—"the tidal swell / Particle and wave / Wave and particle / Distances"[37]—holds no hope of relief. Gilbert Sorrentino has a witty poem called "The Mathematics,"[38] Barbara Guest questions the aesthetic discourse of progress and its "heavy and pure logic" in "The Blue Stairs"[39] and, from this perspective, the poems of James Koller and Gary Snyder seem positively zoological and geological. Even John Ashbery might be talking, in "The Ecclesiast" (and perhaps also "These Lacustrine Cities"), about the need for a new scientific revolution: "you see how honey crumbles your universe / Which seems like an institution."[40] A similar emphasis is much harder to find amongst the poems Allen chose for the original anthology. The inclusion of Zukofsky in the Allen and Creeley anthology is particularly apt, because in a passage from *Bottom: On Shakespeare*, first published in *Origin* in July 1961 and therefore more widely circulated than most of the rest of the work, Zukofsky quotes Charles Sanders Pierce as saying that long "contemplation and study of the physico-psychical universe can imbue a man with principles of conduct analogous to the influence of a great man's works or conversation,"[41] an ethics of natural science that might be justification for the emulations and transformations of science in New American poetry.

Turning back to *The New American Poetry*, what new light does Creeley's interpretation of the poetry, and the choice of poets in the later revised picture of the movement, shine on Allen's anthology? There are several ways to understand this question. We could look individually and then collectively at the careers of these poets and at the bodies of work they produced in order to decide whether science played a part in their poetics. I will claim without further explanation here that the careers of some of these poets, including Olson, Creeley, Duncan, Snyder, McClure, and the later Baraka, do provide extensive evidence of such interests, and that an active suspicion of science can be discerned in O'Hara, Ashbery, and others. But this doesn't quite address our question, since in many of these instances the poets only became articulate about science later in their careers. What evidence is there that the very possibility of assembling this diverse yet interlocking group of poets under the name New American poets was partially due to their active engagement with ideas of research and models of the material universe that were current in the public reception of the natural sciences around 1960? My argument will be that in order to be perceptive enough to register signs of scientific interest amongst the poets we need now to reflect on what the sciences meant to Americans around 1960, and then to bring this knowledge together with Creeley's special synthesis of concepts, and reread Allen's anthology, when we will begin to see just how much science meant to these poets. We will also notice that the choice of poems, made by Allen, and the choice of themes for poetics essays made by the poets themselves are slightly at odds. The poets are more interested in the sciences than the poems which have been chosen to represent them.

To an American poet in the 1950s and early 1960s, physics was unavoidable. Vast amounts of government funding, mostly from defense agencies, flowed into physics research, notably the building of linear accelerators for studying high-energy particles. Poets thought of physicists as being in the position of the character Travis in Philip Whalen's 1967 novel *You Didn't Even Try* who, because he "knew a lot about theoretical physics" and "had a lot of ideas about why the current theories were probably all wrong," is "paid a lot of money by Stanford University to sit around discussing why he thought so with another two or three amiable eccentricks [*sic*] like himself"[42] and could earn even more if he wanted to work on military projects for the government or the corporations. *Scientific American* magazines of the period bristle with advertisements about weapons projects: "A New Role for the Mature Scientist . . . in a unique Military Systems Organization created by RCA" (ellipses in original) begins the long copy of an advertisement in the February 1960 issue, reminding us also that the adjective "new" was not only the province of poetry.[43] The heavens too were the province of the new physics. After the launch of Sputnik by the Soviets in 1957, America began its own high-profile space program. This was perceived as a time of great opportunities for the science of matter and energy. In his history of physics in America, Daniel Kevles paints a buoyant picture of the 1950s and most of the 1960s: "It was a time when Americans ranked nuclear physicists third in occupational status—they had been fifteenth in 1947—ahead of everyone except Supreme Court justices and physicians."[44] They had gained this status because they appeared to have direct access to the workings of the universe. Writing in 1949 in the popular journal *American Scientist*, John Dunning, a professor of physics at Columbia who had worked with Enrico Fermi (*American Scientist* describes him as "in the very top rank of modern physicists"[45]), makes a revealing aside as he sets the scene for his account of contemporary nuclear physics:

> It has long been accepted that you and I and all the world around us are made of some 92 basic types of atoms which we call elements.[46]

So not just rocks and chemicals but minds, bodies, and even poems are all ultimately made of the stuff that these physicists have the methods to study. No wonder so many intellectuals were drawn to physics, and scientists like Einstein and Oppenheimer were celebrities whose every move was reported in the press. This attraction was helped by the long-standing philosophical character of particle physics. Physics might in practice be a matter of machines in laboratories remote from the public gaze, but many of the interwar generation of physicists were also very interested in philosophical issues (their successors like Richard Feynman would be much less so), and this made their writings interesting to public intellectuals, including poets.

As Heisenberg had demonstrated, understanding the complex role of observation had become central to modern science. We can see how this could be developed in poetics by reflecting on Thomas Kuhn's summary of the scientific doxa of 1962, the year when *The Structure of Scientific Revolutions* was first published:

> [T]he scientist must, for example, be concerned to understand the world and to extend the precision and scope with which it has been ordered. That commitment must, in turn, lead him to scrutinize, either for himself or through colleagues, some aspect of nature in great empirical detail. And, if that scrutiny displays pockets of apparent disorder, then these must challenge him to a new refinement of his observational techniques or to a further articulation of his theories.[47]

New American poets were also committed to understanding, finding implicit order, and to observing whatever constituted the familiar world. In her 1965 essay "Some Notes on Organic Form," Denise Levertov explained that the new poetics of what she uniquely, and somewhat misleadingly, called "organic form" rests on a belief that "there is a form in all things (and in our experience) which the poet can discover and reveal [. . .] inherent, though not immediately apparent, form."[48] What to literary readers may seem just a familiar blend of Neo-Platonism and Gerard Manley Hopkins's idea of "inscape" is also indebted to the self-understanding of science in the 1960s. Another philosopher of science, Ernest Nagel, speaks to this in 1961 (in *The Structure of Science*):

> Scientific thought takes its ultimate point of departure from problems suggested by observing things and events encountered in common experience; it aims to understand these observable things by discovering some systematic order in them; and its final test for the laws that serve as instruments of explanation and prediction is their concordance with such observations.[49]

Levertov's vision of the poem as an organic whole was a commitment to such ideals of observation.

Observation was unfortunately not all that the physicists were doing. They were also in control of energies capable of destroying the planet, as well as ensuring America's protection from overseas attack. A program to develop a successor to the atomic bomb, a "superbomb" or hydrogen bomb, created enormous controversy in the early 1950s, and led to the demotion and public humiliation of the most famous physicist after Einstein, J. Robert Oppenheimer, for his opposition to its development. The bomb created a climate of anxiety about the imminence of total assured destruction, and added to a sense that there was something Faustian about nuclear physics though, as Edward Brunner has argued, as a theme the bomb tended to elude poets of all kinds. Brunner believes that this was because of the tendency of much of the poetry of the time towards what Donald Hall identified in 1959 as "a pattern among us of provinciality and evasion, which results in a reliance on the domestic at the expense of the historical."[50] Brunner's argument finds support in Ginsberg's *Howl*, perhaps the most famous and the least evasive poem in the anthology, which does wittily acknowledge the fatalism induced by the nuclear threat. Ginsberg imagines his generation of Beat poets "listening to the crack of doom on the hydrogen jukebox"[51] as if waiting to see if the system will select a safe sound or the explosion of the bomb, though later in the poem he writes as if the outcome is a foregone conclusion, and the fate of his monstrous personification of American society will certainly be "a cloud of sexless hydrogen!"[52]

Poets in the immediate postwar period did however acknowledge the power of physics. Wallace Stevens wrote in his 1948 essay "Imagination as Value" that American poets were living in "a civilization based on science," and he ended the lecture on philosophy and poetry he gave in 1951 at the University of Chicago by saying that the physicist Max Planck, the founder of quantum theory, is a "truer symbol of ourselves"[53] than a philosopher such as Blaise Pascal, because Planck, despite his physicist's commitment to material causality and determinism, recognizes the importance of imagination as an unexplained factor in the constitution of the material universe. As a doctor and therefore a scientist, William Carlos Williams was always interested in scientific developments, and notably so in the late 1940s, when he gave a lecture at the University of Washington on "The Poem as a Field of Action," in which he proposed "sweeping changes from top to bottom of the poetic structure." Unlike Olson, Williams offered no specific application of the analogy between the electromagnetic field and the construction of poems, seeming content with the idea of the poem as a field or space for the enactment of experience.[54]

Science was also a strong theme in John Ciardi's 1950 anthology *Mid-Century American Poets* which brought together Robert Lowell, Richard Wilbur, Richard Eberhart, Muriel Rukeyser, and other prominent younger poets of the time and, although it contained many fewer poets, anticipated the poems plus poetics essays format of *The New American Poetry 1945–1960*. Ciardi asked fourteen poets to make their own selection of poems and to preface them with an essay about the principles shaping their poetic practice which was to be guided by twelve questions on such "technical" topics as structure, prosody, audience, and performance, flattering his contributors with the claim that "the most generally acknowledged leaders of this generation are being asked to record their attitudes toward the problems of writing."[55] In his poetics statement, Richard Eberhart treats the scientist as a further evolved poet:

> If one could know anything definitely, accurately, or perhaps "scientifically" (in the lesser sense of measure, not in the greater sense of imagination, where science and poetry join, as in Einstein's Unified Field Theory) one would not write a poem. The poem is an erection from primitive complexities, involvements and engagements.[56]

Randall Jarrell is more skeptical of the value of science to poets:

> Naturally the terms of scientific explanation cannot have these poetic and emotional effects, since it is precisely by the exclusion of these effects that science has developed. (Many of the conclusions of the sciences are as poetic as anything in the world, but they have been of little use to poets—how can you use something you are delighted never to have heard of?)[57]

In her note, Muriel Rukeyser cites Einstein's anticipation of the future, more complete causal laws of physics, and adds that "one suggestion of such law is to be found in the process of poetry."[58] Ciardi's poets vary between enthusiasm and hostility towards the increasingly dominant natural sciences, but their interest is pervasive. The anthology was reviewed in *Poetry New York* by one of the editors, Rolf Fjelde, in the same issue that first published Olson's "Projective Verse," who characterized this mid-century poet as "part of this world, socially aware," and therefore able to "construct an image around a bomb-sight and employ test tubes, tabloid headlines, and X-rays as the natural props of poetry."[59] The mid-century poet was a scientific American, and as I have been arguing, the New American poet of 1960 remained so.

Literary theorists of poetry were also caught up in this attraction to physics. How could one defend the value of poetry in 1960 to Americans for whom the power of science is indisputable? One way would be to begin by saying that "poetry gives us knowledge," as Cleanth Brooks and Robert Penn Warren do at the start of the preface to the third edition of *Understanding*

Poetry, the most influential poetry textbook in America for many years and itself an extended defense of poetry. Having started so boldly, Brooks and Warren are soon surprisingly defensive about their opening claim.

> We know that to conceive of poetry as knowledge is not the only possible way of conceiving it. It is, however, our basic assumption, clung to for many years, and it would be disingenuous not to state it as the assumption behind this book.[60]

The discussion that follows is dominated by the idea that their anticipated young readers of 1960 are, if anything, more familiar with science than with poetry. "The value of science we all know," they go on to say, acceding to its claim to be the primary source of modern knowledge, but poetry exists in a separate sphere and readers therefore have to realize that "what makes science valuable cannot be held to make poetry valuable also."[61] They don't necessarily expect this admission to be won easily. A textbook on the nature of poetry is needed because "people are constantly confusing the two sorts of communication. This confusion that causes people to judge formal poetry as if it were science is the source of most of the misunderstandings of poetry and of literature in general."[62] Science "represents an extreme degree of special-ization of language in the direction of a certain kind of precision"[63] whereas poetry clarifies in its own precise articulations the "attitudes, feelings and interpretations"[64] found in everyday speech.

Michael Polanyi famously wrote in 1958 that scientific discovery depends upon "a passionate pouring of oneself into untried forms of existence."[65] Awe, wonder, untried forms of existence: these are just what many of the poets in Allen's anthology aspired to. It is time to look back at the anthol-ogy itself for explicit signs of recognition of scientific method and theories.

The back pages of the typical academic codex reveal in their notes and bibliographies the construction plans, the sources, and the indices of reli-ability of the more public pages where arguments are won and lost. So when Donald Allen announced that his new anthology presented a third genera-tion of modernist American poets, "the true continuers of the modern move-ment in American poetry," who collectively have just "one common char-acteristic," their aversion to "those qualities typical of academic verse,"[66] his readers might have expected a volume with no such apparatus at all. Instead of further demonstrating these anti-academic allegiances by abandoning all notes and appendices, Allen decided instead to print an extensive selection of expository prose materials by a significant proportion of his selected poets to act as "aids to a more exact understanding of literary history."[67] What did this apparatus, whose justification sounds disconcertingly academic, for what else are the academic literary critics attempting to achieve than ever more precise understandings of literary history, actually amount to? In quantitative terms, fifteen out of the forty-four poets provided "statements on poetics," and everyone had to provide "biographical notes," "notes" which in several cases amount to further short essays or manifestoes. Allen's briefing to his readers tells us that we can find an explanation of "the dominant new double concept: 'composition by field' and the poet's 'stance toward reality,'" as well as make distinctions between different poetic commitments, learn about the "ambience" of the New York poets, and read the reports "sent back from the fronts on which they are engaged."[68] Reference to Allen's account demands quotation marks, not just for the sake of accuracy, but because so many of these terms, these "notes," these "statements," these "aids," and these "qualities," like the more idiosyncratic terms, "field" and "fronts" for instance, are words under pressure, a strain due the way these terms are pulled conceptually in different directions by both the literary world and the scientific one. These back pages reveal intertextual allusions and epistemological manoeuvrings by the poets in a field of literary composition that is not simply defined by its antithesis to literary norms, and underwrite Creeley's later use of concepts derived from the dominant scientific paradigms of the late 1950s. Here too are unmistakable traces of the impact of these paradigms, as well as strategies for countering their authority and for positioning poetry alongside them. Just as the incorporation of an archetypal scholarly architecture into the volume indicates a more complex relation to academic definitions of verse than simple opposition, so this insistent preoccupation with science also points to interrelations of both assimilation and resistance.

Scientific discourse appears at the very start of the final sections of the book, in Charles Olson's essay "Projective Verse" (correctly printed here so that its title extends over four lines and includes that dominant military figure, the "projectile") which is emphatic about the scientific possibilities: "the poem, itself, must, at all points, be a high-energy-construct and, at all points, an energy-discharge."[69] This makes the poem sound like one of the new giant condensers or "atom-smashers," an engineered construction like a synchrocyclotron for testing the fundamental constituents of the universe. His other key compositional proposal is the idea that the new poetry should be derived from "composition by field." At the time he wrote the essay in 1950, fields were big news. It had been claimed wrongly that Einstein had finally developed a unified field theory and, less well known, but also widely reported was the construction of a new quantum field theory known as Quantum Electrodynamics (or QED as it was punningly known) by a group of young physicists including Richard Feynman. Field analogies were also adopted in other disciplines including the gestalt psychology of Kurt Lewin, and the philosophy of W. V. O. Quine. Olson's celebration of the new poetry as a high-energy discharge amounts to little more than an attempt to regain some of the prestige for poetry that had flowed to the nuclear physicists whose high-energy discharges had brought threats of annihilation as well as new insights into the construction of the universe, but his notion of "composition by field" implicitly offered the possibility that a poem could employ scientific methodologies for poetic ends. The field concept in physics was a means of representing transformations of energy and behaviour in particles. Could poems similarly represent the paths of their subjects across time and space? The impact of the science in "Projective Verse" is reinforced by a second poetics statement, his breathless concatenation of current preoccupations in the short "Letter to Elaine Feinstein" dated nearly ten years later. This not only makes connections with physics, it also discusses history in poetry by means of allusions to the increasingly visible field of genetics that had been opened up in 1953 by James Watson and Francis Crick's discovery of the codable structure of DNA. Heritage and history, says Olson, can be understood as "chromosomic"[70] processes for transmission of speech and etymology.

Other poets are generally more sparing of such fulsomely scientific rhetoric, although many of them do acknowledge the growing significance of science for contemporary life, even if only to question its authority, cultural and epistemic. In his poetics statement, "Pages from a Notebook," Robert Duncan actually gives one section the subtitle "On Science," where he takes issue with Giambattista Vico's idea that poetry is the earliest stage of philosophy, "primitive to science."[71] No, says Duncan, poetry is not the first step towards some other kind of more advanced art or knowledge, poetry is a distinct realm, and he then turns the tables on science, saying that "for the poet, science seems like poetry itself a primitive conceiving of things."[72] The remainder of this section of Duncan's statement argues that medicine's authority over disease should be challenged, that disease may be a form of aesthetic expression, and that therefore Freud was right to emphasize self-knowledge rather than cure. Duncan may be questioning the medical metaphors of illness as the invasion of pathogens and the disruption of norms of health, and counter-intuitively suggesting that from a poet's standpoint, cancer could be "a flower, an adventure, an intrigue with life"[73] in a manner that anticipates the analyses of Susan Sontag (though she would surely demur at the re-introduction of the "romanticizing" metaphors that she attributes to tuberculosis), but he is more interested in challenging in a coded manner the rhetorics of pathology by which homosexuality was frequently described as an illness. As he says later in the statement, "our taboo is at root against unintelligible passions,"[74] for which read homosexuality. Later in his statement, Duncan explores his identification with Faust, that early figure of the scientist who defies theogony in the search for knowledge.

Robert Creeley approvingly cites Olson's description of the high-energy poem, and adds that this new poetics "breaks the line of aesthetics, or that outcrop of a general division of knowledge."[75] Since his next sentence affirms that "a sense of the KINETIC impels recognition of force,"[76] we can interpret his somewhat less than clear reference to an "outcrop of a general division of knowledge"[77] to mean that poetry aims to be cross-disciplinary and encompass what have traditionally been divided, the arts and sciences, and that its warrant for doing so is that poetry has its own access to the "forces" whose study has been central to physics and the natural sciences.

Philip Whalen compares the poem's representation of psychic process to the machinery used to detect atomic particles:

> This poetry is a picture or graph of a mind moving, which is a world body being here and now which is history . . . and you. Or think about the Wilson Cloud Chamber, not ideogram, not poetic beauty: bald-faced didacticism moving, as Dr. Johnson commands all poetry should, from the particular to the general. (ellipses in original)[78]

By the time this statement was published, the fiddly temperamental Wilson cloud chamber, a sealed container of supersaturated gas that could reveal the ionizing traces of nuclear particles as trails of mist to be photographed, had been superseded in the 1950s by more reliable bubble chambers.[79] Dr. Johnson complains in his "Life of Cowley" that in the work of some of the metaphysical poets, "all the power of description is destroyed by a scrupulous enumeration, and the force of metaphors is lost, when the mind, by the mention of particulars, is turned more upon the original than the secondary sense."[80] Whalen is intimating that the poems he writes can record the traces of particulars as precisely as the cloud chamber registers atomic particles, a link that depends on the punning reference to both particles and particulars.

Some references to the sciences might easily pass us by. Allen Ginsberg may seem to be a poet uninterested in the sciences, yet he is insistent that his poems are "a series of experiments with the formal organization of the long line."[81] It is as much the use of the phrase "a series" as the idea of experiment that suggests he has in mind an analogy with laboratory science. The idea that a work of art can be legitimately called an experiment has been central to modern aesthetics, and however unlikely it is that such work would be accepted as scientific by scientists, this axiological use of a concept central to modern science tacitly endorses the status of scientific method. As Dewey's pragmatist aesthetic in *Art as Experience* (1934) (which could be described, recalling William James's *The Varieties of Religious Experience*, as the "varieties of aesthetic experience") would have it:

> There is a tendency among lay critics to confine experimentation to scientists in the laboratory. Yet one of the essential traits of the artist is that he is born an experimenter. . . . Only because the artist operates experimentally does he open new fields of experience and disclose new aspects and qualities in familiar scenes and objects.[82]

Do we also hear a premonition of Olson's aesthetic of the "open field" foreshadowed in Dewey's rhetoric? Ginsberg's allusion to a "series of experiments" continues the Deweyan belief that art can hold its head high in an age of experimental science.

Not all science is based on experiment; many areas of science such as biology and geology depend on field work. Gary Snyder's allusion to field work in his brief account of the origins of *Myths and Texts*, which explains that "'Riprap' is really a class of poems I wrote under the influence of the geology of the Sierra Nevada,"[83] can easily go unnoticed as a reference to scientific method, since in the remainder of the statement the influences he outlines are native American folktales, religious experiences, and what he calls "symbols and sense-impressions."[84] Although Michael McClure actually mentions science in his statement, where he insists (like Denise Levertov, who does so less explicitly) on the role of the body or what he calls "physiology" as a ground to the poem, here too the significance of the connection with science might not be noticed. Physiology, says McClure, is a partner to the emotions and intellect, adding that: "The intellect will be the wit, discipline and truth of it— also the hanging to Science, of the known true part of the writing, that which I say I know to be true (and that is also a message)."[85] What troubles McClure about the emphasis on intellect in Olson and Duncan, he tells us, is that if he follows the prescriptions of "projective verse" he risks losing contact with the affects, and his experience of poetry tells him that "the emotions push me to discoveries that afterwards I recognize intellectively to be truths."[86] Despite seeming to turn away from intellect, McClure actually endorses the same objectives as science, discovery leading to truth, and even appears to be willing to identify science with "the known true part of the writing"[87] though he wants to find a non-scientific method of inquiry to do so.

In Allen's choice of poems, science is generally a much less evident feature than it is in the statements made by the poets, although the very first poem in the anthology, Olson's "The Kingfishers," certainly sets a strong scientific tone. It is permeated with scientific allusions to biology, archaeology, and cybernetics and, more significantly still, has a structure that emulates the process of scientific inquiry, of blundering about in the face of new empirical information or, as Kuhn describes it, recognizing that if "scrutiny displays pockets of apparent disorder, then these must challenge him to a new refinement of his observational techniques or to a further articulation of his theories and trying to find patterns within it."[88] So the unnamed protagonist at the start of Olson's poem wakes to considerable disorder both within and without, and begins to work towards an understanding of the origins of human violence. The entire poem enacts a process of inquiry that begins with conversational hints, struggles with epistemological uncertainty, and then has to take account of its own implication in any process of inquiry (in Creeley's words, the protagonist of Olson's poem "cannot assume some 'not being' so as to 'talk about it.'"[89]

The encroachment of scientific method into all areas of human life over the past century has increasingly led poets to feel a need to demonstrate the continuing relevance of poetry to investigate human affairs in the face of the dominant belief that "the methods of natural science are applicable in every area of inquiry"[90] and increasingly render all others obsolete.[91] Olson's poem attempts to demonstrate that poetry is as capable of inquiry as the sciences of cybernetics, archaeology, or psychology. The poetic complexity that results from this ambition is best revealed by examining the passage in "The Kingfishers" that cites the cybernetic principle of information. It follows a discussion of the ancient philosophical question of how it is that human beings retain an identity despite constant change:

> We can be precise. The factors are
> in the animal and / or the machine the factors are
> communication and / or control, both involve
> the message. And what is the message? The message is
> a discrete or continuous sequence of measurable events distributed in time.[92]

Who, a reader might reasonably ask, is speaking and from what community standpoint: we moderns, we scientists, we cyberneticists, or we poets? The passage appears to make the large claim that the puzzle articulated by the ancients has now been solved, and yet what we are given as the solution is curiously empty, as if we had been told that the message is a series of words placed in order across a medium. We readers don't know how to read this passage because we lack contextual direction as to whether to accept the speaker's authority as a scientist that it is now possible to be precise (accurate, truthful, factual) about the causes and consequences of change, or to question the right of the poet to make claim to such authority. Our uncertainty is exacerbated by Olson's literary critical joke. Literary pedagogy is notorious for encouraging students to look for the message in a poem and here the poem thoughtfully offers a readymade statement of its message, except that it is entirely unhelpful because what is described is the material structure rather than the semantic content. We are left with no message, which is the point. What we are being offered is Olson's version of what a poetics equal to scientific method might look like.

A similar analysis of the remaining poems in Allen's anthology would fill out the picture of how these poets engaged with the sciences, but is beyond the scope of this essay. What I can do here is outline several different kinds of interrelation between science and poetry that can be found at work in *The New American Poetry*. Firstly, contemporary natural science provides a materialist account of the universe that many of the poets allude to as the taken for granted furnishings of the cosmos. Even the poets best known for seeking anti-materialist transformations through "Holy Signs"[93] or "a gathering together of spirit"[94] also acknowledge the materialist scientific vision of the cosmos as a "starry dynamo in the machinery of night"[95] and that "Scientia" holds a light for understanding "the information flows / that is yearning."[96] These poets live in a world of subatomic particles, electromagnetic fields, endless receding galaxies, a world located in an almost unimaginable stretch of time and space. Secondly, scientific practice offers them an ideal of truthfulness about the state of the world, through its insistence on accuracy and on a sincerity based on mutual trust. Scientific research is always open to correction by new findings, new observations. The "nature of the writing" of Olson and his contemporaries is similarly, according to Creeley, able "to move in the field of its recognitions" and "the nature of the life it *is* demands a possibility which no assumption can anticipate."[97] The writing resembles science because it too requires accuracy in its treatment of experience and its commitment to respond to what is discovered, not what it wishes were real.

A third connection between this poetry and contemporary science is to be found in the ways these poets understand their commitment to what Ginsberg calls in his anthology statement "unconditioned Spirit,"[98] a spirit of creativity that is not conditioned by the many powerful psychological pressures to conform. As many commentators have said, New American poetry celebrated spontaneity, and both Allen and Creeley emphasize the importance of a present moment as the source of a poem, not recollection or tradition. Current scientific ideas provided several models of spontaneity as other than simply divine or unconscious inspiration, notably the cybernetic model of feedback that Olson drops into "The Kingfishers." A fourth connection between this poetry and science is its emulation of what it understood to be the character of scientific inquiry, often in order to resist the encroachments of scientific methodology into hitherto humanist areas of everyday life. This is the great era when sociology, psychology and related disciplines openly celebrate their status as social *sciences*, and adopt many of the experimental, mathematical, and even conceptual techniques of the natural sciences. Several of the best known poems in the anthology can be read as claims for the continuing relevance of poetry as a site of investigation.

The New American poets were a heterogeneous group assembled for the purposes of an anthology, and the commonalities between them were various too, including a resistance to conformity, an interest in the aesthetics of spontaneity, opposition to the politics of the Cold War, sexual radicalism, modernist sensibilities, friendship networks, and shared metropolitan experiences. I have argued here that an alert responsiveness to the sciences of their time, and an interest in emulating some types of scientific inquiry, also played a part in helping this network of poets articulate itself, although Allen was either unaware of this or unwilling to acknowledge it. Given the rapid expansion of the natural sciences after the Second World War, and the scientization of the study of human society and the human mind, poets could not avoid encountering scientific interpretations of the world at almost every turn. The late essays of Stevens and Williams, and the preoccupations of the poets in Ciardi's anthology, demonstrate just how pervasive science had already become when Olson started writing poetry. But I am arguing something stronger than the claim that this was a scientific era. Olson and Creeley believed that the best poets of their generation were not just swept along by the *zeitgeist*, they were actively attentive to "those particulars of time and space of which one is a given instance, equally present," an orientation towards the phenomenal world that required forms of inquiry as rigorous as any scientific investigation. They were wary of the institutions of science, so they borrowed terms from scientific discourse and reframed them within the authority of their own poetics. I am claiming that New American poetry could not have achieved so much if it had not been driven as much by a passionate curiosity about science as by a belief that the scientists should not be allowed to take over all areas of inquiry into human affairs. They shared with Zukofsky the belief that "oneself" was as open to discoveries made by poetic inquiry as it might seem be to the new methods of scientific investigation.

Notes

1. Donald Allen and Robert Creeley, *The New Writing in the USA* (Harmondsworth: Penguin, 1967), 305.

2. See also Louis Zukofsky, "A" (Berkeley: University of California Press, 1978), 291–292.

3. Allen and Creeley, *The New Writing in the USA*, 11.

4. Ibid., 10.

5. Ibid., 19.

6. Creeley's introduction was republished in his *Collected Essays* (Berkeley: University of California Press, 1989), 89–96.

7. Allen and Creeley, *The New Writing in the USA*, 9.

8. Ibid., 10.

9. Ibid.

10. Ibid., 9.

11. Ibid., 10.

12. Ibid.

13. Ibid., 17.

14. Ibid., 18.

15. Ibid., 19.

16. Robert Duncan, *A Selected Prose* (New York: New Directions, 1995), 25.

17. Richard Bernstein, *The Pragmatic Turn* (Cambridge, UK: Polity Press, 2010), 147.

18. Ibid., 150; Bernstein cites this from a collection of Dewey's writings, *On Experience, Nature and Freedom* (New York: Liberal Arts Press, 1960), 85–86.

19. Allen and Creeley, *The New Writing in the USA*, 19.

20. Ibid., 20; The quotation from Olson's essay can be found in his *Collected Prose* (Berkeley: University of California Press, 1997), 121.

21. Allen and Creeley, *The New Writing in the USA*, 20.

22. Ibid., 22.

23. Ibid.

24. Robert Brandom, *Reason in Philosophy: Animating Ideas* (Cambridge, MA: Harvard University Press, 2009), 7. This passage is cited from an essay by Wilfrid Sellars, "Counterfactuals, Dispositions, and the Causal Modalities," *Minnesota Studies in the Philosophy of Science*, vol. 2. eds. H. Feigl, M. Scriven, and G. Maxwell, (Minneapolis: University of Minnesota Press, 1957).

25. Brandom, 7.

26. Ibid.

27. Ibid., 13.

28. Werner Heisenberg, *Physics and Philosophy* (Harmondsworth: Penguin, 1958), 46.

29. Ibid., 43.

30. Allen and Creeley, *The New Writing in the USA*, 24.

31. William Bronk, *Life Supports: New and Collected Poems* (San Francisco: North Point Press, 1981), 64.

32. Erwin Schrödinger, *What is Life?: With Mind and Matter and Autobiographical Sketches* (Cambridge: Cambridge University Press, 1992), 3.

33. Ibid., 68.

34. Allen and Creeley, *The New Writing in the USA*, 185. For the source of the quotation see Charles Olson's *Collected Prose* (Berkeley, University of California Press, 1997), 155.

35. Lew Welch, "Hermit Poems," in *The New Writing in the USA*, eds. Donald Allen and Robert Creeley (Harmondsworth: Penguin, 1957), 278.

36. Jack Spicer, "Love Poems," in *The New Writing in the USA*, eds. Donald Allen and Robert Creeley (Harmondsworth: Penguin, 1967), 269.

37. Ibid.

38. Gilbert Sorrentino, "The Mathematics," in *The New Writing in the USA*, eds. Donald Allen and Robert Creeley (Harmondsworth: Penguin, 1967), 264.

39. Barbara Guest, "The Blue Stairs," in *The New Writing in the USA*, eds. Donald Allen and Robert Creeley (Harmondsworth: Penguin, 1967), 102.

40. John Ashbery, "The Ecclesiast," in *The New Writing in the USA*, eds. Donald Allen and Robert Creeley, (Harmondsworth: Penguin, 1967), 25.

41. Louis Zukofsky, *Bottom: On Shakespeare* (Berkeley, University of California Press, 1987), 90.

42. Philip Whalen, *Two Novels: You Didn't Even Try and Imaginary Speeches for a Brazen Head* (Somerville, MA: Zephyr Press, 1985), 19.

43. Radio Corporation of America advertisement, *Scientific American*, 202 no. 2 (February 1960): 113.

44. Daniel Kevles, *The Physicists: The History of a Scientific Community in Modern America* (Cambridge, MA: Harvard University Press, 1995), 391.

45. Untitled Article. *American Scientist* (October 1949): 475.

46. J. R. Dunning, "Atomic Structure and Energy," *American Scientist* (October 1949): 507.

47. Thomas Kuhn, *The Structure of Scientific Revolutions*. 2nd edition. (Chicago: University of Chicago Press, 1970), 42.

48. Denise Levertov, *The Poet in the World* (New York: New Directions, 1974), 67. This essay was originally published in the September 1965 issue of *Poetry*.

49. Ernest Nagel, *The Structure of Science: Problems in the Logic of Scientific Explanation*, (London: Routledge and Kegan Paul, 1961), 79.

50. Donald Hall, "Ah, Love, Let Us Be True To One Another!: Domesticity and History in Contemporary Poetry," *The American Scholar* 23 (March 1959): 311.

51. Allen Ginsberg, "Howl." In *The New Writing in the USA*, eds. Donald Allen and Robert Creeley (Harmondsworth: Penguin, 1967), 183.

52. Ibid., 189.

53. Wallace Stevens, *Collected Poetry and Prose*. (New York: Library of America, 1997), 728.

54. William Carlos Williams, "The Poem as a Field of Action," *Selected Essays*. (New York: New Directions, 1969), 281. This essay began as a lecture given at the University of Washington in 1948, but was not printed until 1954 when it appeared from Random House in the *Selected Essays*. Although it seems plausible that Olson might have heard about the lecture either from Williams or other members of Williams's extensive network of correspondents, what the coincidence of interest in the idea of the poem as field in the two essays demonstrates is the attractiveness of developing a literary concept of the poem as field given the increasing prominence of physics, and the wish on the part of these poets to avoid conventional aesthetic discourse.

55. John Ciardi, *Mid-Century American Poets* (New York: Twayne, 1950), xxvii.

56. Richard Eberhart, "Statement of Poetics," in *Mid-Century American Poets*, ed. John Ciardi. (New York: Twayne, 1950), 227.

57. Randall Jarrell, "Statement of Poetics," in *Mid-Century American Poets*, ed. John Ciardi. (New York: Twayne, 1950), 166.

58. Muriel Rukeyser, "Note," in *Mid-Century American Poets*, ed. John Ciardi (New York: Twayne, 1950), 50.

59. Rolf Fjelde, "Mid Century American Poets," *Poetry New York* 3 (1950): 38.

60. Cleanth Brooks and Robert Penn Warren, *Understanding Poetry*, 3rd edition, (New York: Holt, Rinehart and Winston, 1960), xiii. By the time they produced the fourth edition in 1976 they had apparently lost confidence entirely in this formulation, which is not mentioned. The early reflections on the limits of scientific discourse are repeated, but the general emphasis is much more on pedagogy than before.

61. Ibid., 20.

62. Ibid., 8.

63. Ibid., 5.

64. Ibid.

65. Michael Polanyi, *Personal Knowledge: Towards a Post-Critical Philosophy* (Chicago: University of Chicago Press, 1974), 207–208.

66. Allen and Creeley, *The New Writing in the USA*, xi.

67. Ibid., xiii.

68. Ibid., xiv.

69. Charles Olson, "Projective Verse," in *The New Writing in the USA*, eds. Donald Allen and Robert Creeley (Harmondsworth: Penguin, 1967), 387.

70. Ibid., 398.

71. Robert Duncan, "Pages from a Notebook," in *The New Writing in the USA*, eds. Donald Allen and Robert Creeley (Harmondsworth: Penguin, 1967), 403.

72. Ibid.

73. Ibid.

74. Ibid., 406.

75. Robert Creeley, "To Define," in *The New Writing in the USA*, eds. Donald Allen and Robert Creeley (Harmondsworth: Penguin, 1967), 408.

76. Ibid.

77. Ibid.

78. Philip Whalen, "Statement on Poetics," in *The New Writing in the USA*, eds. Donald Allen and Robert Creeley (Harmondsworth: Penguin, 1967), 420.

79. Luis Alvarez, a pioneer in the use of these evolving devices, says the "Wilson expansion chamber had two difficulties that rendered it unsuitable for the job": it was very slow and became slower still if you tried for greater precision by increasing the pressure in the chamber. He talks of how "unsuitable for the job" it was. See Luis W. Alvarez, "Recent Developments in Particle Physics," *Science* New Series 165, no. 3898 (1969): 1074.

80. Samuel Johnson, *The Lives of the Poets: A Selection*. Edited by John Mullan and Lonsdale, (Oxford: Oxford University Press, 2009), 37.

81. Allen Ginsberg, "Notes for *Howl* and Other Poems," in *The New Writing in the USA*, eds. Donald Allen and Robert Creeley (Harmondsworth: Penguin, 1967), 416.

82. John Dewey, *Art as Experience* (New York: Perigee, 2005), 149.

83. Gary Snyder, "Statement of Poetics," in *The New Writing in the USA*, eds. Donald Allen and Robert Creeley (Harmondsworth: Penguin, 1967), 420.

84. Ibid., 421.

85. Michael McClure, "From a Journal," in *The New Writing in the USA*, eds. Donald Allen and Robert Creeley (Harmondsworth: Penguin, 1967), 423.

86. Ibid.

87. Ibid.

88. Kuhn, *The Structure of Scientific Revolutions*, 42.

89. Allen and Creeley, *The New Writing in the USA*, 22.

90. Hilary Putnam, *Philosophy in an Age of Science: Physics, Mathematics, and Skepticism*. (Cambridge, MA: Harvard University Press, 2012), 110.

91. In a brilliant critique of naturalism, Putnam cites this definition of naturalism from Boyd *et. al.* (778), claiming that such explicit definitions are relatively rare and the implications of naturalism need to be explored more fully than they have been.

92. Charles Olson, "The Kingfishers," in *The New Writing in the USA*. eds. Donald Allen and Robert Creeley (Harmondsworth: Penguin, 1967), 5.

93. Allen Ginsberg, "Sather Gate Illumination," in *The New Writing in the USA*. eds. Donald Allen and Robert Creeley (Harmondsworth: Penguin, 1967), 191.

94. Robert Duncan, "This Place Rumord to have been Sodom," in *The New Writing in the USA*, eds. Donald Allen and Robert Creeley (Harmondsworth: Penguin, 1967), 44.

95. Ginsberg, *Howl*, 182.

96. Robert Duncan, "A Poem Beginning with a Line by Pindar," in *The New Writing in the USA*, eds. Donald Allen and Robert Creeley (Harmondsworth: Penguin, 1967), 54, 57.

97. Allen and Creeley, *The New Writing in the USA*, 22.

98. Ginsberg, "Notes for *Howl* and Other Poems," 417.

Bibliography

Allen, Donald, and Robert Creeley, eds. *The New Writing in the USA*. Harmondsworth: Penguin, 1967.

Alvarez, Luis W. "Recent Developments in Particle Physics." *Science*. New Series 165, no. 3898 (1969): 1071–1091.

Ashbery, John. "The Ecclesiast." *The New Writing in the USA*. Edited by Donald Allen and Robert Creeley. Harmondsworth: Penguin, 1967.

Bernstein, Richard. *The Pragmatic Turn*. Cambridge, UK: Polity Press, 2010.

Boyd, Richard, Philip Gasper, and J. D. Trout, eds. *The Philosophy of Science*. Cambridge, MA: MIT Press, 1991.

Brandom, Robert. *Reason in Philosophy: Animating Ideas*. Cambridge, MA: Harvard University Press, 2009.

Bronk, William. *Life Supports: New and Collected Poems*. San Francisco: North Point Press, 1981.

Brooks, Cleanth, and Robert Penn Warren. *Understanding Poetry*. 3rd edition. New York: Holt, Rinehart and Winston, 1960.

Brunner, Edward. *Cold War Poetry*. Chicago: University of Illinois Press, 2001.

Ciardi, John. *Mid-Century American Poets*. New York: Twayne, 1950.

Creeley, Robert. *The Collected Essays of Robert Creeley*. Berkeley: University of California Press, 1989.

———. "To Define." *The New Writing in the USA*. Edited by Donald Allen and Robert Creeley, Harmondsworth: Penguin, 1967: 408.

Dewey, John. *Art as Experience*. New York: Perigee, 2005.

———. *On Experience, Nature and Freedom*. Edited by R. J. Bernstein. New York: Liberal Arts Press, 1960.

Duncan, Robert. "A Poem Beginning with a Line by Pindar." *The New Writing in the USA*. Edited by Donald Allen and Robert Creeley. Harmondsworth: Penguin, 1967.

———. *A Selected Prose*. Edited by Robert J. Bertholf. New York: New Directions, 1995.

———. "Pages from a Notebook." *The New Writing in the USA*. Edited by Donald Allen and Robert Creeley. Harmondsworth: Penguin, 1967.

———. "This Place Rumord to have been Sodom." *The New Writing in the USA*. Edited by Donald Allen and Robert Creeley. Harmondsworth: Penguin, 1967.

Dunning, J. R. "Atomic Structure and Energy." *American Scientist* (October 1949): 505–527.

Eberhart, Richard. "Statement of Poetics." *Mid-Century American Poets*. Edited by John Ciardi. New York: Twayne, 1950.

Fjelde, Rolf. "Mid Century American Poets." *Poetry New York* 3 (1950): 38–40.

Ginsberg, Allen. *Howl*. *The New Writing in the USA*. Edited by Donald Allen and Robert Creeley. Harmondsworth: Penguin, 1967.

———. "Notes for *Howl* and Other Poems." *The New Writing in the USA*. Edited by Donald Allen and Robert Creeley. Harmondsworth: Penguin, 1967.

———. "Sather Gate Illumination." *The New Writing in the USA.* Edited by Donald Allen and Robert Creeley. Harmondsworth: Penguin, 1967.

Guest, Barbara. "The Blue Stairs." *The New Writing in the USA.* Edited by Donald Allen and Robert Creeley. Harmondsworth: Penguin, 1967.

Hall, Donald. 1959. "Ah, Love, Let Us Be True To One Another!: Domesticity and History in Contemporary Poetry." *The American Scholar* 28 (March, 1959): 310–319.

Heisenberg, Werner. *Physics and Philosophy.* Harmondsworth: Penguin, 1958.

Jarrell, Randall. "Statement of Poetics." *Mid-Century American Poets.* Edited by John Ciardi. New York: Twayne, 1950.

Johnson, Samuel. *The Lives of the Poets: A Selection.* Edited by John Mullan and Roger Lonsdale. Oxford: Oxford University Press, 2009.

Kevles, Daniel. *The Physicists: The History of a Scientific Community in Modern America.* Cambridge, MA: Harvard University Press, 1995.

Kuhn, Thomas. *The Structure of Scientific Revolutions.* 2nd edition. Chicago: University of Chicago Press, 1970.

Levertov, Denise. *The Poet in the World.* New York: New Directions, 1974.

McClure, Michael. "From a Journal." *The New Writing in the USA.* Edited by Donald Allen and Robert Creeley. Harmondsworth: Penguin, 1967.

McDowell, John. *Mind and World.* Cambridge, MA: Harvard University Press, 1996.

Nagel, Ernest. *The Structure of Science: Problems in the Logic of Scientific Explanation.* London: Routledge and Kegan Paul, 1961.

Olson, Charles. *Collected Prose.* Edited by Donald Allen and Benjamin Friedlander. Berkeley: University of California Press, 1997.

———. "Projective Verse." *The New Writing in the USA.* Edited by Donald Allen and Robert Creeley. Harmondsworth: Penguin, 1967.

———. "The Kingfishers." *The New Writing in the USA.* Edited by Donald Allen and Robert Creeley. Harmondsworth: Penguin, 1967.

Oppen, George. *Of Being Numerous.* New York: New Directions, 1968.

Polanyi, Michael. *Personal Knowledge: Towards a Post-Critical Philosophy.* Chicago: University of Chicago Press, 1974.

Putnam, Hilary. *Philosophy in an Age of Science: Physics, Mathematics, and Skepticism.* Cambridge, MA: Harvard University Press, 2012.

Rukeyser, Muriel. *The Speed of Darkness.* New York: Random House, 1968.

———. "Note." *Mid-Century American Poets.* Edited by John Ciardi. New York: Twayne, 1950.

Schrödinger, Erwin. *What is Life?: With Mind and Matter and Autobiographical Sketches.* Cambridge: Cambridge University Press, 1992

Sellars, Wilfrid. "Counterfactuals, Dispositions, and the Causal Modalities." *Minnesota Studies in the Philosophy of Science.* Vol. 2. Edited by H. Feigl, M. Scriven, and G. Maxwell. Minneapolis: University of Minnesota Press, 1957.

Snyder, Gary. "Statement of Poetics." *The New Writing in the USA.* Edited by Donald Allen and Robert Creeley. Harmondsworth: Penguin, 1967.

Stevens, Wallace. *Collected Poetry and Prose*. New York: Library of America, 1997.

Sorrentino, Gilbert. "The Mathematics." *The New Writing in the USA*. Edited by Donald Allen and Robert Creeley. Harmondsworth: Penguin, 1967.

Spicer, Jack. "Love Poems." *The New Writing in the USA*. Edited by Donald Allen and Robert Creeley. Harmondsworth: Penguin, 1967.

Stevens, Wallace. *Collected Poetry and Prose*. New York: Library of America, 1997.

Untitled Article. *American Scientist* (October 1949): 475.

Welch, Lew. "Hermit Poems." *The New Writing in the USA*. Edited by Donald Allen and Robert Creeley. Harmondsworth: Penguin, 1967.

Whalen, Philip. *Two Novels: You Didn't Even Try and Imaginary Speeches for a Brazen Head*. Somerville, MA: Zephyr Press, 1985.

———. "Statement of Poetics." *The New Writing in the USA*. Edited by Donald Allen and Robert Creeley. Harmondsworth: Penguin, 1967.

Williams, William Carlos. "The Poem as a Field of Action." *Selected Essays*. New York: New Directions, 1969.

Zukofsky, Louis. "A". Berkeley: University of California Press, 1978.

———. *Bottom: On Shakespeare*. Berkeley: University of California Press, 1987.

CHAPTER TEN

~

Aurality and Literacy: The New American Poets and the Age of Technological Reproduction

Seth Forrest

In a recent mailing announcing the Spring 2010 schedule of events at the Poetry Center and American Poetry Archives at San Francisco State University, director Steve Dickison describes his first visit to the Poetry Center:

> What I was treated to in that little room with funky couches was a first opportunity to listen to the voices [. . .] *The New American Poetry* anthology was talking, amplified by fresh young voices. I'd tapped the motherlode.[1]

Since Dickison's encounter in the 1980s, that "motherlode" of recorded voices has expanded as scholars like Steve Evans, Charles Bernstein, and Al Filreis have unpacked and cataloged the contents of reel-to-reel and cassette tapes left by poets to university archives.[2] Now recordings of the New American poets abound in archives across the country. Significant collections in the Archive for New Poetry at the University of California at San Diego, the Poetry Collection at the University of Buffalo, the Woodberry Poetry Room Collection at Harvard's Houghton Library, and of course the American Poetry Archives at San Francisco State University contain hours of readings, lectures, and discussions. For the past five years, the PennSound project of the University of Pennsylvania's Center for Programs in Contemporary Writing has made digital versions of hundreds of poetry readings available on the Internet for listeners to stream and download.[3] The importance of PennSound has been to make what are often aging reel-to-reel tapes easy for anyone to hear and to collect for more intensive analysis. The vast majority of these readings have been separated into individual "tracks" containing a single poem along with any related commentary. As founding editor Charles Bernstein says in the manifesto that accompanied PennSound's 2003 launch, "MP3s of song-length poems could become a very appealing format for poetry. The implications for audience, listenership, critical thinking, poetics, and poetic production are great."[4] Bibliographic information is embedded in the ID3 tag for each file, allowing these recordings to be widely accessible far beyond the necessary protective restrictions that traditional archives and libraries must observe. The casual listener and serious student alike now have access to recorded materials that once could only be heard by research scholars in a special collections listening room.

The digital archive of mp3 files at PennSound specializes in contemporary poetry but extends historically to include significant readings by the New Americans. With the exceptions of Jack Kerouac, Frank O'Hara, and Gary Snyder, the major poets gathered in the anthology that has come to define the postwar avant-garde in American poetry are well represented. Though it doesn't yet include the first known recording of *Howl* recently unearthed at Reed College, PennSound has made available four recordings of Ginsberg that date from the late 1950s, including the San Francisco State University re-creation of the famous reading at the Six Gallery and another private reading at Robert Creeley's home in 1959, a tape from Creeley's own personal collection. The site includes a studio recording made by Creeley at Black Mountain College in 1954 during his brief teaching appointment there as well. Recordings of Creeley and Olson reading at the San Francisco State University Poetry Center date from 1956 and 1957, and early readings by Robert Duncan are also available. John Ashbery's "The Instruction Manual" is included in two different recordings, and "How Much Longer Will I Be Able to Inhabit the Divine Sepulcher" appears in a recording made in 1973 at the Library of Congress. We also have access to many readings, lectures, and discussions from the Vancouver and Berkeley Poetry Conferences on PennSound, and the entirety of the Vancouver events is available from Philadelphia's Slought Foundation.

Today, *The New American Poetry* anthology is indeed talking, but what, exactly, is it saying? We might also ask how we are hearing it and, perhaps an even more intriguing question, how the poets were hearing themselves? These questions are posed in a more general manner by three key collections of essays—*Close Listening*, edited by Charles Bernstein; *Sound States*, edited by Adelaide Morris; and, most recently, *The Sound of Poetry/The Poetry of Sound*, edited by and based on the MLA Presidential Forum organized by Marjorie Perloff. These volumes contain essential reading for any scholar of poetry and poetics preparing to work with audio recordings. The essays, however varied they may be in their focal points, show that recorded poetry is much more important to scholarship and criticism in recent years. As sound studies scholars often assert, from the perspective of our own time of entrenched and omnipresent electronic multimedia, the audio archive has been neglected for too long.[5] However, the poets and archivists have been recording poetry since the days of the wax cylinder, and it is criticism and scholarship that have been slow to engage with these recordings. The reasons why scholars have avoided audio are various, but for now it must suffice to demonstrate my assertion that the poets were very quick to realize the usefulness of audio recording technology and, in so doing, to show some of the important material from the New American period that is available on the audio archive and to theorize how the age of mechanical reproduction affected the sense of aurality that informs the poetics of the New Americans. In what follows, I have several purposes in mind. The first is simply to give some examples of how audio recordings have added to the literal textual condition with which editors and scholars need to engage. The second is to provide a demonstration of the sort of close listening that is afforded to students and critics by the opportunity to hear the poets read their writing. And finally, I want to argue that understanding the principles of recording and the habits of listening that develop in response to audio recording is instrumental to understanding the New American poetry. Writing at a time in which audio recording technology altered our habits of listening and indeed our entire conception of the oral/aural dynamic, the New American poets developed prosodic innovations that continue into contemporary experimental writing practices, what I want to call a poetics of aurality.

Tape Recordings and (Audio)Textual Scholarship

In *Theory of Literature*, a book as vast in scope as in its influence on New Critical thinking, René Wellek and Austin Warren seek to determine the "mode of existence of a literary work of art."[6] Wellek and Warren's complicated early accounting of the textual condition would eventually be overshadowed by W. K. Wimsatt and Monroe Beardsley's insistence on the "enduring object," their parsing of the poem into layers of strata consisting of print copies, performances, or "soundings."[7] The various contexts out of and through which the poem might be read and understood bears considerable similarity to recent work by theorists of contemporary poetry. That is, they must balance their analysis of print and performance and of the problem of the "original" in a time when manuscripts, typescripts, mimeograph and Xerox copies, digital word processing files, Adobe PDF documents, hypertexts, Flash animations, oral performances, tape and digital recordings and even digital copies of tape recordings or edited versions of digital recordings can exist of a single Robert Creeley poem.[8] We need only examine two major examples of variation among recordings and printed versions to understand the role that recordings can have in complicating the work of textual scholars and editors of the New American poetry. The two examples I have in mind are poems of unquestionable importance in defining the New American style, Allen Ginsberg's *Howl* and Charles Olson's "I, Maximus of Gloucester, to You." In both examples, early recordings add to the rich history of manuscript and published versions, in addition to providing an opportunity to analyze qualities of the poem beyond what we can read in the anthology.

Edward Foster claims, "Black Mountain poetry is located in time, in the occasion of its composition."[9] And in the famous phrase from "I, Maximus of Gloucester, to You" Olson suggests the same, that the poem is composed, "by ear, he sd."[10] Olson's manuscripts and publication record, however, tell a different story. The most well-documented example of Olson's revision practices must be this first Maximus poem. As Ralph Maud has written in *The Minutes of the Charles Olson Society*, the poem's earliest appearance is in a letter to Frances Boldereff:

> The genesis of "I, Maximus of Gloucester, to You," the first of the Maximus poems, is still, to my mind, conjectural, though it might be thought perfectly obvious that the poem began in Olson's letter to Frances Boldereff of 17 May 1950. Isn't its inception there right before our eyes? In the second paragraph (see Appendix A for a facsimile of the letter) Olson declares himself scared that he might never write another poem after "The Morning News":

> It is the craziest sort of feeling, this, of not being able to match the done! (I suppose this plane is the sex of writing art, the underpart, the nervousness because love is not born. One loves only form, and form only comes into existence when the thing is born. And the thing may lie around the bend of the next second. Yet, one does not know, until it is there, under hand.

> Tom Clark in his *Charles Olson: The Allegory of a Poet's Life* (p. 166) supposes—and it is a very reasonable deduction—that Olson was at this point in the letter moved to stop and turn his last few sentences into verse, gliding right there and then into:

> the thing may lie

> around the bend of the next

> second

> —where, Clark conjectures, Olson hit the "s" key instead of "x," accidentally turning "next" into "nest," and then, Clark's hypothesis goes (p. 166), deciding

to retain the typo: "From the 'nest' mischance issued a key image: 'the bird! the bird!'" which then immediately gets us to the seagulls of Gloucester:

o Anthony

of Padua sweep low and bless the roofs,

the gentle steep ones on whose ridge

gulls sit . . .

And so on for the rest of that page of the letter and another full page after that. This theory proposes that Olson composed the poem impromptu on the typewriter without pause. Well, so it might be.[11]

Facsimiles of the letter in question, attached to the online copy of Maud's short article, show the letter shifting immediately into lineated verse, with the left margin of the nascent poem indented from the margin of the prose above. After drafting parts of the poem, Olson finishes his love letter to his erstwhile mistress, saying that he speaks out from "islands hidden in the blood which, like jewels and miracles, you invoke" and calling himself "a hard-boiled instrument, a metal hot from boiling water" and her "o kylix."[12] The poem, as Maud and Tom Clark deftly reveal, comes together, if piecemeal, in this letter. Spontaneity, it seems, has been at the poet's service in this case, as the first lines of the letter indicate that he had not been writing at all of late. One could easily make the claim that Olson is in fact playing "by ear" here.

But this is not the last stop for this poem. In a series of decade-long revisions, "I, Maximus of Gloucester, to You," the first of Olson's Maximus poems, would go through major changes. The first version, which begins with "Off-shore," was the first to be published, in the first issue of Origin in 1951. The second version, with the first line "By ear, he sd." was first published in Jonathan Williams's Jargon Press edition of Maximus 1–10 in 1953. Olson would publish both versions once again in 1960, the "Off-shore" version in Totem/Corinth Press's Maximus 1–22 and the "By ear" version in The New American Poetry. Butterick's comprehensive edition of The Maximus Poems contains the first version. Olson, Maud tells us, made the decision to publish each version, sending Williams a revised copy of the poem that first had appeared in Origin I and later reverting back to the original for inclusion in the Totem/Corinth edition of 1960, without apparent reason, though he suspects that a review by Ed Dorn, critical of the "By ear" introductory lines, might have pushed Olson to favor the original.

Given the editorial rigor that scholars like George Butterick and Ralph Maud have shown in combing special collections for any statement regarding Olson's selection process, it seems unlikely that a clear-cut justification of Olson's revisions will come to light, but the audio archive reveals Olson in the midst of these revisions, providing a third version to add to the two published instances of the poem. In a performance of the poem at San Francisco State's Poetry Center, Olson reads from a poem that begins with, "Off-shore, by islands in the blood, I, Maximus, a metal hot from boiling water // By ear, he sd."[13] The remainder of the poem follows the "By ear" version until the final section, where the lines are changed to "Off-shore / (As I see it" so as to mark the poem's conclusion by a return to the first words. Minor as the changes might be, they have the significant effect of lending the poem a circularity of structure, returning to the speaker's initial watchful position "Off-shore," therefore reflecting Olson's interest in continuing to edit his work. On this tape, then, Olson is clearly at work on his arrangement, and the poem exists in a state of revision far from the "occasion of its composition." If anything, the composition is in flux, not improvised but tried and tested and retried.

The "Off-shore" version begins with the voice of Olson's speaker, the vaunted Maximus, "a metal hot from boiling water," an image that comes, as Maud's article shows, directly from the letter to Frances Boldereff, an image originally fraught with sexual tension from the context of the letter. Opening the poem with this bold sense of statement presents the speaker in a far-off position, putting himself above and beyond Gloucester while building his own sexualized mythology. In the "By ear" version, the speaker is much more difficult to place. "By ear, he sd," is the narration of a remark made in an indistinct past by an unidentified speaker; Maximus is only revealed as the narrator/speaker of the poem near the final lines. The tone of this version is much less turgid and high-pitched (in both senses of the word) than the "Off-shore" version. Whereas the "Off-shore" version has a fairly clear introduction and conclusion, "By ear" circles around its themes and images, going and coming in a cycle of apostrophes. The recording from the Poetry Center reading, though, offers a medium between the original and "By ear" versions, introducing Maximus right away, though the speaker does not purport to "tell you / what is a lance, who obeys the figures of / the present dance." We lose the voice of the speaker and, significantly, lose the iambic rhythm of "I, Maximus, a metal hot from boiling water," in the abrupt return to "By ear, he sd," in the subsequent lines.

It is this middle ground that captures a sense of what makes Olson so difficult to place and that hints at a major point I want to make later in this essay, which is the paradoxical tendency that belongs to the poetics of aurality that emerges in the age of technological reproduction, in the New American poetry. This is a tendency to blur the function of the poet, who becomes more a receiver or transmitter than an autonomous creator, more a recorder. We hear this tendency in Jack Spicer's notion of the poet as a radio and see it in his suggestion that a poem is a camera, the tendency of the poet to become a medium, in both senses of the word. We hear it in Robert Duncan's channeling of poets within his "made place" of correspondences. We hear it in Allen Ginsberg's Bardic lines that both record scenes and take the form of entranced chanting. Poets as different in temperament and subject matter as Paul Blackburn and James Schuyler share this sensibility. Both Blackburn and Schuyler, though their styles and their approach to the poem's form on the page are vastly different, present the sounds and images of everyday life in their poetry. Recordings then provide new instances of poems, which belong in the editor's files alongside the various manuscript copies. The activity of recording provides a model which affects changes in the dynamic of speaking and listening at the same time it shifts the poet's understanding of the relationship between speech, hearing and text. Our second example of recordings that add to the textual archive does much to demonstrate this point.

The story of Allen Ginsberg's copious revisions to *Howl* are rather well-known by now, and the recent discovery of what is now the earliest recording of Ginsberg reading the poem in the archives of Gary Snyder's undergraduate alma mater, Reed College, offers another glimpse into Ginsberg's revision process.[14] The Reed tape was made in February of 1956, only five months after Ginsberg read the initial drafts of the poem at the legendary Six Gallery reading made famous by Kerouac's descriptions in *The Dharma Bums*. This was also one month before the "re-creation" of the Six Gallery reading, which was recorded by the San Francisco State Poetry Center and had previously been the early recording. Significantly, though, the Reed tape comes only three months before Ginsberg gave Lawrence Ferlinghetti the manuscript that would go to print.[15] On the Reed recording, Ginsberg has completed most of the major revisions to the original manuscript drafts.[16] The section devoted exclusively to Carl Solomon has already been removed to a third part, which Ginsberg declines to read on this occasion. The signature long line is polished, the poet having long since abandoned the triadic line structure with which he initially experimented, following W. C. Williams's preferred form in *The Descent of Winter*. But the timing of this reading means that Ginsberg was still in the act of preparing the manuscript for its final published form. Most of the differences between the published text and the Reed recording consist of lines that were shuffled around slightly. Most of this reshuffling comes near the end of Part I. A large chunk of lines beginning with "who walked all night with their shoes full of blood" show the most rearranging, perhaps indicating that Ginsberg was around three-quarters of the way through his final revisions of *Howl*, Part I.

In a poem with such paratactic movement from one line to the next, the rearrangement of lines, admittedly, does not present much for the textual scholar to explain in terms of the subject matter. Though the revisions do not appear to be driven by relationships in content, we might productively imagine Ginsberg moving a line or even a short sequence of lines back or ahead a few lines in the poem in order to allow more literal breathing room. This would keep lines that require especially long breaths spaced out in the poem so as not to overtax the poet's considerable lungs during performance. Ginsberg has compared the poem's structure on many occasions to a legendary performance by Lester Young, often recounted by Kerouac, in which he played seventy consecutive choruses of "Lady Be Good" before a blown-away audience.[17] If we think of *Howl*'s prosody in this way, then we understand Ginsberg's late revisions better. On the recording, by this section of the poem, again roughly three-quarters into Part I, Ginsberg sounds entranced. His voice has become more monotone, allowing the texture of the words to take primacy over the emotional timbre of the performance. Ginsberg's revisions, which are in process on the Reed recording, should be heard, then, as attempts to fine-tune the poem's prosody. The recording becomes a means for Ginsberg to evaluate his revisions, to listen to his own performance and identify sections that could be subject to further rearranging. Recording allows the text of the poem to become a locus of the interconnectedness of poetic language, a score for oral performance that Ginsberg tweaks to perfection using tools and conceptions of orality and aurality that relate directly to the technology of audio recording.

Paul Blackburn understood this function of audio recording perhaps better than any other poet among the New Americans. Although most of his recordings are only accessible through the listening room at the Archive for New Poetry at the University of California at San Diego, Blackburn's massive collection of homemade tape recordings serves as perhaps the largest single audio archive of the New American period. And while the archive contains hundreds of recordings Blackburn made of other poets reading, some of the most fascinating tapes document Blackburn's use of the tape recorder as an integral step in his composition process. In a recent interview with Steve Evans, Robert Kelly recalls Paul Blackburn's ritual of composing poems by writing, then recording, then repeatedly playing back one line at a time and making revisions according to his ear:

You wanted to hear about Paul Blackburn and his tape recording. As you said, it was legendary. Every time he went into a reading in New York [. . .] whenever he gave a reading or came to a reading, he would bring his tape recorder, which in those days I recall as being a massive Roberts tape recorder, which was fairly high quality as such things went. Wollensack was another option; I think he may have had that once upon a time. But he came with his Roberts, which must have weighed thirty pounds—it was a tube operated amplifier in it and all that. He'd carry it in and set it up and record. When you visited Paul in his apartment [. . .] when you'd go to see Paul you'd see him taping a lot. He'd write his poems and then he'd read them into the tape recorder and listen over and over again to what he had said, in no sense narcissistic. He didn't enjoy his listenings, he was trying to attune the relationship between the paper and the ear. No poet I've ever met, even Jackson Mac Low, not even Jackson, was as concerned with the scoring, the paper as score for the performance. The performance was not in Paul's sense [. . .] he was not especially musical in the sense of an orotund, vocal delivery, but he was a master of pause, holding inflection, quickness, slowness. He loved all that, and he recorded to make sure he got it right [. . .] He was, to my knowledge, the first poet to put the tape recorder to a genuine compositional function, not archival, not documentation; he collaborated with the tape recorder, he collaborated with his own voice to restore the poem on the paper to its proper indexical function.[18]

Of the 260 tapes in the Blackburn Collection, most contain public poetry readings in which poets deliver their work before an audience. The graphic text is vocalized and rendered into the oral/aural dimension. The audience interacts occasionally, and the poet may offer some comments on the composition or publication history. As with the Olson and Ginsberg recordings discussed above, these delivery instances sometimes offer a new version of a poem and therefore become part of the textual condition of that poem. But in many of Blackburn's own recordings, he reads alone, speaking directly to the recorder, using the recording process, as Robert Kelly recalls, to create an aural text, a permanent record of oral speech that is stored and subject to (depending on the medium) nearly endless playback.

The tape, on which magnetized marks are made and then "read" by a diaphragm and converted into sound waves, becomes another text. The recorder becomes a technologized amanuensis, producing an exact copy of the poet's voice. We know from Blackburn's collection that he used this process extensively to edit his lineation and his spacing. Poems like "The Continuity," then, take on new significance:

> The bricklayer tells the busdriver
> and I have nothing to do but listen:

> The holdup at the liquor store, d'ja hear?
>   a detective
> watch't 'm for ten minutes
>   He took it away
> Got away down Broadway.   Yeah?
> Yeah.
>   And me:
> the one on the Circle?
> Yeah.
> Yeah? I was in there early tonight.
>   The continuity.
>   A dollar forty-
> two that I spent on a bottle of wine
> is now in a man's pocket going down Broadway.
>
> Thus far the transmission is oral.
>
> Then a cornerboy borrows my pencil
> to keep track of his sale of newspapers.[19]

Knowing that Blackburn has worked from graphic text to oral delivery to aural text and back to graphic text shows us that a poem like this documents a very complex web of orality, aurality and literacy. If Blackburn is attempting to highlight "natural," "oral" language, as critics and reviewers have suggested, then he does so with the utmost understanding of the dimensions of language, as we can come to see that the final, authoritative version of the poem is really a graphic representation of a carving made of linguistic sound.

Close Listening

The recording, then, offers an instance of a poem that can add to and complicate the textual archive, a sort of audio-manuscript of sorts, and it provides an opportunity, through the poet's vocalization, to experience the material of the poem as something heard as well as seen on the page. In recordings of Olson, we hear his deep, crackling voice intoning the long vowels and stammering over his signature clusters of consonants and parallel phrases. We hear Ginsberg's emotions build in his voice and then ebb towards monotone chanting. In a recording made at the Library of Congress in January of 1973, John Ashbery reads a poem from *The New American Poetry*, "How Much Longer Will I Be Able to Inhabit the Divine Sepulcher."[20] His vocalization emphasizes the contours of syntax in such a way that makes the surrealism and illogic of the content all the more noticeable, a sort of poetic deadpan.

James Schuyler's reading of "Freely Espousing" from 1986 is particularly notable for the way it demonstrates the point I discussed earlier, that recording served as a model for new methods of poetic composition, that the poet's were becoming like recorders. In the reading, we might expect the poet to use an array of intonations to vocalize from one line to the next in response to the extremity of the collage arrangement of the poem's content:

> a commingling sky
> > a semi-tropic night
> > that cast the blackest shadow
> > of the easily torn, untrembling banana leaf
> or Quebec! what a horrible city
> o Steubenville is better?
> > the sinking sensation
> when someone drowns thinking, "This can't be happening to me!"
> the profit of excavating the battlefield where Hannibal whomped
> > the Romans
> the sinous beauty of words like allergy
> the tonic resonance of
> pill when used as in
> "she is a pill"[21]

Yet Schuyler reads with the same flatness of voice across the lines, some of which suggest a poet-speaker, while others would appear to be quotations, bits of conversation overheard and reframed as found poetry. Treating each line with the same intonation, Schuyler's performance of the poem recalls the regularizing effect of technological reproduction. Even if sections of the poem appear to be "speech-based," it should be clear from his performance that the poet understands the transposition that occurs when spoken language is converted to writing. Schuyler's momentary attention to the "sinuous beauty" and "tonic resonance" of words also recalls the sense of close audition that is the result of an age in which we have learned to listen to sounds made permanent by way of recording. When we listen to recorded sound, we tend to experience the sound more directly, as I will discuss in more detail below. In the case of Schuyler's poem, we hear this kind of audition in the poem itself, and we experience it ourselves when we are able to focus on the grain of the reader's voice.

For another example of close listening, I want to turn to a reader whose performance style has been as influential as his formal technique, Robert Creeley. Creeley's style has been recognizable from very early on in his artistic career, a spare but sinewy, hypotactic syntax that is broken into lines of usually less than ten syllables. The influence is clearly from Williams and Zukofsky, though the enjambment that does much to dramatize Creeley's sentences can be traced back to Wordsworth's formal innovations. However, listening to Creeley reading suggests that he has reconceived the function and effect of enjambment.

For Wordsworth, enjambment was a tool to speed up the poem from line to line, a way to avoid the stilted and halting syntax of the end-stopped line, which created much of the artifice of poetry that Wordsworth felt should be abandoned in poetry that would fit the egalitarian ethos of the late eighteenth century. For Williams, who made the next great innovations with enjambment in poetry in English, enjambment is a way to change the way we pay attention to different words in a given poetic sentence. Take the repetition of "they taste good to her" in "To a Poor Old Woman":

> They taste good to her
> They taste good
> to her. They taste
> good to her[22]

The first line here offers the full sentence, while the second and third lines in the stanza are enjambed. The line breaks give the reader reason to pause, shifting our attention to the last word in the line and the first word of the next line so that in line 5 we attend to the goodness and in the beginning of line 6 we focus on the woman's perception of that goodness, "to her." The break at "taste" perhaps causes us to linger over that verb long enough to consider its paradoxical nature, used as an active verb but requiring the indirect object "to her" in order to make any logical sense. Seeing the poem's form on the page, we perceive enjambment as a disruptive technique, but Williams reads the poem quickly, taking no appreciable pause whatsoever at his carefully wrought line breaks. The lines that are so evocative on the page are rendered as though they are unbroken when the poet voices his work.

However, anyone who has heard Creeley read has likely been struck by the significant pause with which he approaches every line break. While he does not pause the same length at every line break, we can clearly hear that, in lines like

> . . . the darkness sur-
> rounds us, what[23]

In "I Know a Man," the word "surrounds" is forcefully and decisively broken into its two syllables. In fact in some recordings, the pause is long enough that we can just barely hear Creeley briefly exhale and draw breath in the acoustic space between "sur-" and "rounds." Creeley, then, takes a step beyond what Williams did with enjambment. If Williams sought to insist that we pay a bit more attention to the various but equally important parts of a sentence, then Creeley seeks to interrupt and complicate our reading by representing silence with his line breaks.

What we hear in that silence is somewhat more difficult to place. Every time I play a recording of "The Whip" for students, I have a very insistent group who hears Creeley's hesitancy and pausing as sobbing or other similar markers of a speaker who is choking over words. Creeley often reads with a serious, plaintive quality in his very singular voice. This response is most often the initial reaction of a listener who tries to hear the oral cues of extra-linguistic meaning in the voice, and especially with regard to poems that are as minimalist as Creeley's, this kind of reaction is helpful in making meaning. But the recording helps us access other dimensions of audition. Listening to the poem repeatedly, we are able to habituate to the point that the emotional cues in the voice become less and less salient. In the absence of the actual speaker, we begin to attend to the aural dimensions—what we hear—more than we attend to the oral dimensions—what the speaker says. The difference is subtle, but the principle is similar to what happens when we listen to, say, a Coltrane solo over and over again. We may think of the emotional power of the music and the virtuosity, but these qualities become less salient with repetition over time such that we begin to hear structures even in the free improvisations. Recording removes the presence of context; we can listen to the recording an infinite (give or take the durability of the recording medium) number of times, and we can listen in a theoretical vacuum, far from the moment of the original performance. We hear Creeley's poem not in the poet's home in early 1970s Bolinas or in the ritualistic space of the auditorium at the 92nd Street YMCA but in the more sterile, analytic space of our offices, our classrooms, or indeed anyplace given the paradoxical intimacy of headphones and earbuds.

The editors of PennSound, especially Michael S. Hennessey and Steve McLaughlin, have helped in the process tremendously by grouping together Creeley's performances of the same poem, notably "I Know a Man." As a result, listeners can hear the poem read repeatedly but also hear how Creeley's reading style might have altered over time. Of particular interest are the well-known poems from *For Love*, which Creeley read again and again in performances that date from the late 1950s all the way up to the 1970s and just before his death in 2005.[24] When we listen closely to recordings of "I Know a Man" and "The Whip" from a 1956 reading at the San Francisco

State Poetry Center and compare them to later readings, from the Vancouver Poetry Conference of 1963 and a reading at Harvard in 1966, we can hear a dramatic difference in the pause at the end of each line. The enjambment that disrupts the syntax of the poem becomes a silence that allows the words to recombine paragrammatically in unexpected ways. Creeley's signature device, with these more extensive silences, appears less mimetic; the hesitations no longer sound like sobbing or, in the case of "I Know a Man," drunken stammering. Instead of imitating speech, these poems shape language such that it becomes uncanny, rich with a sense of strange familiarity. The kind of audition that these recordings allow and encourage us to undertake results in this kind of close, formalist listening.

The Poetics of Aurality

While the modernist poets were affected by the changes in the sonic environment and in conceptions aurality that were wrought by electronic sound and sound recording, the New Americans represent the first generation of poets to live and write in the age of mechanical *sound* reproduction.[25] Olson famously speaks of working towards a poetics that runs counter to the "poetry that print bred." Even so, it is somewhat misleading to think of the New American poetry as an *oral* poetics as is so often asserted, especially with respect to the Black Mountain School and the Beats, by the critical tradition.[26] As Walter Ong has theorized, recuperation of some aspects of primary orality, such as a completely non-literate culture might experience, was made possible by the development of electronic media in the early twentieth century. He calls this "secondary orality":

> When I first used the term "secondary orality," I was thinking of the kind of orality you get on radio and television, where oral performance produces effects somewhat like those of "primary orality," the orality using the unprocessed human voice, particularly in addressing groups, but where the creation of orality is of a new sort. Orality here is produced by technology. Radio and television are "secondary" in the sense that they are technologically powered, demanding the use of writing and other technologies in designing and manufacturing the machines which reproduce voice. They are thus unlike primary orality, which uses no tools or technology at all. Radio and television provide technologized orality. This is what I originally referred to by the term "secondary orality."[27]

Secondary orality complicates the sense of presence that Ong argues is foregrounded in primary oral communications and in primarily oral cultures, the immediate presence of the speaker and the dialogic partner and the immediate and fleeting presence of the spoken utterance itself.

The concepts of orality and secondary orality have received considerable attention in literary studies. As Ong and other scholars related to the Toronto School of Media Studies, especially Eric Havelock, have shown, orality shows up in style, and residual oral styles can be observed even in very literary prose writing. Orality, as Ong and Havelock understand it, imparts a sense of powerful imminence to the spoken word, and language is treated with a sense of ritualistic ardor. The parallel syntax that marks some New American writing—*Howl* is perhaps the most obvious example—seeks to consciously recuperate some of the incantatory power of primary orality. Certainly the rise of the public poetry reading in the New American period speaks to a similar desire to regain some of the social collectivism and much of the spiritual and, therefore, political power of the poem by reestablishing the ritualistic context of the poem. But the accompanying sense of *aurality* has been less well studied until recently with the interdisciplinary connections being made between the New Formalism and sound studies. As Ong recognizes, "radio and television provide *technologized* orality" [my emphasis]. Whereas primary orality involves the co-presence of speaker and listener, when we think of this relationship with respect to technologized, secondary orality, the gap in presence affects the auditor more than the speaker. Technologically mediated speech, like writing, presumes the absence of either the speaker or the auditor, even if the communication—via telephony, radio or television—occurs in something close to "real time." Technologically mediated orality almost always results in acousmatic audition, a condition in which the listener listens to an absent or unseen speaker. Indeed, the term "loudspeaker," more commonly used in its shortened form, "speaker," which denotes the ubiquitous device that converts electric pulses into sound waves, reflects our desire to erase conceptually this gap in presence; the term "speaker" personifies and anthropomorphizes the electronic driver that recreates the speech of a once-but-no-longer-present human speaker, a perfect example of electronic age *prosopopeia*.

French composer Pierre Schaeffer has been among the earliest and best theorists of the effects of acousmatic listening, arguing that the "acousmatic situation" made common by electronic sound technologies, especially radio and recording, has transformative effects on the previous norms of listening. Schaeffer, by asserting the separation of an audio signal from its source, coins the term *objet sonore*, the sonorous object:

> In listening to sonorous objects whose instrumental causes are hidden, we are led to forget the latter and to take an interest in these objects for themselves. The dissociation of seeing and hearing here encourages another way of listening: we listen to the sonorous forms, without any aim other than that of hearing them better, in order to be able to describe them through an analysis of the contents of our perceptions.[28]

The recorded poetry reading allows this transformation in listening, whereby the experience of the poetry reading becomes emphatically more aural than oral. The reception of the sound signal now takes precedence over its delivery; we listen to the poem instead of listening to the poet, or at the very least, we listen to the poet's voice instead of listening to the poet, a distinction that is subtle but significant. The distinction is paramount since such refocused listening theoretically elevates the analysis of form and prosody over the analysis of the poet. We hear what Roland Barthes called the "grain of the voice," the hearing of which allows us to perceive the "fringe of contact between language and music."[29] This "fringe of contact" is precisely the site of poetry according to Louis Zukofsky's poetics of the integral, "upper limit music, lower limit / speech."[30] This is not to say that when listening to a recording one *must not* attend to the personality of voice or even the personality of form. In fact, the listener has greater choice and, of equal importance for the study of poetry, greater access to the kind of close listening that provides us with finer critical distinctions. Michael Davidson reminds us that

> "Technologies of presence" will always offer a hybrid voice—a voice in a machine—that cannot speak entirely for itself, even though it posits self-presence as its ground [. . .] When the complicity between presence and technology is acknowledged [. . .] the tape recorder ceases to be a passive receptacle for a more authentic speech but an active agent in its deconstruction."[31]

Indeed, as Schaeffer is aware, the *aura*, to adapt Walter Benjamin's very apt vocabulary, of the source is not entirely eliminated, yet, with regard to recording and playback, repetition helps the listener in bypassing the aura:

> In fact, Pythagoras' curtain is not enough to discourage our curiosity about causes, to which we are instinctively, almost irresistibly drawn. But the repetition of the physical signal, which recording makes possible, assists us here in two ways: by exhausting this curiosity, it gradually brings the sonorous object to the fore as a perception worthy of being observed for itself; on the other hand, as a result of ever more attentive and more refined listenings, it progressively reveals to us the richness of this perception.[32]

The aura of the poet, then, may be as present in a recording as we wish it to be, though I am inclined to agree that a threshold for repetition exists wherein that aura inevitably is, to use Schaeffer's descriptive verb, exhausted. And once that aura is exhausted, the sound of the poem is that much more palpable, more material than, perhaps, ever before.

This is same process that led contemporaneous artists like John Cage and Vladimir Ussachevsky to begin to question the possibilities in music of sounds that had previously been considered noise. The recording process is indiscriminate, inscribing all sounds within range. The recorder hears all sounds, but it does not listen to any sounds in particular. For Cage, who began using tape recorders in his compositions at least as early as 1955, with his "Williams Mix," this represents a massive "opening of the field" of available sounds to such an extent that divisions of time began to serve as the only limitations necessary to delineate a piece of music. We can see parallels particularly in the work of Schuyler and Larry Eigner, whose poems frequently demonstrate such a radical openness of content—and form in Eigner's later work—that they are markedly noisier than the most dissonant collages of Pound, Oppen or even Zukofsky. In "Freely Espousing," Schuyler's range of listening is exceptionally wide, incorporating a multitude of untraceable voices. Consider Larry Eigner's "Do it yrself," published in *Look at the Park* and in *The New American Poetry* (I keep Eigner's Courier typeface in order to be consistent with the spacing):

```
Do it yrself

Now they have two cars to clean
the front and back lawns
bloom in the drought

        why not turn the other radio on the
    pious hopes of the Red Sox

yes, that's a real gangling kid coming down the street

he'll grow up

        He'll fill out

    sponges with handles

        we got trinaural hearing

-they are taller than their cars³³
```

Here a number of observations are thrown together paratactically, the neighbors with their cars and their overwatering, the proposal to listen to the game on the radio, the awkward boy walking by, back to the cars, to a very oddly placed reference probably to a hearing aid, and then back to the cars again. The spacing on the page reinforces the cognitive and grammatical distances between the lines in the poem. The poem is at all points open. The discrete, grammatically fragmented even-handedness with which the poem moves from one object to the next suggests the destabilization of lyrical subjectivity, the "I" that focuses closely and singularly on the object or event that is the poem's primary concern. The effect is achieved by rendering a graphic representation of hearing as opposed to listening, of open aurality like that of the indiscriminate tape recorder. As such, Eigner's poems are perhaps the purest demonstration of the poetics of aurality. Creeley's equation of form and content finds its most literal manifestation in Eigner's paratactic distribution of grammatical and semantic units, as does Olson's notion of "Composition by Field." The appearance of black typescript sprawling across the page space demonstrates the notion that the poem can be an open field, and the arrangement of disconnected objects, observations and quotations of found poetry evince a poetry that embraces an open field of thought not a closed, focused system. Because the "content" of Eigner's poetry is so often clipped from its context, any easy distinction between what is usually termed form and content is incredibly complicated. Is the clipping and placement of words and phrases in "Do it yrself" a function more of content or form? In Eigner's work, Williams's "machine made of words" has become self-sustaining and autonomous, unconcerned with referring to any "absolute object" outside the poem. The poem is a recording comprised of all the noise that can be heard on the many tapes in which Paul Blackburn leaves the recorder on between poems, bits of traffic sounds, thunderstorms, footsteps, swatches of phone conversations, and refrigerator doors opening and shutting. We hear the same things when the recorder is left on at the end of a reading, when multiple conversations are heard simultaneously above the shifting of chairs and the laughter of the poet, now relaxing after the performance.

The New American period represents the first generation of poets to be so exhaustively recorded, as the audio archive shows. "Poets," says Brian Reed in his masterful analysis of Hart Crane's relationship with his Victrola gramophone, "listen to the world around them. Their verse records not only what they hear but how they hear it. The job of the critic is to unpack the interdependency of that 'what' and 'how' in the name of achieving a more accurate account of the poetry, its genesis, and its significance."[34] For the New Americans, the age of recorded sound means an age of increasingly mediated orality, which, as I have been arguing, shifts the focus in fact away from the oral qualities of the voice towards the heard-ness of those qualities. The voice, which can now be stored, removed from the immediacy of its context, played back infinitely and manipulated during both recording and playback, is experienced as an aural phenomenon. Poetry, then, recording what poets hear and how they hear it, becomes likewise more aural. The function of the poet starts to change from creator to recorder, and the materiality of the poem shifts towards sound, whether that sound is inscribed in the marks on the page or vocalized in performance. The result is a poetics of aurality that came into very rigorous experimentation in the 1970s and 1980s by the loosely-termed Language writers and that continues to be developed today by writers like Christian Bok, Caroline Bergvall, and Kenneth Goldsmith. These are all poets whose relationship to the New Americans has at times seemed ambivalent. Considering the New American poetry in the audio archive opens up new ways to understand trends in innovative poetics over the last half-century while cementing the importance of this generation of writers and the anthology that made them famous.

Notes

1. Steve Dickison, Poetry Center Mailing, San Francisco State University, December 20, 2009.

2. Evans cataloged and re-mastered dozens of tapes in the Paul Blackburn Collection of the Archive for New Poetry at UC San Diego's Mandeville Library, and Charles Bernstein and Al Filreis have been instrumental in establishing the PennSound archive, which is now managed by Michael S. Hennessey.

3. http://writing.upenn.edu/pennsound/

4. Charles Bernstein, "PennSound Manifesto," *PennSound*, (2003), http://writing.upenn.edu/pennsound/manifesto.php.

5. See Douglas Kahn, *Noise Water Meat*, Cambridge, MA, MIT Press, 1999.

6. René Wellek and Austin Warren, "The Mode of Existence of a Literary Work of Art," in *Theory of Literature*, 2nd edition, New York: Harcourt, Brace and Co., 1956, 129–145.

7. W. K. Wimsatt, Jr. and Monroe C. Beardsley, "The Concept of Meter: An Exercise in Abstraction," *PMLA* (December 1959): 593.

8. I am thinking especially of Steven Clay and Jerome Rothenberg's collection, *The Book of the Book: Some Works and Projections about the Book and Writing*, New York: Granary Books, 1999.

9. Edward Halsey Foster, *Understanding the Black Mountain Poets*, Columbia, SC: University of South Carolina Press, 1995, 18.

10. Charles Olson, "I, Maximus of Gloucester to You," in *The New American Poetry 1945–1960*. ed. Donald Allen, Berkeley: University of California Press, 1999, 8.

11. Ralph Maud, "The First Maximus Poem." *Minutes of the Charles Olson Society* 29 (April 1999).

12. Ibid., *Appendix A*.

13. Charles Olson, "I, Maximus of Gloucester to You" (Recorded at San Francisco State University, 1957). *PennSound*, 2004–2007, University of Pennsylvania Center for Programs in Contemporary Writing.

14. Available only as streaming audio at Reed Multimedia, http://www.reed.edu/news_center/multimedia/2007–08/ginsbergreadings1.28.08.html.

15. In a letter to his father, dated April 26, 1956, Ginsberg says that he has "set a deadline for this weekend for City Lights and said I'd bring it in." Bill Morgan and

Nancy Joyce Peters, *Howl on Trial: The Battle for Free Expression*, San Francisco: City Lights, 2006, 39.

16. Allen Ginsberg, *Howl: Original Draft Facsimile*, New York: Harper, 2006.

17. Daniel Belgrad, *The Culture of Spontaneity: Improvisation and the Arts in Post-War America*, Chicago: University of Chicago Press, 1998, 196.

18. Robert Kelly and Steve Evans, "Robert Kelly Remembering Paul Blackburn," (2007), http://media.sas.upenn.edu/pennsound/authors/Kelly/Kelly-Robert_Remembering-Blackburn_The-Lipstick-of-Noise_4–07.mp3. Evans originally posted the interview on his weblog, *The Lipstick of Noise*, http://www.thirdfactory.net/lipstick.php.

19. Paul Blackburn, *Collected Poems*, New York: Persea Books, 1985.

20. http://media.sas.upenn.edu/pennsound/authors/Ashbery/Songs-We-Know/Ashbery-John_11_Divine-Sepulcher_The-Songs-We-Know-Best_1973.mp3.

21. James Schuyler, "Freely Espousing," *The New American Poetry*, ed. Donald Allen, New York: Grove Press, 1960, 223.

22. William Carlos Williams, "To a Poor Old Woman," *Collected Poems: 1909–1939, Volume I*, New York: New Directions, 1991.

23. Robert Creeley, "I Know a Man," *The Collected Poems of Robert Creeley 1945–1975*, Berkeley, University of California Press, 1982.

24. See Creeley's Author Page at PennSound, http://writing.upenn.edu/pennsound/x/Creeley.html

25. Brian Reed, in *Hart Crane: After His Lights* (Tuscaloosa: University of Alabama Press, 2006), includes an excellent discussion of Crane's use of the Victrola in his compositional process, and Juan A. Suarez relates T.S. Eliot's formal arrangements and prosody to the experience of listening to recordings of ragtime in his *Pop Modernism: Noise and the Reinvention of the Everyday* (Urbana: University of Illinois Press, 2007). We could also point to the repetition in Gertrude Stein's poetry as evidence of the influence of film and sound recording and, likewise, to the radical collage of Oppen and Zukofsky. Williams's poems, "The Defective Record" and "To a Poor Old Woman," with their use of repetition, offer a telling example of his awareness of the effects of listening to recorded sound.

26. Readers will have to forgive me for not including citations here of such analyses. I hope my point can be granted without listing what would be a very large number of book chapters and articles.

27. Michael Kleine and Fredric G. Gale, "The Elusive Presence of the Word: An Interview with Walter Ong," Composition FORUM 7.2 (1996): 80.

28. Pierre Schaeffer, "Acousmatics," *Audio Culture: Readings in Modern Music*, eds. Cristoph Cox and Daniel Warner, New York: Continuum, 2004, 78.

29. Roland Barthes, "The Grain of the Voice," in *Image, Music, Text*, trans. Stephen Heath, New York: Hill and Wang, 1978, 180–181.

30. Louis Zukofsky, "A-12," *A*, Baltimore: Johns Hopkins University Press, 1993.

31. Michael Davidson, "Technologies of Presence: Orality and the Tapevoice of Contemporary Poetics," *Sound States: Innovative Poetics and Acoustical Technologies*, ed. Adalaide Morris, Chapel Hill, NC: University of North Carolina Press, 1997, 100.

32. Schaeffer, "Acousmatics," 78.

33. Larry Eigner, *Look at the Park*, Swampscott, MA, Independently Published, 1958, 8.

34. Reed, *Hart Crane*, 121.

Bibliography

Ashbery, John. "How Much Longer Will I Be Able to Inhabit the Divine Sepulcher." Recording. http://media.sas.upenn.edu/pennsound/authors/Ashbery/Songs-We-Know/Ashbery-John_11_Divine-Sepulcher_The-Songs-We-Know-Best_1973.mp3.

Barthes, Roland. "The Grain of the Voice." In *Image, Music, Text*. Translated by Stephen Heath. New York: Hill and Wang, 1978.

Belgrad, Daniel. *The Culture of Spontaneity: Improvisation and the Arts in Post-War America*. Chicago: University of Chicago Press, 1998.

Bernstein, Charles. "PennSound Manifesto," *PennSound* (2003). http://writing.upenn.edu/pennsound/manifesto.php.

Blackburn, Paul. *Collected Poems*. New York: Persea Books. 1985.

Clay, Steven and Jerome Rothenberg. *The Book of the Book: Some Works and Projections About the Book and Writing*. New York: Granary Books, 1999.

Creeley, Robert. "I Know A Man." Recording. Author Page. PennSound. http://writing.upenn.edu/pennsound/x/Creeley.html.

———. "I Know A Man." *The Collected Poems of Robert Creeley 1945–75*. Berkeley: University of California Press, 1982.

Dickison, Steve. Poetry Center Mailing. San Francisco State University, December 20, 2009.

Davidson, Michael. "Technologies of Presence: Orality and the Tapevoice of Contemporary Poetics." *Sound States: Innovative Poetics and Acoustical Technologies*. Edited by Adalaide Morris. Chapel Hill, NC: University of North Carolina Press, 1997.

Eigner, Larry. *Look at the Park*. Swampscott, MA: Independently Published, 1958.

Foster, Edward Halsey. *Understanding the Black Mountain Poets*. Columbia: University of South Carolina Press, 1995.

Ginsberg, Allen. *Howl: Original Draft Facsimile*. New York: Harper, 2006.

———. "Howl." Part 1. Recording. http://www.reed.edu/news_center/multimedia/2007–08/ginsbergreadings1.28.08.html.

Kahn, Douglas. *Noise Water Meat*. Cambridge, MA: MIT Press, 1999.

Kelly, Robert, and Steve Evans. "Robert Kelly Remembering Paul Blackburn." (2007). http://media.sas.upenn.edu/pennsound/authors/Kelly/Kelly-Robert_Remembering-Blackburn_The-Lipstick-of-Noise_4–07.mp3.

Kleine, Michael, and Fredric G. Gale. "The Elusive Presence of the Word: An Interview with Walter Ong." Composition FORUM 7.2 (1996).

Maud, Ralph. "The First Maximus Poem." *Minutes of the Charles Olson Society* 29, 1999.

Morgan, Bill and Nancy Joyce Peters. *Howl on Trial: The Battle for Free Expression*. San Francisco: City Lights, 2006.

Olson, Charles. "I, Maximus of Gloucester to You." *The New American Poetry 1945–1960*. Edited by Donald Allen. Berkeley: University of California Press, 1999.

———. "I, Maximus of Gloucester to You" (Recorded at San Francisco State University, 1957). *PennSound*, 2004–2007. University of Pennsylvania Center for Programs in Contemporary Writing. 30 July 2007.

Reed, Brian. *Hart Crane: After His Lights*. Tuscaloosa: University of Alabama Press, 2006.

Schaeffer, Pierre. "Acousmatics." *Audio Culture: Readings in Modern Music*. Edited by Cristoph Cox and Daniel Warner. New York: Continuum, 2004.

Schuyler, James, "Freely Espousing." *The New American Poetry 1945–1960*. Edited by Donald Allen. New York: Grove Press, 1960.

Suarez, Juan A. *Pop Modernism: Noise and the Reinvention of the Everyday*. Urbana: University of Illinois Press, 2007.

Williams, William Carlos. "To a Poor Old Woman." *Collected Poems: 1909–1939, Volume I*. New York: New Directions, 1991.

Wimsatt, W. K. Jr., and Monroe C. Beardsley. "The Concept of Meter: An Exercise in Abstraction." *PMLA* (December 1959).

Wellek, René and Austin Warren, "The Mode of Existence of a Literary Work of Art." *Theory of Literature*. 2nd edition. New York: Harcourt, Brace and Co., 1956.

Zukofsky, Louis. "A-12." A. Baltimore: Johns Hopkins University Press, 1993.

~

CHAPTER ELEVEN

The New American Poetry's Objectivist Legacy: Linguistic Skepticism, the Signifier, and Material Language

Burt Kimmelman

Donald Allen's monumental, game-changing anthology he baldly titled *The New American Poetry* proclaimed, in effect, a new order of writing and thinking in North America and beyond. Conceived of not long after the Second World War, Allen's collection contained "new" poetics, aesthetics, and otherwise theorizing about how poetry might authentically exist in a new time. It was indeed a new time. Published in 1960 (its full title was *The New American Poetry: 1945–1960*),[1] Allen had drawn from several of the cutting-edge journals of the 1940s and 1950s—not least of them were the *San Francisco Review*, the *Black Mountain Review*, and *Origin*—in whose pages the work of a young John Taggart would appear in 1969. Taggart, along with Rachel Blau DuPlessis, Ron Silliman, and Michael Heller, are the focus of this chapter, and how their work evolved in tandem with and in consequence of the evolution in poetry embodied in this book reveals a great deal about the nature of poetry and thought in the book as well as about both its roots and branches[2] that extend even into the present moment.

In these and other journals of the period could be found, too, poems by Louis Zukofsky, George Oppen, and other Objectivist poets. This inclusion is noteworthy, since particularly the work of that group of late Modernists, the Objectivists (so named from Zukofsky's 1931 special issue of *Poetry* magazine), informed all the writing in the Allen anthology and both the poetry and poetics of these four younger poets. To be sure, the work in the Allen book was of immense importance to Taggart (b. 1942) and his fellow poets of a third generation: Heller (b. 1937), DuPlessis (b. 1941) and Silliman (b. 1946). They were too young to have been anthologized by Allen, and the question of whether or not, had they published substantially by the late 1950s, they would have been included by Allen is not an idle one. While the work of these relatively younger practitioners could not have appeared in the book, neither did the work of the older Objectivists whose aesthetics and ideology, I am arguing here, sponsored the book, giving rise in large measure to what is now thought of as "the New American Poetry."

On the other hand, the poets who were featured by Allen—such as Robert Duncan, Charles Olson, Robert Creeley, and others affiliated with them who came to influence the four "third generation" poets and whose writings are key to understanding the greater evolution of the avant-garde in both Allen's time and ours today—did break new ground. And Taggart, Heller, DuPlessis and Silliman—like the poets Allen valorized—revered the Objectivists, studying their work closely. I would also say that, together with these "NAP" poets, they played a role in the formation of a second generation of "neo-Objectivists" (the work of Olson, Creeley, Duncan et al., comprising a next stage, as it were, of Objectivist poetics).[3] What is fascinating, however, is the fact that the Objectivists' writings were first encountered by these four younger neo-Objectivists before there was any digging by them into the Allen book. And yet, despite their chronology—possibly better to say because of this chain of events—the output of the four younger poets provides new insight into the achievement of the Allen collection overall as well as, perhaps, into the collective achievement of Louis Zukofsky, George Oppen, and the other Objectivists as they came to be known (principally Lorine Niedecker, Charles Reznikoff, and Carl Rakosi), and both William Carlos Williams and Gertrude Stein. Furthermore, the four younger poets tell us a great deal about why the Allen book is still very much alive for us today and, too, why we need to keep it before us when considering the avant-garde of the present, in the early years of the twenty-first century.

Surveying the anthology, from within that broad collection, however, it is the work of the Black Mountain poets, as Allen named them, which especially represents a neo-Objectivist generation. In accounting for that work we are able to appreciate fully the sway the anthology still holds over a great many poets, indirectly or directly, more than a half century later. When we look out on the literary landscape through the eyes of the new generation of neo-Objectivists, we can understand what "new" can really mean today.

To tell the story of these four younger poets will require both contextualizing and analyzing their work, arising out of their first discovery of their own potential about the time when the anthology was first being read. Examining their work today discloses four distinct versions of neo-Objectivism needing still to be re-understood as avant-garde—a poetics that reveals filiation and, as will be discussed later, cross- and counter-influences within a still larger picture of North American experimental poetry in the last century. Hence, the question arises as to whether or not the Allen collection can still be seen as residing at the heart of this avant-garde. In order to provide a full accounting of the impact of the anthology—and, as already suggested, to fill in the picture of what the "new" in poetry has been since 1960 (to echo Ezra Pound's famous imprecation to "make it new")—we must consider the effects of the respective work of these four recent neo-Objectivists on newer avant-garde movements.

It is probably best to begin the mapping of the various influences by discussing the relationships between the Objectivists and these four younger poets, inasmuch as this set of relationships is pivotal in comprehending the avant-garde trajectory beginning in the early 1900s. It may seem ironic to account for the Objectivists' involvement in the growth of Taggart, Heller, DuPlessis, and Silliman as poets apart from the poetry of the first neo-Objectivists, so to speak (i.e., the NAP poets), as if to leap over them. To be sure, the poets of the generation following the Objectivists, those whom Allen included in his book, have been and still are of great importance to these younger practitioners. Poets like Duncan, Creeley, Jack Spicer, Denise Levertov, Olson, Robin Blaser and others strikingly inflected the development of the post-anthology poets; again, their reading of their immediate elders, who themselves were enamored of the Objectivists, provides us with a vital entrance into the Objectivists' work and a deeper comprehension of their achievement which, in their turn, allows us to appreciate fully the poets of the anthology as well as the anthology itself as a socio-literary event, both in its own time and ours.

This reading backward is not new. In fact, just as the Objectivists read and revered their immediate predecessors—namely, along with the High Modernist Stein, others of her time such as "the Philadelphia Three"[4]—so too did the NAP poets alert a wider reading public to their Objectivist forebears. Within this complex of influences the avant-garde who preceded the Objectivists needs also to be discussed in order to complete the picture of Modern and postmodern experimentalism. Indeed, one achievement of the Allen anthology was, directly or indirectly, to secure both the modernist (the writings of poets like Marianne Moore, T.S. Eliot, and Wallace Stevens aside) and Objectivist legacies, although the poets succeeding the anthology especially called attention to this fact and, by dint of their own achievements, celebrated it. The Objectivists proved to be life-changing for them. Even so, it would be difficult if not impossible to overstate the effect the anthology had on this younger generation of avant-garde poets (specifically, as Allen grouped them, the poets associated with the San Francisco Renaissance, the Beats, and the New York School, but especially the Black Mountain School that was named after the famous experimental college in North Carolina in which many of the poets in this grouping participated—whose rector, Olson, would exercise a great deal of influence on Allen)[5] by way of either a simultaneous or prior engagement with the poetry and eventually the theoretical writings of the Objectivists.

One question that arises, given this web of inter-influences, is why the Objectivists were not included in the anthology. Might we also ask why Allen didn't include any of the High Modernists? After all, the avant-garde strain in North American poetics arguably begins with them. What, if anything, was really "new" in *The New American Poetry*? Was Allen merely thinking of chronology, wanting to include, let's say, the avant-garde poetry of a younger generation—or did he perceive how the work of these younger, post-war, poets constituted a sea change yet may have been beholden to the Objectivists and their predecessors? Not only does poetry of the generation following the Allen anthology not negate the crucial filiation coming out of these older poets, this later work also reveals the importance of the middle generation, who were lauded in a way the Objectivists could but only have envied, in shaping the work of their successors. Moreover, in a twist, the poetry (and critical prose) of the third generation may very well have affected the writing of poets who became known as hallmarks of that anthology and who continued to write for many years after its publication, such as, most notably, Robert Creeley. Hence, at least his later work ought to be attended to in this light. Considering how these four younger poets, along with a mature Creeley with whom they each enjoyed a nurturing relationship, provide their own vital path toward a complete comprehension of the Objectivists' heritage allows for a deeper appreciation of Allen's accomplishment.

Heller, DuPlessis, Taggart, and Silliman came to writing poems at about the time when the anthology first appeared. In thinking about inter- or cross-influence, a comment by DuPlessis is particularly telling, which speaks directly to her development as a poet and, possibly by inference, how Taggart, Heller, and Silliman also began their writing lives. When asked about the poetic influences on her, she corrected the question by saying that she

> prefer[s] the words "affected by" to the word "influence" which suggests a one-way street. And actually etymology gives something even more strange—

"influence" is a flowing into—as if the person to be influenced were a kind of vessel or vat or holding pot. In fact there is a lot of agency involved in "influence" or in "being affected by" another person. You choose. And you also shape the narrative or contribute to it.[6]

Could DuPlessis's writing—or that of the other three—possibly have had an effect on Oppen (a mentor for both her and Heller), or perhaps Zukofsky or Rakosi who, along with Creeley, were writing well into the period when these younger poets first started making their mark?

The anthology proposed an alternative conceptualization of poetry which was radical in its time; simultaneously, it bestowed both fame and notoriety upon Pound, Williams, and the other earlier Modernists—while calling attention to Zukofsky, Oppen, and the other Objectivists. The fact that DuPlessis and her peers first awoke to and became enthused by the possibility of the *new* as integrally involved with the Objectivists does not at all negate the enormous role played by the middle generation who were the first and principal readers of the Objectivists and Stein (as well as, principally, Pound, Williams, and H.D.): Olson, Creeley, Levertov, Duncan, Spicer, and others of their generation such as Paul Blackburn (who, like Olson, visited Pound over a number of years and carried on a brilliant correspondence with him). The NAP poets were acknowledging their roots in all these Modernists and late Modernists (or perhaps better to think of them as our early Postmodernists)—it might be said that they worshipped them—at a time when none of them was being anthologized or taught in universities. Thus the "grandchildren" may have had the sense of a time frame and within it of their own instrumentality that they envisioned as helping to effect a turning point in their century. In other words, to put it plainly, they looked ahead in their writing, not necessarily concerned with wanting to replicate prior work, even what they saw as prior avant-garde work.

Once again, this self-positioning created a "new," not unlike what Pound and the other Modernists had called for at the start of the twentieth century. And the grandchildren created a possible "back formation" in which older, still surviving poets such as Creeley unconsciously or purposely revised the mid-century "new." Together with DuPlessis, Heller, Silliman, and Taggart, they helped to establish the conditions for a fourth generation—still younger poets who claim to be or are seen to be avant-garde in some sense—within a chronology that not only comes readily to hand but also discloses a lineation that may be useful as concerns the very question of influence proper over younger poets and then their inflection of the later work of their surviving elders (i.e., in the case of the third generation, Creeley but also Oppen). And so the late work of a poet like DuPlessis might be usefully read in comparison with the work of Flarf or Conceptual poets (Flarf poets like Sharon Mesmer or K. Silem Mohammad, for instance, and Conceptualists like Rob Fitterman or Vanessa Place, among others). Time frames co-exist and may overlie discursive frames that take as their guiding question the continued existence of an avant-garde—if, in the present, we can still speak seriously of an extant avant-garde in North American poetry—if we can seriously talk about, in the words of Paul Mann, "an outside of the inside, the leading edge of the mainstream, and thus marginal in both senses: excluded and salient."[7] The argument may be interjected here to the effect that there will always be an avant-garde. Whether or not that avant-garde would be powerful enough to inflect a mainstream over time, however, is another matter.

Classic literary-critical periodization, for all its limitations, may be of use in this contrast, while I realize that there is the ever present danger in envisioning or explaining a society's literary developments within the context of a standard periodization, and yet a special dispensation might be granted anyone who tries to come to terms with the modern era, especially anyone who might wish to speak of the twentieth century as a time frame that just may happen to have been bounded by the dates of our calendar. Some justification is in order for seeing this century as having gotten underway at about 1900, when Modernism is first taking root, and when great technological and scientific changes took place, changes that altered the nature of life and the way the world was viewed and that may have encouraged people's notions about their entering a radically new world, as acutely aware of the calendar as people were (the awareness and attention to particulars a part of the modern sensibility). Indeed, when we look back from the vantage point of the early twenty-first century, it is interesting to note how much of the material and intellectual world normally associated with *modern* living was already in place by 1900.

Cities, for example, the incubators of high culture, were growing quickly. Skyscrapers were already being constructed, and over distances people could communicate by telephone. Work began on New York City's rapid transit "subway" system and the photostatic copying machine was invented, while the "Brownie" camera was being marketed. Fundamental change was rampant. As Richard Gray has noted in his history of twentieth-century American poetry, none other than Henry Adams had written in 1900 that "his historical neck [was being] broken by the irruption of forces totally new."[8] Life was becoming more complicated. Adams felt that the "child born in 1900 would [. . .] be born into a new world which would not be a unity but a multiple."[9]

Discoveries in science, especially in physics and biology, in the later years of the twentieth century revealed vast landscapes of possibility and multiplicity, inevitably to become the substance of some poetry; these discoveries were presaged in the century's early years. The idea that the universe is comprised of twelve dimensions, for example, as is held by some String Theorists today, represents a departure from classical physics, a physics that still holds great sway over everyday language—yet poems, one by one, can work to reshape language and meaning. The rift in the laws of nature as they were propounded by Newton in the late seventeenth and early eighteenth century appeared with Einstein's Theories of Relativity (1905, 1916) and then Heisenberg's Uncertainty Principle (1927). Tangibility, objectivity, and subjectivity were to be understood in new ways; predictability came to be conditional. Here, then, is a very different world than the one being articulated in Robert Browning's "Pippa Passes" (1841), for instance in the declamation that "God's in His Heaven—/ All's right with the world."[10] 1900 is also the year when Sigmund Freud published *The Interpretation of Dreams.* In another two years Wassily Kandinsky would inaugurate abstract painting with the showing of his *Blue Rider,* a work that may have anticipated Marcel Duchamp's *Nude Descending a Staircase* that was put on view at the famous 1913 Armory Show in New York City. Would Williams have otherwise postulated, as he did subsequently after attending the show, that a poem was a "machine made of words," and would the "machine aesthetic" have gained ground in his and others' poetry?

Transformation continues within a world predicated on transformation. What is important to see in these developments is that the last century discovered a radically new world, and the century produced a unique art expressing this new awareness. In his landmark book *Disjunctive Poetics: From Gertrude Stein and Louis Zukofsky to Susan Howe,* Peter Quartermain also turns to Adams's eloquent witnessing of that turn-of-the-century moment. Framing the developments of the time as constituting a paradigm shift, Quartermain sees much of the new writing of Modernism as not only a symptom of great changes but also as instrumental in making them. Laying out the scientific and technological background of the poetry he examines in his book allows him to talk about what he sees was "the central preoccupation" of the then experimental writers who were intent on responding to the new world. The radically new led them to recognize "that in preconstituting the world we de-liberate our experience, thereby foreordaining the real; [thus] their central insistence [was] on the autonomous nature of the poem as part of an indeterminate physical and socioeconomic world."[11] The Objectivists, he explains, conceived of poems as "objects," while their poetics was a working toward a fundamental decontextualization—not unlike, perhaps, the undermined sense of order Adams confronted, his feeling of not fitting neatly into his world, possibly because the world of his forebears was no longer coherent and because a new world needed to be understood, albeit its explanation was not coming readily to hand. Quartermain observes that "such objects"—that is, Objectivist poems—

> are difficult to read, because they challenge our assumptions about the processes of reading, about what constitutes "value," about knowledge and about "knowing." A poem as a decontextualized object creates enormous problems for the reader, and it is the experience of these problems which constitutes that of the poems.[12]

These are works not only by the Objectivists, but also by Stein as well as the later Creeley, Duncan, and others of the Allen anthology, and finally Susan Howe, of the third generation. Rather than any precept that has been put forth from the "School of Quietude" (à la Silliman—his snarky epithet for mainstream poetry),[13] Quartermain delights in quoting Olson's imprecation "Go / contrary, go // sing,"[14] as well as the third-generation poet and critic Bob Perelman's pronouncement that "'real history' refuses to place the 'I' in a privileged position"[15] and, too, a remark by his contemporary, the poet Bruce Andrews, regarding "the necessity to abandon the controls of hermeneutic for the multiplexity of behavioural reading."[16]

The monumental signals of a new century, in other words, may have remained salient in the modern American consciousness long after the early 1900s. And a temporal structure in which we can evaluate the peculiar triangulation of the second-generation neo-Objectivist poets, the NAP poets (this first generation of neo-Objectivists), and the original Objectivist poets is not without value, especially given the backdrop of High Modernism. The triangulation is the real subject of this essay, in a way, yet so is, in explicating this configuration, the realization of how under appreciated Objectivist poetics has been, especially within the context of readers coming to terms with today's avant-garde and in their appreciation of how this third generation has contributed to an understanding of what Objectivist poetics was and is—a comprehension of how the later poets have appropriated and reimagined this poetics, taking it on as their responsibility, as it were. Without this orientation, the extraordinary breakthrough of *The New American Poetry* cannot be fully comprehended.

We can see how Allen and the NAP poets might have viewed their work as constituting a radical break with the old, how they would have seen their writing as "new" (paradoxically, since they all embraced Pound's notion of the "new"), and how they might have imagined a trajectory into the future, on to the end of the century and beyond—how they might have imagined their work not only occupying a position along that trajectory, but also continuing to be a vital influence.

Within this framework it is especially important, I believe, to take into account the psychological and other effects on American society (thereby on its poets) of World War Two. We can appreciate these consequences for what they were in and of themselves; however, we can also consider how post-war, psychosocial conditions created the immense and radically "new" writing of the New American poetry that evolved starting in the 1940s—particularly in relation to how people may have been aware of themselves as living in an uncannily calendar-defined midpoint of their unique century, and so how they may have viewed the war and its immediate aftermath when poets who were to appear in the Allen anthology were striking out in new aesthetic and philosophical territory. The century's ostensible midpoint, that is, had already proven itself to have been singularly outsized. Where exactly that midpoint was can be debated, yet I am suggesting that there was a palpable sense of a turn or pivot.

One obvious "midpoint" of the twentieth century, glaringly demarcating a *before* and *after*, is the Second World War. A good deal of the writing in the Allen collection is produced immediately after the war, and some of it in the wake of the closely subsequent Korean War (the two wars actually straddling the mid-year of 1950). Whatever the psychological effects of the wars on these poets, and on American society as a whole, I think we can say that the NAP poets simply had no patience for a received literature that failed to comprehend the implications of the wars, especially World War II. The young poets of the Allen anthology aimed to respond authentically to the midcentury world cataclysm and all it called up in people's minds. Also—for poets like Olson, Creeley, Duncan, and Spicer—there was the need to write from within a new philosophical paradigm underwritten by certain scientific breakthroughs such as in physics, the need to engage and integrate new intellectual developments beyond the literary[17] (which were, furthermore, popularly and grimly typified by the atomic bombing of Japan). The impact of the wars is a topic requiring more room to explore than this essay allows, except to state the obvious here, which is that the war had a profoundly sobering effect on all Americans.

"The Great War," the First World War, gave birth to Robert Graves's book *Goodbye to All That*, what at the time was a testament to the end of innocence.[18] Likewise the Second World War produced Theodor Adorno's 1949 observation that, after the German death camps, "to write poetry" would be "barbaric"[19] (attendant to that was Hannah Arendt's famous coinage of the phrase "the banality of evil"[20] when speaking of Adolph Eichmann whose later trial in Israel she covered as a journalist—*banality* being the operative term, also significant as a way to account for what the Allen anthology was *not*). It was as if clarity was needed or, at a minimum, a new framework in which clarity might be possible once again was needed, predicated by a profound skepticism, as may have been seen in the heady days of the immediate post-World War II experimentation—a clarity for the first time that was born out of the sense of loss, the sense of desolation or abjection a writer like Samuel Beckett anticipated.

This need for clarity—within a new context, within a new world manifest in the anthology—was later to be epitomized in Oppen's famous *cri de coeur*, "Clarity, clarity, surely clarity is the most beautiful thing in the world, / A limited, limiting clarity // I have not and never did have any motive of poetry / But to achieve clarity"[21] (Oppen's combat experience in the Second World War possibly acting as a catalyst here).[22] The need, the drive for clarity, moreover, underlies the development of a linguistic skepticism in the work of the four poets of the third generation. It has not been out of keeping with a general post-war skepticism over human possibility, perhaps a delicate yet profound sense of despair caught in the web of widespread disillusionment and disorientation the NAP poets must have lived with, which is keenly expressed by Creeley's brief poem "I Know a Man" that was written about the time when Allen Ginsberg penned his long and overpowering, painful cry *Howl*.[23] Yet the skepticism, in respect to language, actually arises with the far-sighted Objectivists. This linguistic skepticism, traceable back through the New American poets to the Objectivists, distinguishes them from the High Modernists. And it is most significant in situating the second-generation neo-Objectivists within the greater North American poetry landscape of the present, hence taking us more deeply into our consideration of a continuing avant-garde.

While recognizing this skepticism, we ought also to acknowledge a continuing neo-Romantic strain in post-World War II poetry (despite the abjuration of the Romantic on the part of Pound, Williams, Stein, and the Objectivists as well as their progeny). Viewed in contrast, the poetry of celebrated poets like John Berryman, Anne Sexton, Robert Lowell, or Theodore Roethke—all marvelously accomplished—is essentially nostalgic. More to the point, however, it exudes a sense of comfort and discloses a complacency that was inherent in these poets' working practices as regards their linguistic limits. This circumscribed reach is evident in their work's language *per se*—a language not fully scrutinized by them and, important in considering both the present and past avant-gardes, a language that was not understood by them in terms of its materiality. It may be fair to claim that they were unaware of, and otherwise would not especially care about, what Creeley once called "the thingness of language" when reviewing the 1987 Language poetry anthology *In the American Tree* (edited and introduced by

Silliman).[24] Creeley may have been aware of Marjorie Perloff's 1984 article "The Word as Such" in the *American Poetry Review*,[25] which, in her writing about Language poetry, develops a similar concept.

This neo-Romantic tradition in twentieth-century American poetry was being violently repudiated by the poets in the Allen anthology. Instead of mainstream poetic practices, there had developed a poetry written under a new sign, one anticipated by Pound and H.D., then suggested by Williams. While not many other poets or readers at the time were aware of him, it was first being established by the Objectivist poet Charles Reznikoff. This neo-Romanticism is alive and well in a great deal of poetry still being written a century later. Even so, Pound, Williams, H.D., Stein, and others, who were virtually unrecognized by the poets and critics of the 1950s and 1960s mainstream are now part of the fabric of university education and a great many poets make sure to read them. What must also be noted, in order to appreciate fully the role the Allen book played in revolutionizing American poetry and American society more broadly, is that the poets of nostalgia, so to speak, were celebrated and canonized, particularly in an anthology contemporaneous with *The New American Poetry*. First published in 1957, edited by Donald Hall, Robert Pack and Louis Simpson, *New Poets of England and America*[26] contained work written not by a single poet included in the Allen anthology, and vice versa. Most of America read this highly-lauded mainstream collection that is now all but forgotten. It was this anthology most of all that was to be taught in the universities at the time when the Allen book appeared and for a while thereafter.

In contrast, the skepticism resulting in part from the war, coupled with the new insights in physics that led to the undeniability of uncertainty as a central factor in people's lives, informed the avant-garde's attention to language in and of itself. Inherited from the Objectivists and carried forward in a demonstrated awareness of *language as such* (to echo both Perloff's title "The Word as Such" and Creeley's phrase "the thingness of language"), Heller, Taggart, DuPlessis, and Silliman found four distinct ways to embody their awareness of *linguistic thingness*, both in their poetic practices and critical prose.

In Heller's earliest work we see his sensitivity to the thingness of language in a penchant for isolating words on the page, for instance in his poem "7 Praises" where he singles out the monosyllabic "be"; the poem's lines play off of this verb (beginning with "Be drunk. / Be the body / drunk. Drunk. // Move to become; / be /ruffled."[27] As his work evolves over the years it tends to be increasingly philosophical, couched in a rhetoric of meditation or contemplation. His tendency toward making philosophical pronouncements does show up in the early work yet it is full throated in the late—for example in the iconic poem "Space." In "Space" Heller "[hopes] for the promise of an infinity // that would leave

a foreground for the finite, / for [. . .] an entwine of emotion // and object";
and later he asks, "who now could live only by a word or by an image; / who
could stand back, look and speak, only to fall silent? / Who, in these times, did
not sense death and non-being / as a shadow, something brushed against the
cranial wall?"[28] In this poem a serialism we find in earlier work has disappeared
(although a good deal of the late work is comprised of poems structured by a
gripping anaphora).

In "Space" and other poems like it the awareness of the thingness of
language is more prominent in other ways, such as in the employment of a
term like "entwine," a special if not singular usage (here a verb turned into
a noun), which is meant to call attention to itself, and is an invitation to
the reader to savor and contemplate the word for its own sake. This fascination with one or another word and how it might work within a statement
is anticipated by the kind of repetition to be found in the earlier "Praises."
In another early poem, "OK Everybody, Let's Do the Mondrian Stomp,"[29]
Heller also creates a serialism, one reminiscent of the minimalist music of
Steve Reich or Philip Glass; hence the word "block" is repeated in a manner
sympathetic with Mondrian's aesthetics (the topic of the poem, presumably),
downplaying the word's semantic charge while calling attention to its sheer
look and sound.

As I've suggested, however, especially in Heller's most recent work, serialism has been abandoned but for some insistent anaphoric poems such as
"Looking at Some Petroglyphs in a Dry Arroyo Near a Friend's House,"[30] in
which deft use is made of the sentence fragment structure as a ploy to make
palpable the sense of place, which moves the persona to deep reflection:

> if our words are off not by being
> in another place but in a nowhere
>
> of no help to our selves or anyone,
> if they are just stuff and the proof of stuff,
> but might as well be vanished or banished,
>
> if they are the proverbial, music of the cosmos
>
> but no longer sing of a self, and if the footprint
> is just something to aestheticize and to remember
>
> those tribes who lived here but now go unrecorded, [etc.]

It is interesting that the poem ends metapoetically:

if to see

the petroglyph as just *there*, exposing all this
and we are deluded for thinking elsewise

as someone, me, you, those we care for try to round
the horn of this thought because only love is the at the end of it.[31]

The poem has a momentum, felt nonetheless when arriving at its asyntactic conclusion; and in this movement the language becomes especially muscular, vivid in its self-awareness, although, as seen here, for all their musical lilt Heller's poems do not possess the swaying, the overwhelmingly incantatory feel of many of Taggart's poems (as we shall see). One exception might be Heller's "City: Matrix: Bird: Collage," containing lines that seem to allude to, or comment on, Taggart's work, perhaps especially his book *Dodeka* (1979): "thousands of birds screaming down the sun / their tremendous noise as though they took up // our polyphony, dodecaphony of voices who despair / and sing bird cries, music of the caged birds [etc."[32] Another late poem, "Ready for Sunset," might be read as something closer to Taggart's work, and the poem does in fact pull Heller's *oeuvre* together insofar as, in its minimalist use of "Mars," it recapitulates to a degree the tactics in his early work:

> Mars is not at perihelion.
> Mars is not near you.
> Mars is arrayed on a skyline
> as though waiting for dark.
>
> Mars is up there, neither accepting
> nor barring.
>
> For all we know, Mars has its visor shut.
>
> Mars—so many for Mars, all we could ask for.
>
> Mars, Mars, somewhere floating over mountaintops.
>
> Soon we will see Mars. We will see its light,
> blood-tinged all the way to Sheol.[33]

Heller's engagement with the textures of language and most of all its thingliness comes through subtly but unequivocally, all the same, in the obvious delight disclosed in using complex words in appropriate even if in unusual ways.

His poems, indeed, investigate language. They philosophize about the limits of both language and poetry. As I have said elsewhere, moreover, in his "fundamental relationship with language there is a powerfully creative tension between embracing the word and being alienated from it, and thus the poet exists at a vantage point from which the limitations of language are glaringly apparent."[34]

Possibly of the four younger poets DuPlessis's work provides the most useful contrast to Heller's, and between the two we might better see the problem of language for all the Objectivists and their offspring. While occasionally DuPlessis may comment on the linguistic limits of her poems' language, to be precise, her poetics on the page is what does the real work of interrogating not merely language but also inscription (and in doing so she raises the issue of the Derridean claim for writing's priority over speech). This enacting of her belief about both language and writing takes is privileged, for her, over any theorizing. In her serial poem *Drafts*, which has been written over decades, and in early versions of its first installments, she demonstrates even more than Heller a concern with writing, perhaps as much as with words themselves, and with sounds and speech. This concern is most dramatically evident in the way her poems behave, but it is also to be found in the themes expressed within them.

There is, for instance, her fondness for erasure, for smudge, diacritical marking, and so on—all possibly designed, at least in part, to point out a crucial difference between chirographics and print (she will even juxtapose the two on the page). This contrast, however, might lead back to voice as the source of an unmitigated utterance. It is this voice which is contested by flows of power in society as reflected in her work, a society that is essentially phallocentric. In *The Pink Guitar* (in an essay originally published in 1980) she defines the

> "Female aesthetic" [as] the production of formal, epistemological, and thematic strategies by members of the group Woman, strategies born in struggle with much of already existing culture, and overdetermined by two elements of sexual difference—by women's psychosocial experiences of gender asymmetry and by women's historical status in an (ambiguously nonhegemonic group.[35]

The third-generation poets, it might be said overall, have all been interested in the foregrounding of language, and collectively, as part of a neo-Obectivist generation, they have moved together in a certain direction first established by their forebears. Yet they possess a deeper skepticism about language and poetry, and I would say an affection for the written word and material language overall, than either the NAP poets or the Objectivists. DuPlessis's theoretical prose confirms this outlook. In her poetry too she has contributed instrumentally to this shared ideology and, broadly speaking, aesthetics; and her feminist perspective on language and rhetoric has seemed to sharpen the questions the work of all four poets has posed overtly and implicitly at various times.

In her earliest work she does not really concern herself with the problem of language, but it is not long before she is expressing a diffidence about language and very quickly moving to address the act of writing. On the one hand this focus invites comparison most with Silliman, among the four third-generation poets, especially his huge poem *The Alphabet* (also composed over decades), comprised of serial poems.[36] On the other hand her point of view, in many respects, suggests an affinity with Heller. In either case, though, it might be said that she has operated under the sign of a salient remark her one-time mentor Oppen makes in his Daybook: "words are a constant enemy: the thing seems to exist because the word does";[37] in his poem "A Language of New York," furthermore, he writes that it is "Possible / To use / Words provided one treat them / As enemies."[38]

Even before DuPlessis's own massive serial poem *Drafts* (not totally unlike Silliman's *The Alphabet* inasmuch as various sections of it have been collected and published in a number of consecutive volumes) gets truly underway,[39] she writes a proto "draft" in the second section of her early volume of poems *Tabula Rosa* (1987)[40] which signals a radical deconstruction of writing and language she will continue to implement. The first poem in the grouping titled "Writing" begins as follows: "Smudge, ballpoint, iridesces / behind the."[41] The opening lines of this poem's third section, in the same style and discourse, reflects back on the poem's initial lines in order to solidify the experience of the poet being recorded: ".A wri- / ting marks the / patch of void."[42] And, as she says further on, "Impossible maybe to write / the techne of dailiness [etc.]"[43] Some lines later she reflects, "anyway / all this has been 'the' / just where I thought I began / beyond,"[44] and then further on she notes, in starting to conclude this section:

To write into silence. *The*. And the *t*. Narrative and experience. "Narrative" and "experience." Poetry too pretty; creating 'beauty'? Creating chora. Beginning-middle-end, ha. [And so on.][45]

DuPlessis is taking not only syntax but also discourse apart. Of the four second-generation neo-Objectivists she stands out as the one whose work embodies and perhaps enacts, practices, the Derridean idea of the priority of writing set out in *Of Grammatology*[46] and elsewhere—which, again, runs counter-conceptually, it might be said, to the thinking about oral utterance and inscription put forth by Walter Ong[47] and others, and furthermore which likely runs counter not only to Heller's and Taggart's work, but also, possibly, Oppen's, Zukofsky's, even Stein's or maybe Silliman's in the final analysis.

When *Drafts* proper gets underway, DuPlessis deepens her exploration, now also pushing beyond the accepted perimeters of formal speech in great part to find, or rather to create, a female subject position not conditioned by phallocentric speech or writing's formalism. Thus "Draft 58" postulates that "all words dismember into invention. / For in (or by) the act of starting (staring, stating), / something else takes shape"[48] And earlier, in "Draft 39," we get a passage like this:

> No verbs. No words.
> No writing. Nothing there but
> – – lessness and angry, back and front
>
>   but also look around thee.
>
> At undecipherable Graffiti
> sloppy scribble over the Focus
>
>   Group poster's high-end dewy-eyed design.
>
> dark vandal slash marks on the photograph of Things
> whose gem-like research Codes are not thereby undone.[49]

And this: "It is this: // You made a dot because you are a dot."[50] DuPlessis will also deconstruct the aesthetics of patriarchal linguistic architecture:

> We wanted poetry known for lavishness and brightness
> fierce streaky brightness –
> plus minimize dreck
> and the too-pretty by far
>
> we wanted access
> open places out of solid praxis
> ate our joy and joyous anger held our, gripped our laser hunger
> we wanted women!
> back channel me . . .[51]

At times she presents the reader with a deconstructed inscription that suggests the tension between, on the one hand, existential albeit inchoate awareness, and on the other hand elegant if fragmented articulation:

>   rranged
>   ne of anguage
>   nger, mean

glot

grns, sighs

o stop
consider step,

orm of me.
f
r
avine[52]

So how does DuPlessis, or Heller, compare with Taggart and Silliman? DuPlessis's poetry fundamentally is not, akin to Heller's, *procedural* in any real sense of
this descriptor; to be sure, her poetry strenuously avoids being so. Yet Silliman's
work, and Taggart's, is decidedly so. In Taggart we see something not unlike
that early Heller poem "Ok Everybody" that might recall the music of Glass or
Reich, but Heller does not want to be overtly musical—whereas DuPlessis does,
often in complex ways, and Taggart's music, no less subtle, of the four poets
seems most of all to be nearly of a piece with musical minimalism.

Heller's version of what comes to be known in music as minimalism, for
instance in "OK Everybody," is on full display in Taggart's work throughout
his career, arguably more relentlessly so in his later work. I would say that
the effect of his poetics is akin to that found in much of the poetry of Silliman where he employs proceduralist measures of one form or another—for
instance his use of the Fibonacci sequence of numbers as a blueprint for line-
by-line wording in a poem like *Tjanting*.[53] It is difficult to avoid thinking of
Zukofsky's earlier procedures when reading Silliman, such as the older poet's
five-word lines in a number of sections of "A" (some other sections contain
different pre-set line lengths in which words are being counted). Silliman's
notion of what he has called "The New Sentence,"[54] however, like other procedures, also foregrounds words in and of themselves; this privileging calls a
reader's attention to words for the sake of their material properties. If it does
not exactly exemplify Oppen's sentiments then at least it fulfills their promise
as embodied in his now famous comment about "[t]he little words I like so
much";[55] something much the same can be said for Zukofsky's musing, in his
introduction to Oppen's *Selected Poems*, that "one might spend a lifetime considering the difference between 'the' and 'a', the particular and the general."[56]

In undermining syntax "The New Sentence" leaves the reader with
the words although without the ordering of lineation that would create

an overriding organization of its own. As Alan Holder has commented, "Silliman's new sentences simply hang us up. They appear to be all *torque* [Silliman's favored, key term] with no semantic completions."[57] Or there is DuPlessis's comment about *The Alphabet*, that in it "there is little sense of foreground and background as conventionally positioned; rather, everything is foreground."[58]

Overt musicality, which in some instances might be likened in its action to procedural practices of one sort or another, can also vitiate syntactic rigor. Of the four poets we find this dynamic most often and most vividly present in Taggart. While Taggart may be more often thought of in connection with Oppen, it is difficult not to think of Zukofsky's life-long attachment to the fugue as idea and as a structure to be put into practice, beginning early with his pronouncement in the 1931 Objectivist issue of *Poetry* magazine, wherein he speaks of "A" as possessing two salient vectors that would run through each of the poems in this long epic or serial work, out of which there arises his "approximate attainment of [a] perfection in the feeling of the contra-puntal design of the fugue transferred to poetry."[59] (Pound, too, as Sandra Kumamoto Stanley reports, had "compared the form of *The Cantos* to a fugue."[60]) Along with Pound and the more overtly sonorous Zukosfky, it is Duncan's poetry, of all the writing that emerged from within the Black Mountain School, which is the most obviously musical, sonorous. And Duncan, as Peter O'Leary has said, "is one of Taggart's acknowledged masters in poetry, along with Oppen and Zukofsky."[61]

Taggart's "Precious Lord," observes O'Leary, is "a fugue that is ultimately a threnody for a friend recently passed away."[62] Overall, Taggart's "use of a cantillation effect that draws upon twentieth-century minimalism as well as medieval music"[63] is comparable with some of Duncan's work such as *A Poet's Masque*. Michael Davidson has shrewdly written of Duncan, that "[u]nlike the work of many postwar poets, [his] is not self-expressive or confessionalist but rather a 'structure of rime' that repeats in its architectonics the history of mimetic acts."[64] Duncan, in his introduction to Taggart's volume *Dodeka* (1979), points out that "[f]or those post-Zukofsky and post-Olson, the lure of the poem is to find an extension of what speaks to us. For Taggart, where the *particles* themselves speak, he must follow his hearing to find what they have to say."[65]

The particles of language, a concern for poets like Zukofsky, Oppen, and earlier both Williams and Stein, are later brought to the reader's attention through Taggart's overtly sonorous musicality that, if anyone's is commensurate, has its match in some of Zukofsky's poetry, exemplifying his gravitation to what he called the "Upper limit music."[66] Taggart's musically structured lines and stanzas isolate and foreground words, and thereby particles. Music, maybe especially as manifested in the fugue structure, overrides syntax in

Taggart's poems and is meant to do so. It might be better to say that syntax is obliterated, yet not through the writerly strategies employed by either Silliman or DuPlessis—strategies that, while in obvious ways they announce their intention to undermine or override syntax, do not succeed in carrying out this intention as palpably as can be seen in Taggart's poetics, a *modus operandi* that in the end may possibly be more subtle (what this may say about the capacities of sonorous music I leave off commenting upon).

This success of Taggart's might also be measured against poems like Creeley's *Gnomic Verses* (1993). Creeley's modulations of syntax are both subtle and haunting but they are generally of another order than those employed by these three other younger poets, possibly being closer to work by fellow poets of the Black Mountain group (like, say, Joel Oppenheimer, Levertov or Blackburn). Nevertheless, the *Gnomic Verses* has brought out Creeley's natural propensity for overt melody beyond the simple end-rhymed forms he favored occasionally. And some of this late work, line for line, could almost be intermixed particularly with Taggart's, escaping the notice of a casual reader, such as with the ironic title "Words":

> Driving to the expected
> Place in mind in
> Place of mind in
> Driving to the expected[67]

Of course, in these verses Creeley continues to foreground and celebrate even the smallest particles of language, celebrating them—a poetics set in motion with Williams's placing of the preposition "upon" on its own line in "The Red Wheelbarrow,"[68] perpetuated by Stein and the Objectivists, and later all the NAP poets to one degree or another. This is a poetics and philosophy the third generation has embraced fully.

Here, then, to underscore this point, is "Oh Oh," another of Creeley's "gnomic" verses:

> Now and then
> Here and there
> Everywhere
> On and on[69]

Similar to "Oh Oh," in the present context, is "Fat Fate" (note the play on the title with the added letter "e"):

> Be at That this
> Come as If when

> Stay or Soon then
> Ever happen It will[70]

There is also Creeley's poem "Loop," in this series of short lyrics, which echoes Taggart's book *Loop* not only in title:

> Down the road Up the hill Into the house
> Over the wall Under the bed After the fact
> By the way Out of the woods Behind the times
> In front of the door Between the lines Along the path[71]

What O'Leary has called Taggart's "cantillation effect" in his poetry,[72] which evolves into a serial musicalism that either is a fugue or is fugue-like, begins early in his career. O'Leary sees Duncan along with Oppen as influences and "acknowledged masters" for Taggart;[73] and one might also consider if late-Creeley poems such as his "gnomic verses" not only recall Duncan, his peer, but also his progenitors Oppen and Zukofsky—and, too, in this regard, we might think of, as I've suggested, Taggart's poetic project and maybe those of other poets his age (occasionally, in his work, Silliman can possibly be included in this context, e.g., both thematically and sensually in lines like "words warm / or warn / where meaning wanes // crouch to carve / ink into pages" in *Non*,[74] or in the muscular statement that begins *Garfield*, "The tropic treacle tripped over the derivation causing Lit").[75]

It is worth comparing, then, early and late Taggart. What can be said overall about his poetry, however, is that he often creates a spiraling or rather—as echoed in the introduction to his book on Edward Hopper—a möbius strip-like movement carrying a poem's rhetoric to a conclusion that both can be and is not anticipated.[76] In *Dodeka* Taggart weaves terms and concepts like "seed" and "light" through a poem that looks ahead to a later, more pronounced musical serialism. For example, Taggart will set out a composite of the lines that are recapitulated in a number of iterations later on. Thus we first read this series of lines: "Face cut: seeds spill / seeds within seeds / on fire, white sparks / in a dark house."[77] And a good deal further on we read: "Seeds within seeds / burn in stripper music, his / music, fire eyes has his own music."[78] The fact that lines like these contain a meta-poetical burden only adds to their circularity. *Dodeka* is also procedural in nature, inasmuch as it's structured according to a dodecahedron. Duncan precisely characterizes Taggart's poetics when he writes in his introduction to the poem—which in effect links the poem to Creeley as well as Pound, Williams, Zukofsky, and Olson—that "Number, for John Taggart, is the threshold of world-dance."[79]

By 1993, the second section of "In the Sense Of," a poem within Taggart's collection *Standing Wave* (the semantic weight of both titles should be noted), begins as follows.

> The vibration there is the vibration the vibration of a fan
> there is the vibration there is the continuous vibration
> there is the continuous the continuous dull vibration
> continuous vibration of a fan small fan on the wooden floor
> the vibration the continuous the dull vibration
> there is the continuous vibration there is the vibration
> the vibration of a fan the vibration there is the vibration
> there is the vibration the vibration on the wooden floor
> vibration on the floor in the midst of stifling heat[80]

As in other of his serialisms, musical structure and otherwise relentless circles of sequences of words override syntactic possibilities; individualized words are thrown up to the reader, which in their isolation not only attract the reader's attention to their linguistic thingliness but also act as the radicals that propel the poem forward musically and semantically. The final poem in Taggart's 2010 volume, *Is Music* (a collection of selected and new poems), may serve as a consummating postscript to a lifetime's project. Here is the poem in its entirety:

You've solved the problem with splendid wings and different directions. The one wing each solution. One each, each a little less splendid. Smaller.

You're walking. You're not climbing ladders. That's what the two of you are doing, two angels who are walking together.

It's the music, isn't it? Someone changed the music. Or the music changed itself like the sky changes itself. So it doesn't have to be the same music over and over. Pulse and throb, parched and plangent trumpet echo against pulse and throb is the same over and over. The sky changes. Doesn't have to be the same. Not even bird in flight, the song of that bird. Doesn't have to be imploring words over and over.

I know it's not the happy ending because it's not ending. The sky changes. The music changes and is not ending. It is not unfinished. It is unending.[81]

What "[d]oesn't have to be imploring words over and over"—the poet's act or, more likely, the poem itself?

This final poem in this monumental collection, by virtue of its placement, invites us to consider it as an *ars poetica*. It may be just that, but more to the point it is the metapoetical description of the work in the collection from one poem to the next and overall. And "[i]t is not unfinished"; still, "[i]t is unending." That the process never ends, arguably, is another way in which syntax and possibly even semantics are undermined, and so the process places the material word in the foreground of the poem and in the reader's experience of it, even before the word "means" anything. While Taggart's work must reside on the page, and in the voice of a reader reading aloud, in its poetics it does share, all the same, an affinity with digital poetry in which "materiality emerges as a dance," to borrow from N. Katherine Hayles, "between the medium's physical characteristics and the work's signifying strategies [. . .] materiality itself [coming] to be seen as more an event than a preexisting object."[82] In this way we might say, furthermore, that Taggart's work has anticipated Flarf too. Music here, however, in this poem of Taggart's, in its phenomenal nature, is stipulated as sponsoring, as a paradigm for, Taggart's epistemological procedures.

As for Silliman, the relentless drive of his procedural writing, no less so than we see in Taggart's serialisms (Zukofsky's musicality aside, not least of all in his poems of five-word lines)—in which there can be syntactical arrangements suggesting the influence of both Zukofsky and Stein—is singularly inflected and is modulated by his own disjunctive syntax. Of all the Modernist and late Modernist progenitors, it may be upon Stein's rather than, say, Zukofsky's repeated words and their sounds, within lines and in subsequent lines, which Taggart has based his singular poetics. We might be quick to say something like this about Silliman. Yet his serialism is of another order, arising out of his commitment to procedural poetics. Here, for instance, are the opening lines of "Force" (the "F" installment of *The Alphabet*):

The audients of politics
in the -torium of sounds
eye is for fours
is thus tragedy first
then farce, majestic speech
muttered under morning's breath
while brushing. Against news, noise. Against toys, few respectable chariots, blue as cribbage, ocker as in Rx, Delaware's a warning. No-load, after a long illness or preventive strike, thunder allegro in the woodwinds converts the spare, hiring from within, primer coat. Interservice flea-flicker absent deicing refunds the smoking intitlement. How teacher
taught himself unthoughtfully spoken
toward the sake of
particulars, few nouns breaking
predawn stillness but songs
toward the sake of
particulars, few nouns breaking

predawn stillness but songs
from red garbagetrucks's hydraulics[83]
[etc.]

The *torqued* syntax (to twist Silliman's term) in this passage helps to force
a reader's attention to the individual words both free of and simultaneously
caught within a net. While the disjunctive nature of this arrangement does
not lend itself to anything resembling a traditionally mellifluous quality, the
passage does actually have an ebb and flow, not only when Silliman leads his
statement out of the four-word lines into prose justified both left and right
on the page, and then back to the set number of words per line, but also in
the tensions he creates between the lines with greater and fewer numbers
of syllables. Along with this arrangement he is aware of, from line to line,
whether or not he's setting down substantives or accidentals, nouns or verbs
versus prepositions or articles (he even wants to play a joke on us in order to
emphasize this operation when he makes "garbage truck" into one word in
"garbagetruck's hydraulics"). His play recalls passages in Zukofsky's "A" (for
instance "A"-11) such as when he writes of a "[speaking] / toward the sake of /
particulars, few nouns breaking / predawn stillness but songs / toward the sake
of /particulars, few nouns breaking predawn stillness but songs."[84] But Silliman's passage also echoes Zukofsky's *ars poetica* "An Objective" that begins
by expressing a *"Desire for what is objectively perfect, inextricably the direction
of historic and contemporary particulars"*;[85] and we might not be able to avoid
hearing Oppen's praising of "all the little words."[86]

In *Tjanting*, as has been mentioned, each paragraph has a set number of
sentences, following the model of the Fibonacci progression. In this poem,
as William Watkin has observed—not unlike what we see in Taggart's pulses
and undulating waves—"repeated sentences nearly always go through some
sort of modification to alter their sense or reveal new links with the sentences that surround them within the paragraph."[87] If we consider the procedural action in this poem, which actually turns the poem in some sense into a
kind of serialism, then we can contrast the poem to Taggart's, in a loose sense
"procedural" serial poems, which seem, when set against Silliman's work, to
possess a sense of closure after all, although what one feels often enough in
reading a Taggart poem is that it could go on and on. In the case of *Tjanting*,
however, as Watkin comments,

> [d]ue to this choice of procedurality the structural demands of the procedure
> mean the poem body expands at such a rate that it literally spirals out of
> 'control' if we take control to mean certain taken for granted qualities of struc-
> tural cohesion. The final paragraph is so long that one's conception of it as a
> structure of sense cohesion, which is what after all the paragraph is, becomes
> hopelessly compromised.[88]

It may be that what Silliman particularly provides us finally, in his procedural practices, given their "disjunctive" nature at times (to borrow from Quartermain), that is to say given their sending up of any readerly expectation of traditional rhetorical structures, is the baring of otherwise unnoticed tendencies of language, along with the textures and inherent *suchness* of words and phrases, which we would not appreciate in a different milieu.

Postscript

Thus far in this chapter I have attempted to demonstrate an avant-garde continuum in North American poetry which has included the four poets who represent a second neo-Objectivist wave, and I have tried to account in brief for the emergence of the Allen anthology along this continuum. In the remainder of this chapter I would like to establish the anthology as the most significant moment in our literary history's moving forward in time—a moment when the very terms of what the avant-garde meant were recast—and to look beyond what I have been calling the third generation of avant-garde poets (more to the point, the third generation of "Objectivists") to more recent experimental work as a way to bring to bear a full comprehension of what Heller, DuPlessis, Silliman, and Taggart have achieved. Let's return, then, first, to that mid-twentieth century sea change discussed already, and begin there by observing that, while the Second World War serves as an obvious socio-political midpoint of the twentieth century, the literary-historical midpoint followed it by a few years, to a great degree for the reasons already mentioned, which include the psycho-social effects of the war.

There were actually four literary events, occurring almost in lock-step after the war and all within a decade, which collectively make up this other midpoint. In effect they bifurcated the poetics of the twentieth century as it had come to be imagined in the modern North American mind—certainly within the avant-garde, but over time they have also had a long-lasting, in fact a jarring effect within the mainstream (and maybe they will be the root cause of the eventual end, for all intents and purposes, of the mainstream as it exists today). The four events, together, changed the course of writing and certainly of avant-garde poetry. Allen's anthology played an instrumental role in this tectonic shift.

The first of these events was the 1950 publication in the journal *Poetry New York* (its editor was Harvey Shapiro whom we might think of, if not Jerome Rothenberg, as the first of the third-generation poets to emerge) of Olson's landmark essay, a statement of poetics he titled "Projective

Verse." A decade later the essay was being taken most seriously by the NAP poets and was to be given prime place by Allen in the poetics section of his anthology. It was as if Olson, his poetry and theory, and perhaps his outsized personality that matched his six foot nine-inch bulky frame, was presiding over the book, Olson the spiritual father or patron saint. The fact that he had close ties to Pound, Williams, and Zukofsky could but only have been a factor in the poetry world's view of him. Apart from being a kind of guide for writing a radically different kind of poem from that which was being produced in the mainstream—in some respects from that which had been produced by the high and late Modernists—the essay was an intellectual testament that was read assiduously by the next generation of experimental poets (as well as by the younger poets). The essay was not just a clarion call whose soaring rhetoric insisted upon a new notion of writing and stirred the poets who read it to what at the time was radical action. It was also a penetrating explanation of what was at hand and implicitly of what the Modernists had been about. While it confirmed some of their practices and aesthetics, though, in it Olson provided a vision and map of how to move beyond them. Whether by this map the territory of younger neo-Objectivism could be negotiated is another matter; but Olson was surely demarcating where the New American poets were picking up from their forebears, and he may finally have hinted at directions the still younger poets could strike out in.

The second of the four events was, to my mind, the 1955 inaugural reading of Allen Ginsberg's Howl (in San Francisco). By this time Creeley had written his poem "I Know a Man"—that composition comprising the third of the four pivotal events (Creeley also produced the first typewritten copy of the Ginsberg poem), [89] even as its powerful influence grew only gradually until its appearance in the anthology. A portion of Ginsberg's long declaration was also to appear there. Of the two poems, it is Creeley's that looks ahead to help to define the practices of the second Objectivist wave.

It is important to think not so much about the social impact of either poem—most obviously in the wake of the midcentury's conflagration—but rather about the breaking of the rules, so to speak, most obviously having to do with the decorum a poem should maintain. In the case of Creeley's poem we see how the notion of the thingness of language can actually manifest. Yet both Ginsberg and Creeley had taken to heart the famous dictum "no ideas but in things" set out by Williams (who had mentored them both variously)—the importance of the word and concept *thing* having grown over the years since he first wrote it. In the years before the Allen book appeared many of the poets in it followed Williams; belonging to the different groupings Allen created, they were not so aware of these categorizations beforehand and were living and working closely together, so there was a lot of what in hindsight seems to have been cross fertilization,[90] while on their respective ways to becoming representatives of schools established for them in *The New American Poetry*—whose 1960 publication was the last of these pivotal events, and the culmination of them all. The event announced the gestation of radically new poetical practices taking place over more than a decade. Beyond the particularities of its poetry and poetics, the book offered a broad alternative vision of what a poem could be.

In its own way, the book stood as a repudiation of the social conservatism of the fifties—the reactionary politics of the McCarthy hearings, the black lists, the ramped up Cold War rhetoric, the threat of nuclear militarism and/ or annihilation, the subtle and not-so-subtle impositions of Eisenhower-era conformity—and championed an already emerging social and political counterculture, to say nothing of the dramatic changes in the other arts. The élan of this new culture was on display in the poems. Hence the cataclysm of world war as well as, at bottom, world science—even if they affected the New American poets only distantly or indirectly (in the case of some of them, like Olson, Creeley, Spicer, and others, as has been said, there was direct influence)—set off a new, fecund period of creativity. The Allen anthology marked its public attention, even as it was boosting it.

Of the four events, the publication of the Allen book was the one to proclaim overtly the "new direction" poetry was taking among practitioners who made up a new wave of experimentalism (to echo the name of James Laughlin's press, *New Directions*—Laughlin having sat at Pound's feet to learn what there was to learn, then bringing to light still relatively unread Modernists and eventually others). This new direction was seen to have been authentic to a new reality on the ground, one operating under a new conceptual paradigm that attracted poets who had grown tired of the essentially neo-Romantic Modernism of poets like Eliot and W.H. Auden, Robert Frost, and even Stevens; rather, Williams and H.D., but fundamentally Pound, had been the root of the "new" work.

Collectively these four events, this literary-historical midpoint, marked the sea change that would inaugurate what people thought at the time, and still feel was the beginning of the second half of a century to be imagined as having gotten underway at about 1900, whose birth was graced by the advent of Modernism—a movement that strove to sever ties with its Romantic past, the Romantic impulse that for some poets was more successful than for others. Yet it is important to consider that the new century's avant-garde movement, with the possible exception of Stein and the Objectivists (Williams might also be included here), did not succeed fully in effecting the separation. The fact that the mainstream Hall-Pack-Simpson anthology was being taught in college classrooms—while Pound, Williams, H.D., Stein, Laura Riding Jackson, and others were still pretty much unheard of and/or were not taken seriously in the academy, and that *The New American Poetry* also escaped academic notice—goes a long way toward explaining what remains a basic divide among North American poets today. Whatever the differences are among contemporary poets who can be associated with the Allen anthology, differences at times fought over with great zeal, they all share a root in Pound most of all, and as he underwrites the Objectivists who, in turn, more than anyone else, I would say, are the progenitors of the Allen collection. There was another important avant-garde anthology that followed closely upon the heels of Allen's; edited by Paris Leary and Robert Kelly, *A Controversy of Poets*[91] also had a great influence on young explorative poets of the time, and it is recalled with fondness by many of today's older poets. But the anthology that remains as *the* monument of its moment is Allen's. Baldly titled as it was, it proclaimed a new conceptual and aesthetic order for writing poetry and, without meaning to do so, it reflected the reality of that new conceptual paradigm fueled by post-Newtonian and post-Kantian thinking. The poems Allen included embraced a new sense of time and the possibility of form, or, within the moment of the book's appearance, perhaps it is better to speak of the possibilities of formlessness (not unlike how, for instance, a contemporaneous Jackson Pollock drip painting, an event, can be said to be about nothing, or nothingness, rather than a pictorial scene).

The 1940s and 1950s were a most extraordinary artistic period, not just as seen in the context of the twentieth but rather of any century. Of course it may be argued that, on one level, poets simply write their poems, and only after the fact of the writing do they try to justify or explain their compositions—but when their work is anthologized, even if the poets whose work appears in an anthology might resist a critical framework being constructed around it, one will appear. Within the writer-reader dynamic that is key to any textual community (poets and readers, some of whom are poets themselves, listeners at poetry readings, literary critics, etc.), a way of mentally situating a poem or an entire *oeuvre* comes to the fore, and the poet becomes hard pressed to remain ignorant of that. Poets may indeed be influenced over the course of a career, furthermore, by a critical reception, so that their work continues though it has been subject to a resonance engendered by, a reaction from, its readers. Poets may also be vulnerable to the memorialization and celebration of their work in a book of the stature of Allen's, even the eventual canonization of it, due to the very facticity and historicizing the anthology provides it, so that their future writing is influenced by that socio-literary reception. It is fair to say that the poet who is not understood (and at times eventually not self-understood) within some lineation of influence, milieu or whatever, is rare.

In this regard, then, if we think about the second-generation neo-Objectivists—Silliman, Taggart, DuPlessis, and Heller—and their successors as well, and if we revisit the question of a contemporary avant-garde's viability today, it is useful to remind ourselves of how the Hall-Pack-Simpson book, so prevalent in its time, never was seen as a landmark after that, while it had been the center of the attention of the majority of the North American poetry world. DuPlessis, who at the time was enrolled in a course taught by Pack, recently recalled the sense of futility she felt about his book. "[I]f that was IT," she writes, "—you can imagine that one needed something else—desperately."[92] The anthology was what she as a student at Barnard was supposed to read, presented to her as if all contemporary poetry resided within it.

While the Objectivists loomed large for them, all four poets of this third generation were quite deeply affected by the Allen anthology, yet they came to it either concomitantly with their discoveries of the Objectivists (as well as, principally, Pound, Williams and Stein) or shortly thereafter; the book was and remains, even so, of huge importance to them. They have viewed it as an integral force in the avant-garde world that their own work has now helped to define. A remark by Silliman about this sphere of influence and inter-influence may aptly sum up the experiences of all four poets in this respect. There was "not [a] direct heritage situation," and even though he knew of the Allen anthology in 1965, he "didn't know how to read it until January 1966" when Oppen gave a reading in Berkeley.[93]

For Taggart and Heller, both somewhat older than Silliman, the situation was a bit different. The two were each aware of Zukofsky before the appearance of the anthology, and saw the work in it as part of a greater poetic experience, however much each of them eventually zeroed in on the Objectivist work.[94] In comparison, DuPlessis's early engagement with the avant-garde was more complex. She was "very struck by the Allen anthology, which [she] first read in maybe 1964 (just in [her] first year of grad school)."[95] Yet her meeting Oppen the following year was momentous.

The anthology was nevertheless a breakthrough. In talking about the "new" she was encountering, which saved her from "the tight, tidy, domesticated poetry of [her] college years," it was "particularly 'Poem Beginning with a Line from Pindar' [by Duncan and included by Allen] that transformed

[her] sense of poetry."[96] Her meeting Oppen in the following year was in its own way transformative, however, and he became her mentor. As in the case of Creeley, whose work continues after the emergence of the third generation and may have been affected by these later poets, Oppen straddled both generations of neo-Objectivists.

"In 1965," DuPlessis has recalled, Oppen sent her an early draft of his great long poem "Of Being Numerous":

> I was a graduate student sort of, and sort of a poet, wayward, conflicted, yearning—and, of course, female. I had met Oppen for the first time barely two months before. Nothing, absolutely nothing had prepared me for this experience—of knowing instantly that I had received a major poem, a work of great poetic force and intellectual originality. It was like having a meteor land in your backyard. Should I use the word "masterpiece," even all deconstructed? Should I bother to say "genius" when I disagree with that concept? Let's at least say—*this poem was sufficient to the day.*[97]

Oppen solicited her reaction and included her language in the poem's revision (at the start of the poem's ninth section).

The older Oppen finally wishes to remain as both elder statesman and mentor (his self-positioning a contrast to Creeley's). He held off on cutting a key passage the young DuPlessis failed to see the significance of: "My main mis-step? I had suggested that George drop section 7," she reports.[98] Here is that section:

> Obsessed, bewildered
>
> By the shipwreck
> Of the singular
>
> We have chosen the meaning
> Of being numerous.[99]

"What was I thinking, exactly?" DuPlessis's question leads to the following conjecture:

> Well, probably overvaluing the Poundean-ly hermetic, the not-overt, the clandestine. I think the section appeared too bald or 'obvious' to me at the time. How wrong can one be? At least with my being so wrong, Oppen defended, in an important letter, his choice to keep the section that—after all—articulates his major theme.[100]

DuPlessis may have second-guessed herself then and afterwards in her reminiscence of this period in her life, but we see her ennobling Oppen's work and projecting the potential in it, the poetics and principles in it, forward into her own poetry—even as her attention to inscription in and of itself, as well as the implications of that attention and of writing, might recall the work of someone like Creeley (more so than Duncan), and the matter of her poetry's indebtedness to Creeley is also to be contemplated. But Oppen stands as an undeniably major, progenerative force in her work, even now, while the Allen anthology, a spark lighting a bonfire, is also to be remembered when reading her.

The sense that radical and exciting alternatives were available to DuPlessis was shared by her three peers. In remembering his evolution as a young poet, Taggart recalls that he "was a little suspicious of" the Allen book when he first laid eyes on it in about 1963. He remembers "how mixed and molten a time it was," and he had an "equal enthusiasm for [John] Berryman and Oppen and Duncan and Levertov [and] liked [James] Dickey, [and] Jerry Rothenberg was going to publish Don [Donald] Justice."[101] The time was "molten" for Heller too, who entered into the world of poetry not in college, as did DuPlessis and Taggart, but through relationships with some of Zukofsky's students with whom he worked after graduation. He had studied engineering at RPI and then, in 1959, living in New York City, he began to work as a technical writer. Zukofsky had been teaching courses at Polytechnic University in Brooklyn—courses attended by, among others, Hugh Seidman, whom Heller met in 1961 or 1962 (the start of a life-long friendship both personal and artistic).[102] First reading Zukofsky, Heller almost immediately began to read Olson, Creeley, and others. Dickey or Justice probably did not know of Zukofsky—while poets like Rothenberg, or Olson or Creeley did, and it was natural in Heller's situation to have been led, through Zukofsky, to the NAP poets.

These poetic encounters of Heller's all occurred before the anthology appeared, however. "It was that environment of the new that really interested me," Heller has said. In fact he was "awakened by all of them at the same time," while "Zukofsky was definitely a model, an exemplar."[103] When the Allen collection was first published, Heller and his poet co-workers raced to the Eighth Street Bookshop in Greenwich Village to buy it. A lot of discussion ensued as to why the Objectivists were not in it. It may be safe to say that, in their minds, due to their reading of the work of the various poets, they could but only have marked the conspicuous absence.[104]

Even with Zukofsky's influence being what it was, Heller's careful reading of Oppen's work in 1965, and then his meeting Oppen the following year, were "decisive" events for him.[105] One aspect of Oppen's poems at that time, which can be seen in the writing of someone like Creeley, was spacing on the page. While this was not likely the most important thing for the young poet, as it manifested in the older poet's work, it was nonetheless significant. In Heller's eyes this aesthetic and epistemological textual evidence pertained to Zukofsky's poetry too: "Two or three words on a line was interesting and I said, 'Hey, I can do that.'"[106] Heller's reaction suggests his early experience was very like DuPlessis's when she first read the Allen anthology in about 1964. She was struck by "[t]he page space freedom and the sense of notational fragment." This way of writing, she felt, "was liberating formally. The information seemed so new—or so confirming of intuitions that I had."[107]

Wallace Stevens, who can be usefully contrasted to Pound, Williams, Zukofsky, and Oppen (to say nothing of poets like Berryman or Justice), was important for DuPlessis—as he was for Taggart and Silliman in their early days (and for Heller starting in about 1970). Yet it may very well be, as can be taken from subsequent remarks made by her, that the new news, for all four of these young poets, was being announced by other Modernists such as Williams, and in the Allen anthology, particularly by the Black Mountain poets. It is worth noticing that Stevens appeared regularly in journals like *The Black Mountain Review* and *Origin*. "I was desperately trying to find out 'things' that were not the tight, tidy, domesticated poetry of my college years—in which Robert Pack instructed the 'girls' at Barnard College," DuPlessis has said. "His heroes were Richard Wilbur, Howard Nemerov, and [W. D.] Snodgrass—that kind of zone; he did love Wallace Stevens, however, and so do (so did and do) I; that was a help from him, in a pedagogy otherwise so dismal to recall."[108] Actually, she had started reading the avant-garde poets in the late fifties, in little magazines at the New York Public Library's main branch reading room.

With this preparation she came to Allen's collection, and within it Duncan first and foremost, at that time. Her experience of that poetry, vivid and profound, was instructive and instrumental. She still remembers experiencing "the first HIT of" Duncan: "that person, the absolute gasp and sense of desire—to do something like THAT!"[109] Was there anything in Duncan's poems that might have come out of Williams? Would DuPlessis, a young poet, be able to play with tendencies in the work of them both, as well as in that of other poets of the avant-garde? In 1966 she read Williams's *Spring and All* "in the Rare Book Room of Columbia University" (as she remembers after delving into her daybooks of that period). "There are stars on those pages of [her] notes" from that time, she has said. "It was a VERY important discovery—for the elegance and wildness at once, and a discovery of the hybrid text. Of the poet-critic text, one might say."[110]

In considering DuPlessis's memories especially, yet also in thinking about our map of avant-garde cross-influences and its fundamental triangulation, we might begin to understand how the relevant poets of the Allen anthology were most responsible—aided by the Objectivists—for the eventual legitimization and academic acceptance not only of Modernists like Pound, Williams, H.D., and Stein (rather than someone like Stevens whose general readership emerged through the mainstream). The poets of the Black Mountain and San Francisco Renaissance schools were most responsible for calling to the attention of both younger poets and a wider reading public the work of these same Objectivists. As has been suggested already, the fact that some of the Objectivists remained alive during a considerable creative period for Heller, Taggart, DuPlessis, and Silliman, furthermore, cannot be overlooked. Likewise what must be kept in mind in thinking about the impact of the Allen anthology on today's younger writers and readers, is the influence these "third generation" poets came to have on their anthologized elders who lived on well past the 1960s and 1970s (such as, principally, Creeley).

A way forward in considering the implications of the writing of our four representative younger poets, especially in relation to the writing of Creeley and his contemporaries who joined him in the Allen anthology, therefore, might very well be to further adumbrate the framework in which we can view them all clearly. I would say that they themselves were not only aware of this framework of the various inter-influences that I have sketched already; they also sought to employ it for their own ends. Finally, the framework allows for the assessment, moreover, of the state of avant-garde poetry today.

What might, then, does a possible avant-garde look like now—provided we can legitimately stipulate that an avant-garde still exists? This question is not meant to be facetious. To be sure its implication, once the question itself is answered, provides us with a key insight, since it takes us back to the poets of the Allen anthology and, as has been established, the second-generation neo-Objectivists. That is, we might begin to answer what is actually a complex of questions before us by acknowledging, as I have been saying in other ways, the very fact of the book in which this essay appears, titled *The New American Poetry: Fifty Years Later*. Does the very existence of a book such as this one indicate that what was once experimentation, that was once unusual, has now become the norm? Is the poetry—and theory as well—being written today really any different from the avant-garde work of a more than half a century ago—setting aside, for the moment, recent poetic movements like Flarf and Conceptual poetry?[111] No doubt caught in my own time warp, I do tend to think of a North American avant-garde as like that which can be found in the Allen anthology or work stemming from it. In this regard, some remarks about Flarf and Conceptual poetry are warranted, first of all in order to situate these movements within the larger avant-garde field, and secondly to define more subtly the historical and conceptual nature of that field from the period of the Allen anthology going forward in time.

A theme struck on a panel that was a part of the Denver 2010 conference of the Association of Writers and Writing Programs (AWP) had to do with how Flarf and Conceptual poetry are extensions or continuations of the experimentalism of Language writing. As K. Silem Mohammad whimsically remarked, in introducing the panel, Flarf and Conceptual poetry were finishing the job Language writing began ("Flarf and Conceptual poetry perform the opposite of damage control: they try to do the damage that didn't get done enough before").[112] And on that panel Vanessa Place, in contrasting Flarf and Conceptualism, insightfully proclaimed that while "Flarf still loves poetry" (which for her was a shortcoming) "conceptualism loves poetry enough to put it out of its misery."[113] In one respect we might see her sweeping and at the same time brilliantly incisive attack, if that is what it was, as coming out of a basic stance toward language such as was expressed on that same panel by Christian Bök who spoke of "language itself" as being already "a form of infidelity."[114]

In some respects, as I have said in this essay about the Objectivists and their offspring, we might understand the avant-garde of Modernism and thereafter as embodying a basic distrust of language. I've been maintaining that the four third-generation poets generally work out of this experience or understanding. Nevertheless, there may be another *sine qua non* that ultimately is more useful to us in responding to the present question I am now posing. It may be that foregrounding the material nature of writing is an artistic impulse that arises out of a linguistic skepticism; nevertheless the skepticism itself can be viewed as a separate issue. Whether or not the awareness of the material existence of writing or language can arise without an attendant skepticism is another line of (related) inquiry. What seems to me to be an obvious reason to associate Flarf and Conceptual writing with Language writing, therefore, may be the palpable syntactic disjunction in the earlier work, certainly as is theorized in Silliman's notion of "the new sentence" and in his own poetic practice. Yet the avant-garde tradition, which comprehends disjunctive syntax as a mode of poetry, is broader than this, and these younger, post-Language poets have wanted to establish themselves within this poetics more broadly and variously.

A recent comment by Kenneth Goldsmith, who is now a principal spokesperson for and practitioner of Flarf and Conceptual writing, spells out their lineage and how it serves as a precondition for what we can entertain as yet another "new." Discussing avant-garde history from this perspective, Goldsmith finds "[t]he touchstones [to be] always the same." He explains what he means in the following way:

> You could go back—it's actually the same lineage from which all experimentation emerges. Our roots are not that much different than Language poetry. We love Stein, we love Pound, we love Joyce. You know, that lineage. But then it breaks. Because what's more important then is Fluxus, Pop Art, Sound Poetry, Visual and Concrete Poetry; of course sampling and hip hop are all very important tenets behind it; situationism is really big; and Language poetry is a real influence as well.[115]

That language per se might be more fundamental to Stein or Pound than to an artist like Andy Warhol (whom Goldsmith cites as an important influence on him) may go without saying. It's interesting to think about, for instance, Warhol's series of images—be they portraits of Marilyn Monroe or Mao Tse Tung, or objects like Campbell's soup cans—as establishing or re-establishing the continuous that the early mid twentieth-century avant-garde poets needed to disrupt. In his article "Flarf is Dionysus. Conceptual Writing is Apollo," Goldsmith writes, perhaps wryly, that "Disjunction is dead. The fragment, which ruled poetry for the past one hundred years, has left the building. Subjectivity, emotion, the body, and desire, as expressed in whole units of plain English with normative syntax, has returned."[116] So far so good—but we are learning to look out for the proviso. Coherent statement is possible, Goldsmith teases, "[b]ut not in ways you would imagine."[117]

Shall we think of these new poetics as fulfilling a promise made by, say, Pop Art or an ultimately aloof serialism we might associate with Warhol, an insouciance or aleatory playing with situation inherent in a collective like Fluxus? Goldsmith goes on to explain the new radicalism he has helped to set in motion by explaining that

> [t]his new poetry wears its sincerity on its sleeve . . . yet no one means a word of it. Come to think of it, no one's really written a word of it. It's been grabbed, cut, pasted, processed, machined, honed, flattened, repurposed, regurgitated, and reframed from the great mass of free-floating language out there just begging to be turned into poetry. Why atomize, shatter, and splay language into nonsensical shards when you can hoard, store, mold, squeeze, shovel, soil, scrub, package, and cram the stuff into towers of words and castles of language with a stroke of the keyboard? And what fun to wreck it: knock it down, hit delete, and start all over again.[118]

Would there be Flarf without the Internet? It seems not. Yet Conceptual poetry, too—Conceptual Art preceding though possibly anticipating the digital age of coding and thereby the unsecuring of our physical substrate—might be an authentic response to a culture undermined and remade by computing. Where then, how does someone like Goldsmith emerge out of the avant-garde procession of which he is a part, of which he claims to be a part? "There's a sense of gluttony, of joy, and of fun," he says.

> Like kids at a touch table, we're delighted to feel language again, to roll in it, to get our hands dirty. With so much available language, does anyone really need to write more? Instead, let's just process what exists. Language as matter; language as material. How much did you say that paragraph weighed?[119]

How one "feels" ultimately about fungible language may be the question at hand, really. To "process" a glut of language—maybe language, like the material world itself, unmoored by an awareness of an inherent instability of the coding that holds it in place—is at least, metaphorically perhaps, to "feel language again" (above). Goldsmith may want to reject the material existence of language, finally.

Fine-tuning the notion of picking up where Language poetry has left off, in his talk at the AWP conference in Denver, Mohammad's quip was, "the first times, they didn't take,"[120]—which we may take to mean that the very potential of Language writing was not realized by the Language writers but is now being brought to fruition by the Flarfists. And yet a Flarf poet's typical appropriation of search engines in order to gather "pre-written text in the far flung corners of the Internet," its aggregation "often with no clear limit in sight" yet so that "[w]ords are fused and isolated, phrases are redacted and rearranged,"[121] strikes me as predicated on an understanding of a hypermediated culture, a high-tech culture that was anticipated by some of the earlier Language writing (Silliman's, and possibly Barrett Watten's, for example). How to engage, or to ignore, or repudiate our present media-enfiladed culture, in any case, was not part of the basic rationale for the Language project whose *raison d'etre* involved neo-Marxist or Structuralist or Deconstructionist thinking and otherwise socio-political relations that arose concomitant with, prior to, or in succession to the Language poem.

If we can acknowledge Flarf as a present form of avant-garde writing then we should also include Conceptual writing in this embrace, and what has been said now about Flarf in relation to Language writing can in fact be said for the Conceptualist project. Consider, for example, the totemic nature of Mathew Timmons's huge and for all practical purposes unreadable tome *Credit*,[122] a physically heavy book (à la Goldsmith's teasing rhetorical question "How much did you say that paragraph weighed?").[123] The book is prohibitively expensive, moreover. Aesthetically striking, it is a willy-nilly collection of credit card company solicitations and dunnings. Of course Silliman is one of the founding creators of Language Poetry, and at times DuPlessis has been associated with practices intrinsic to the work of that large and rather amorphous group known generally as Language poets.[124] Whether or not we should call Timmons's work an *objet d'art*, a work or a gesture of conceptual art, or a conceptual poem, let's say, is really an academic exercise. Whether or not we can call Silliman's equally weighty, in the physical sense at the very least, monumental book *The Alphabet* a Flarfist's or Conceptualist's provocation is not merely academic (the heft of Silliman's book comports with the experience of reading the poems within, and has an aesthetics all its own), and anyway it is clear that its aims are very different, which is not to take away from the book's importance. Something the same can be said for DuPlessis's decades-long serial, epic project *Drafts*. However, what is common among all these works is the awareness of, the thoughtfulness about, and the inclusion of the material nature of writing as a founding aesthetic—despite any protestations Flarf or Conceptual poets might make to the contrary, and admitting the supra-tangible nature that can be part of either Conceptual poetry or Conceptual art for that matter. Hence, in this we see these respective writings in consonance with, for instance, the work of the Black Mountain poets.

On the other hand, to return to what appears to be merely a theatrical question about the demise of the avant-garde, some people have suggested that the ways of poetry embodied in the Allen book have now been assimilated into the mainstream poetry world—what the Language poet Charles Bernstein has called "Official Verse Culture." As the reasoning goes, while there had been a chasm between mainstream and experimental, in a gradual tectonic shift this chasm has closed. Borrowing the terms *otherstream* and *knownstream*, which were coined by Bob Grumman in the 1980s, Jake Berry has said recently in *The Argotist Online*, for instance, that "[a]fter a long struggle the academy in many places has accepted that both movements are significant enough to be taught [. . .]"[125] in universities.

If there is still a widely practiced experimentation, in opposition to or as a turning away from mainstream poetics, then it now must be comprised of a very large minority, it must be assumed, although a recent blog post at *Silliman's Blog*, on the occasion of a new edition of Paul Hoover's anthology *Postmodern American Poetry*, contradicts this notion. Silliman describes the attempt "to pull together a broad-based anthology in 2013" as a "hopeless task. It is one thing," he points out,

> to attempt what Donald Allen achieved in the 1950s, a decade for which no estimate made at the time of the number poets publishing in English in the US market exceeded 100. Allen's gathering of the "other" tradition, the counter formation to the anglophiliac imitators of the mainstream that then ran all of the major institutions of American verse, incorporated 44 poets. (The Donald Hall, Robert Pack Louis Simpson New Poets of England and America, the Quietist counter to the Allen—tho note its broader reach—was itself just 52 poets in the 1957 first edition, 62 in the expanded 1962 "second selection."[126]

In contrast, it seems as if every citizen now self-identifies as a poet. This sociological shift is not necessarily to be lamented. Yet for the anthologist it is a nightmare, asleep or awake. Recent "estimates of the number of publishing poets in English start at 20,000." Silliman concludes: "the notion that anyone could represent the progressive side of American verse with just 115 poets is, on its face, preposterous."[127]

Citing scholarship by Jed Rasula, in an article titled "Poetry on the Brink: Reinventing the Lyric" (which was occasioned by the recent publication of Rita Dove's controversial Penguin anthology), Perloff takes issue with this reformation. Similar in point to Silliman's comments made after his own, Rasula lays out statistics suggesting that there are now too many people involved in the creative writing industry. His summation of the evidence—he says "[he doesn't] need to spell out the truly exorbitant numbers involved"—leads Perloff to proclaim that that "[t]he demand for a certain kind of prize-winning, 'well-crafted' poem has produced extraordinary uniformity."[128] Reading this, I wonder if in many instances this poem (be it "well crafted" or not) resembles work in the Allen anthology. Perloff then posits Language poetry as the pressure point in a quite a plausible literary historiography.

In "the 1980s, after Language poetry came on the scene," Perloff writes,

> The poetry wars were renewed, although the context for the debate became more specialized than it was in the 1960s. Language poetry provided a serious challenge to the delicate lyric of self-expression and direct speech: it demanded an end to transparency and straightforward reference in favor of ellipsis, indirection, and intellectual-political engagement. [Yet by] the late '90s, when Language poetry felt compelled to be more inclusive with respect to gender, race, and ethnic diversity, it became difficult to tell what was or was not a "Language poem."[129]

Fast-forward to 2011. Susan Howe wins the Bollingen Prize, not long after Rae Armantrout has won the Pulitzer. Moreover, a handful of years ago Creeley and Perloff, who would become president of the preeminent professional organization of literary scholarship, the Modern Language Association (rather than Helen Vendler), came to sit on the Board of the Academy of American Poets. That very year its new prestigious prize went to the influential experimentalist Jackson Mac Low. So, beyond what Perloff has said in that article, how have we gotten from what was seen to be a radical "new" in the Poundian sense, in fact "revolutionary" in the Language poetry sense of this word, to the presumed acceptance and homogeneity of today? Or is there still an avant-garde, one that drives our thinking and writing? Of course, given my discussion of Goldsmith *et alia*—whatever tendencies coming out of the Language movement have been appropriated by a mainstream—I think we can stipulate that at least Flarf and Conceptualism remain beyond its pale.

And where does that leave our neo-Objectivists (Silliman included)? Whatever poets of subsequent generations are doing today, it is fair to say that the third-generation avant-gardists have always thought of themselves as working in sympathetic response to the achievements of the Objectivists as well as those of the poets making up the New American poetry; and these two groups of elders have always been considered to have been avant-garde.[130] Furthermore, the third-generation poets, these new neo-Objectivists, as it were, who were inspired and at times mentored by these older poets, have conceived of what they were doing as poets to have been avant-garde, cutting-edge, pushing at the frontiers sighted by the earlier groups of experimentalists.

Finally, then, how does the work of this third generation relate to Flarf and Conceptual poetry? The elevation of language in and of itself for its own sake as the ultimate experience of the poem—the shared basis for all these poetics—spells materiality. Hence this basic element of Flarf, for all its inherent potential for wittiness, and of Conceptual poetry, for all its often claimed attempts to be boring or unreadable, takes us back not only to the NAP poets, but also to the Objectivists, Stein, and arguably Williams.

My surprise at the claim that the job of Language poetry still needs to be completed (cf. above) occurs in spite of the Conceptualists' position, such as has been described by Matvei Yankelevich who has written that, while "Conceptualism may reframe discourse, [. . .] it doesn't usually insist on aesthetic autonomy of its parts."[131] Instead, he continues, "for the Conceptualist, the goal is revelation of the framework which governs the text."[132] By this reasoning Yankelevich must maintain that the materiality of language is not to be foregrounded or, if it is to be foregrounded, then it is still not the goal of Conceptualist writing. His argument has been made in response to Perloff's "Poetry on the Brink" article, and it received a reply from Perloff three days after it appeared.

In countering him, she hearkens back to Marcel Duchamp's artwork *Fountain*, the first of his series of *readymades*. The fact that too often the ideation inherent in Duchamp's provocation is what attracts the most critical attention only further obscures what I would suggest was at least partially Duchamp's reaction to industrialization, and as such we should recognize the continuing development of his own form of a "machine aesthetic," which is evident in a number of preceding paintings, including his famous *Nude Descending a Staircase*, most likely unintentionally in parallel with the machine aestheticism of Williams and the Objectivists. "[T]he effect of the readymade," Perloff writes in answering Yankelevich, "is based on a prior conception or idea not directly visible in the work, [yet] its material embodiment also matters."[133]

While Perloff is not necessarily thinking of the objectness or thingness of the mass-produced, machine-produced object such as a urinal (turned upside down to become a *fountain*), she is acknowledging its physical presence, such as when she quotes Yankelevich to argue that for his claim to be valid, he must "divest the Conceptualist work of its most radical feature, that of the *dematerialization* of the art object."[134] Yet if "dematerialization were a Conceptualist requisite," Perloff reasons, then "why do Sol Lewitt's and Donald Judd's non-works, not to mention Duchamp's own, prompt such reverential attention, not to mention such high prices? Why do people travel to Beacon, N.Y. or to remote Marfa, Texas to see Conceptualist 'sculpture?'"[135] The logic here is compelling, notwithstanding Yankelevich's well-founded claim.

It strikes me that not only the theorizing of various Language poets—which gives rise to various styles of writing ranging from work by Andrews and Lyn Hejinian, to Barrett Watten and Carla Harryman, to Bernstein (somewhere in this range Silliman is to be found, and his notion of the New Sentence is to be seen as a key methodology, to say nothing more of DuPlessis who is at times placed critically in sympathy with Language writing)—but also their practices are different from those of the Flarfists whose rationale can barely accommodate the ideas of someone like Frederic Jameson, important to the LangPo project, while the two kinds of writing do test or undermine syntactically grounded ideation (despite Goldsmith's instance otherwise); as for the Conceptualists, especially, syntax or the lack of it really is beside the point. If Stein is to be seen as a progenitor for the stylistic practices of Language writing and Flarf in her testing of language's syntactical tensions, moreover, then the example she sets really has to do with her foregrounding of language *qua* language, certainly through manipulation of syntax—a practice that, along with a poet like Zukofsky's (rather than say, Williams's), sets the condition for later experimental writing of various persuasions, in the final analysis.

I think Perloff's point about Place's *Statement of Facts*,[136] that it *can* be compared with Reznikoff's *Testimony*,[137] is quite revealing (yet I would offer the contrast between Williams and either Pound or H.D. as being most instructive, and it takes no great effort to see Williams's use of prepositions reprised in a more evolved way in Levertov's or Creeley's writing). In both Place and Reznikoff the presence of the language of testimony is palpable and it's the very point. Perloff does add an insight in her comparison, however, useful in the present discussion—which is that Place's book creates a condition for a reader to enter into the book's materiality as well as its discourse too (no matter what effort may have been made by Place to make it unreadable, even boring, let's say): "I must take issue," Perloff writes, referring to Yankelevich's notion that "Place's book 'offers no position, no critique.' Again, this is to mistake simulation for actual truth. What the 'flat' surface of *Statement of Fact* achieves *critically* is to force its reader to wonder whether we can trust any of the 'factual' statements we are given in police reports and court testimony."[138]

Perloff's use of the term *trust* here is to be noted—the reliability of language and thus testimony even to the degree of its physical presence. In 1960 if we were to imagine reading the poetry in the Allen anthology, along with all the poetry's visual strategies on the page, the seeming disruptions in some cases, the irruptions in others, the undermining of lyric diction in others, and so on, then the question of trust would very much have come to the fore. And what the third generation did, in these younger poets' various fascinations with the "new" to be found in the work before them (for convenience let's assume Flarf and Conceptual practices represent a fourth generation), was to make the leap. That these young poets, these new neo-Objectivists, would not fall in love with avant-garde poetry radical in its later Modernist time and still so well into the 1960s, is finally unimaginable. In hindsight we can say that their embrace of the work in the Allen anthology is a given. The fact that their work in one way or another, moreover, helped to create the ground for later experimentations—however different they may be in their various aspects from the unique poetries of Taggart, Heller, DuPlessis, and Silliman—should surprise no one.

It may not be the case that every era will give rise to or host radical experimentations, an avant-garde. The twentieth century, its various periods, did sustain just that, however. Perloff may be right about the present-day absorption by the mainstream of what was once a radical poetics, and I would argue a neo-Objectivist poetics, an avant-garde that first established itself after the Second World War. All the same, there *is* an avant-garde today, which in its own way is radical, yet it is rooted in a larger experimentalism that to a great extent is now being taken for granted. And yet the Allen anthology, coming along at the midpoint of the century, inflecting deeply the avant-garde trajectory of the time, continues to enjoy the attentions of readers, and continues to attract criticism because of its two-fold, acute, awareness of its moment as well as its commitment to "make it new."

Notes

1. Donald M. Allen, ed., *The New American Poetry: 1945–1960* (New York: Grove Press, 1960).

2. I borrow, here, the title of a poetry collection by Robert Duncan, *Roots and Branches* (New York: Scribners, 1964) containing poems written contemporaneously with the poems of his included in the anthology.

3. I'm not wishing to ignore or finesse Ron Silliman's widely known and influential article "Third Phase Objectivism" that sees Objectivist poetics as, in a way, more absent than present, and which is emblematized by George Oppen's return to writing poetry after the long hiatus marked by his and Mary Oppen's political activism that in part caused them to live in Mexico, in exile, during the McCarthy era. Nor do I want to reject Silliman's point that a voice-based poetics was tempered in the 1960s by writing. This matter is too much to have to take up in this chapter; in any case, it does not lessen the point I am trying to make about an attention to language (not least of all to written language) in its material presence, which we find in the work of his generation. See Ron Silliman, "Third Phase Objectivism," *Paideuma* 10.1 (Spring 1981): 85–9.

4. This is Burton Hatlen's reference to the key poets Ezra Pound, H.D., and Williams, who first met at the University of Pennsylvania in 1902. See Burton Hatlen, "Foreword," *The Facts on File Companion to 20th-Century American Poetry*, ed. Burt Kimmelman (New York: Facts on File, 2005), vi-xiii.

5. Peter Middleton's recent essay on Modernist poetry and its legacy provides telling evidence and discussion of Olson's privileged opinions, which Allen sought, regarding the formation of this anthology; which poets might not be included, etc. See especially pages 185–88 in "Conclusion: The History and Interpretation of Modernist Poetry," Nicky Marsh and Peter Middleton, eds., *Teaching Modernist Poetry* (London: Palgrave, 2010), 179–201.

6. Rachel Blau DuPlessis, "An Epistle for Burt Kimmelman," Email to Author, December 17, 2011. Printed with the Permission of Rachel Blau DuPlessis, All Rights Reserved.

7. Paul Mann, *The Theory-Death of the Avant-Garde* (Bloomington: Indiana University Press, 1991), 13.

8. Henry Adams, *The Education of Henry Adams*. Int. D. W. Brogan (Boston: Houghton Mifflin, 1946), 382; compare Richard Gray, *American Poetry of the Twentieth Century* (New York: Longman, 1990), 30.

9. Adams, *The Education of Henry Adams*, 457; c.f. Gray, *American Poetry of the Twentieth Century*, 30.

10. Robert Browning, "Pippa Passes," *The Poems of Robert Browning* (Norwalk, CT: Easton Press, 1979), 39.

11. Peter Quartermain, *Disjunctive Poetics: From Gertrude Stein and Louis Zukofsky to Susan Howe* (Cambridge, UK: Cambridge University Press, 1992), 1.

12. Ibid., 2.

13. See, for example, Ron Silliman and Thomas A. Vogler. "Ron Silliman Interview [with Thomas A. Vogler]." *The Argotist Online*, Accessed August 5, 2011. http://www.argotistonline.co.uk/Silliman%20interview.htm.

14. Quartermain, *Disjunctive Poetics*, 5; Charles Olson, "Songs of Maximus," *The Maximus Poems*, ed. George Butterick. Berkeley: University of California Press, 1981, 19.

15. Bob Perelman, "The First Person," *Hills* 6/7 (1980): 156; qtd. in Quartermain, *Disjunctive Poetics*, 6.

16. Bruce Andrews, "Misrepresentation," $L=A=N=G=U=A=G=E$ 12 (June 1980): 5; qtd. in Quartermain, *Disjunctive Poetics*, 9.

17. For example, see Steven Carter, *Bearing Across: Studies in Science and Literature*, 2nd edition (Washington, D.C.: International Scholars Publications, 2002), and Burt Kimmelman, "'Equal, That Is, to the Real Itself': The New Physics, Charles Olson, and Avant-Garde Poetics," *Restoring the Mystery of the Rainbow: Literature's Refraction of Science*, eds. Valeria Tinkler-Villani and C. C. Barfoot (Amsterdam: Rodopi, 2011), 641–67.

18. Robert Graves, *Goodbye to All That*, (London: Penguin, 2000).

19. Theodor Adorno, "Cultural Criticism and Society," reprinted as the first essay in *Prisms* (Cambridge, MA: MIT Press, 1983), 17–34.

20. Hannah Arendt, *Eichmann in Jerusalem: A Report on the Banality of Evil* (New York: Viking, 1963).

21. George Oppen, "Of Being Numerous," in *New Collected Poems*, ed. and intr. Michael Davidson, pref. Eliot Weinberger (New York: New Directions, 2002), 163–88.

22. As is spelled out in Eric Hoffman, *Oppen: A Narrative* (Bristol, UK: Shearsman Books, forthcoming), a draft of which I have read in manuscript (sent to the author, February 2010).

23. Robert Creeley, "I Know a Man," in *The Collected Poems of Robert Creeley 1945–1975* (Berkeley: University of California Press, 2002), 132; Allen Ginsberg, *Howl*, in *Collected Poems 1947–1997* (New York: Harper Collins, 2010), 134–41.

24. Robert Creeley, "From the Language Poets," *Sunday Review, The San Francisco Chronicle* (September 28, 1986), 347. Ron Silliman, ed. and intr., *In the American Tree*, (Orono, ME: National Poetry Foundation, 2002).

25. Marjorie Perloff, "The Word As Such: L=A=N=G=U=A=G=E Poetry in the Eighties," *American Poetry Review* 13.3 (May/June 1984), 15–22.

26. Donald Hall, Robert Pack and Louis Simpson, *New Poets of England and America* (New York: Meridian Books, 1957).

27. Michael Heller, "7 Praises," in *This Constellation is a Name* (Callicoon, NY: Nightboat Books, 2012), 3.

28. Heller, "Space," *This Constellation*, 479.

29. Heller, "OK Everybody, Let's Do the Mondrian Stomp," *This Constellation*, 4.

30. Heller, "Looking at Some Petroglyphs in a Dry Arroyo Near a Friend's House," *This Constellation*, 385–86.

31. Ibid.

32. Heller, "City: Matrix: Bird: Collage," *This Constellation*, 515; John Taggart, *Dodeka* (Milwaukee: Membrane Press, 1979).

33. Heller, "Ready for Sunset," *This Constellation*, 507.

34. Burt Kimmelman, "'The 'Heartlessness' of Words': Michael Heller and Hugh Seidman, Objectivist Poetry and the Problem of Language," *Textual Practice* 25.2 (September 2011), 869.

35. Rachel Blau DuPlessis, *The Pink Guitar: Writing as Feminist* Practice (Tuscaloosa: University of Alabama Press, 2006), 5; compare David W. Huntsperger, *Procedural Form in Postmodern American Poetry: Berrigan, Antin, Silliman, and Hejinian* (New York: Palgrave MacMillan, 2010), 10–11.

36. Ron Silliman, *The Alphabet* (Tuscaloosa: University of Alabama Press, 2008).

37. George Oppen, *Selected Prose, Daybooks and Papers*, ed. and intr. Stephen Cope (Berkeley: University of California Press, 2007), 53; compare Hoffman, *Oppen: A Narrative*, 372.

38. George Oppen, *New Collected Poems*, ed. Michael Davidson, pref. Eliot Weinberger (New York: New Directions, 2002), 116; compare Stephen Cope, *George Oppen: Selected Prose, Daybooks and Papers* by George Oppen, ed. and intr. Stephen Cope (Berkeley: University of California Press, 2007), 250, n. 2.

39. Rachel DuPlessis, *Drafts 3–14* (Elmwood, CT: Potes and Poets Press, 1991); *Drafts 15–XXX, The Fold* (Elmwood, CT: Potes and Poets Press, 1997); *Drafts 1–38, Toll* (Middletown, CT: Wesleyan University Press, 2001); *Drafts 39–57, Pledge*, with Draft Unnumbered: Précis (Cambridge, UK: Salt Publishing, 2004); *Torques: Drafts 58–76* (Cambridge, UK: Salt Publishing, 2007); *Pitch: Drafts 77–95* (Cambridge, UK: Salt Publishing, 2010).

40. DuPlessis, *Tabula Rosa* (Elmwood, CT: Potes and Poets Press, 1987).

41. DuPlessis, "Writing," *Tabula Rosa*, 55, 57.

42. Ibid., 57.

43. Ibid., 65.

44. Ibid.

45. Ibid., 85.

46. Jacques Derrida, *Of Grammatology*, tr. Gayatri Spivak (Baltimore: Johns Hopkins University Press, 1997).

47. See Walter J. Ong, *Orality and Literacy: The Technologizing of the Word* (London: Routledge, 1982).

48. DuPlessis, "Draft 58," 1.

49. DuPlessis, "Draft 39," 4.

50. Ibid., 5.

51. DuPlessis, "Draft 43," 50.

52. Ibid., 51–52.

53. See among many commentaries on this William Watkin, "Projective Recursion: The Structure of Ron Silliman's *Tjanting*," *Jacket* 39 (Early 2010), accessed April 22, 2013, http://jacketmagazine.com/39/silliman-watkin.shtml.

54. Silliman lists the "qualities" of "The New Sentence" as follows: 1) The paragraph [rather than the stanza] organizes the sentences; 2) The paragraph is a unit of quantity, not logic or argument; 3) Sentence length [rather than the line] is a unit of measure; 4) Sentence structure is altered for torque, or increased polysemy/ambiguity; 5) Syllogistic movement is (a) limited (b) controlled; 6) Primary syllogistic movement is toward the paragraph as a whole, or the total work; 7) Secondary syllogistic movement is toward the paragraph as a whole, or the total work; 8) The limiting of syllogistic movement keeps the reader's attention at or very close to the level of language, the sentence level or below. See Ron Silliman, "The New Sentence," *The New Sentence* (New York: Roof Books, 2003), 63–93.

55. George Oppen, "George Oppen [Interview with George Oppen conducted by L. S. Dembo on April 25, 1968]" in "The 'Objectivist' Poet: Four Interviews." *Contemporary Literature* 10 (1969), 162.

56. As recalled by Creeley (in Creeley, "Introduction to the Selected Poems [of George Oppen]" Electronic Poetry Center, par. 5, accessed April 22, 2013, http://epc.buffalo.edu/authors/oppen/oppen_creeley.html). Compare Robert Creeley, "Introduction," in *George Oppen: Selected Poems* (New York: New Directions, 2003), ix–xvi.

57. Alan Holder, *Rethinking Meter: A New Approach to the Verse Line* (Lewisburg, PA: Bucknell University Press, 1995), 142; my emphasis. See Ron Silliman, "The New Sentence," *The New Sentence* (New York: Roof Books, 2003), 63–93.

58. Rachel Blau DuPlessis, "Notes on Silliman and Poesis" (unpublished ms. sent to author, forthcoming in *The Poetic Front*), 13.

59. Louis Zukofsky, "Notes and Books Received," 294, qtd. in Sandra Kumamoto Stanley, *Louis Zukofsky and the Transformation of Modern American Poetics* (Berkeley: University of California Press, 1994), 100, n. 51.

60. Ibid., 100.

61. Peter O'Leary, *Gnostic Contagion: Robert Duncan and the Poetry of Illness* (Wesleyan University Press, 2002), 220.

62. Ibid., 220.

63. Ibid., 219.

64. Michael Davidson, "Foreword," in *Robert Duncan: The Ambassador from Venus* by Lisa Jarnot (Berkeley: University of California Press, 2012), xv.

65. Robert Duncan, "In Introduction," in *Dodeka* by John Taggart (Milwaukee: Membrane Press, 1979), vi; my emphasis.

66. "I'll tell you. / About my *poetics*—/ music / speech // An integral / Lower limit speech / Upper limit music[.]" Louis Zukofsky, "A"-12, "A" (Berkeley: University of California Press, 1978), 138.

67. Robert Creeley, *Selected Poems, 1945–2005*, ed. Benjamin Friedlander (Berkeley: University of California Press, 2008), 252.

68. "So much depends / upon // a red wheel / barrow [etc.]." William Carlos Williams, *The Collected Poems of William Carlos Williams, Vol. 1: 1909–1939*, ed. A. Walton Litz (New York: New Directions, 1991), 224.

69. Creeley, *Selected Poems, 1945–2005*, 248.

70. Creeley, *Selected Poems, 1945–2005*, 247.

71. Robert Creeley, *Selected Poems, 1945–2005*, 246; John Taggart, *Loop* (Los Angeles: Sun and Moon Press, 1991).

72. O'Leary, *Gnostic Contagion*, 219.

73. Ibid., 220.

74. Silliman, *Non*, 334.

75. Silliman, *Garfield*, 49.

76. John Taggart, *Remaining in Light: Ant Meditations on a Painting by Edward Hopper* (Albany, SUNY Press, 1993).

77. Taggart, *Dodeka*, No pag.

78. Taggart, *Dodeka*, No pag.

79. Duncan, "In Introduction," *Dodeka*, iii.

80. Taggart, "In the Sense Of," *Standing Wave* (Providence: Lost Road Publishers, 1993), 26.

81. Taggart, "Meditation," *Is Music: Selected Poems* (Port Townsend, WA: Copper Canyon Press, 2010), 351.

82. N. Katherine Hayles, "The Time of Digital Poetry: From Object to Event," in *New Media Poetics: Contexts, Technotexts, and Theories* (Cambridge: MIT Press, 2006), 206.

83. Silliman, "Force," 43.

84. Zukofsky, "A-11," 124.

85. Zukofsky, "An Objective," in *Prepositions: The Collected Critical Essays of Louis Zukofsky, Expanded Edition* (Berkeley: University of California Press, 1981), 12.

86. Ibid.

87. Watkin, "Projective Recursion," par. 2.

88. Ibid., par. 4.

89. As mentioned by Penelope Creeley in a session on Language writing and neo-Objectivist poetics in the 1980s, which was a part of the Poetry in the Eighties conference held in Orono, Maine, in the spring of 2012 (sponsored by the National Poetry Foundation, University of Maine).

90. See Burt Kimmelman, "From Black Mountain College to St. Mark's Church: The Cityscape Poetics of Blackburn, di Prima, and Oppenheimer," *Rain Taxi* (Spring

2002), accessed April 24, 2013, http://www.raintaxi.com/online/2002spring/poetry-project.shtml.

91. Paris Leary and Robert Kelly, eds., A *Controversy of Poets: An Anthology of Contemporary American Poetry* (Garden City, NY: Anchor/Doubleday, 1965).

92. DuPlessis, Email to author, December 17, 2011.

93. Ron Silliman, Telephone conversation with author, December 23, 2011.

94. John Taggart, Telephone conversation with author, February 18, 20012; Michael Heller, Telephone conversation with author, July 8, 2012.

95. DuPlessis, Email to author, December 17, 2011.

96. DuPlessis, Email to author, December 12, 2011.

97. DuPlessis, "Oppen from Seventy-Five to a Hundred, 1983–2008," *Jacket* 36 (Late 2008), par. 27.

98. Ibid., par. 35–37.

99. Oppen, *New Collected Poems*, 166.

100. DuPlessis, "Oppen from Seventy-Five," par. 35–37; Oppen, *The Selected Letters of George Oppen*, ed. Rachel Blau DuPlessis (Durham: Duke University Press, 1990), 121. See also Michael Davidson's notes in Oppen, *New Collected Poems*, 382–83.

101. John Taggart, Telephone conversation with author, February 18, 2012.

102. See Kimmelman, "'The 'Heartlessness' of Words': Michael Heller and Hugh Seidman, Objectivist Poetry and the Problem of Language," *Textual Practice* 25.2 (September 2011): 867–92.

103. Heller, Telephone conversation with author, July 8, 2012.

104. Ibid.

105. Ibid.

106. Ibid.

107. DuPlessis, "An Epistle for Burt Kimmelman," Email to Author, December 17, 2011.

108. Ibid.

109. Ibid.

110. Ibid.

111. Not digital poetry, which I would argue would be better thought of as art rather than literature, although, unlike Conceptual poetry perhaps, it calls into question what writing really may be, as demonstrated in some artworks by, let's say, Jenny Holzer, yet which shares with Flarf and Conceptual writing, I am maintaining here, a great awareness of language as material, and which privileges this, as do Objectivist and neo-Objectivist poetry (but see C. T. Funkhouser, *New Directions in Digital Poetry* [New York: Continuum, 2012]) for the argument that digital poetry is poetry rather than art). Considering the vastness of it as an artistic phenomenon in the broadest sense at least, I'll refrain from further comment on it, given that such commentary must be too extensive and out of proportion in the present discussion.

112. K. Silem Mohammad, "Introduction," Flarf and Conceptual Poetry panel, AWP Conference in Denver (April 13, 2010); compare *Limetree*, par. 5, http://lime-tree

.blogspot.com/2010/04/awp-2010–flarf-conceptual-poetry-panel.html, accessed April 27, 2013.

113. "Flarf still loves poetry [whereas] Conceptualism loves poetry enough to put it out of its misery." Vanessa Place, "Why Conceptualism is Better Than Flarf," Flarf and Conceptual Poetry panel at the AWP Conference, Denver (April 13, 2010). Compare http://www.youtube.com/watch?v=PBTPXbIVbTk, accessed April 27, 2013.

114. "Flarf and Conceptual Poetry" panel at the AWP Conference, Denver (April 13, 2010); compare http://www.youtube.com/watch?v=Ci9Nvfa7VFQ, accessed April 27, 2013.

115. Kenneth Goldsmith, "'Against Expression': Kenneth Goldsmith in Conversation," Academy of American Poets, http://www.poets.org/viewmedia.php/prm MID/22407, accessed April 27, 2013.

116. Goldsmith, "Flarf is Dionysus. Conceptual Writing is Apollo: An Introduction to the 21st Century's Most Controversial Poetry Movement," *Poetry* [Poetry Foundation online], par. 1, http://www.poetryfoundation.org/poetrymagazine/article/237176, accessed April 27, 2013.

117. Ibid.

118. Ibid.

119. Ibid.

120. Mohammad, "Flarf and Conceptual Poetry," Flarf and Conceptual Poetry panel, AWP Conference in Denver (April 13, 2010); compare *Limetree*, par. 5, http://lime-tree.blogspot.com/2010/04/awp-2010–flarf-conceptual-poetry-panel.html, accessed April 27, 2013.

121. Kaplan Harris, "Introducing Flarf," *ArtVoice*, par. 2, http://artvoice.com/issues/v7n12/introducing_flarf, accessed April 27, 2013.

122. Matthew Timmons, *Credit* (Los Angeles: Blanc Press, 2009).

123. Goldsmith, "Flarf is Dionysus," par. 1.

124. For the latest discussion of this see Charles Bernstein, "The Expanded Field of L=A=N=G=U=A=G=E," *Routledge Companion to Experimental Literature*, eds. Joe Bray, Alison Gibbons, and Brian McHale: (London: Routledge, 2013).

125. Jake Berry, "Poetry Wide Open: The Otherstream (Fragments In Motion)," *The Argotist Online*, par. 12, accessed April 20, 2013, http://www.argotistonline.co.uk/Berry%20essay%203.htm.

126. Silliman, [blog entry], *Silliman's Blog*, February 15, 2013, par. 2, accessed April 20, 2013, http://ronsilliman.blogspot.com/2013_02_10_archive.html.

127. Ibid.

128. Marjorie Perloff, "Poetry on the Brink: Reinventing the Lyric," *The Boston Review* (May/June 2012), par. 7. Accessed April 20, 2013, http://www.bostonreview.net/BR37.3/marjorie_perloff_poetry_lyric_reinvention.php.

129. Ibid., par. 6.

130. It should be noted at this point, in passing, that in 2000 Silliman said in effect that he'd moved beyond the NAP sensibility, epistemology, poetics ("Ron Silliman Interview [with Gary Sullivan]," par. 20 and following, http://home.jps

.net/~nada/silliman.htm, accessed April 27, 2013), and that specifically Projective Verse poetics became "claustrophobic" for him by the end of the 1960s (just as an intense engagement with Levertov arose when she was teaching at Berkeley). That he maintained relationships with the poets I'm calling the neo-Objectivists throughout the many years since his initial encounter with their work is a matter of record. In any case, he tells Gary Sullivan that he was "indeed completely under the spell of the Projectivists for several years, roughly 1966 through 1970, and it was an extraordinarily useful apprenticeship in that sense. There is no question in my mind that those poets were the ones asking the most demanding questions of themselves and of poetry in the period when I first really began writing." I know of no comment of his suggesting an eventual disaffection with the Objectivists, however.

131. Matvei Yankelevich, "The Gray Area: An Open Letter to Marjorie Perloff," *Los Angeles Review of Books* July 13, 2012, par. 4, accessed April 20, 2013, http://lareviewofbooks.org/article.php?id=762&fulltext=1.

132. Ibid., par. 5.

133. Marjorie Perloff, "A Response to Matvei Yankelevich," *Los Angeles Review of Books* 16 July 2013, par. 6, accessed April 20, 2013, http://lareviewofbooks.org/article.php?id=768&fulltext=1.

134. Yankelevich, "The Gray Area," par. 6.

135. Perloff, "A Response," par. 7.

136. Vanessa Place, *Statement of Facts* (Los Angeles: Blanc Press, 2010).

137. Charles Reznikoff, *Testimony: The United States 1885–1890—Recitative* (New York, New Directions, 1965).

138. Perloff, "A Response," par. 8.

Bibliography

Adams, Henry. *The Education of Henry Adams.* Int. D. W. Brogan. Boston: Houghton Mifflin, 1946.

Adorno, Theodor. "Cultural Criticism and Society." Reprinted in *Prisms.* Cambridge: MIT Press, 1983: 17–34.

Allen, Donald M., ed. *The New American Poetry: 1945–1960.* New York: Grove Press, 1960.

Andrews, Bruce. "Misrepresentation." *L=A=N=G=U=A=G=E* 12 (June 1980): 5.

Arendt, Hannah. *Eichmann in Jerusalem: A Report on the Banality of Evil.* New York: Viking, 1963.

Bernstein, Charles. "The Expanded Field of L=A=N=G=U=A=G=E." *Routledge Companion to Experimental Literature.* Edited by Joe Bray, Alison Gibbons, and Brian McHale. London: Routledge, 2013.

Berry, Jake. "Poetry Wide Open: The Otherstream (Fragments In Motion)." *The Argotist Online,* par. 12. Accessed April 20, 2013. http://www.argotistonline.co.uk/Berry%20essay%203.htm.

Blau DuPlessis, Rachel. "An Epistle for Burt Kimmelman," Email to Author, December 17, 2011.

———. Email to author, 12 December 2011.

———. *Drafts 3–14.* Elmwood, CT: Potes and Poets Press, 1991.

———. *Drafts 15–XXX, The Fold.* Elmwood, CT: Potes and Poets Press, 1997.

———. *Drafts 1–38, Toll.* Middletown, CT: Wesleyan University Press, 2001.

———. *Drafts 39–57, Pledge,* with Draft Unnumbered: Précis. Cambridge, UK: Salt Publishing, 2004.

———. "Notes on Silliman and Poesis" (unpublished ms. sent to author, forthcoming in *The Poetic Front.*

———. "Oppen from Seventy-Five to a Hundred, 1983–2008." *Jacket* 36 (Late 2008).

———. *Pitch: Drafts 77–95.* Cambridge, UK: Salt Publishing, 2010.

———. *Tabula Rosa.* Elmwood, CT: Potes and Poets Press, 1987.

———. *Torques: Drafts 58–76.* Cambridge, UK: Salt Publishing, 2007.

———. *The Pink Guitar: Writing as Feminist Practice.* Tuscaloosa: University of Alabama Press, 2006.

———. "Writing." *Tabula Rosa.* Elmwood, CT: Potes and Poets Press, 1987.

Bok, Christian. "Flarf and Conceptual Poetry" panel at the AWP Conference, Denver (April 13, 2010). Compare http://www.youtube.com/watch?v=Ci9Nvfa7VFQ. Accessed April 27, 2013.

Browning, Robert. "Pippa Passes." *The Poems of Robert Browning,* Norwalk, CT: Easton Press, 1979.

Carter, Steven. *Bearing Across: Studies in Science and Literature.* 2nd edition. Washington, D.C.: International Scholars Publications, 2002.

Cope, Stephen. *George Oppen: Selected Prose, Daybooks and Papers by George Oppen.* Edited and Introduced by Stephen Cope. Berkeley: University of California Press, 2007.

Creeley, Penelope. "Language Writing and neo-Objectivist poetics in the 1980s." The Poetry in the Eighties conference, Orono, Maine, Spring 2012.

Creeley, Robert. "From the Language Poets." *Sunday Review, The San Francisco Chronicle* (28 September 1986), 347.

———. "I Know a Man." *The Collected Poems of Robert Creeley 1945–1975.* Berkeley: University of California Press, 2002.

———. "Introduction to the Selected Poems [of George Oppen]." Electronic Poetry Center, par. 5. Accessed April 22, 2013. http://epc.buffalo.edu/authors/oppen/oppen_creeley.html.

———. "Introduction." *George Oppen: Selected Poems.* New York: New Directions, 2003.

———. *Selected Poems, 1945–2005.* Edited by Benjamin Friedlander. Berkeley: University of California Press, 2008.

Davidson, Michael. "Foreword." *Robert Duncan: The Ambassador from Venus by Lisa Jarnot.* Berkeley: University of California Press, 2012.

———. "Notes." *George Oppen: New Collected Poems.* Edited by Michael Davidson. Preface by Eliot Weinberger. New York: New Directions, 2002.

Derrida, Jacques. *Of Grammatology*. Tr. Gayatri Spivak. Baltimore: Johns Hopkins University Press, 1997.

Duncan, Robert. "In Introduction." *Dodeka* by John Taggart. Milwaukee: Membrane Press, 1979.

———. *Roots and Branches*. New York: Scribners, 1964.

Funkhouser, C. T. *New Directions in Digital Poetry*. New York: Continuum, 2012.

Ginsberg, Allen. *Howl*, in *Collected Poems 1947–1997*. New York: Harper Collins, 2010.

Goldsmith, Kenneth. "'Against Expression': Kenneth Goldsmith in Conversation." Academy of American Poets, http://www.poets.org/viewmedia.php/prmMID/22407. Accessed April 27, 2013.

———. "Flarf is Dionysus. Conceptual Writing is Apollo: An Introduction to the 21st Century's Most Controversial Poetry Movement." *Poetry* [Poetry Foundation online], par. 1, http://www.poetryfoundation.org/poetrymagazine/article/237176. Accessed April 27, 2013.

Graves, Robert. *Goodbye to All That*. London: Penguin, 2000.

Gray, Richard. *American Poetry of the Twentieth Century*. London: Longman, 1990.

Hall, Donald, Robert Pack, and Louis Simpson, *New Poets of England and America*. New York: Meridian Books, 1957.

Harris,Kaplan. "Introducing Flarf." *ArtVoice*, par. 2. http://artvoice.com/issues/v7n12/introducing_flarf. Accessed April 27, 2013.

Hatlen, Burton. "Foreword," *The Facts on File Companion to 20th-Century American Poetry*. Edited by Burt Kimmelman. New York: Facts on File, 2005.

Hayles, N. Katherine. "The Time of Digital Poetry: From Object to Event." *New Media Poetics: Contexts, Technotexts, and Theories*. Cambridge: MIT Press, 2006.

Heller, Michael. "City: Matrix: Bird: Collage." *This Constellation is a Name*. Callicoon, NY: Nightboat Books, 2012.

———. "Looking at Some Petroglyphs in a Dry Arroyo Near a Friend's House." *This Constellation is a Name*. Callicoon, NY: Nightboat Books, 2012.

———. "OK Everybody, Let's Do the Mondrian Stomp." *This Constellation is a Name*. Callicoon, NY: Nightboat Books, 2012.

———. "Ready for Sunset." *This Constellation is a Name*. Callicoon, NY: Nightboat Books, 2012.

———. "Space." *This Constellation is a Name*. Callicoon, NY: Nightboat Books, 2012.

———. Telephone conversation with author, 8 July 2012.

———. "7 Praises." *This Constellation is a Name*, Callicoon, NY: Nightboat Books, 2012.

Hoffman, Eric. *Oppen: A Narrative*. Bristol, UK: Shearsman Books, forthcoming.

Holder, Alan. *Rethinking Meter: A New Approach to the Verse Line*. Lewisburg, PA: Bucknell University Press, 1995.

Huntsperger, David W. *Procedural Form in Postmodern American Poetry: Berrigan, Antin, Silliman, and Hejinian*. New York: Palgrave MacMillan, 2010.

Kimmelman, Burt. "'Equal, That Is, to the Real Itself': The New Physics, Charles Olson, and Avant-Garde Poetics." *Restoring the Mystery of the Rainbow: Literature's*

Refraction of Science. Edited by Valeria Tinkler-Villani and C. C. Barfoot. Amsterdam: Rodopi, 2011.

———. "From Black Mountain College to St. Mark's Church: The Cityscape Poetics of Blackburn, di Prima, and Oppenheimer." *Rain Taxi* (Spring 2002). Accessed April 24, 2013. http://www.raintaxi.com/online/2002spring/poetry project.shtml.

———. "'The 'Heartlessness' of Words': Michael Heller and Hugh Seidman, Objectivist Poetry and the Problem of Language." *Textual Practice* 25.2 (September 2011): 869.

Leary, Paris and Robert Kelly, eds. *A Controversy of Poets: An Anthology of Contemporary American Poetry*. Garden City, NY: Anchor/Doubleday, 1965.

Mann, Paul. *The Theory-Death of the Avant-Garde*. Bloomington: Indiana University Press, 1991.

Marsh, Nicky and Peter Middleton, eds. "Conclusion: The History and Interpretation of Modernist Poetry." *Teaching Modernist Poetry*. London: Palgrave, 2010.

Mohammad, K. Silem. "Flarf and Conceptual Poetry." Flarf and Conceptual Poetry panel, AWP Conference in Denver (April 13, 2010); cf. *Limetree*, par. 5. http://lime-tree.blogspot.com/2010/04/awp-2010–flarf-conceptual-poetry-panel.html. Accessed April 27, 2013.

O'Leary, Peter. *Gnostic Contagion: Robert Duncan and the Poetry of Illness*. Wesleyan University Press, 2002.

Olson, Charles. "Songs of Maximus." *The Maximus Poems*. Edited by George Butterick. Berkeley: University of California Press, 1981.

Ong, Walter J. *Orality and Literacy: The Technologizing of the Word*. London: Routledge, 1982.

Oppen, George. "George Oppen [Interview with George Oppen conducted by L. S. Dembo on April 25, 1968]" in "The 'Objectivist' Poet: Four Interviews." *Contemporary Literature* 10 (1969): 162.

———. *New Collected Poems*. Edited by Michael Davidson. Preface by Eliot Weinberger. New York: New Directions, 2002.

———. "Of Being Numerous." *New Collected Poems*. Edited by Michael Davidson. Preface by Eliot Weinberger. New York: New Directions, 2002: 163–88.

———. *Selected Prose, Daybooks and Papers by George Oppen*. Edited and introduced by Stephen Cope. Berkeley: University of California Press, 2007.

———. *The Selected Letters of George Oppen*. Edited by Rachel Blau DuPlessis. Durham: Duke University Press, 1990.

Perelman, Bob. "The First Person." *Hills* 6/7 (1980): 156.

Perloff, Marjorie. "A Response to Matvei Yankelevich." *Los Angeles Review of Books* 16 (July 2013): par. 6. Accessed April 20, 2013. http://lareviewofbooks.org/article.php?id=768&fulltext=1.

———. "Poetry on the Brink: Reinventing the Lyric." *The Boston Review* (May/June 2012): par. 7. Accessed April 20, 2013. http://www.bostonreview.net/BR37.3/marjorie_perloff_poetry_lyric_reinvention.php.

———. "The Word As Such: L=A=N=G=U=A=G=E Poetry in the Eighties." *American Poetry Review* 13.3 (May/June 1984): 15–22.

Place, Vanessa. *Statement of Fact.* Los Angeles: Blanc Press, 2010.

———. "Why Conceptualism is Better Than Flarf." Flarf and Conceptual Poetry panel at the AWP Conference, Denver (April 13, 2010). c.f. http://www.youtube.com/watch?v=PBTPXbIVbTk. Accessed April 27, 2013.

Quartermain, Peter. *Disjunctive Poetics: From Gertrude Stein and Louis Zukofsky to Susan Howe.* Cambridge, UK: Cambridge University Press, 1992.

Reznikoff, Charles. *Testimony: The United States 1885–1890—Recitative.* New York: New Directions, 1965.

Silliman, Ron. "Force." *The Alphabet.* Tuscaloosa: University of Alabama Press, 2008.

———. *Garfield. The Alphabet.* Tuscaloosa: University University of Alabama Press, 2008.

———, ed. and intr. *In the American Tree.* Orono, ME: National Poetry Foundation, 2002.

———. *Non.* In *The Alphabet.* Tuscaloosa: University of Alabama Press, 2008.

———. "Ron Silliman Interview [with Gary Sullivan]." http://home.jps.net/~nada/silliman.htm. Accessed April 27, 2013.

———. Silliman's Blog, [blog entry]. February 15, 2013, par. 2. http://ronsilliman.blogspot.com/2013_02_10_archive.html. Accessed April 20, 2013.

———. Telephone conversation with author, December 23, 2011.

———. *The Alphabet.* Tuscaloosa: University of Alabama Press, 2008.

———. "The New Sentence." *The New Sentence.* New York: Roof Books, 2003: 63–93.

———. "Third Phase Objectivism." *Paideuma* 10.1 (Spring 1981): 85–9.

Silliman, Ron and Thomas A. Vogler. "Ron Silliman Interview [with Thomas A. Vogler]." *The Argotist Online.* http://www.argotistonline.co.uk/Silliman%20interview.htm. Accessed August 5, 2011.

Taggart, John. *Dodeka.* Milwaukee: Membrane Press, 1979.

———. "In the Sense Of." *Standing* Wave. Providence: Lost Road Publishers, 1993: 26.

———. *Loop.* Los Angeles: Sun and Moon Press, 1991.

———. "Meditation." *Is Music: Selected Poems.* Port Townsend, WA: Copper Canyon Press, 2010.

———. *Remaining in Light: Ant Meditations on a Painting by Edward Hopper.* Albany: SUNY Press, 1993.

———. Telephone conversation with author, February 18, 2012.

Timmons, Matthew. *Credit.* Los Angeles: Blanc Press, 2009.

Watkin, William. "Projective Recursion: The Structure of Ron Silliman's *Tjanting.*" *Jacket* 39 (Early 2010). http://jacketmagazine.com/39/silliman-watkin.shtml. Accessed April 22, 2013.

Williams, William Carlos. *The Collected Poems of William Carlos Williams, Vol. 1: 1909–1939.* Edited by A. Walton Litz. New York: New Directions, 1991.

Yankelevich, Matvei. "The Gray Area: An Open Letter to Marjorie Perloff." *Los Angeles Review of Books*. July 13, 2012: par. 4. http://lareviewofbooks.org/article. php?id=762&fulltext=1. Accessed April 20, 2013.

Zukofsky, Louis. "An Objective." *Prepositions: The Collected Critical Essays of Louis Zukofsky, Expanded Edition*. Berkeley: University of California Press, 1981.

———. "Notes and Books Received." *Louis Zukofsky and the Transformation of Modern American Poetics* by Sandra Kumamoto Stanley. Berkeley: University of California Press, 1994.

———. "A-11." "A." Berkeley: University of California Press, 1978.

———. "A-12." "A." Berkeley: University of California Press, 1978.

CHAPTER TWELVE

~

Afterword

Carla Billitteri

In considering this collection, we might carry with us Michel Foucault's idea that "[c]ommentary's only role is to say, *finally*, what has silently been articulated *deep down*. It must—and the paradox is ever-changing yet inescapable—say, for the first time, what has already been said, and repeat tirelessly what was nevertheless, never said."[1] Several works gathered in this collection, playing off the title of the Allen anthology, speak of the tradition of the new, of the jolt of what was created and explicitly branded as new; how the new was received, how it was recognized. In a parallel fashion, several works address what "stays new" (to cite the title of Terence Diggory's chapter), what seems to have not changed, and still others confront the problematic aspects of the legacy of that new: its narrowly defined group identity (as discussed by Diggory and Megan Swihart Jewell), its irredentist political design (the here, the nowhere: the dream of redeeming America from itself, as indicated by David Herd), its awkward dispatching of the old (as Paul Cappucci suggests). Although the circumstances are varied, these chapters speak of a poetic tradition that hypostasized itself as absolute present, a poetics of the *now* even more than the new. As Robert Creeley writes in one of his statements in this anthology, "Tradition is an aspect of what anyone is now thinking, not what someone once thought."[2] This tradition is not only present but inherent ("an aspect of what anyone is thinking"), and pertinent in so far as it expresses the concerns of the group. "A tradition becomes inept," Creeley concludes, "when it blocks the necessary conclusion; it says we have felt nothing, it implies others have felt more."[3] A tradition, even if conceived in the mode of the new and of the present, can be seen as a transitive begin-ning, a point of departure for other traditions, or other experiences, for what Creeley calls "the necessary conclusion."

I adopt the term "transitive" from Edward Said, whose discriminating discussion of beginnings distinguishes between transitive and intransitive aspects. The former emphasizes transmission and continuity. In the latter, the beginning preserves "its identity as radical starting point"—radical in the sense of root—and offers itself to the reader as a "conceptual" project demanding "constant clarification."[4] These two aspects coexist in the act of writing as well as in the act of reading and responding to writing. Indeed, many of the contributors gathered by John R. Woznicki in this collection of essays address both aspects of *The New American Poetry*. As Woznicki writes in his introduction, what motivates this collection is the expectation that new continuities will be discovered, and that the conceptual design will yield new insights. Thus, when Ben Hickman, Joe Moffett, Burt Kimmelman, and Seth Forrest—as well as Diggory and Jewell—talk about the metamorpho-sis of *The New American Poetry* in a broad range of later movements and technologies, the Allen anthology is taken as a transitive beginning. When Joshua Hoeynck discusses the influence of Whitehead, David Herd surveys the articulation of new political spaces, Peter Middleton illuminates the interlacing of scientific and poetic discourses, the anthology is seen in its conceptual design, as an intransitive beginning.

Edward Said, borrowing a suggestive word from Paul Valéry, says that all beginnings should be read as "implexes": as having an involved, complicate plot in which the transitive and intransitive are entwined. The two forms of beginning, Said explains, "animate one another."[5] What is unique or at least noteworthy about the Allen anthology is its reflection on this twofold, ani-mated quality of writing, already glimpsed in Allen's introduction, intermit-tently visible in the poems, and fully manifest in the statements of poetics. To my mind, this self-reflexivity regarding the nature of beginnings is the lasting legacy of the anthology, of its tradition, to recall Creeley's statement.

For my part, I will not touch further on the transitive aspects of this im-plex, which are taken up so ably by the majority of the contributors to this collection. The impact of *The New American Poetry* on later writers and its continued visibility in new literary milieus is of course one of the principal reasons we are drawn back to the anthology again and again. Drawn back, we engage with the intransitive, and it is this aspect of the implex I would like to take up briefly in this postface, making a few tentative gestures toward what I mean by the self-reflexivity of the anthology's poetics. Like Hoeynck I would place these poetics in a Whiteheadean matrix.

In strong contrast to the product-oriented poetry and poetics associated with the New Critics (famously typified by the "well wrought urn") the poets of *The New American Poetry* were process-oriented, and the anthology itself is structured in a processual way. The poets are grouped by community, which highlights the circumstances of creation, preparing us to see each poem as responding to the conditions of its own occasion, as an actualized "prehension," Whitehead's term for the act of cognition. For Whitehead, the highest form of cognition, arrived at after a sequence of individual acts of prehension, is "satisfaction." This too is built into the anthology's structure, not only in the ordinary way of all anthologies whereby the multiple poems of individual poets yield a deeper understanding of the individual's project (and here, of course, the multiple individuals yield a deeper understanding of the community's projects,) but also in Allen's original—and highly influential—decision to include statements of poetics. For a select number of poets, ranging across all of the communities, the groupings of poems are supplemented in a final section of the book with critical prose (manifestoes, journal entries, theoretical notations, addresses to the reader). The statements are a reflection on process and, at their best, the culmination of years of thinking about the practice of poetry—satisfaction in Whitehead's sense. Moreover, for a reader who engages with the anthology in its totality, the juxtaposition of all these acts of prehension produces "society" as Whitehead uses this word: a nexus of occasions that are not only mutually informed and informing but self-sustaining.

As the function of its communities, the anthology is the record and result of a transitive beginning, one that continues to yield results in the communities that receive it. The self-sustaining society of the anthology in itself is where we discover and rediscover the intransitive.

Speaking of the anthology in this way, as a society in itself, does risk a sterile formalism, a freezing of the process, turning the book into another kind of verbal icon. What distinguishes *The New American Poetry* from its product-oriented antitheses is not just the commitment to process, which of course did result in discrete and memorable works of art, but the forms of subjectivity that the work embodied and helped to produce. These forms of subjectivity have much to do with the anthology's enduring popularity—its transitive aspect—and these too can be understood as an intransitive beginning: a conceptual nexus that awaits constant clarification—the clarification of commentary, of "say[ing], for the first time, what has already been said . . . repeat[ing] tirelessly what was nevertheless, never said."[6]

There is, then, for all the wealth of commentary collected here in the volume at hand, much more to be said. This collection continues the work of *The New American Poetry* and more work, surely, will continue from here.

Notes

1. Michel Foucault, *The Archeology of Knowledge*, tr. by A.M. Sheridan Smith (New York: Pantheon, 1972), 221.

2. Robert Creeley, "To Define," in *The New American Poetry*, ed. Donald Allen (New York: Grove Press, 1960), 408.

3. Ibid.

4. Edward Said, *Beginnings: Intention and Method* (New York: Columbia University Press, 1975), 72–73.

5. Ibid.

6. Michel Foucault, *The Archeology of Knowledge*, 221.

Bibliography

Allen, Donald, ed. *The New American Poetry 1945–1960*. New York: Grove Press, 1960.

Creeley, Robert. "To Define." *The New American Poetry 1945–1960*. Edited by Donald Allen. New York: Grove Press, 1960.

Foucault, Michel. *The Archeology of Knowledge*. Translated by A.M. Sheridan Smith. New York: Pantheon Press, 1972.

Said, Edward. *Beginnings: Intention and Method*. New York: Columbia University Press, 1975.

Whitehead, Alfred North. *Process and Reality*. Edited by David Ray Griffin and Donald W. Sherburne. New York: The Free Press, 1978.

Index

~

About the Contributors

About the Editor

John R. Woznicki is the author of the book *Ideological Content and Political Significance of Twentieth-Century American Poetry*, as well as articles focusing on the poetry of L=A=N=G=U=A=G=E, Charles Olson, Ezra Pound, Wallace Stevens, and the fiction of Stephen King. He is currently provost and assistant vice president of Academic Affairs at Union County College in New Jersey.

About the Contributors

Carla Billitteri is associate professor of English at the University of Maine, and a member of the editorial collective of the National Poetry Foundation. She is the author of the critical study, *Language and the Renewal of Society in Walt Whitman, Laura (Riding) Jackson and Charles Olson*, as well as of numerous essays on modern and contemporary poetry that have appeared in *Aerial, Arizona Quarterly, Gravesiana, How2, The Journal of Modern Literature, Open Letter, Paideuma, Textual Practice,* and *The Worcester Review*. She is also active as a translator of contemporary Italian poetry, with work in *Aufgabe, Boundary2, How2, Fascicle,* the *Atlanta Review,* and the *Farrar Straus Giroux Book of Twentieth-Century Italian Poetry*. An edition of her translations from Alda Merini's aphorisms was published by Hooke Press in 2008. A book of her translations of Maria Attanasio's poetry will be published by Litmus Press.

Paul Cappucci is professor of English at Georgian Court University in Lakewood, New Jersey. He has published two books: *William Carlos Williams, Frank O'Hara, and the New York Art Scene* and *William Carlos Williams' Poetic Response to the 1913 Paterson Silk Strike*. He also has published articles in the *Journal of Modern Literature*, *Papers on Language and Literature*, and the *William Carlos Williams Review*.

Terence Diggory is emeritus professor of English at Skidmore College. He is co-editor (with Stephen Paul Miller) of *The Scene of My Selves: New Work on New York School Poets* and editor of the *Encyclopedia of the New York School Poets*.

Seth Forrest is assistant professor of English at Coppin State University in Baltimore. He has published articles on Charles Olson and Larry Eigner. His current project considers the ways in which the age of audio recording alters our sense of voices and noises and, in so doing, the way that poetic form in American poetry responds to the new aurality ushered in by recorded sound.

David Herd is the author of two critical works, *John Ashbery and American Poetry* and *Enthusiast! Essays on Modern American Literature*. His collections of poetry include *All Just* and *Outwith*. His recent writings on poetry and politics have appeared in *PN Review*, *Parallax*, and *Almost Island*. He is professor of Modern Literature at the University of Kent, where he directs the Centre for Modern Poetry.

Ben Hickman is lecturer in Modern Poetry at the University of Kent, having studied at Kent and University College, London. His *John Ashbery and English Poetry* was published in 2012, and his new book, entitled *Poetry and Real Politics: Crisis and the U.S. Avant-Garde*, will be published in 2014.

Joshua S. Hoeynck researches American poetry and poetics, with a particular focus on the experimental forms that emerged after World War II. He is at work on a book tentatively titled *The Process of Poetry: Alfred North Whitehead and the Black Mountain Poets*, which charts the influence of Whitehead's process philosophy on Charles Olson, Robert Creeley, Robert Duncan, and Denise Levertov. His other articles have appeared in *The Journal of Process Studies* and *Contemporary Literature*. Currently, he teaches writing, American literature, and film as a lecturer in Case Western Reserve University's English Department.

Megan Swihart Jewell teaches in the English Department at Case Western Reserve University, where she also directs the university's writing center. She has published essays on poets Charles Bernstein and Rachel Blau DuPlessis. Her current research focuses on the intersections between experimental poetics and writing pedagogy.

Burt Kimmelman is the author, co-author, editor, or co-editor of thirteen books—the sole author of two literary-critical studies (including The "Winter Mind": William Bronk and American Letters) and of eight collections of poems—with two more literary-critical volumes he is co-editing forthcoming, and the author of approximately ninety articles on medieval, modern, or postmodern poetry. He is professor of English at New Jersey Institute of Technology.

Peter Middleton has produced several books on modern poetry, including Distant Reading and Teaching Modernist Poetry (co-edited with Nicky Marsh), as well many essays on contemporary poetics. One of the most recent of these is an account of L=A=N=G=U=A=G=E magazine for Among Friends, edited by Anne Dewey and Libbie Rifkin. A study of American poetry and science in the Cold War is forthcoming. He teaches at the University of Southampton, UK.

Joe Moffett teaches at Northern Kentucky University. He is the author of Understanding Charles Wright and The Search for Origins in the Twentieth-Century Long Poem: Sumerian, Homeric, Anglo-Saxon. He has co-edited a special issue of Genre: Forms of Discourse and Culture and his essays have appeared in such journals as The Southern Literary Journal, The Journal of the Midwest Modern Language Association, LIT: Literature Interpretation Theory, and North American Journal of Welsh Studies. He is currently completing a manuscript titled Contemplation of the Divine: Mysticism in Contemporary Long Poems.

www.ingramcontent.com/pod-product-compliance
Lightning Source LLC
Chambersburg PA
CBHW021505110726
47899CB00001BA/308